JEWS
and American
Popular Culture

Associate Editor

Dave Wagner

Board of Advisers

Joyce Antler
Brandeis University

Daniel Czitrom
Mount Holyoke College

Bernard F. Dick
Fairleigh Dickenson University

Hasia Diner
New York University

Danny Goldberg
Gold Village Entertainment, Inc.

Elliott Gorn
Brown University

Michael Kazin
Georgetown University

David Marc
Syracuse University

Anthony Michels
University of Wisconsin

Harvey Pekar
American Splendor

Riv-Ellen Prell
University of Minnesota

Judith Rosenbaum
Jewish Women's Archive

Henry Sapoznik
Living Traditions

Susan Smulyan
Brown University

Judith Thissen
Utrecht University

Alan Wald
University of Michigan

JEWS and American Popular Culture

Volume 1
Movies, Radio, and Television

Edited by Paul Buhle

Praeger Perspectives

Westport, Connecticut
London

Library of Congress Cataloging-in-Publication Data

Jews and American popular culture / edited by Paul Buhle.
  p. cm.
  Includes bibliographical references and index.
  ISBN 0-275-98793-0 (set : alk. paper) — ISBN 0-275-98794-9 (v. 1 : alk. paper) — ISBN 0-275-98795-7 (v. 2 : alk. paper) — ISBN 0-275-98796-5 (v. 3 : alk. paper) —
  1. Jews—United States—Intellectual life. 2. Jewish entertainers—United States. 3. Judaism and literature—United States. 4. Jewish athletes—United States. 5. Popular culture—United States. 6. Jews in popular culture—United States. 7. United States—Ethnic relations. I. Buhle, Paul, 1944–
  E184.35.J5 2006
  305.892′4073—dc22   2006031050

British Library Cataloguing in Publication Data is available.

Copyright © 2007 by Paul Buhle

All rights reserved. No portion of this book may be
reproduced, by any process or technique, without
the express written consent of the publisher.

Library of Congress Catalog Card Number: 2006031050
ISBN: 0-275-98793-0 (set)
      0-275-98794-9 (vol. 1)
      0-275-98795-7 (vol. 2)
      0-275-98796-5 (vol. 3)

First published in 2007

Praeger Publishers, 88 Post Road West, Westport, CT 06881
An imprint of Greenwood Publishing Group, Inc.
www.praeger.com

Printed in the United States of America

The paper used in this book complies with the
Permanent Paper Standard issued by the National
Information Standards Organization (Z39.48-1984).

10 9 8 7 6 5 4 3 2 1

Every reasonable effort has been made to trace the owners of copyright materials in this book, but in some instances this has proven impossible. The author and publisher will be glad to receive information leading to more complete acknowledgments in subsequent printings of the book, and in the meantime extend their apologies for any omissions.

Contents

	Acknowledgments	vii
	Introduction *Paul Buhle and Harvey Pekar*	ix
	A Cartoon Introduction *Harvey Pekar and Barry Blitt*	xv
1	The Movies: Notes on the Ethnic Origins of an American Obsession *Dennis B. Klein*	1
2	National and Local Movie Moguls: Two Patterns of Jewish Showmanship in Film Exhibition *Judith Thissen*	13
3	The Studio System *Bernard F. Dick*	25
4	The Social Film and the Hollywood Blacklist *Dave Wagner*	37
5	Jews in Hollywood Musicals *Bernard F. Dick*	61
6	Making a Scene: Jews, Stooges, and Censors in Pre-War Hollywood *Dan M. Bronstein*	73

7	Animation *Tom Sito*	85
8	The Jewish Film Festival *Deborah Kaufman and Janis Plotkin*	109
9	A Brief Introduction to Jewish American Radio *Henry Sapoznik*	123
10	Jews on the Radio, 1920–1953 *Ari Y. Kelman*	145
11	Jewish Talk Radio: Programming in Our Time and Place *Ariana Green*	155
12	Television Drama of the Golden Age *Judith Smith*	183
13	Intellectual Pogrom: How the Blacklist Purged Political and Cultural Discourse in Early Television *Steven W. Bowie*	199
14	Jewish Comedy Writers of the 1950s and 1960s *Kathy M. Newman*	213
15	Bring in the Klowns: Jewish Television Comedy since the 1960s *Vincent Brook*	237
Index		261
About the Editor and Contributors		277

Acknowledgments

These volumes owe everything to the collaboration of our authors in the happy spirit of mutual accomplishment, and a great deal to Lisa Pierce of Praeger Publishers for seeing the work through to completion.

To select individuals special to myself and not the other authors would be a mistake. However, a large handful of us, it is fair to say, have crossed paths in person or through books with the late George Mosse, a dean of Jewish studies. A smaller but not insignificant number have felt the influence of Itche Goldberg, 102 years old at this writing, a teacher, editor, and scholar of Yiddish and *Yiddishkayt* for around eighty years. Beyond these, every contributor doubtless has had friends and influencers whose names and books appear in numerous "Further Reading" references.

Introduction
Paul Buhle and Harvey Pekar

Jews and American Popular Culture is an intellectually engaged collection of essays on a subject that has long awaited comprehensive treatment. The contributors, it is useful to note, range in age from their early 20s to their late 70s, representing among themselves three generations of Jewish life. The subjects range from surveys of well-trod zones, literature and film, to those extremely familiar in daily life but most unfamiliar in scholarship, for example, amateur athletics, food, and others in the emerging field of "material culture." Although frequently unstudied, nothing here is really unfamiliar, because it involves the first-hand experiences of ordinary people, especially, but not only, Jewish Americans themselves.

No set of volumes, not thirty or even a hundred, could exhaust the subject, and no such claim is made for these 900-odd pages. Nor is a claim made to the single, definitive answer to the inevitable question, "Why have Jews had such a central impact upon American popular culture?" Claims to a unitary answer would be shallow at best, fraudulent (or perhaps anti-Semitic) at worst.

The following chapters nevertheless offer a serious, many-sided contribution to the answering of that question long unasked, or asked only with a mixture of anxiety and *entre nous* secrecy. At a recent San Francisco Jewish Film Festival, during the break after a panel, an elderly lady approached this editor during the reception and said in a troubled but almost kindly manner, "I agree with everything you say, but I resent terribly your having said it." In other words: Jews had not only an artistic contribution but also (in the case of this festival, devoted to the films of Hollywood blacklistees) a large and sympathetic one, endeavoring to raise public consciousness and conscience on matters of class, race, and gender. However, for me to have said so directly, to have noted Jewishness as a key element of the story, was to court trouble. It is better that secrets or semi-secrets are left unsaid.

We, that is, the newer generations of scholars and a great many Jewish Americans at large—not to speak of a wider interested public—no longer accept this limitation. The sense of comfort has become far greater when Jews so often play Jews on television and in films. Besides, the time is long overdue to ask the hard questions. When the populations of the world at large express a deep suspicion of so many aspects of the U.S. global policy, but also eagerly accept the popular culture produced in Hollywood and New York, an unwillingness to treat the seriousness of the issue invites not only misunderstanding but also disaster. On a smaller scale, ignorance simply begets ignorance, untold tales die with their holders, and so much precious knowledge and insight is unnecessarily lost. The talents of cultural contributors for generations, making audiences laugh or cry, refashioning themes as old as campfire stories (love, adventure, mystery, etc.) into current tellable narratives, *must* have something important to do with the tellers being Jewish.

A certain measure of responsibility or blame for this significant lapse falls rightfully on Jewish intellectuals, mostly but not entirely on older generations. American popular culture observed by educated Jews from the 1890s onward seemed not only tainted by commercialism's siren appeal to the unwary but also positively ridden with violence, lust, and other unworthy values. Uneducated Jews, fathers and mothers eager for their children's success, attainable through education and right living, very often felt much the same. The crowds of immigrant Jews of various classes who flooded the museums on Sundays also wanted for themselves what the Germans called *Bildung*, self-improvement. Night school was ideal, whereas popular culture was a wasteful diversion at best. Worse regions of popular culture, like boxing, were frequently viewed as a horror—its regulars on their way to perdition.

The resulting contradiction, creatively developed repeatedly in different venues within the chapters that follow, was inherent, and its expressions legion. First, thousands of Jews were making a living in the very venues of popular arts on Broadway, actually fashioning the emerging vision of sophisticated living, with Greater New York, the global Jewish capital, epicenter of modern civilization and democratic evolution. Second, many more Jews provided the key audience for the entertainments inevitably centered in the world's greatest metropolis. Movies, later television, radiated outward from New York in audience owing to the concentrated humanity eager for entertainment. Baseball, basketball, and boxing fans were legion among Jewish populations, including fashion-wearing women (and men), as well as gourmet cooks before "gourmet" slipped into household vocabularies. Every class had its own popular culture.

A third element of the contradiction was fatefully entwined with the assimilating generations of the 1930s through the 1950s and this one seems, in retrospect, the most contradictory of all. American Jews have never had such a hero as Franklin D. Roosevelt (and arguably never would again, except for Martin Luther King, Jr.), the last item in a famous Depression Era quip about the worlds of Jewish life: *diese velt* (this world), *yenne velt* (the afterlife), and Roosevelt.

The vision of a great democratizing assimilation, bigger and better New Deals to follow the heroic victory over Fascism, was, however, wrapped up with another largely Jewish creation: the Popular Front. Prompted or at least blessed in Moscow, completely refashioned in the United States into a mixture of liberals and radicals, the Popular Front embraced and (through a combination of artists, publicists, and audience) emphatically created widely beloved versions of "Americanism"—Paul Robeson and Woody Guthrie to Humphrey Bogart and Katharine Hepburn, Aaron Copland to Norman Corwin. These versions seemed to the hostile, mostly Jewish critics around the *Partisan Review*, as unworthy, worse than comic books or boxing. *Bildung* had evidently been turned on its head, making citizens into mere consumers of a *kitsch* or pseudoculture that corrupted folk and high culture alike.

The presumed conspiracy soon unraveled amid Red Scares, disillusionment with Russia, fresh bursts of homegrown anti-Semitism and counter-avowals of Jewish loyalty to what were deemed "American values." But the central contradictions remained unresolved. What did it mean that so many elements of popular culture heavily inflected by so many Jewish Americans' inclinations and careers would be perceived as harmful, many of their creators, only yesterday highly lauded professionals, dastardly subversives?

So determined was the hostile response to a surging popular culture that in the Cold War years such recent or newer developments as comic books, television, and rock 'n' roll music became a veritable counterpart to global Communism, an enemy from within. Jewish upward mobility had meanwhile accelerated most astonishingly, and yet well-paid professors and distinguished cultural critics felt their surroundings besieged by dumb fads, teenage idols, and the wider sense that young people including their own children simply could and would not appreciate the sacrifices made on their privileged behalves. Or, for that matter, sit and listen, with pleasure, to good classical music.

This picture may seem somewhat overdrawn, because even a certain share of those prominent young Jewish intellectuals who denounced popular culture during the 1950s found themselves coming around to student interests (and more to the point, student enrollments) as their careers advanced. But, of course, the later 1960s and early 1970s had intervened, changing almost everything. The result was vastly worse, according to that new and disproportionately Jewish category of intellectual, the neoconservative. Or ambiguously better, according to rebellious younger Jews and their sympathetic elders. In any case, as a French student-participant of the May 1968 Paris revolution remarked a decade later: after the uprising, a professor thought twice before declaring a dissertation on comic books to be off limits and, indeed, entirely out of the question.

The same counter-cultural upheaval created previously inconceivable opportunities for jobs and hobbies in and around the entertainment world, along with a fresh generation of consumers. When *Rolling Stone* magazine surpassed *Time* magazine in circulation, the times really had changed. Younger Jewish cultural creators and packagers flourished in the face of an often disdaining, ardently conservative "red state" political culture, and perhaps because of it. Standing categories in the official art world also faded away. If "modernism" had been an uncertain title for the collective work of intellectuals and artists seeking ever-purer forms of expression, "postmodernism" was a more unambiguous cognomen for the abandonment of purity once and for all.

In what would become known as the "Age of the Cassette" (until cassettes themselves became obsolete), images—visual and verbal—would be available everywhere, permitting each consumer to create a personal *cinematique* of various sorts. Access has, of course, expanded continuously since. And yet, the change was poorly represented in scholarship, usually remaining at the level of journalism, documentary presentation, or classroom anecdote than sustained work in primary sources.

The older generations of intellectuals, but especially those coming to notable prestige during the 1950s, had been above all specialists in the essay. The new generations had perhaps skipped that writing course and rarely bothered with the genteel preoccupations of the past. But in time, they began to discover the pleasures of heavy-duty research unknown to the self-consciously cerebral essayist. Archives of Jewish athletic societies and other assorted clubs; archives of record creators, radio and television corporations, and writers; and new kinds of archives, created through oral history of old-timers still on hand to recall their participation at all levels of popular culture. As yet another generation of intellectuals took their Ph.Ds, the popular culture scholar finally came of age. His subject or hers (the drastic shift in the gender demography of academic life, steadily diluting the proportion of white males, became crucial here) was no longer so likely to be ridiculed as "cowboys and comic books," the laughable oddity of American Studies departments for the hobbyist unlikely to get tenure in either English or History proper. Now she or he was more likely to be the lecturer who packed in the students looking for something that connected with their own lives.

Slowly but surely, popular arts were also being accepted as real arts. Some eighty years since the appearance of *The Seven Lively Arts* (1926) by Gilbert Seldes and a half-century after the ponderous, mostly disdaining *Mass Culture: The Popular Arts in America* (1957), cartoonist Ben Katchor was an honored guest at museums around the world and a MacArthur Fellow as well. Film had long since been nudged up from its old, lowly status of escapism by the appearance of television, a worse escapism. Some would say that Woody Allen films had become a totemic cinematic and notably Jewish art of the waning twentieth century. At any rate, film scholarship, film departments, global film history conferences, all proliferated, followed by similar developments in sports history, comics history, and so on.

Introduction

Was *Seinfeld* or *Curb Your Enthusiasm* likely to become art for the ages? Probably not, but they were art for this age, when the lines between fans and scholars had become less apparent and a lot less interesting.

***

These volumes, as studies within American culture, do not pretend to explore the taproot of creativity in the Old World. The scholarly work here is far more preliminary; the conclusions destined to be debated for decades more, as scholars set themselves for vastly more work in Yiddish sources. Yet the subject is undeniably connected with our own. The reader will tolerate, I hope, some tentative suggestions.

First of all, within the European Jewish diaspora, over the course of centuries, the Yiddish language with its correlative, *Yiddishkayt* (i.e., Yiddishness), was itself a popular culture, distinctively vernacular and accorded the same lack of respect as the popular cultures to follow. New pressures in mid-nineteenth-century industrialization and urbanization prompted inhabitants in village or city to begin stepping on a path to be traversed ever farther by those who followed them.

No one could at the time have possibly predicted that a generation or two after departure from the *shtetl* and urban ghettoes, the immigrant children of the inhabitants would frame the internal logic of the emerging popular cultures, severely mediated—but never completely controlled—by the forces of the market. The suggestion that nothing can be seen in retrospect as predicting that upsurge would not only be foolish but would connote a stubborn resistance to examining one of the most influential developments of modern times.

The examination of popular culture as anything but an object of contempt has some genuine genteel (as well as emphatically Gentile) roots in the old hostility toward capitalistic commercialization. But it also reflects the Haskalah determination, mainly of German Jews, to purge Jewish populations of their folkish culture and language, thus preparing them for proper assimilation and upward mobility, in a word "normalization." Thus Yiddish itself was, for the modernizer, an obstacle, and a contemptible "jhargon," a language neither Hebrew nor German nor Slavic but something mongrelized and unclean. It symbolized the unwillingness to rise to the challenge of gentility and upward mobility, where Judaism might exist as religion (and for some, a Jewish homeland remain a vision) but vernacular Jewishness as widely understood would disappear.

Rising Yiddishists of the late nineteenth century offered a custard pie in the face to this version of propriety. The legendary Yiddish writers Mendele and Sholem Aleichem brought literary Yiddish to life as they sought to prod the community forward. Humor was a crucial means for making existence bearable but also understandable. Yiddish writing also reflected the deep resentment by the dispossessed against the elite, religious, and secular.

Introduction

The Yiddish aphorisms *di velt iz eukh a velt* (this world is also a world) and *di gantse velt iz a khlum, nokh esser iz a guter khlum, eder a shlekhter* (the world is a dream—but better a good dream than a bad one) date at least to the middle of the century and in spirit, perhaps far earlier. The jokester's corresponding satire on the proclamations of the righteous—whose dualism never allowed flesh-and-blood existence much leeway except to face discipline, suffer, and be punished—were to be matched by the contempt for the commercial pseudorationalism and social bullying by the Jewish merchant class of poor and working class Jews.

In the voice of the satirist, there emerged a counter-narrative, closer perhaps than anything else in Jewish life to the carnivals held by the Gentiles (with furtive Jewish participation), turning all the social rules upside down for a short time. The raucous laughter of the vulgar Jewish crowd at the mockery of kings and religious leaders presaged, at any rate, published Yiddish humor attacking politicians, the rich, and the get-along-go-along rabbinate.

Darker theories about the kinship of Jews and comedy or humor developed in the cerebral corners of anti-Semitism during the last third of the nineteenth century, that is, shortly after Jews began leaving the Pale in larger numbers and making their presence felt in European capitals. According to perceptive scholars, the condemnation of humor, satire, and similar merriment to the literary gutter was strongly associated with the connections of Jews and sexuality. True and dignified humor, according to the savants of the day, had to be transcendent; the Jew was purported to suffer from a kind of deformity that manifested itself in mere mockery.

Otto Weininger, the most distinguished of anti-Semites, granted that Jews had great talent for all manner of superficial arts, but reasoned that this merely compensated for their lack of depth, that is, their inability to create real art. Essentially unbelievers (Judaism could not be granted status as a real religion), they were hypercritical of everything, mere cultural parasites on civil society and the arts wherever they gathered and expressed themselves.

It has taken five generations or so, rich with Jewish participation in popular arts and culture, to prove the slander false, and more than false. In the grasp of that vulgar vernacular, Jewish artists and Jewish audiences have fashioned a proper response to anti-Semites and to the haughtiness of history's upper classes, a response in practice. If the accompanying market impulses and salesmanship have often corrupted the response, it has survived that corruption with some of the finest moments of civilized response to the common disaster of our time. No more could properly be asked.

Perhaps, by now, the residual effects of the old hostility toward popular culture in particular have ceased to count for much. If the collective contribution of these volumes adds to a contrary view, an appreciation of Jewish generations to make fresh discoveries in culture and to fashion a more democratic vision out of them, then surely my fellow contributors will feel, as I do, that they have not wasted their efforts.

Chapter 1

The Movies: Notes on the Ethnic Origins of an American Obsession

Dennis B. Klein

The motion picture industry, we all know, is deeply indebted to the ingenuity of one man—Thomas Alva Edison. He supplied the indispensable hardware: cameras, film, and projectors. However, technology alone fails to explain the way the industry initially courted Americans, exactly who among Americans first fell in love with the movies, and how the industry eventually created an American obsession. For this, it is necessary to look beyond the spectacle of motion pictures to the time and place where men and women transformed a clever idea into a national passion. This is not a simple matter: at the human heart of the nascent industry exist two half-forgotten facts.

The first is the setting where movie studios first migrated to form a critical mass of film production. Though East Coast operations were scattered in New York City, Long Island, and throughout New Jersey, Fort Lee, N.J., emerged toward the end of the first decade of the twentieth century as the vital production center. Few traces survive from the days when thousands of "photoplays" were filmed every year along the Palisades overlooking the Hudson River and New York City: an innocuous office building that once was home to Champion studios, a forerunner of the Universal Film Manufacturing Company (Universal Studios); a surviving stone wall that formed the perimeter of another studio; and a street named after Theda Bara, an early actor. Even movie buffs may not be aware that the Palisades, a steep, rocky, majestic overhang used for suspenseful early drama, provided the memorable movie term "the cliffhanger." Fort Lee's obscurity is enshrined in its omission as a separate entry in the otherwise comprehensive *Encyclopedia of Early Cinema* (Abel).

Fort Lee emerged as the incubus of the motion picture industry for two reasons: it offered a range of backdrop scenery that Manhattan and nearby studios could not match. As a summer resort for the well-to-do, it had a saloon, a hotel, and forests throughout the region. There was even an Indian village that became important for the Westerns. As the movies grew from an exhibition showing the novelty of pictures in motion and lasting just a few minutes, to longer narratives telling epic stories, Fort Lee was the perfect setting. Although remote, it was also accessible by ferry from Manhattan's 125th Street pier and, once in Jersey, by trolley scaling the Palisades to Fort Lee village. The ferry came to symbolize Fort Lee's ascendance. Its boats took on the names of the industry's earliest movie stars—Mae Marsh, Maxine Elliot, Mary Garden, Jane Cowl, and Madge Kennedy.

However, the real story of Fort Lee was the kind of people the studios drew. From 1907 on, Fort Lee became a magnet for social outcasts, a mix of immigrants and foreigners, where women and blacks could find a niche. It was already a town where Italian immigrants found jobs catering to the resort crowd and the nearby Palisades Amusement Park. Like other amusement parks at the turn of the last century, the Palisades anticipated Fort Lee's enthusiasm for the movies by screening the earliest, crude productions during the summers when urban theaters went "dark" due to the overbearing heat. Among the early studios, several were owned and operated by French movie entrepreneurs (they lived together in their community). Along with bizarre street occurrences, like "auto loads of Fiji Islanders ... or a string of camels ... and then a bevy of 'leggy' chorus girls," as one contemporary Fort Lee resident reported, the panoply of America's pariahs who made the movies set the early, offbeat tone. As Carl Laemmle, a maverick entrepreneur in the early movie business, recalled, alluding in part to the early industry's intimate association with the amusement park, "It was a business which sheltered a variegated collection of former carnival men, gamblers, ex-saloon keepers, medicine men, concessionaires of circus side shows, photographers, and peddlers who were attracted by reports of lurid profits made in the operation of nickelodeons."

Not surprisingly, the subjects of the early movies were often ribald and risqué, eventually a source of considerable consternation for the moral police who feverishly campaigned to impose censorship regulations. Twice in 1908 Progressive-era reformers exerted pressure on the industry to sanitize what seemed to them as the movies' unfettered vulgarity. In March, movie studios agreed to collaborate with the People's Institute to create the National Board of Censorship—a self-regulating gatekeeper that avoided government intervention. However, the industry would remain under a cloud of suspicion. Just nine months later, New York City mayor George Brinton McClellan ordered all nickelodeons closed for their invidious influence on children, women, and immigrants. Only after the studios consented to new laws that included wider police jurisdiction and control over children's attendance did city authorities permit the theaters to reopen. Nevertheless, as columnist Maude McDougall

The Movies: Notes on the Ethnic Origins of an American Obsession

observed in 1913, concern over the influence of "cheap shows" seemed as grave as ever. Nothing less than "the entire raw material of future citizenship" was at stake.

The second fact that forms the hidden history of the early motion picture industry is the pivotal role Jewish immigrants played. Neal Gabler, in his *An Empire of Their Own: How the Jews Invented Hollywood* (1988), in important respects called positive attention to the role of Jews in the movie industry, but he mistakenly referred to the 1920s through the 1940s as the "first generation" of Jews in film. Additionally, film historians are right in maintaining, contrary to Gabler's argument, that the emerging industry constituted filmmakers from a variety of backgrounds, not just Jewish. Above all, Gabler's argument that Jews in the industry submerged their Jewish backgrounds to a single-minded pursuit of the American dream erringly diminishes the organizing, self-consciously Jewish influence on the industry.

During the Fort Lee period, from 1909 to 1922, that is, from its first to its last major production studio, Jews became studio owners and movie producers in impressive numbers. Of Hollywood's "Big Eight"—the studios that, by 1940, controlled 95 percent of all movie rentals paid by U.S. theaters—six can trace their origins to Jewish entrepreneurs who got their start in Fort Lee: Paramount, 20th Century Fox, MGM, Universal, United Artists, and RKO. Moreover, the collective effect of their activities was greater than the sum of their individual parts: a Jewish extended family of sorts existed in Fort Lee that goes a long way toward explaining the industry's dramatic ascendance. In addition, the "opposition" these Jews cultivated to compete with Edison's movie trust—a war that gave birth to independent studios and, eventually, many of the Big Eight, as well as to indelible movie innovations such as the star system, feature-length films, the integration of movie production and distribution, and construction of grand movie houses—was fundamentally a culture war between Jews and Edison's oligopoly of mainly Protestant studio owners.

As Jewish immigrants, Carl Laemmle, William Fox, Adolph Zukor, Lewis J. Selznick, Marcus Loew, Louis B. Mayer, Samuel Goldwyn, and others possessed an unexpected advantage over the studios that formed the movie trust—the Motion Picture Patent Company, or MPPCo: they knew the people who delighted in the early silent nickelodeons because most lived among them. According to *Statistical Sources for Demographic Studies of Greater New York*, published in 1913, Jewish immigrants loved the movies more than any other ethnic group, constituting the largest part of the nickelodeon audience in Manhattan. Indeed, a significant number of movie theaters (really, storefronts) were located in their Lower East Side and Brooklyn neighborhoods. As one trade report from 1906 noted, Jews would exploit their Sabbath holidays to gather at moving picture exhibitions—an observation that incidentally suggests that immigrants who were keen on the movies were receptive to cultural innovation and social change.

Jewish-immigrant studio owners therefore acquired a unique understanding of the early industry's evolving market forces. Like movie theater exhibitors generally, who, by 1909, were largely Jewish, they knew what their patrons wanted—cheap entertainment that did not require English literacy to understand, and the chance to feel like respectable, middle-class Americans as they were ushered to their seats, in theaters that were evolving into elegant movie palaces, in anticipation of watching Broadway stars on the big screen. (Loew named his first nickelodeon theater, in 1908, the "Royal" [Gabler 27]; one reporter covering the opening in 1914 of Strand Theater in Manhattan made note of "an idealization of the dreams of life" painted above the proscenium arch "New Strand Opens; Biggest of Movies," *New York Times*, April 12, 1914.) For Zukor, who made the study of audiences into a fine art, discerning immigrant tastes was the key to the industry's swift successes. This intimate relationship would have important practical consequences. When the trust acquired virtually absolute control over patent rights, raw film, and film distribution by 1911, the independents maintained their connections with their patrons by managing to control one-third to one-half of the nation's movie theaters.

The "in-between" liminal place Jewish-immigrant entrepreneurs inhabited in America's early twentieth century is also significant: their uneasy negotiation of the Jewish past and the American future suggests the reasons for the seminal bond they forged with their audiences and with each other. In socially dynamic terms, like many of those who were drawn to watching the movies these movie-makers were eager to escape from their inherited Jewishness, but they also recognized and affirmed the value of something inescapably Jewish. Their immediate backgrounds show just how proximate their Jewishness was. Fox, born Wilhelm Fuchs, grew up in the United States in an Orthodox-Jewish household and attended a *cheder*, a school for Orthodox Jews. Goldwyn, born Schmuel Gelbfisz, came from a Hasidic family. Selznick, born Zeleznik, would recall the harsh conditions for Jews during his early life in Kiev. Zukor's uncle, Kalman Liebermann, a Judaic scholar who raised him after Zukor's father and his mother died by the time he was eight, wanted him to become a rabbi. Another source of influence, Samuel Rosenberg, Zukor's school headmaster in Hungary who taught him the Bible, apparently had a lasting effect. According to his son, Eugene, Zukor's Jewish and filial attachment to Rosenberg was his "secret self." In an interview he gave years later, Zukor remarked that had he been exposed less to Orthodox piety and more to the attenuated Jewishness epitomized by American Jews, he would have been "a very devout Jew."

As a whole, they seemed embarrassed by their Jewish associations and wanted nothing more than to blend into the American, middle-class mainstream. Indeed, there is scant evidence of their Jewish heritage in their memoirs and other reminiscences. Fox's biographer observed that Fox was not interested in religion. Goldwyn and Mayer eventually crossed the divide to the non-Jewish world, Goldwyn through marriage and Mayer through developing a deep interest in Christianity. Zukor recalled with contempt his Jewish upbringing with Liebermann. Laemmle also appeared determined to erase his Jewish past. Gilbert Max Aaronson, co-owner of the trust's Essanay company who was known affectionately to film viewers as "Bronco Billy" Anderson, chose not to speak openly about his Jewish American roots. Together, they have hidden their Jewish origins as much as Universal Studios has neglected its Fort Lee origins, which is one important reason why a good part of the story of the early motion picture obsession has practically disappeared.

However, this does not mean that their Jewishness did not matter to them. To be sure, Judaism meant little. But in other respects that had more to do with the company they kept and preferred to keep, and even with the movies they made, being Jewish was important. Laemmle, for example, hired scores of his relatives, exhibiting, as one observer noted years later, "an intense love for all those to whom he is tied by blood." Other filmmakers who were Jewish met each other years on sales routes years before they entered the film business and remained friends or became partners in the industry. Mark Dintenfass, who built Champion studios in 1909—Fort Lee's first—and joined Universal three years later, met Selznick in Pittsburgh and introduced him to Universal that led to Selznick's role as Universal's first general manager. Judith Thissen, elsewhere in this compendium, suggestively refers to a network of Jewish investment companies, partnership firms, and amusement companies, a network that twinned Loew with brothers Nicholas and Joseph Schenck, who benefited from his investments first in their amusement park then in United Artists and MGM, their respective Hollywood film corporations; and with Zukor, who joined Loew in managing movie theaters. Lee Shubert, an immigrant from a Polish Jewish family, also invested heavily in the movies, including millions in 1914 in the World Film Corporation, which Selznick was managing. Not only were Zukor and Loew in business together, Zukor's daughter, Mildred, eventually married Loew's son, Arthur, at a ceremony officiated by Rabbi Stephen S. Wise. Zukor, himself, married Lottie Kaufman, the niece of his partner, Morris Kohn, in the fur business and, later, in the movie arcades (Gabler 16). Goldwyn's marriage to Blanche Lasky in 1910 foreshadowed the partnership he formed with her brother and Cecil B. DeMille three years later in the Jesse L. Lasky Feature Play Company. The Selznick and Mayer families reinforced the Jewish kinship that started in Fort Lee when David O., the son of Lewis J., married Mayer's daughter, Irene, in 1930. It may be significant as a reflection of the tight Jewish bond that existed in the nascent industry that DeMille, who was a devout Episcopalian, recalled how uncomfortable he felt in this ancestral as well as professional circle of Jews (Brackman 4).

This extended family embraced a wider circle. Siegmund Lubin, who belonged to Edison's trust (the only one in the trust unmistakably recognized as a Jew), often breached trust boundaries to help Jews in the independents, such as Dintenfass and Goldwyn, and studio partners Charles O. Baumann and Adam Kessel (on Baumann and Kessel, Eckhardt, 74+). During the war, while still in Fort Lee, Lasky, Loew, Fox, Zukor, Joseph Schenck, and L.J. Selznick joined the New York Community Campaign to raise money for the support of Jewish troops and Jews in the European war zone. Loew, Fox, and Zukor made substantial donations and appealed to their peers in the theatrical business. Two years later, in 1919, Lewis Selznick, who stayed in Fort Lee until 1922 after others left for Hollywood, joined Laemmle and Loew in contributing financially to Jewish social service and charitable organizations. He contributed to the Zionist Organization of America the following year.

The movies they made and the audience they sought to court also hints at the importance of a Jewish self-consciousness. Reading film for autobiographical evidence is a hazardous endeavor to be sure, and a facile conflation of a work of art with its ethnic origins is a mistake. However, the work of film historians Patricia Erens and Richard Abel in this area is compelling. In her study of films with Jewish themes made during this period—many in Fort Lee—Erens observed that those by Jewish production companies or by Jewish authors show Jews making their way in America and up the social ladder, but not at the expense of their Jewish backgrounds. Indeed, Jewish studio owners appeared to regard America as mainly heterogeneous, a cultural mosaic that could accommodate Jews and other distinctive groups—though not blacks (who often had to sit in segregated theater balconies, as well)—on their own terms. Fox derived joy from observing the way "the rich [moviegoers] rub elbows with the poor, . . . forming a distinctly American institution"—something few in Edison's trust regarded as worthy of comment, let alone jubilation. Kathy Peiss, in *Cheap Amusements*, noted how Goldwyn praised the movies' carnival of pleasure, which in his opinion duly Americanized the working class.

Conversely, Abel shows an inclination in films made by non-Jewish-owned studios to project an image of American homogeneity, known widely from this period on as the melting pot. Abel does not distinguish between Jewish- and non-Jewish-owned studios, but in passages from "The 'Imagined Community' of the Westerns, 1910–1913" (2004) dealing with the image of a mythic, one-America national identity in film, his frequent references to two, Essanay and Selig (Selig was based in Chicago), suggest a Protestant-establishment shading of these themes. (Anderson complicates Essanay's ethnic makeup, but both his Jewish concealment and co-owner George Spoor's documented hostility toward Jews confirm the company's American-nativist credentials; Selig's ethnicity is a matter of some disagreement, but Lary May, consulting primary source documents, maintained that William Selig, like Spoor, was Protestant.)

Abel studied the "imagined community" implicit in the westerns, which proliferated against the background of fatal conflict between the MPPCo and the independents for industry supremacy during the years 1910 to 1913. In these particularly relevant passages, he observed that films mainly depicted threatened white settlers fighting Indians not only for their own survival but also for the triumph of a "new 'imperial' nation." Essanay's Anderson, whose portrayals of the outlaw cowboy "with a conscience" thrilled audiences, himself "offered a model of assimilation" into an emerging social order. (Indeed, as Abel maintains, Anderson's on-screen social reintegration reflected his own Jewish assimilation.) It is possible, then, to discern competing visions of America in early-narrative films made by Jews and non-Jews.

There is evidence that, as intense as the independents' legal battles were against Edison's monopoly over film making and distribution—and they were intense: Laemmle took part in 289 legal actions in all—the ethnic undercurrent was even stronger and may well have fueled the more public conflict. This is significant. It is well-documented that the trust controlled film production and distribution by 1910. By threatening legal suits under Frank L. Dyer's overall direction, it induced most filmmakers to acquire the requisite license to use, at least legally, Edison's patents. Dyer expressed complete satisfaction in his 1910 exultant biography of Edison: "All the principal American manufacturers of motion pictures are paying a royalty to Edison under his basic patents." But by 1912, the independents already succeeded at halving the trust's once-complete control over the film supply and Laemmle and Fox were making their way through legal channels toward defeating General Film Company, which had managed the MPPCo's near-monopoly of film distribution. It is also recognized that the independents and those associated with them not only went on to dominate movie-making in America (though not without its own internecine warfare) but also took extraordinary steps toward igniting its market appeal. However, there is little recognition of the role of a self-consciously culture war in galvanizing these key developments. It is pointless to determine which side started the war. It is more important to understand that, like any conflict, both sides were responsible and, indeed, were constituent parts of mutual recrimination. MPPCo's members were consistently hostile toward Jews in the early industry. Edison expressed this view, though he was not the most tendentious. In a 1911 letter he observed the tendency among Jews toward greed and "clannishness," an optic that could only have darkened his opinion of Jews who led the anti-film-trust campaign. Reflecting a wish-fulfillment in the movies made by at least some in the trust, he hoped the Jew would someday assimilate, or at least "not carry to such extremes his natural advantages." Others nurtured deeper antagonisms. Court records show that most trust members apparently did not want Jews in the business. In legal testimony, William Swanson, a film distributor, testified that George Spoor of MPPCo's Essanay studio had expressed contempt: he "didn't want any God damn Jews in the Company," a comment that raises other questions about his relationship with

Anderson. Apparently more summary was Frank Dyer of the Edison Company, who also presided over the General Film Company. According to Swanson, he maintained there was no room in the motion picture industry for Jews. Indeed, there appeared to be an effort to expel Lubin from the trust. (Film historians render different opinions about Swanson's testimony: Eileen Bowser questioned his credibility; Joseph Eckhardt believed that there was "a core of truth" in Swanson's direct examination. Unlike Laemmle, who gave up playing by the trust's rules after a couple of months in early 1909, Lubin remained in the trust, putting up with the anti-Jewish sentiment to avoid legal entanglements over patent infringements.)

Dyer's strong opinion against Jews, if true, may well have had a decisive shaping effect on what was called the U.S. patent wars—the legal offensives and counter-offensives that menaced film production during the first fifteen years of the twentieth century. After all, as a patent attorney, he represented Edison in legal battles over 17 years, from 1897 to 1914. He was a driving force in organizing the MPPCo in December, 1908, and served as its first president during the apogee of conflict with the independents, from 1908 to 1912. From 1912 to 1914 he led the General Film Company as its president. He returned to private law practice in 1914.

Vitagraph's Albert Smith and John Stuart Blackton were especially hostile toward Jews. Kalem's George Kleine, in a 1908 letter to Selig, vilified one film exchange owner as following the "Hebraic rule of taking everything that is allowed and then some." (Selig received a letter that year from a distributor that expressed similar invective even more crudely.) To make sure no one assumed he was Jewish, he insisted on pronouncing his surname's German final "e." There is no doubt that the trust framed the struggle for industry preeminence in volatile, ethnic terms: their ads in *Moving Picture World*, in response to Laemmle's public assault on the trust, consisted of cartoons showing the independents as ghetto junkmen.

Years later, Zukor recalled the pain he felt as a result of this kind of social rejection, as did Fox, who said he had been uncomfortable in "fashionable culture." But Jews in the industry were not innocent. They were not just victims. As the political philosopher Hannah Arendt observed, Jews in the modern era possessed "as much responsibility for world events as anyone else" (Canovan 44), and this insight certainly applies to the industry's nascent stage. To begin with, the bond Jews formed amounted to a powerful subculture; just as Edison remarked, the independents were largely "clannish." Indeed, when studio partners Charles O. Baumann and Adam Kessel joined Laemmle in 1910 to form the Motion Picture Distributing and Sales Company, some denounced it as a "trust" because it controlled the distribution of nearly all films made by the independents. The sense of resentment was strong enough to split apart the Sales Company two years later into three competing firms—Laemmle's Universal Film Manufacturing Company, the Mutual Film Company, and the Film Supply Company

(*Encyclopedia of Early Cinema*). But the independents ultimately succeeded at controlling the industry, a phenomenon periodically confirmed by attempts over the years to break up this "empire" that culminated in the government's 1947 decision against the Hollywood "Big Eight."

D.W. Griffith's notorious production of *Birth of a Nation*, which his Triangle Film Corporation released in 1915, is emblematic of this competition for the soul of America. In it, he depicted the Ku Klux Klan's white crusade against an American fifth column—blacks, Catholics, and Jews who represented a danger to the nation's moral firmament. Jews, however much they needed a common defense against an intolerant film trust, appeared to heighten the stakes of war: they liked to see themselves in the opposition. It was Laemmle who branded the MPPCo as a "trust," a term of certain opprobrium during this era of government trust-busting. He first used the term after deserting the MPPCo in early 1909 (Eckhardt 72). Given his natural association with other Jews, his campaign expressed a good fight he and other Jews were waging against what he continued to call "the gigantic trust."

Arendt argued that Jews in the nineteenth and twentieth centuries partly incited a hostile reaction because they never asked about the political implications of their conduct. It apparently never occurred to Jews in their drive for independence that they confirmed the suspicions of their detractors. The provocative blend of Jewish kinship and their declaration of war fueled the belief that Jews "were held together by mysterious ties," aspiring "to a mysterious rule 'behind the scenes'" (Canovan 44). Their enlistment of the government in the legal dismantlement of the MPPCo similarly suggests Jewish control of the state for legal and cultural supremacy (Canovan 44). In this light, the neglect in memoirs and other reminiscences by Jews in the early industry of the formative influence of their Jewishness seems to reflect an element of shame for their role as Jews in the relentless hostilities that gave birth to the modern movie industry.

The early motion picture industry was troubled in a way not often grasped by historians. There were hard feelings, distrust, crass competition, and winners and losers. While winners in any endeavor deserve credit on their own merits, it is surely significant that many in the emerging film industry were Jews. As Jews they were energized by common purpose strengthened by ethnic kinship. Fort Lee, the bohemian world of early movie makers, was a setting that helped immigrant Jews feel at home in America, one that was conducive to movie innovations that set the industry on its ascent to international eminence.

Why, then, did not Jews in the nascent industry and their supporters affirm the owners' Jewish attachments, at least in retrospect? The desire to escape what seemed like an irrelevant or narrow Jewish past provides one answer, though that does not explain why they still could not just revise their inherited Jewishness to make it agree with a modern American ethos the way Progressive-era jurist and Jewish Zionist leader Louis Brandeis did, or, for that matter, the way Zukor said he wanted to. The main reason has more to do with image, or rather image control. Anti-Jewish hostility was the infant movie business's subtext. Its exponents succeeded at defining the industry as Jewish and anything Jewish as repugnant. For them, the only good Jew was a former Jew. How could anyone Jewish in the business claim their formative Jewish attachments when opinions like screenwriter Harold Hoadly's were so prevalent? In a risible 1913 letter, Hoadly referred to Lewis Selznick as "a little fat, sawed off, undersized, hook-nosed Jew simp by the name of Selznick (you don't pronounce it, you sneeze it)."

The twin assault on the movies and on Jews accreted and became a worldview after World War I, owing in large part to Henry Ford. His scurrilous February, 1921, *Dearborn Independent* articles were among the first to make note of the Jewish predominance in the film industry, indeed, to assert that "the movies are Jewish." His contemporary, William Sheafe Chase, who belonged to the New York Civic League, agreed: "The motion picture industry is in the despotic control of four or five Hebrews, such as Messrs. Lasky, Loew, Fox, Zukor, and Laemmle."

Ford and Chase were right to a point: Jews did play a formative role. But by blaming Jews for corroding American morals grounded in "faith and quietness," by branding Jews as "foreign to America"; in short, by denouncing Jews for subverting sacred religious, racial and sexual conventions, Ford's steady diatribes have made it next to impossible to revisit the subject without evoking his characterization of the movies as "Jewish supremacy" or a Jewish conspiracy. Kleine liked what he read in these articles so much that he requested reprints and, in a classic stroke of psychological projection, published a letter to the editor about New York's City College, his alma mater, where "Gentiles . . . have been frozen out." It may seem a bit apologetic, but it is also understandable under these circumstances why Laemmle, instead of promoting the exhilaration and sensuousness of film, would characterize his first production, *Hiawatha*, just three years after its 1909 release, as "instructive and educational." As Ford would make clear, "sensuous" was code for Jewish corruption while "educational" was code for American decency. Yet the governing enthusiasm for filmmaking and the filmmakers' progressive determination to manufacture an eager market—the seeds of an American obsession—indeed, the explanatory power of the movies' lightening ascendancy, will remain shrouded in obscurity until we restore to the industry's early history the vital role Fort Lee and its Jewish independent filmmakers played.

ACKNOWLEDGMENT

The author wishes to thank Karen Lynch and Joanna Sliwa for their assistance with this article, and Kean University for supporting the research with a faculty/student research grant.

FURTHER READING

Abel, Richard. "The 'Imagined Community' of the Westerns, 1910–1913." *America's Transitional Era: Audiences, Institutions, Practices.* Eds. Charlie Kiel and Shelley Stamp. Los Angeles: University of California Press, 2004. 131–170.

Bowser, Eileen. *The Transformation of the Cinema, 1907–1915.* Berkeley: University of California Press, 1994.

Canovan, Margaret. *Hannah Arendt: A Reinterpretation of Her Political Thought.* Cambridge, UK: Cambridge University Press, 1992.

Eckhardt, Joseph P. *The King of the Movies: Film Pioneer Siegmund Lubin.* Madison, WI: Fairleigh Dickinson Press, 1997.

Encyclopedia of Early Cinema. Ed. Richard Abel. London: Routledge, 2005.

Erens, Patricia. *The Jew in American Cinema.* Bloomington: Indiana University Press, 1984.

Gabler, Neal. *An Empire of Their Own: How the Jews Invented Hollywood.* New York: Crown Publishers, 1988.

Koszarski, Richard. *Fort Lee: The Film Town.* Rome, Italy: John Libbey Publishing, 2004.

May, Lary L. *Screening Out the Past: The Birth of Mass Culture and the Motion Picture Industry.* New York: Oxford University Press, 1980.

"New Strand Opens; Biggest of Movies." *New York Times*, 12 Apr. 1914.

Peiss, Kathy Lee. *Cheap Amusements: Working Women and Leisure in Turn-of-the-Century New York.* Philadelphia: Temple University Press, 1986.

Chapter 2

National and Local Movie Moguls: Two Patterns of Jewish Showmanship in Film Exhibition

Judith Thissen

In the early twentieth century, the emergence of moving picture theaters dramatically altered the ways most Americans spent their leisure time. Nowhere was the impact of the nation's new pastime more visible than in New York City, where the rapid proliferation of penny arcades and nickel shows redefined the cityscape and provided the working classes in particular with unparalleled access to commercial entertainment.

The growth in popularity of the movies began with the nickelodeon. Around 1905, the cinema found its own exclusive outlet in small storefront theaters, which offered a half-hour program of moving pictures and illustrated songs for five cents. The shows ran continuously from morning to evening. People went day after day, and from one show to another. In December 1908, New York's police commissioner Theodore Bingham, in a memo to Mayor McClellan, reported 194 storefront nickelodeons for Manhattan alone. In three years, there were approximately 750 motion picture shows in Greater New York. It seemed that Jewish immigrants, who constituted about 25 percent of the city's population, loved the movies more than any other ethnic group. "The success of the moving pictures in our neighborhood is amazing. Soon more houses will open. Everywhere, hundreds of people are standing in line, waiting to get a chance to see a show," the leading Yiddish daily reported in May 1908. This enthusiasm for the movies is confirmed by the fact that the Lower East Side and Jewish Harlem had the highest density of nickelodeons and by the prominence of Eastern European Jews in the early film exhibition business. Sixty percent of the nickelodeon operators in Manhattan were Jewish. Three of them would become leading figures in American industry: Marcus Loew, Adolph Zukor, and William Fox.

Together with Louis B. Mayer and the Warner brothers, Loew, Zukor, and Fox have become synonym with the Golden Age of Hollywood and the era of the picture palaces. Even today, their road of success from humble immigrant origins to captains of industry still stands as a symbol for the Jewish pursuit of the American Dream. By contrast, the names of many other Jewish film exhibitors have been forgotten, even though they played an important role in the first decades of motion picture exhibition. The career of Charles Steiner, for instance, offers a different model of Jewish showman, that of the independent film exhibitor who invested in medium-sized neighborhood theaters for a working-class clientele. Steiner never went to Hollywood. He stayed in New York and managed to fashion a niche in the nation's largest movie market. By 1925, he and his business associates controlled almost all moving picture theaters on the Lower East Side, as well as half a dozen in Harlem and several more in Brooklyn.

This chapter, then, investigates the crucial contribution that Jewish film exhibitors made to the entertainment revolution of the early twentieth century by focussing on two complementary patterns of Jewish showmanship. It details the rise to power of Loew, Zukor, Fox, and Steiner and explores the logic of their success, taking up a decade of film exhibition in New York City from the beginning of the nickelodeon boom to the late 1910s. To understand their early careers is to learn how the movies captured America.

Adolph Zukor (1873–1976), the later head of Paramount Pictures, came from Hungary. He was born into Jewish family of small shopkeepers and migrated to America in 1888. Within a decade or so, the young immigrant worked his way up from an apprentice in a fur store to ownership of a prosperous fur business. At the age of thirty, he had already accumulated a small fortune. Zukor perceived the potential of low-cost entertainment several years before the nickelodeon boom hit New York. In those days, storefront theaters specialized in projected movies for collective audiences were still an exhibition form of limited viability, but penny arcades with peepshow movies for individual viewers, phonographs, and other slot machines were steadily rising in popularity. In March 1904, Zukor incorporated with three business partners the Automatic Vaudeville Company and set up a large and elegant $75,000 arcade on East Fourteenth Street near Union Square, the heart of the downtown entertainment and shopping district. Above the entrance, which was decorated with an extravagantly inlaid dome roof, a huge electric sign invited the passerby into the arcade. In *The Public Is Never Wrong* (1953), his autobiography, Zukor gives us some idea of what visitors saw when they entered:

The long room was decorated with bright colours and flashing lights. A hundred or more peep machines were installed, about sixty percent of them phonographs and the rest motion pictures. The phonographs were the more popular because changes of records were available. Sufficient film was hard to get. Other slot machines delivered peanuts, candy, and the like. Everything cost a penny, a penny to get in and a penny a look, a listen, or a handful of food. Morris Kohn [one of the partners], in an inventive turn of find, rigged up a small locomotive which ran around a track and released the coins into itself.... From the beginning the enterprise was a success, the daily take ranging from five to seven hundred dollars.

A year later, the company converted the floor above the arcade into a small moving picture theater for screen shows. To reach it, they devised a spectacular glass staircase filled with water that cascaded over lights of changing colors. The "Crystal Hall" was one of the first movie theaters as we know them today. Expansion, however, took place with other penny arcades, including a small storefront arcade on Grand Street, in the heart of the Jewish quarter. By November 1905, Zukor and his business partners operated more than a dozen arcades in New York, Buffalo, and Boston.

Marcus Loew (1870–1927) was to become the owner of New York's largest movie exhibition circuit and the founder of Metro-Goldwyn-Mayer, the most renowned movie-making company of its day. He was born on the Lower East Side in 1870, the son of a Viennese waiter and a German widow. Like many immigrant families, the Loews lived at the minimum level of subsistence. As a child, the young Marcus sold lemons and newspapers to contribute to the household income. When he reached working age, he found a job in the needle trades. After several years at a wholesale fur company, he had scraped together enough capital to go into business for himself. Loew entered the film industry in the footsteps of Adolph Zukor. At the time, the two were friends and neighbors, living in a wealthy German Jewish section of New York's Upper West Side. Searching for a ripe area of investment, Loew and Broadway star David Warfield (his next-door neighbor) bought a joint $20,000 share in Zukor's Automatic Vaudeville Company in 1904. After a few months, however, the new stockholders sold their holdings and opened their own penny arcade on 23rd Street (November 1904), the first in a chain that became known as the People's Vaudeville Company. When the moving picture craze began to spread outward from the Midwest to the East Coast during the 1905–1906 season, Loew was among the first in New York City to convert his penny arcades into storefront movie theaters. Zukor soon followed. The Automatic Vaudeville on Grand Street, for example, was turned into an "attractive little theatre" during the summer of 1906. According to one trade journal, "the result was very gratifying. The place commenced to do a rushing business and is doing it yet." Films were changed frequently to keep the East Side public interested.

William Fox (1879–1952) was the youngest of the three Hollywood moguls who started their career in New York. This son of German Jewish immigrants from Hungary, came to America as an infant. Like Loew, Fox grew up on the Lower East Side and went to work in the needle trades. Eventually he set up his own garment business and was fairly successful. In 1904, Fox acquired a nickelodeon in Brooklyn and soon developed his enterprise into a chain of fifteen moving picture venues. Realizing that even bigger profits were to be made in distribution, he started his own film rental exchange in March 1907. In film exhibition, both Fox and Loew expanded rapidly, in part because they displayed a great attentiveness to new trends and developed a keen awareness of the ways in which middle-class consumers wanted to be treated. As early as 1907, Loew "sensed that he might get a jump on the competition" if he could offer a combination of moving pictures and vaudeville in more sophisticated quarters than his storefront theaters. Seeking higher profits, he decided to move into larger and more luxurious theater buildings. So did Fox, his main rival. Their strategy was simple: they either bought or leased a deserted playhouse designed for high class vaudeville or legitimate drama, and after renovation, reopened it as a cut-rate vaudeville theater, in which moving pictures and life acts were presented in more or less equal proportions, for admission prices ranging between 10 and 25 cents. This new form of exhibition, which became known as "small-time" vaudeville (as opposed to "big-time" or "high-class" vaudeville), only remotely resembled the nickelodeon: it infused the filmgoing experience with the aura of luxury, with ornate prosceniums, plush chairs, and uniformed ushers. At the Dewey, Fox's theater on East 14th Street, which opened in the fall of 1908, the program lasted about two hours and included five reels of film and four acts of vaudeville. The 1000-seat Dewey had a total of fifty employees, including twelve ushers who were attractively outfitted in red uniforms. This luxury assured the better classes, yet it also made lower-class patrons ("the unwashed") feel a little out-of-place, if they came at all (many working people could simply not afford an admission price at least double that for a storefront show). In any case, the formula proved a success. By the end of 1910, Fox operated nine large capacity theaters in Manhattan alone, which were operated along similar lines.

However, the acknowledged "small-time king" was Marcus Loew. The first theater that Loew transformed into a small-time vaudeville theater was Watson's Cozy Corner, a former burlesque house in Brooklyn. In January 1908, after a month-long renovation, the newly decorated building reopened as the Royal Theater with a program starring Italian actor Antonio Moro in scenes from Shakespeare. The formula of marketing moving pictures in combination with live entertainment for relatively low prices in the large capacity theaters put Loew on the cutting edge of film exhibition. It proved an immediate success and marked a new stage on his way to become a theater magnate. Many former burlesque and "legitimate" houses followed. In September 1909, Loew and Zukor secured the lease of the 2,000-seat Grand Theater, the first playhouse in New York especially built for Yiddish performances. The takeover triggered highly emotional responses in the Yiddish press because for several years this legitimate playhouse had been the home of Yiddish literary drama. Many immigrants, especially the community's cultural elite, found it difficult to put up with the idea that moving pictures were to replace the great Jacob P. Adler staring in the *Jewish King Lear*. The *Jewish Daily Forward* and the United Hebrew Trades tried to retain the playhouse for Yiddish performances, but Adler accepted the generous offer that the future Hollywood moguls made him and the pride of the East Side was turned into a 5-10-15-cent moving picture and vaudeville house.

By the end of 1910, Loew operated a chain of forty theaters in the New York area. That same year, Loew and Zukor pooled their holdings in a new company, Loew's Consolidated Enterprises, which was capitalized at $1,500,000. In March 1912, the company opened the 1,700-seat Delancey Street Theater on the Lower East Side. It was one of the first theaters that Marcus Loew actually built, and not a takeover of an already existing one. A year later, he erected a few blocks north, on the very site of the tenement building where he was born, the even more luxurious Avenue B Theater. This $800,000 picture palace was designed by Thomas W. Lamb and opened in January 1913. In his opening night speech, Marcus Loew said, "This is the most pretentious of the houses on our string, because my better judgment was over-balanced by my sentimentalism and my longing to do something better here than I ever did before." Initially, the Avenue B, like Loew's Delancey Street Theater, presented a mixed program of vaudeville sketches and short movies. There were at least three shows a day and the bill was changed twice a week. Admission prices ranged from a dime on a weekday afternoon to fifteen and twenty-five cents at night. The Avenue B was the top Loews house on the Lower East Side until the late 1920s, when the circuit took over the independently owned Commodore Theater on Second Avenue. The Avenue B was reduced to playing movies at the end of their Loew's circuit run and remained so until its closure around 1957.

While Loew concentrated on refining the package in which movies were presented to the audience, his friend Zukor decided to concentrate on improving the film product itself. Zukor's goal was to make first-rate films based on the standards of the theater. Initially, he merely imported quality features from Europe, such as Sarah Bernhardt's *Queen Elizabeth*, but in the fall of 1912, Zukor burst into the vanguard of feature film production, when he founded the Famous Players Company, with Daniel Frohman as managing director and Edwin Porter as first director. The company produced "Famous Players in Famous Plays," four- and five-reel features starring the big names of the Broadway stage. Over the next few years, Zukor would take the company to the acme of Hollywood production through a series of mergers, notably with the Lasky Feature Play Company of Jesse Lasky and Samuel Goldwyn.

The early career paths of Zukor, Loew, and Fox in the motion picture business have several aspects in common. First, they started out as film exhibitors after a relatively successful career in the garment trades. Second, drawing on a rich commercial experience and considerable capital acquired in the garment trades, they quickly gained a regional reputation as amusement entrepreneurs. Third, equal in importance to their commercial experience was the network of friends and associates willing to invest in their new undertakings. In line with modern capitalist business methods, almost all their enterprises were organized as corporate businesses, allowing outside participation to finance expansion. Finally, and this may well be the single most important factor accounting for their success as immigrant entrepreneurs: their ambitions ranged far beyond the needs of New York's Jewish community from where they originated. Right from the outset, Loew, Zukor, and Fox showed little interest in the ethnic entertainment market. Right from the outset, their business strategies aimed at conquering the mainstream market with a standardized, broad-based entertainment product, which emphasized mainstream American values and middle-class sensibilities. The first penny arcades and movie theaters that they opened were not located in Manhattan's working-class immigrant neighborhoods, but in traditional entertainment and retail districts such as Union Square/East 14th Street, Herald Square, 23rd Street, and 125th Street. These theaters catered primarily to a "floating clientele," that is, patrons drawn from outside the immediate neighborhood of the theater: day-trippers, out-of-town-tourists, and shoppers from nearby department stores on Ladies' Mile. In fact, Fox never ventured below East 14th into the tenement district, where he grew up. Zukor briefly operated a storefront picture show on Grand Street, which he closed in 1909 when he and Loew took over the 2,000-seat Grand Theater next door to convert it into a small-time vaudeville house. Only Loews Inc. firmly established itself in the downtown Jewish quarter, with the opening of the Delancey Street and Avenue B theaters, in 1912 and 1913, respectively. However, in sharp contrast to the popular myth, it was not the nickels and dimes of the East Side Jews that vaulted Marcus Loew to the top of the local exhibition business. On the contrary, the Avenue B and Delancey Street were built with the profits made from uptown theaters. In fact, according to corporate histories, the Avenue B was never successful, but the company kept it running for decades as a memorial to its founder. The strength of Loew's circuit came from its interests in small-time vaudeville houses in higher-income residential areas, suburban shopping centers, and from its flagships in New York's established theater districts.

A skillful manager and showman, Charles Steiner (1883–1946) established the locus of his power by catering to the very people in whose patronage the future Hollywood moguls showed little interested: the five- and ten-cent audience. The circuit he built had its origins on the Lower East Side, from where expansion took place, but only into other densely settled, low-income neighborhoods with a large immigrant Jewish population.

Charles Steiner was born in America, the son of Jewish immigrants from Hungary. Before he ventured into the film exhibition business at the age of twenty-five, he ran a stable at 133 Essex Street, with his father. It was this stable that Steiner Junior turned into a 250-seat nickelodeon in 1908. During the opening week, one could still smell the horses. In many respects, Steiner's Essex Street Theater was the archetypal Manhattan storefront show, which one trade journal described as "no larger than the ordinary store or shop of the neighborhood and plainly furnished with chairs facing the screen." For a nickel, audiences saw three or four short movies, along with an illustrated song or two and perhaps a Yiddish vaudeville sketch. The neighbourhood was literally dotted with this type of *muving piktshur pletser*, as they were called in Yiddish. On the corner of Essex and Rivington streets, "brightly lighted fronts blink at each other at such close quarters that it seems as if the spectator could not be quite sure exactly which house he was getting into; but the neighboring six square blocks with their 50,000 population keeps the managers far from starving," the *New York Sun* reported in 1909.

Whereas Zukor, Loew, and Fox had been men of some means when they entered the entertainment business, Charlie Steiner evidently fits the profile of the impoverished but enterprising young man of immigrant background who first had to scrape together the few hundred dollars that he needed to launch a nickelodeon. But Steiner did better than many others. Two years after he opened his first nickelodeon, he launched a Yiddish music hall with Abraham Minsky, the oldest of the legendary Minsky brothers who were to become leading burlesque producers in the 1920s. With Minsky, he also briefly operated the roof garden of Boris Thomashesky's National Theater on East Houston Street. The real break through, however, came with the American Movies Theater. In 1914, Steiner opened a brand-new movie theater in the middle of the Hungarian Jewish district, north of East Houston Street. It was one the first purpose-built medium-sized movie theaters on the Lower East Side: a modest hall with a sloped floor that could seat around 550 people. In sharp contrast to Loew's much larger and luxurious Avenue B and Delancey Street theaters, the simple design of the American Movies, inspired by the architecture of retail stores, revealed a concern with efficiency and economy over aesthetics and lavishness. The American Movies presented its patrons with a middle ground between the movie palace and the old-style storefront picture show. A marvel of modern-day engineering, the roof was constructed in such way that it could be opened during hot summer nights. Thus, Steiner offered working-class Jews surroundings where they could feel at home while participating in the American dream of abundance.

As a manager, Steiner took direct aim at the varied interests of the targeted clientele of East Side Jews. Admission prices were kept down to suit everybody's purse: the American Movies Theater presented moving pictures for five cents in the afternoon and ten cents in the evening. Steiner was one of the first film exhibitors on the Lower East Side who made the switch-over to feature film presentation. In addition, to serve the cultural interests of the Jewish immigrant community, Steiner specialized in programming Jewish theme films. In July 1914, for instance, he promoted the following program in the Yiddish press:

URIEL ACOSTA
This is the name of the famous historical drama of Jewish life in the Middle-Ages, written by the famous Jewish author Karl Gutzkoff. For decades, it has been performed all over the words, on the major theatrical stages. This drama about the lives of the Jews in Holland several hundred years ago and the tragic but interesting story of Uriel Acosta will be presented in moving pictures by a troupe of the best and most popular Yiddish actors. The troupe with mr. Adler, mrs. Rosetta Cohen and mr. and mrs. Menne has been created especially for this occasion.
You can see this drama for just a nickel if you visit the
American Movies
238–240 East Third Street
Today Friday and tomorrow Shabbat
The American Movies—the coolest place on the East Side—cooler than Coney Island

The formula of offering low-budget entertainment tuned to ethnic taste in a modest yet modern setting proved a success. Throughout the following years, Steiner continued to expand, backed by local real estate investors. A few months after the opening of the American Movies Theater, the old Essex Street nickelodeon, where he had started out, was demolished to make way for the Palace Theater. The Palace was followed by the New Fourteenth Street Theater in 1915, and the Clinton and Sunshine theaters in 1917.

In the 1920s, Steiner frequently functioned as a broker, buying and selling leases of suitable building lots, and bringing investors and exhibitors together. Thus, despite the fact that the forces of big business increasingly monopolized the U.S. film industry, with powerful, regionally based chains such as Loew's assuming control over film exhibition, Steiner was able to build an empire of his own. He played a key role in an interlocked network of Jewish investment companies, partnership firms, and amusement companies, which became known as the "Steiner, Weisner & Schwartz and Mayer & Schneider Syndicate," or Greater M & S Circuit. This conglomeration of independent chains operated under different names throughout Manhattan and Brooklyn, but had its base on the Lower East Side. The hegemony of this local "syndicate" was founded on its ability to offer an entertainment product that was adapted to specific local demands: films tuned to Jewish taste, inexpensive admission prices, and proximity to the home. Because of its modern business methods, the group around Steiner gained control over almost all movie theaters on Manhattan's Lower East Side (in that sense, Steiner and his business partners operated very much like the Hollywood moguls). On the other hand, it managed to compete with the Hollywood-controlled theaters, the picture palaces of Marcus Loew and William Fox, because of its ethnically specific programming practices and low ticket prices.

The majority of the movie theaters that Steiner developed during the teens and early twenties were houses with a maximum seating capacity of six hundred and no stage facilities. Larger movie theaters and combination houses that offered life entertainment in addition to films had to comply with far more stringent building and safety rules according to the municipal code that regulated moving picture exhibition. By 1925, however, the M & S circuit of Mayer and Schneider and Steiner's own chains did so well that the business partner began to invest in the construction of picture palaces with seating capacities well over two thousand. In the midst of a citywide construction boom, they launched the million-dollar M & S Commodore on Second Avenue, the Yiddish Broadway and a bustling shopping district. According to the *Jewish Daily Forward*, it was "all gold and silver," "plush and velvet," like in "the big Broadway theatres." Mayer and Schneider marketed their new flagship as a "temple of art" that would only show the greatest "first run" films. The advertisements in the local press suggest, however, that they did not have access to Hollywood's top films. The M & S Commodore opened in September 1926 with the premiere of Ivan Abramson's *Children of Fate*, an independent production about Jewish life in America, dramatizing "the choice between 'love and religion,' " and starring Bessie Thomashefsky and Joseph Schoengold. Its next feature was *Kosher Kitty Kelly*, a film directed by James W. Horne for the Robertson-Cole studios, another independent company. In other words, although the 2,830-seat Commodore was beyond doubt the most beautiful movie theater on the East Side and very well located on top of that, it did not become a showcase for the major Hollywood studios. By choice or not, the M & S circuit continued to rely on Jewish theme films to build up a patronage, whether it was for their newly opened picture palace or for one of the older movie houses that they operated in the neighborhood. In an advertisement for the M & S Odeon (58 Clinton Street), for instance, readers of the *Jewish Daily Forward* who still "remembered something of the old home" were urged not to miss *Tkies khaf* (*The Vilna Legend*), a 1924 Polish movie starring Ida Kaminska and Zigmund Turkov. In addition to its ethnic programming practices, M & S also maintained its democratic admission policy, "same price all days, from ten o'clock in the morning until midnight," boasted an advertisement for the M & S Clinton (88 Clinton Street) and the newly opened 1,300-seat Hollywood Theater on the corner of Avenue A and Tompkins Square.

The third large movie theater that opened on the Lower East Side in 1926 was Steiner's New Apollo Theater at 126 Clinton Street. The main auditorium had 1,788 seats, while the roof theater seated 1,000. Here again either the theme of the film or the live entertainment (or both) gave the moviegoing experience a distinctly Jewish flavor well before the arrival of Yiddish talkies. In the opening weeks of the New Apollo, Steiner programmed Josef Cherniavsky and his Hasidic Jazz Band as a special feature, whereas patrons of his nearby Palestine Theater, which had opened in 1925, could enjoy *Jewish Tears*, "a drama about Jewish life" starring "the great Jewish artist" Nelly Kesman. Throughout his career, Steiner continued to build audiences on the basis of a shared ethnic identity. Yiddish vaudeville and Yiddish talkies attracted crowds to the Palestine and Clinton Theaters during the 1930s. Responding to demographic changes, Steiner also began to program Spanish-language films and Cuban music in some of his neighborhood theaters, bringing in young talent that he had scouted himself in Havana.

As we saw, a number of factors contributed to Steiner's success. The decisive factor was that he understood early on that he would be fighting a lost battle, if he entered into competition with Loew, Zukor, and Fox in their own arena. During the 1910s, he left them the field of upmarket-scale movie exhibition and concentrated entirely on the bottom-price market, drawing his patronage from the segment of the public that could not afford to pay more than a nickel or dime for an evening's entertainment. When Steiner and his business partners eventually tried to break into Loew's territory, they met with fierce resistance. Their newly opened picture palaces remained subrun houses within Hollywood zoning system. Moreover, Marcus Loew never stopped trying to gain control over the top theaters of the Greater M & S Circuit. Even before its opening in September 1926, Marcus Loew had sought to secure the lease of the Commodore Theater on Second Avenue. He was also interested in the New Apollo and Hollywood. By the early 1930s, Loew's Inc. controlled all three.

Unfair competition from Hollywood-owned theaters and the Great Depression forced the Greater M & S Circuit to curtail its activities. Like many other independents, the circuit struggled to survive. Some of its older neighborhood theaters closed down for good. The Palace Theater at 133–135 Essex Street, where Steiner had begun his career, became a kosher restaurant. Like Steiner, the new owner presented a creative merger of old traditions and new world habits: the legendary Bernstein-on-Essex combined under one roof Eastern European Jewish delicatessen and kosher Chinese food. During the 1930s, the "Steiner, Weisner & Schwartz and Mayer & Schneider Syndicate" slowly fell apart into smaller chains. Steiner continued to operate a small independent chain that was called the Manhattan Playhouses.

In 1948, the final verdict in the so-called Paramount Case finally ended the dominance of the Hollywood studios that Zukor, Loew, and Fox had built and that Steiner had opposed throughout his career. The decision of the Supreme Court marked the end of Hollywood's Golden Years and the beginning of better times for independent theater owners and film producers. If only Steiner had lived to see this—but he died in 1946. The *New York Times* remembered him as a prominent film exhibitor and a strong defender of independent theater owners' interest in the age of Hollywood control. The Bijou on Avenue B, one of the last three remaining Steiner theaters, was renamed the Charles to pay tribute to its founder. The Charles survived until 1972 as a late-run "nebe" showing Spanish-language films, art cinema, and exploitation movies to an audience of East Village's hippies and newcomers from Puerto Rico.

FURTHER READING

Bachmann, Gregg and Thomas J. Slater, eds. *The American Silent Film*. Carbondale: Southern Illinois University Press, 2002.

Stokes, Melvyn and Richard Maltby, eds. *American Movie Audiences, from the Turn of the Century to the Early Silent Era*. London: British Film Institute, 1999.

Chapter 3

The Studio System
Bernard F. Dick

If Hollywood was a Jewish invention, as Neal Gabler implies, so was the studio system—or most of it. Hollywood's Golden Age, which extended roughly from the late 1920s to the late 1950s, coincided with the ascendancy of the eight majors—The Big Five (20th Century Fox, Metro-Goldwyn-Mayer, Warner Bros., Paramount, and RKO) and the Little Three (United Artists, Columbia, Universal)—which together dominated film production in the United States during that period. The Big Five were vertically integrated, combining production, distribution, and exhibition under one roof. They had extensive theater chains with flagship movie palaces in major cities. Fox could boast of the Roxy, "the cathedral of movie palaces," on Seventh Avenue and 50th Street in New York; a few blocks away on Broadway and 43rd Street was Paramount's jewel in the crown, appropriately named the Paramount, with its dramatic staircase and crystal chandeliers. In their heyday, both theaters offered audiences a feature film along with live entertainment. Ice shows were popular at the Roxy, and during the early years of World War II, Frank Sinatra was a regular at the Paramount. Although Loew's Inc., the parent company of Metro-Goldwyn-Mayer, had theaters throughout the world, few could compare with Loew's Paradise on the Bronx's Grand Concourse. The Paradise, with its terraces and sky-blue ceiling where stars twinkled on and off, lived up to its name.

The studios were patriarchies in which nepotism was common. Universal's founder, Carl Laemmle, had such a reputation for hiring relatives that Ogden Nash quipped, "Uncle Carl Laemmle, has a large faemmle." Carl found work at the studio for his brothers, brothers-in-law, nephews, nieces, and cousins. His nephews, Ernest and Edward Laemmle, directed a few minor films. Edward's half-sister Carla was featured in Universal's *Phantom of the Opera* and *King of Jazz*. Carl's son, Carl Laemmle, Jr., took over production in 1929, enhancing the studio's reputation with such classics as

All Quiet on the Western Front and *Frankenstein*. Warner Bros. was aptly named. Except for Nicholas and Joseph Schenck, brothers in the industry were rarely role models. Jack Warner hated his brother Harry and would not even attend his funeral. Columbia's Harry Cohn was also at odds with his brother Jack, although he was shattered by the latter's death.

Despotism, ranging from the benign to the tyrannical, was ubiquitous. Carl Laemmle, affectionately called "Uncle Carl," lived up to his sobriquet; Harry Cohn to his, "White Fang." MGM's Louis B. Mayer inspired both extremes. To Helen Hayes, Mayer was "the devil incarnate"; to Ralph Bellamy, "a Jewish Hitler"; and to Esther Williams, "God."

However, patriarchies only survive if they can withstand internal dissension and external threats. Shortly after the end of World War II, the Justice Department challenged the hegemony of the Big Five, accusing them of violating the Sherman Antitrust Act and ordering them to divest themselves of their theater chains, in effect becoming production-distribution companies. Although the Little Three were not affected by the 1948 consent decrees, sometimes called the Paramount Decision because Paramount had the largest theater chain, they were charged with favoring the Big Five as outlets for their films. Still, during the period when the eight majors reigned supreme, they produced between 60 and 70 percent of the movies shown in first-run theaters—a fact that was not lost on the Justice Department, which accused them of monopolistic practices, thus undermining the foundation of the studio system.

Although all the studios made the same kinds of movies (musicals, westerns, woman's pictures, crime films, romantic comedies, and melodramas) in their heyday, each was unique.

20TH CENTURY FOX

Initially, there was no such studio. There was the Fox Film Corporation, the creation of the Hungarian born William Fox, who was an infant when his German Jewish parents, Michael Fuchs and Anna Fried, emigrated to the United States. Michael's inability to find suitable employment forced William to leave school at thirteen. Because his parents could not afford to have his broken arm put in a cast, William went through life with a disability that neither prevented his playing golf nor thwarted his ambition to become an entrepreneur. Growing up on New York's Lower East Side, William soon became aware of the storefront theaters proliferating throughout the city. This was the era of the nickelodeon, and after a brief stint in the textile business, he used his savings, a grand total of $1,600, to buy a Brooklyn nickelodeon in 1904. William went on to buy others, renovating old ones and building new ones, until he had forged a theater chain. It was only a matter of time before he turned to production. Meanwhile, William distributed the films of others through his Greater New York Film Rental Company, which evolved into the Box Office Attractions Company—the forerunner of the Fox Film Corporation.

William's impoverished boyhood turned him into a fighter, who would not capitulate to the Motion Picture Patents Company (MPPCo), a trust formed by ten studios that pooled their patents on cameras and projectors to keep non-MPPCo members, such as William, from obtaining raw film stock and equipment. Despite his limited education, William knew that a trust meant the curtailment of free enterprise. He also needed product for his film exchange, Box Office Attractions, which MPPCo was eager to acquire—but not for Fox's asking price, $75,000. When MPPCo cancelled his license, William resorted to litigation. He was not alone; other exchanges also refused to capitulate to MPPCo.

MPPCo was about to become history by 1912; in 1915, the Fox Film Corporation came into existence. Two of Fox's biggest stars were Theda Bara (born Theodosia Goodman), and western hero Tom Mix. Some of Fox's greatest successes were John Ford's *The Iron Horse*, F. W. Murnau's *Sunrise*, and Raoul Walsh's *The Big Trail*, starring the then unknown John Wayne. An abortive attempt to take over Loew's Inc. to turn Metro-Goldwyn Mayer into Fox-MGM-Mayer cost William the Fox presidency. Financially, Fox was hemorrhaging—a $17 million loss in 1932. Salvation came in the form of Joseph Schenck, a Russian-born Jew like his brother Nicholas. The Schenck brothers started in a business totally unrelated to entertainment (drug stores), graduating to movies through exhibition—specifically, at Palisades Amusement Park in New Jersey, where they leased space to Marcus Loew, president of Loew's Inc., to operate a film concession. A relationship was forged, and the brothers joined Loew's, Inc. Joseph briefly, and Nicholas eventually becoming president after Marcus Loew's death. In 1933, Darryl Zanuck, production head at Warner Bros., left the studio rather than implement Jack Warner's across-the-board salary cut and joined Joseph Schenck, then president of United Artists, to form Twentieth Century Pictures. Meanwhile, the Fox Film Corporation needed a *deus ex machina*, while Zanuck and Schenck needed Fox's theater chain. The result was 20th Century Fox. The merger favored Twentieth Century Pictures.

20th Century Fox was called the "*goy* studio" because Zanuck was a Episcopalian-Methodist from Wahoo, Nebraska. None of the studio's major stars (Shirley Temple, Tyrone Power, Betty Grable, Alice Faye, John Payne, Gene Tierney, Don Ameche, and Henry Fonda) were Jews. Still, Fox had three of the greatest directors of Hollywood's Golden Age who were—Joseph L. Mankiewicz (*The Ghost and Mrs. Muir*, *A Letter to Three Wives*, and *All About Eve*); briefly, Ernst Lubitsch (*Heaven Can Wait* and *Cluny Brown*); and the Vienna-born Otto Preminger (*Laura*, *Fallen Angel*, and *Whirlpool*).

To his credit, Zanuck did not shy away from controversial material. He produced *Gentlemen's Agreement*, with Gregory Peck as a Christian masquerading as a Jew to write an exposé of anti-Semitism in America.

Although *Gentlemen's Agreement* may have lost some of its relevance, it awakened postwar America to the existence of religious prejudice. Ironically, of the three principals—Peck, Dorothy McGuire, and John Garfield—only Garfield, born Jacob Julius Garfinkle, was a Jew. So was the screenwriter, Moss Hart, who adapted Laura Z. Hobson's novel of the same name. The Zanuck era ended in 1970 when the conglomeratization of Hollywood was underway, with Fox eventually becoming a cog in the wheel of Rupert Murdoch's News Corp.

METRO-GOLDWYN-MAYER (MGM)

Although Metro-Goldwyn-Mayer was another hyphenated studio, there was one name associated with it during its glory days: Louis Mayer, whose preferred birthday was July 4, 1885 (the month and day being Mayer's bid for acceptance as an American). Born in a small village near Kiev, Lazar (later Louis) Mayer underwent the Lower East Side experience in Saint John, New Brunswick where his parents, Jacob, and Sarah, moved in 1892. Once Louis discovered show business through vaudeville, he had no intention of remaining a collector of scrap metal. The purchase of one theater in Massachusetts led to that of another; and exhibition to distribution, where Mayer was so successful that he was ready for the next phase: Louis B. Mayer Productions.

Meanwhile Marcus Loew was empire building; Loew left school at nine, worked in the fur trade, and then moved into exhibition, with penny arcades that grew into a theater chain, Loew's Inc. In 1920, Loew bought Metro Pictures, of which Mayer was secretary. Four years later, Loew bought Metro and then Louis B. Mayer Productions to form Metro-Goldwyn. Since Mayer's contract called for his name to be "prominently displayed," the new studio became Metro-Goldwyn-Mayer.

The studio boasted of having "more stars than there are in the heavens," which was true: Greta Garbo, Robert Taylor, Norma Shearer, Joan Crawford, Rosalind Russell, Spencer Tracy, Clark Gable, Katharine Hepburn, Judy Garland, Mickey Rooney, Lana Turner, Greer Garson, and Walter Pidgeon—among many others. The MGM musicals were unique, particularly those from the Arthur Freed unit such as *Meet Me in St. Louis*, *The Harvey Girls*, *Singin' in the Rain*, and *The Band Wagon*.

MGM's image was greatly enhanced during the brief tenure of Irving Thalberg, who came on board in 1924 as production head and died twelve years later. Although he was widely respected within the industry, Thalberg's name never appeared on his films, most of them masterpieces (e.g., *Mutiny on the Bounty*, *The Good Earth*, and *Camille*). Thalberg had an uneasy relationship with Mayer, who respected his creativity but not his obstinacy. Supposedly, Mayer said en route to Thalberg's funeral service, "Isn't God good to me?"

"I will only make pictures that I won't be ashamed to have my children see" was Mayer's credo. MGM's films idealized family life, best illustrated by the Andy Hardy series and such glorifications of domesticity as *Mrs. Miniver, The Human Comedy, Meet Me in St. Louis, Mrs. Parkington,* and *Our Vines Have Tender Grapes*. Not every MGM film revealed an America of white picket fences and churchgoing families with acne-less children. Occasionally, Mayer granted audiences a look at the dark side (e.g., *Lady in the Lake, The Postman Always Rings Twice,* and *The High Wall*), but not as often as Warners and RKO did.

Like the other Hollywood patriarchs, Mayer resorted to nepotism. When Twentieth Century Pictures was in the formation stage, Mayer agreed to invest over $1 million in the company if there was a place for his son-in-law, William Goetz. His other son-in-law was the distinguished producer, David O. Selznick, the creative force behind *Gone with the Wind*. Of Mayer's two daughters, Edith and Irene (the latter known as Irene Selznick after her marriage to David), Irene was better known because she produced *A Streetcar Named Desire* and *The Chalk Garden* on Broadway.

The end of World War II presaged the end of the Mayer regime. In 1951, unable to cope with a Hollywood in transition, Mayer was replaced by Dore Schary, known for his message films with B-list casts. Mayer died in 1957 of leukemia. In his eulogy at the funeral service, Spencer Tracy summed up Mayer's legacy: "The story [Mayer] wanted to tell was the story of America." It was not accidental that Mayer, not knowing the date of his birth, chose July 4.

During the intervening years, MGM was bought, sold, amalgamated with United Artists, orphaned, and finally lost its prized location to Sony Pictures Entertainment, which became its owner in 2005.

WARNER BROS.

The brothers Warner were Jack, Harry, Abe, and Sam—the sons of Polish immigrants, Ben and Pearl Warner, whose original surname is unknown. When Jack inquired what it was, Ben replied, "I don't remember." The brothers entered the business in the usual way: exhibition, purchasing theaters, and establishing exchanges. The buying spree culminated in a major theater chain, First National.

Production was the last stop on a journey that began when the brothers and their sister Rose, armed with a projector and film, traveled around Youngstown, Ohio, showing their movies wherever they could. As an added treat, Jack would sing, accompanied by Rose at the piano. Believing that *My Four Years in Germany* (1918) by former U.S. ambassador to Germany, James W. Gerard, could be a successful film, Harry offered Gerard a quarter of the profits. The film grossed $1.5 million, and Warner Bros. was about to become a real studio.

In 1925, Sam Warner attended a demonstration of a sound-on-disk system called Vitaphone, in which the sound was recorded on $33\frac{1}{3}$ rpm disks and synchronized with the film. Believing that Vitaphone would be a boon to exhibitors who could not afford live accompaniment for their films, Sam persuaded his brothers to adopt the Vitaphone system. The result was *Don Juan*, followed by *The Jazz Singer*—the latter with eight sound sequences, six of which with Al Jolson singing such favorites as "Toot, Toot, Tootsie," "Blue Skies," and "Mammy." The sound era had begun.

While MGM specialized in high gloss productions, Warners emphasized the three T's: "timely, topical, and not typical." The crime film was its specialty, and the Warners musical had a working-class look. The chorus girls in *42nd Street* and *Gold Diggers of 1933* behaved as if they knew that when they went out the stage door, they would encounter World War I's forgotten men and the victims of the Great Depression.

Of the four brothers, Harry and Jack were the key figures: Harry as president of Warner Brothers, based in New York; and Jack, as vice president of production in Los Angeles. Golden Age Hollywood was a tale of two cities: New York, where distribution was based, and budgets determined; and Los Angeles, where production took precedence over all else. Compromise was inevitable, and so was rancor. The antagonism between Jack and Harry Warner was legendary, although it existed mostly on the part of Jack who was unrelenting.

In the 1960s Warners, like the other studios, realized that Hollywood's golden age had changed to silver and was on the way to iron. The transformation began when Seven Arts Productions bought Warner Bros. in 1967, the result being Warner Bros.-Seven Arts; next Warner Bros.-Seven Arts transformed into Warner Communications in 1971; and finally Warner Bros. become a subsidiary of the largest media conglomerate, Time Warner.

PARAMOUNT

The name always associated with Paramount Pictures is Adolph Zukor, a Hungarian Jew, whose father was a storekeeper, and his mother, a rabbi's daughter. Both of them had died by the time Zukor was eight. With little incentive to remain in Hungary, he emigrated to America in 1888, where he achieved modest success in the fur trade. The opportunity to invest in a nickelodeon on East 14th Street, then New York's "Broadway," led to the creation of a theater chain. Zukor then teamed up with the ubiquitous Marcus Loew, combining his circuit with Loews to form Loews Consolidated Enterprises, soon to become Loews Inc.

Once Zukor decided he no longer wanted a partner, particularly Loew, he entered production. Interested in featuring stage actors in their hit plays, he christened his company Famous Players in Famous Plays, distributed through W. W. Hodkinson's Progressive film exchanges. Hodkinson preferred another "P" word for the company: Paramount, which Zukor grudgingly accepted. There could only be room for Hodkinson or Zukor—and it would not be the former. Once Zukor deposed Hodkinson, he merged Famous Players and the Jesse Lasky Feature Play Company into Famous Players-Lasky, the forerunner of Paramount. Zukor's goal was a vertically integrated company; not only did he create the largest theater chain of any of the studios (1,424 venues) but he was also determined to get Paramount's films in theaters through two practices that were eventually outlawed: block booking (the package arrangement vs. selecting one's preferences) and blind bidding (bidding on the film, sight unseen).

From the 1920s through the 1950s, Paramount had an impressive array of talent: stars such as Gloria Swanson, Mae West, Marlene Dietrich, Gary Cooper, Bing Crosby, Bob Hope, and Claudette Colbert; directors such as Cecil B. DeMille, Preston Sturges, Mitchell Leisen, and one the industry's greatest, writer-director Billy Wilder. Like other studios, Paramount was adversely affected by the Great Depression, so much so that in 1933 it was on the verge of bankruptcy, which was averted by a change of leadership. Zukor was given the honorific of board chairman, with Barney Balaban eventually assuming the title of Paramount president. The studio was back on its feet, remaining independent until 1967 when it was taken over by Gulf + Western, the first of several owners, the latest being Viacom. In 1976, Zukor, then 103 years old, took a nap from which he never awoke.

RKO

Of the Big Five, RKO was not only the smallest but also the one that underwent the greatest number of regime changes. RKO was the brainchild of David Sarnoff, the Russian-born son of Leah and Abraham Sarnoff, the latter leaving for America when David was five. Four years later, in 1900, David, his mother, and his two brothers joined their father in New York. David was immediately impressed by the impact of radio on American life. Once David became general manager of the Radio Corporation of America (RCA), which eventually became the parent company of NBC, he envisioned a corporation that would house radio, film, and live entertainment (hence the name "Radio City Music Hall") under one roof. In need of a theater chain, he bought KAO, the result of the merger between two vaudeville circuits, the Keith-Albee and the Orpheum, whose theaters were converted into movie houses, with films supplied by the Film Booking Office of America (FBO). Sarnoff then bought FBO, merging KAO and FBO KAO/FBO. Out of this amalgamation came a new studio in 1928: Radio-Keith-Orpheum (RKO).

Although RKO released some of America's greatest films (e.g., *King Kong, Citizen Kane, The Magnificent Ambersons, The Little Foxes,* and *The Best*

Years of Our Lives), it had trouble keeping talent. Katharine Hepburn began her career at RKO, but eventually found MGM more to her liking, as did director George Cukor. Directors such as John Ford, George Stevens, and William Wyler gave RKO a couple of distinguished films, but did not remain there for any length of time. Unlike the other studios, RKO did not have a distinctive image, nor did it inspire the same kind of confidence that existed elsewhere.

Apart from Sarnoff, who had nothing to do with film production, the Jewish presence at RKO was intermittent. The Jews who passed through RKO were among the greatest in the industry: George Cukor (*What Price Hollywood?*, produced by David Selznick, *A Bill of Divorcement*, and *Little Women*); William Wyler (*The Little Foxes* and *The Best Years of Our Lives*); and the undervalued Pandro S. Berman, who produced most of the Fred Astaire–Ginger Rogers musicals (*The Gay Divorcee*, *Roberta*, *Top Hat*, *Follow the Fleet*, *Shall We Dance*, and *Carefree*) and could have become production head had he been willing to go along with RKO's decision to bring in more independent producers—which he was not. Samuel Goldwyn used RKO to release the early films of Danny Kaye (born David Daniel Kaminsky): *Up in Arms*, *Wonder Man*, *The Kid from Brooklyn*, and *A Song Is Born*. Howard Hughes's acquisition of RKO in 1948 signaled the beginning of the end, and by 1957, the studio had ceased production.

COLUMBIA

Little was expected of Columbia, which began as the CBC Film Sales Company. The two C's represented Harry and Jack Cohn; and the B, Joseph Brandt. The Cohn brothers were the sons of Joseph and Bella Cohn, German Jews. The brothers entered the movie business in the usual way—indirectly. Jack was first. Working at an ad agency, he made the acquinatance of Joseph Brandt, who had a law degree that he planned to use to enter the entertainment business. In 1912, the Cohns and Brandt formed the CBC Film Corporation—one Brandt and two Cohns. Eventually there would be one Cohn, Harry, who became both president and head of production of Columbia, after CBC became Columbia Pictures.

During the 1930s, Columbia achieved respectability through the films of its star director, Frank Capra. Respectability was essential, given Columbia's Poverty Row image. When Capra's *It Happened One Night* (1934) won five Oscars, Columbia was no longer "corned beef and cabbage," as CBC had been dubbed.

Jack had now been relegated to New York, where distribution was based. Although New York controlled the purse strings, Harry wheeled and dealed, determined to make Columbia a studio to be taken seriously by producing such classics as *His Girl Friday*, *Gilda*, *The Jolson Story*, *From Here* to *Eternity*, and *On the Waterfront*. Harry's second wife was a B-movie actress, Joan Perry, who scored a coup unique in the annals of Hollywood. When Harry died in February 1958, Perry, a Catholic, convinced a priest that because Harry invoked the Deity before he expired, he harbored a desire to convert to Christianity. Exactly what Harry uttered was unknown. Nonetheless, he underwent posthumous baptism, thus becoming the only mogul to be *bar mitzvahed* and baptized. Harry was blessed for not having to witness the transformation of Columbia into a subsidiary of Coca-Cola, and of Sony Pictures Entertainment. He would never have understood ownership by a soft-drink manufacturer or a Japanese electronics corporation. But he would have been delighted that after the Sony purchase, his studio found a new home: MGM's in Culver City. The studio that boasted of having more stars than there are in the heavens is now home to the studio that once lacked both stars and a firmament in which to showcase them.

UNITED ARTISTS (UA)

United Artists was never a real studio; it did not have its own soundstages, and it could not attract stars, writers, directors, and producers, for the long term. UA was basically a distribution company formed in 1919 by three stars—Charlie Chaplin, Mary Pickford, and Douglas Fairbanks, Sr.; and the director, D.W. Griffith—whose goal was to distribute their own films and those of others, thus making UA an independent production company. There was always a Jewish presence at UA, never as strong as at Warners, MGM, and Columbia; it existed primarily in the form of producers.

Although the founders left their mark on UA (e.g., Chaplin's *The Gold Rush*, Pickford's *Sparrows*, Fairbanks's *The Thief of Bagdad*, and Griffith's *Way Down East*), it was Joseph Schenck who made it a producer's studio after being elected chairman of the board in 1924 and becoming president shortly thereafter. Through his companies, Joseph M. Schenck Productions and Art Cinema, Schenck gave UA a number of distinguished films such as *The Son of the Sheik*, *The Beloved Rogue*, and *Rain*. He cut production-distribution deals with Buster Keaton (*The General*, *College*, and *Steamboat Bill, Jr.*) and Gloria Swanson, the latter resulting in only one decent film, *Sadie Thompson*. Even after Schenck left UA in 1933 to form Twentieth Century Pictures with Darryl Zanuck, UA continued to attract major producers, several of whom were Jews, who enriched the American film with such classics as *Stella Dallas*, *These Three*, *Dodsworth*, *Dead End*, and *Wuthering Heights* (Samuel Goldwyn); *Our Town* and *Stage Door Canteen* (Sol Lesser); *The Man in the Iron Mask*, *The Son of Monte Cristo*, and *The Corsican Brothers* (Edward Small); *A Star Is Born*, *The Prisoner of Zenda*, *Nothing Sacred*, *Made for Each Other*, and *Rebecca* (David O. Selznick); and *You Only Live Once*, *Blockade*, *Stagecoach*, and *Foreign Correspondent* (Walter Wanger).

Despite its unique status, UA experienced the same fate as the other studios. After becoming a subsidiary of Transamerica, UA was merged with Metro-Goldwyn-Mayer to form MGM/UA, the two studios being separate but far from equal. In 2005, MGM/UA became a lesser jewel in Sony's crown, joining the more resplendent Columbia. Such was the fate of a once independent studio.

UNIVERSAL

Before there was Universal Pictures, there was the Independent Moving Picture Company (IMP), the creation of "Uncle Carl" Laemmle. In a business where epithets were rarely complimentary, Laemmle lived up to his. His diminutive stature helped, but his avuncular personality endeared him to the public, especially exhibitors. Born in Laupheim, Germany in 1867, Carl had a better education than most of the moguls. Having learned enough English to correspond with customers and suppliers at a stationery store, and enough arithmetic to keep the stationer's books, Carl was ready to move on—specifically, to America, where he arrived in February 1894 with five dollars worth of gold and a bank draft for $50. When a sales job materialized in Oshkosh, Wisconsin, Carl discovered he had a natural gift for selling. He also married his boss's niece, Recha. However, being a success in Oshkosh was not enough. A trip to Chicago in 1906 exposed him to America's current entertainment craze, the nickelodeon. After seeing how a theater would empty out every ten or so minutes, with one group exiting as another entered, Carl saw the future, and it was movies. Carl's was a familiar scenario: one nickelodeon led to another; exhibition gave way to distribution with the formation of the Laemmle Film Service. Next stop: production. Proud to be an independent, in the sense of being independent of MPPCo (which he actually joined for a brief period to get some decent films to distribute), Carl called his company the Independent Moving Picture Company (IMP). Looking for a star, he discovered one in Florence Lawrence. In 1909, stars' names were never divulged; fans addressed their mail to the "Biograph girl," if Biograph was her home studio. They may not have known the names of the performers, but they knew the companies that released their movies.

Before Laemmle wooed Lawrence to IMP, she was at Biograph, which was part of MPPCo. Laemmle with the aid of his publicist leaked a story to the press that Lawrence was killed in a trolley accident in St. Louis. Carl then informed the press that the "accident" story was MPPCo's way of punishing Lawrence for joining IMP and insisted that Lawrence was not only alive but would also be making a personal appearance in the city of her alleged demise. When Lawrence arrived in St. Louis in April 1910, the fans went wild, the star system was born, and audiences learned the names of the actors.

Reluctant at this stage to form his own studio, Carl proposed a consortium, the Universal Film Manufacturing Company (which suggests an assembly line operation) that would include IMP and other independents, whose common bond was a hatred of MPPCo. However, that was not enough. Carl was determined to gain control of Universal, which he did by acquiring enough stock to impress the stockholders. By 1914, Carl had turned visionary, conjuring up not just a studio but one with its own address: Universal Studios in Universal City, California. In March 1915, Universal City became was a reality; today, it is one of Southern California's leading tourist attractions. Carl would have approved, although he would not have called it a "theme park," a phrase yet to be coined. Yet even in 1915 Universal was on the way to becoming one: Carl provided opening day audiences with a flood scene, a rodeo, and a horse race.

Irving Thalberg was part of Universal for six years, from 1917 to 1923. Never meant to enjoy robust health or a long life (he died in 1936), Thalberg would have been a cardiac invalid if his mother, Henrietta, had not nursed him herself. Henrietta used her friendship with Recha Laemmle to find her son a place at Universal, where he began as a secretary, becoming production head in 1919. Thalberg left Universal in 1923 and moved to MGM, where he established himself as one of the most creative producers in the business.

In 1946, Universal lost its identity when it was taken over by Decca Records and merged with International Pictures to become Universal-International (UI). The name reverted to "Universal" after UI was acquired by the talent agency, the Music Corporation of America (MCA) in 1962. Because a talent agency could not own a studio, MCA chose ownership over representation. Once foreign ownership of the studios began, starting with Sony's acquisition of Columbia, Matsushita, Sony's rival and the world's largest home electronics manufacturer, acquired MCA in 1991, becoming the parent company of Universal until Matsushita realized it had made a mistake and sold MCA to Seagram, which then sold it to Vivendi, a French water distributor and supplier of electric power, in 2000. Vivendi sold MCA to General Electric, NBC's owner, in 2003; what had once been a freestanding studio is now part of NBC Universal.

Neal Gabler was partially correct when he claimed that the Jews invented Hollywood. They really *created* Hollywood, and with it, an art form. Unfortunately, the creators would be completely baffled if they ever saw what happened to their creations.

FURTHER READING

Dick, Bernard F. *City of Dreams: The Making and Remaking of Universal Pictures*. Lexington: University Press of Kentucky, 1997.
Dick, Bernard F. *The Merchant Prince of Poverty Row: Harry Cohn of Columbia Pictures*. Lexington: University Press of Kentucky, 1993.

Eyman, Scott. *Lion of Hollywood: The Life and Legend of Louis B. Mayer*. New York: Simon & Schuster, 2005.

Freedland, Michael. *The Warner Brothers*. London: Harrap, 1985.

Gabler, Neal. *An Empire of Their Own: How the Jews Invented Hollywood*. New York: Crown, 1988.

Herman, Jan. *A Talent for Trouble: The Life of Hollywood's Most Acclaimed Director, William Wyler*. New York: Putnam's, 1996.

Marx, Samuel. *Mayer and Thalberg: The Make-Believe Saints*. New York: Random House, 1975.

Stein, Jean. "West of Eden." *The New Yorker*, 3 Mar. 1998: 150–70.

Zierold, Norman. *The Moguls*. New York: Avon, 1969.

Chapter 4

The Social Film and the Hollywood Blacklist

Dave Wagner

The "secret" of the Jewish role in Hollywood was never much of a secret to anyone except perhaps the semiliterate portions of the movie audience that were unaware of the ethnic identity of the industry's moguls, producers, directors, actors, and screenwriters. Oddly, though, the convention in Hollywood was to *pretend* that it was a secret. From the early sound films until the 1950s, a remarkable convention remained formally intact: the self-constructed collective identity of Jewish film artists and entrepreneurs was to be regarded as merely one within the great human melting pot of the burgeoning film industry, with Jews or characters resembling Jews given "American" or generic immigrant identities, regardless of genre and social content of the movie.

It is no coincidence that it was in 1947 that the pretense began to dissolve. That was the year American movie attendance peaked and when Rep. John Rankin of the House Committee on Un-American Activities warned Congress that many Hollywood actors whose stage names were as reassuringly familiar as Danny Kaye, Edward G. Robinson, and Melvyn Douglas were essentially deceiving the public by hiding their less gentile birth names (David Kaminski, Emanuel Goldenberg, and Melvyn Hesselberg), a practice Rankin considered prima facie evidence of their "Un-American" intentions.

Over the next few years, Congressional hearings that were convened ostensibly to examine the dangers of Communist influence in Hollywood hammered again and again at the "Jewish" role in front of or behind the camera. Not too many years earlier, before World War II, the same committee had invited notorious anti-Semites to testify that Jewish control of Hollywood had led to agitation in popular films for intervention against Nazi Germany; after 1947, the FBI complained in internal memos that the Jewish press was failing in its patriotic duty to support the Hollywood blacklist. That support would come soon enough from the Anti-Defamation League's Los Angeles office and from the American Jewish Committee's *Commentary* magazine, among other sources, but it never managed to persuade the larger Jewish community that the blacklist lacked some larger and more ominous purpose than the defense of "national security."

After all, no one bothered to accuse Hollywood's directors, actors, or screenwriters (its most suspicious elements) of any kind of espionage, stealing state secrets, or any other subversive activities for that matter. What the hearings focused on was the pro-Russian taint in about a half-dozen films, all of them wartime features about an ally that was then taking the brunt of the Nazi attack and for that reason alone was sometimes welcomed by the White House.

The transparent intent of these hearings was to create a dragnet against left-wing political or labor activists and their sympathizers, to drastically narrow the range of acceptable themes in popular film, and to reshape the treatment of subjects in what was then the leading entertainment medium. The tactic has been tried out frequently in Congress since (in recent years, by Senators Larry Pressman and Joseph Lieberman) but never with such devastating results. Movies such as *Gentleman's Agreement*, attacking anti-Semitism; like *Pinky*, appealing for racial egalitarianism; others upholding the dignity of the poor and jeering at the rich or even on occasion appearing to call for a redistributive social justice were evidence of suspicious deviations from the acceptable standards of the Cold War political mainstream. The Los Angeles office of the FBI claimed as much in its reports to J. Edgar Hoover, which by 1947 began to include critical commentaries from literary experts who were paid to pinpoint suspicious qualities in shooting scripts that had been smuggled out of studio lots by friendly hands. After hesitating, Hollywood's power brokers fell in line with the government view and even agreed to conduct the blacklist themselves, with the help of an unusual combination of anti-Semites and a few noted Jewish institutions.

Government and private witch-hunters consistently exaggerated their case, making wild claims for the subversive content of films that in reality contained messages that were nothing more than comfortably liberal or merely patriotic. What was more interesting was the element of reality behind the charges, an element that the blacklisters were largely incapable of articulating. In the late 1930s, when isolationists like Congressman Gerald P. Nye had charged "Hollywood" (meaning Jews as much as liberals) with making films urging U.S. participation in the coming war, he was correct. Director Anatole Litvak's *Confessions of a Nazi Spy* (1939), which had ignited the worries of the German sympathizers among Southern congressmen, was the opening wedge for a new kind of film. Within a decade, Hollywood had changed so dramatically that Jewish left-wing sympathizers *could* write hundreds of pictures, albeit mostly (like *Confessions*) in the genres of "B-movies" best noted for their predictable plots and low production values. Like Gentiles who were also concerned with the appalling fate of Jews in World War II and fascinated with the active role of Jews in contemporary U.S. society, these screenwriters managed first to carve out and then amplify Jewish cinematic roles that were recognizable to anyone who gave them more than a casual look.

Jewish roles had existed from the first moment of film, of course. From the early 1920s onward they had even provided, intermittently, themes for box office hits. However, it was not until the 1940s that what might be called the "crypto-Jewish film" was made in the numbers or variety that approached the potential of the available Jewish talent or invoked with such subtlety. Now dozens of films offered these Jewish experiences and insight. In part because the level of film production began to fall off after 1946, the *implicitly* Jewish roles of certain kinds—from political moralists to soldier-vaudevillians and just plain working stiffs—would never actually rise to this scale of output again.

It is for exactly these reasons that the ghost of John Garfield—the protean proletarian and martyr to the blacklist—has never left the set and is not likely ever to do so. Archetypes of other remembered types likewise persist: Sam Levene, the battered Jew but otherwise cerebral proletarian; Howard Da Silva, the petty criminal (or morally corrupt official); Groucho Marx or Phil Silvers, the fast-talking con man; Sheldon Leonard, the mobster with the heart of gold; master of excess Zero Mostel; not to speak of character actresses like Stella Adler and Gertrude Berg, who helped create the ethnic family relation at her unneurotic loveable best, or of the Jewish writers, directors, and technicians, who made possible in so many ways the laughter and tears of the vast audiences in front of the camera. Lovably annoying cameos of aging Jewish "types" in Woody Allen films, perhaps the most convenient sample of Jewishness on film in recent decades, are properly a last look at (and homage to) what went before. Like their Yiddish American accents and neighborhood slang, they represent an absence in anticipation: soon, no one will remember the life of the *Yiddishe gassen*, the Jewish urban streets, as they once existed. Not even the proletarian neighborhoods of Israel can re-create their counterparts, and not only because the historic moment is gone. "Nothing like it since Valentino," observers pronounced at the 1951 mass mourning of Garfield, dead at 39, in a Jewish working-class New York destined to be Jewish no more, at least in this way.

In the decades to come, as cinematic "Jewish" became matter of fact Jewish, less and less as a semidisguised persona within the framework of a social "problem," it advanced into a more evident part of daily life. Jews had uneasy adolescences, unhappy or happy marriages, silly and occasionally compelling adventures, and so on. Measured in above terms alone, the several hundred American films made in the second half of the twentieth century with Jewish themes certainly marked a considerable step forward. As in the professions and formerly exclusive clubs of real life, they had been "normalized."

And yet there was something unmistakably ambivalent about this coming out. Jewish film makers, from actors to technicians, had wanted since early Hollywood days something more for themselves than a confining or comforting shell of an identity that seemed destined, in one way or another, to limit artistic choices. With relatively few exceptions, they did choose to be "only" Jews, whether they shunned *ghetto* characteristics as embarrassing or (as left-wingers) felt little warmth in a Jewishness dominated by an increasingly wealthy and rightward-drifting Jewish establishment. Not infrequently, the available Jewishness tended to become a template for the immanent critique of the morals and manners that artists abhorred. Nobody did the sixties rebellion fit quite as well as the young man breaking away from the suffocating materialism and the smothering sex-repressed motherhood of home. Dustin Hoffman, Richard Dreyfuss, and dozens of lesser artistic figures were, at their best moments, the new Paul Munis and John Garfields, with all the contradictions implied in the shifts from aspiring homeboy to rootless rebel.

"Another" Jewishness, distanced just enough to dispel maudlin treatment, has had far greater warmth. That "Other" is imaginary as well as historical, closer to the film world's 1940s "hidden Jew" than to the real-life Jewish identity a half century later. Just as the generic ethnics and idealistic intellectuals or workers of earlier films are often not only more interesting and admirable as characters but also more real *as Jews* than the "real" Jews set in films close to the present, so the Jews-as-Other in the recent era often continue to carry the torch of artistic integrity or political morals. Seemingly outdated figures in the New World Order determinedly protecting the lowly against the rich and reclaiming spiritual homelands almost anywhere but Israel bear a relation to a past that bears handholds as well as terrors. If the present, with no more futuristic radical promise or terrible fears for Jews than for anyone else, seems to have less to offer Jewish self-identity, and if even the highly sophisticated Jewishness of David Mamet or Barry Levinson, to take two examples, often dwells within or on the diasporic past, the 1930s–1940s become all the more emblematic. This is, like Hollywood's Golden Age, an experience that remains for Jews and Gentiles alike when so much else slips by. The historical significance of the blacklist, as a Jewish and social-political-aesthetic issue, has never gone away and reappears whenever Hollywoodites make films and television threatening the image of the rich and powerful, oil barons and war-makers, who have no tolerance for criticism.

THE RISE OF THE SOCIAL FILM

The Moguls

The origins of the social film, the film of social issues, lie beyond the scope of this chapter. However, popular themes had certainly been alive in silent cinema. With the advent of the talkies, they had another source: the stage, a most Jewish place in terms of writers in particular. The successes of Sidney Kingsley best showed the transition. A sophisticated New Yorker suited to merge the "documentary" spirit of contemporary artists with winning theatrical plots, Kingsley saw sudden and overwhelming success with *Men in White* (1933), produced by Group Theater. Formed by an overwhelmingly Jewish and left-wing circle of young artists heavily influenced by the Russian example of Constantin Stanislavsky and his American disciple, Lee Strasberg, Group transmitted "Method" acting to the American stage and film—the decisive message that actors needed to understand and internalize their parts rather than acting as directors' automatons or mere showmen with golden voices and interesting bodies.

In *Men In White*, arguably for the first time on the English language stage in America, a workplace was painstakingly reproduced, demonstrated (apart from its soapy but necessary romance features) in the details of operating room procedures, with a set by Mordecai Gorelick and direction by Strasberg. It won Kingsley a Pulitzer. *Dead End* (1935) by Kingsley, the slum saga made into a 1939 film by playwright turned screenwriter Lillian Hellman, director William Wyler and a troupe of actors that included both Humphrey Bogart and core of the future Bowery Boys—archetypal Lower East Siders somehow simultaneously Irish and Jewish—was similarly location-set. This time the action took place below the skyscrapers overlooking the Hudson suites and the tenement dwellers at the bottom. The crippled architect (in Hollywood inevitably gentilized by Joel McCrea) who aspires to rebuild the city New Deal–style is matched to the mobster (played by Bogart) who returns to the scene of his youth to find his mother unforgiving and his old sweetheart a streetwalker with syphilis (in the film, she gives an unconvincing tubercular cough).

That for Frank Capra, the Sicilian-born son of a Los Angeles blue-collar family, the Jewish connection would be decisive for his career with deeply social films condenses a large point usefully. An artist who by no coincidence broke into silent movies owing to his brief marriage to a Jewish actress whose brother owned a tiny studio, Capra hit the formula of the "little guy" film before he joined Columbia in 1929. However, Harry Cohn gave him extraordinary freedom and the permission to work with liberal-to-radical Jewish writers like Robert Riskin and Sidney Buchman on classics like *It Happened One Night* (1934), *Mr. Deeds Goes to Town* (1936), *Mr. Smith Goes to Washington* (1938), *Meet John Doe* (1941), and *It's a Wonderful Life* (1946). That Capra never understood how much he owed either to radicalism or to a certain Jewishness was clear in his later failures. Cohn, who understood better what the loss of relative political and artistic freedom in Hollywood meant, was still trying to stage secret shootings of films with now-forbidden Communist writers like Albert Maltz—only a few years earlier one of Hollywood's favorites—when the blacklist came down tight.

More influential than all these in what might be called Hollywood political aesthetics was Jack Warner. Youngest of twelve children of a Polish Jewish couple, actually born en route from London to America, he grew up mostly in Youngstown, sharing the work of the family bicycle shop business. His folks then bought a nickelodeon operation in Newcastle, Pennsylvania, and young Jack sang during intermission. Four growing brothers attempted repeatedly, over the next decade, to get into film distribution. By 1917, they had set up shop in Hollywood with Jack as a twenty-five-year-old production chief. Acquiring several production companies and many theaters, they were set for the sound era and *The Jazz Singer*.

It was Warner Brothers and above all Jack Warner's response to the social crisis of the Depression that made them and especially him special among the moguls. A Republican like his counterparts, although not as vociferously reactionary as Louis B. Mayer (who cochaired the California Republican Party), he saw the light in 1932—or perhaps glimpsed the changing box office. In September, weeks before the fall election, he staged a Busby Berkeley-style Motion Picture Electrical Parade and Sports Pageant for Roosevelt in Los Angeles' Olympic Stadium, guaranteeing huge waves of added publicity. After winning with FDR, Warners released the New Dealish *42nd Street* to coincide with the inauguration, and with tardily opportunist MGM, provided the starlets and even Tom Mix for the inaugural counterpart parade in Washington.

The moguls at large responded with genius in another way, facing the nation's worst-ever depression. Among the major media, only radio prospered in the early Depression, with falling prices of radios destined to bring down the huge inventory overstock and with continuing profits for the major networks. Most of the major studios, by contrast, lost money during the early Depression years. RKO, Paramount, and Fox all went into bankruptcy by 1933, a trend that accelerated consolidation and control of Wall Street already underway from investment in equipment for the new sound films. Moviemaking, however, soon resumed with a newly burnished corporate-style bureaucracy firmly in place, turning Hollywood from a society of semimavericks into a complex and carefully structured system designed to turn out and (just as important) to market a more regularized product.

Warners, to take a case in point, produced a decade of "social" films with treatment of disillusionment with the system and economic struggle of a type that had been seen only at the margins earlier. It was a shrewd marketing strategy, paired with low budgets and a furious production schedule with no special favors for the directors and writers who turned out respected and profitable films about sympathetic gangsters and slum-dwelling kids, uncaring businessmen, and hardworking chorus girls. Whether Warner was sincere or insincere (he later turned to anticommunist themes as readily as he had turned to reform and wartime antifascist themes) was never the crucial question; as a businessman who also craved the prestige of attachment to the New Deal and the war effort, he accommodated the creative upsurge of Jewish radicals that the era allowed.

The Producers

Below the moguls and substituting in small ways for them were producers, some of them extraordinarily creative, more just carrying out orders. Rather less often Jewish hacks (compared at least to Hollywood's Gentile hacks), the best were far more often Jewish geniuses, like David O. Selznick, Irving Thalberg, and Joseph Pasternak. Thalberg, who claimed to have been a teenaged socialist soapboxer in New York before the war, was supervising the shoot of *The Good Earth* when he collapsed fatally at age 37. Posthumously (by a month), he or his spirit could take credit for *The Story of Louis Pasteur* and *The Great Ziegfeld*, for sympathetic critics the models for the biopic exploring rather than exploiting personalities.

The "Thalberg System" signified integrated production at every level, from bankers' financing to filming, making MGM the masters of the new sound medium. No one else came up to this level. Warners depended on Hal B. Wallis and others for production, using the Depression outbreak and rebound as an opportunity to transform production facilities and expand market shares. "Junior" Laemmle, in effect a surrogate for his father headquartered back in New York, became by force of circumstances a producer for underfinanced Universal, the outsider studio that was about to reemerge as the maker of outstanding weird and horror films with heavy German Impressionist (often immigrant Jewish) influences.

David O. Selznick was the most sincerely aspiring artist of the bunch. Son of mogul Lewis Selznick, leading executive and attempted rebel (his bid for an independent production unit was crushed by multistudio agreements in the early 1930s), he took over the badly wounded RKO that made some of the first Katharine Hepburn films, and then rejoined MGM with a fair degree of autonomy. There he had his success, foreshadowing the postwar efforts of stars, producers, and writers to break off from the suffocating contracts and begin anew. However, the young Selznick was, perhaps, more successful as a model of the artistic filmmaker than in reality. Literary masterpieces became his beat—defying Hollywood wisdom that they could not be done seriously—with *Little Women*, *David Copperfield*, *Anna Karenina*, and *A Tale of Two Cities*, all before he moved on to his own company, Selznick International in 1936. The box-office success (if not the unacknowledged moral and historical disgrace) of *Gone With the Wind* helped him launch Hitchcock (with *Rebecca*) as an American director. His producing of *Spellbound*, *Since You Went Away*, *Portrait of Jennie*, and *The Third Man* remain tributes to his efforts. However, name and influence did not spare him major disappointments. Like many less influential writers and directors, many of Selznick's favorite projects went unproduced and forgotten, his lasting impression on movies slight.

Walter Wanger was another executive genius, in some ways better realized because he was more instinctively cinematic than Selznick. Born Walter Feuchtwanger, the son of a German Jewish salesman and garment producer and nephew of the surrealist painter Florine Stettheimer, he managed to make himself rather more independent and frequently more artistic. He also took more chances. The antifascist *The President Vanishes* (1935), *Blockade* (1938), the "little guy" *Stagecoach* (1939), feminine-alcoholic treatment *Smash-Up* (1947), and the heavily stylized *Joan of Arc* (1948), not to mention his role as a leading Hollywood liberal, drew the enthusiasm of leading intellectuals like Norman Cousins and Carl Sandburg, as well as Hollywood's talented and influential Communists.

Joseph Pasternak was a third and more distinctively European Jewish producer. Born in Transylvania, he returned to Europe and cinematic success and then fled Germany in 1935 for Hollywood; he is credited with the lavish *kitsch* of the Popular Front. Creator of the Deanna Durbin musicals (saving Universal from collapse), he also guided Marlene Dietrich after her preliminary stumble, and made other *sui generis* films that included *Destry Rides Again*, the All-American Western as never seen before, with a distinctly Viennese comic accent. Among the left-leaning crowd, only Joseph Pasternak had the gravity to make films that emphasized New Deal values (for a while, even pro-Russian ones, like *Song of Russia*) of the common man and woman taking their place in society. Only occasionally were they obviously Jewish, but then sometimes in small but vital ways: in *That Midnight Kiss*, Keenan Wynn is the affably Jewish fellow truck driver of Mario Lanza's garage who urges him to take up a singing career, and (naturally) manages it as Mario falls hard for Kathryn Grayson. Credited, for good or ill, with popularizing honeyed versions of classical music through film and for musical extravaganzas like *Anchors Aweigh*, *The Great Caruso*, and *The Merry Widow*, Pasternak's Popular Front *kitsch* may even (as some critics have charged) have foreshadowed Holocaust *kitsch*: one Jewish stylization replacing another.

The Directors

Next, there were directors, perhaps the least Jewish of the Hollywood professions (apart from starlets) but among those best placed to see their own auteurist creations through final hurdles. None was more commercially successful than the gay, Hungarian Jewish George Cukor, none more political in their art than the Russian-born Lewis Milestone, and none more vernacular than bargain basement auteur, Viennese Edgar G. Ulmer.

Cukor, born and raised in New York City, was already a stage manager barely out of his teens, a distinguished theatrical director in his twenties, debuting in Hollywood with *Tarnished Lady* (1930), one of the several kinds of women's films for which he had a great sensitivity. Cukor followed his friend David Selznick to RKO and MGM, leaving in his path such extraordinary Hollywood products as *A Bill of Divorcement, Dinner at Eight, Camille, Little Women*, and *Holiday*. Breaking with Selznick on the set of *Gone with the Wind*, he went on to direct *The Philadelphia Story, A Woman's Face, Adam's Rib, Born Yesterday, Pat and Mike, My Fair Lady*, and so on. The most theatrical of mainstream directors, he had the appreciation of actresses like Hepburn and the rapport that realized the promise of the women's film already strong in the theatrical plots of so many early 1930s films written by Sidney Buchman and others.

Out of that rapport came a kind of sex or gender comedy not quite like any other. Cukor was not just sympathetic to women. He grasped the distortions and hidden weaknesses of male culture as, perhaps, only a gay artist of the time could. His Cary Grant of *Holiday*, Grant and James Stewart of *The Philadelphia Story*, Spencer Tracy of repeated Hepburn–Tracy matchups, did not simply adore Hepburn, as men do with women they place on a pedestal away from the grime and action of life. They came to see something in her character and not just potential uplift that was otherwise lacking within themselves and their world. That unbuxomy Hepburn shone brighter than the Hollywood types around her was in itself a revelation that could hardly be described as Jewish but had much in common with the old Jewish theatrical avant-garde's attachment to the themes of Ibsen.

Milestone was more the showman, but an altogether serious one. Scion of a wealthy Russian Jewish clothing manufacturer, Lev Milstein literally ran away from his family's professional aspirations to immigrate at the age of eighteen in 1913, taking ordinary factory jobs until he managed to become a photographer's assistant. Enlisting in the Army for war service, he was assigned to the Signal Corps' photographic unit, learning about technical shooting, including the possibilities of filming under war conditions. In Hollywood, the very first Oscar ceremonies saw him winning with a comedy direction, *Two Arabian Knights* (including soldiers who escape from a German prisoner of war camp, in Palestine).

This antiwar hit with definite Jewish undertones led him toward the most expensive and (aside from Chaplin films) most radically pacifist film *All Quiet On the Western Front*, in cinematic history. Never had anyone expressed the overwhelming Jewish repulsion at armed conflict so perfectly, or captured the public disillusionment with war that swept across America and Europe by the late 1920s. It is often said that he never returned to this level of accomplishment, but that view fails to recognize the difficulty of what he repeatedly attempted. *The General Died at Dawn*, Clifford Odets' first Hollywood film, *Of Mice and Men*, the second Steinbeck adaptation, *Edge of Darkness* (in which the mass of a Norwegian town rises up heroically against the German occupation, anticipating the crushing response), *Purple Heart* (one of the John Garfield war films ruminating on anti-Semitism), *North Star* (a pro-Soviet musical with score by Aaron

Copland), *A Walk in the Sun* (the most realistic war film made to that date), and the fabled noir *The Strange Love of Martha Ivers*, were among other (actually too many others) lesser efforts to follow.

The Screenwriters

Then there were the screenwriters, Jewish by a considerable disproportion except at the very top levels, where some (by no means most) of the true aristocrats of the trade were Jewish as well. The coincidence of the Depression and the need for real screenwriters (not mere "titlists" as before) with the advent of sound film brought a veritable tidal wave of New Yorkers to Hollywood. A decade or so later, success on Broadway and the boom of wartime cinema prompted newer Jewish playwrights, by the dozens, to make the trip. As in other sections of the entertainment world, supply and demand meant that some prospered while many faced long stretches of unemployment; supply and demand unregulated by the Screen Writers Union, until the achievement of a real contract in 1942, meant that even those working with some regularity often merely scraped by, wondering if they had chosen the wrong line of work.

Success usually came by following well-worn formulas, rearranging parts of melodrama, romance, comedy, and so on to match the image of the stars chosen. Rarely did it mean writing a script that would be used in anything like the version that it left the typewriter, and only occasionally did the writer even appear on the set for production, let alone rewrite for the final take. Those Jewish writers who cared about craft found it perpetually heartbreaking, as they found Los Angeles a pale counterpart to Manhattan. And yet it was, especially with the union in place, a living, sometimes a chance to do something lasting.

Could the studio powerhouses and mere screenwriters have done more to introduce the Jewish character and the Jewish actor, whose talent could be seen everywhere across contemporary theater, the Group to touring WPA troupes? It is an intriguing question. The inner logic of the much-touted "Genius" system of the majors was especially obvious in Hollywood renditions of theater, where the Jewish role could hardly be denied and the cutting edge (as Clifford Odets' explosive mid-1930s hits) sometimes pinpointed a contemporary Jewishness, or reflected on showbiz history full of Jewish ghosts. John Howard Lawson's *Success* (renamed *Success at Any Price*) was especially painful for the playwright, because the very contradiction that bore on the conclusion was the tragic self-denial of the left-leaning Jew who wanted the Bitch Goddess so badly that it ruined him. However, *The Life of Emile Zola* (starring Paul Muni, Hollywood's biggest former Yiddish stage actor), *Golden Boy*, with William Holden playing a Jewish boxer whose Jewishness is just barely suggested.

Not that Jews as Jews disappeared in celluloid, but once more, they usually played a version of themselves in minor or narrowly defined support roles only. *Street Scene* (1931), at the dawn of sound film, actually had a Jewish father preaching socialism to the other inhabitants of the neighborhood. In "foreign" (he reads a Yiddish newspaper) manner, actor Max Montor manages against every expectation to forecast the positive role reserved for upfront (but English-speaking) Jewish progressives in the war film, like militantly antifascist midshipman Sam Levene explaining Americanism to a would-be duty shirker in *Action In the North Atlantic*. Back in 1934, the Oscar-nominated *The House of Rothschild* (for the Best Picture) more typically offers its heroic Jew (he saves the British stock market!) as financial manipulator hiding his fortune from tax collectors. Arguably, the handsome, proletarian-type John Garfield was Jewish for Jewish viewers, Gentile for the Gentiles. Meanwhile, operating considerably under the radar, low-budget B films had more Jewish lawyers, bankers, junk collectors, treasurers of boys' own societies, as well as long-suffering mothers. Perhaps they were made to appeal to urban neighborhood audiences, or perhaps just made to fill out a second bill on the cheap. At any rate, the muscular Jewish hero, the real Jewish intellectual, and the seductive Red Jewess of anti-Semitic lore were late-blooming, from the 1940s to the Cold War era.

In all this, the most prolific and underrated auteur was none other than Edgar G. Ulmer (1904–1972), the director (in this case, "producer" might have been more accurate) of the most successful Yiddish films of all time. At the distant opposite end of production values from Pasternak, who could not imagine a cast of less than hundreds and a budget less than hundreds of thousands—the equivalent of today's blockbuster multimillions—Ulmer's reputed 150 features were mostly shot in under a week with a bare minimum of retakes. That he guided one of the mightiest horror films (and antiwar allegories) ever made, a top Yiddish box office attraction, early "race" films, one of the classic noirs (and later, a classic noir western), as well as several remarkable antinuke sci-fi features surely makes him also the most diverse Jewish filmmaker. More than that, by choosing a most peculiarly vernacular art over the usual Hollywood commerce, Ulmer was in some ways the ultimate popular culture artist and legatee of *Yiddishkayt* that he knew only by second remove.

Born in Bohemia, son of a socialistic wine merchant, he grew up mostly in Vienna, where he eventually studied architecture at the distinguished Academy of Arts and Sciences. Homeless and impoverished by war, he was as much as adopted by the family of later famed actor Joseph Schildkraut. Ulmer began in the film industry as a set-builder, and late in life insisted that his true introduction to the industry had been working on *The Golem* (1920). He came to Hollywood in 1923 with Max Reinhardt, and dividing his time between California and Berlin, worked with many greats: Franz Murnau, Erich von Stroheim, Emil Jannings, Ernst Lubitsch, and others. By the early thirties a refugee, Ulmer directed minor westerns and the first solid documentary about the dangers of venereal disease. He most urgently wanted to make an antiwar film, the kind of project made possible by the great success of *All Quiet On the Western Front*. However, Ulmer, with his background in Expressionism, had a very different notion of how it could be done.

The Black Cat (1934) had virtually nothing in common with Edgar Allen Poe's original story of the same name. Instead, it was an extraordinary revisiting of a battle scene, years after the war stopped, with monstrous consequences. It brought Boris Karloff and Bela Lugosi together for the first time, with great effect. However, Ulmer was sickened by Hollywood and sought his redemption elsewhere. Actually introduced to Yiddish while attending so-called Second Avenue Broadway, he found his new metier in film adaptations of the Yiddish stage drama, comedy, and musical, employing Yiddish stage directors while he oversaw the process.

It was a propitious moment as well as the last extended major moment, for Yiddish film. Actress Molly Picon, who had turned to Broadway in the early 1930s without success, had led the Polish cast in *Yidl Mitn Fidl* (Little Jew with violin), shot in 1936 in Warsaw and in a small Jewish town on the Vistula River. A bittersweet, nostalgic trip through Jewish life with Picon as a daughter, disguised as a boy and featuring real *klezmer* music, *Yidl Mitn Fidl* offered the actress the rare opportunity to display a full repertoire of her vaudeville talents. It even closes with a stage triumph in New York, as befits a proper Hollywood ending. Highlighted by a wedding scene using real-life poor Jews as guests—convinced that they were attending a real wedding—*Yidl* cost $50,000 and was not only the top moneymaker among Polish films that year but also the first Yiddish talkie to play in a major American theater chain.

Ulmer may have been encouraged by this success, but he clearly made his own plans. Raising money from needle trades unions, from former Yiddish actor Paul Muni, and from the Household Finance Corporation on the collateral of his own mortgaged home, he filmed *Grune Felder* (*Green Fields*) in New Jersey in 1937. It is rightly considered the most artistic Yiddish-language film ever made, and was also the most commercially successful. During the next three years, Ulmer also completed *Yankl der Shmid* (retitled in English, *The Singing Blacksmith*), *Die Klatsche* (*The Light Ahead*), and *Americaner Shadchen* (*The Marriage Broker*)—none as successful as *Gruene Felder*. They were sturdy examples of the last wave of Yiddish cinema before the combination of the Holocaust, American assimilationism, and the Israeli demotion of Yiddish (for the exultation of Hebrew: the language of the Ancients and the Gods) had condemned *Yiddishkayt* to generational memory and the ultraorthodox Hasidic communities.

In the above four Yiddish films, Ulmer, the writers, technicians, and above all the actors themselves succeeded in creating a fantasy version of Jewish life of the Pale unseen in Hollywood until *Fiddler On the Roof*. As in all good fantasy, they project a mixture of folklore, unfulfilled aspirations, and keen sensibility of personal fate's merging with that of the collective.

Grune Felder in particular, unsparing in its uncinematic starkness and not only because of the razor-thin budget, is correspondingly excessive in its romanticism for the *Yeshiva bokher* (student) who travels to the *shtetl* of unlettered Jews and falls in love with the land and the local girl. Shot on the barest sets in New Jersey, it drew on the success and the name of the famous play by Peretz Hirschbein. Jacob Ben-Ami, who had starred in a theatrical version fifteen years earlier, cast and supervised the script readings, in effect the dramaturge-adaptor and acting coach, while Ulmer himself oversaw camera work and general direction. He called his intent "the same decision that *Sholem Asch* made, which Chagall made," that is, to create real art from a mixture of folk culture and vaudeville.

Ulmer even had to bargain to get the negative printed, and offered a new theater near Times Square a guaranteed ten-week run, in exchange for 80 percent of the gate (not counting members of the International Ladies Garment Workers Union, whose chief had bought a bloc of seats in a version of the traditional Jewish institution-supported theater). During the first weekend, the manager had to beg filmgoers to leave the theater so that the patrons for the next show could be admitted. Failing that, he called the police. *Grune Felder* broke all film boxoffice records in Jewish neighborhoods, then more characteristically ran (as a somewhat shortened, B-feature with subtitles) on the Keith's circuit theaters at the bottom of a double bill. There had been nothing like it and, sadly enough, there would be nothing like it again.

The evocation of nature's store as the essence of wholeness and of honest labor, the key to achievable paradise, has rarely been equaled, except perhaps in the virtual repeat moments of the otherwise improbable *Jive Junction* (1943)—where patriotic jivers reconcile themselves to classical musicians—Ulmer honoring apple picking (i.e., agricultural production) for antifascist unity, to the sound of the "Bell Song." Ulmer's musical comedy and melodrama *Yankl der Shmid*, based on a David Pinsky play and starring Yiddish stage tyro Moishe Oysher, boasts a plot still more bare, if that is possible: a village smithy who makes the girls swoon. It was his final Yiddish success.

Apart from Yiddish films, Ulmer directed *Moon Over Harlem* (1939), a low-budget melodrama with no white actors, showing the victory of a Popular Front style reformist minister over gangster elements; *Cossacks in Exile* (1939), a musical romance of Ukrainians fleeing into Turkey and then returning to their homeland; and *Clouds in the Sky* (1940), a documentary in English and Spanish about the dangers and treatment of tuberculosis. Over the next few years, he made educational material for the armed forces, and antifascist morale-building melodramas and comedies of other, mostly oddball varieties featuring generational and gender tensions. He was scant few years from making the classic noir *Detour* (1945) and several equally dark films (usually with the participation of his leftwing friends), en route to an obscurity and fantasy and horror series so strange and low budget that he might properly be considered an artistic version of Ed Wood, Jr.—except that even when confined within extremely sharp limits of dreadful scripts and hopelessly small budgets, Ulmer's talent and his redemptive vision never entirely flagged.

One of Ulmer's Cold War films written by Julian Zimet (born Halevy) under a pseudonym and deep in the blacklist illustrates the point. The low-budget and long obscure *The Naked Dawn* (1955) crystallized a theme familiar from the work of other blacklisted screenwriters working in the mid-1950s in exile in Paris, Rome, London, or like Zimet, Mexico City. Appearing less than a year before the Soviet invasion of Hungary, *Naked Dawn* depicts the fate of a double outsider—a Mexican revolutionary disillusioned with the revolutionary party who has not given up on the project for social justice. A social bandit teaches revolutionary ethics by taking what he wants from an exploitive system without succumbing to greed or the code of the gangster (as he says at one point, "People are always more important than money"). Zimet's story was a response to the enormous success of the Western *Shane* (1953), another tale of an outsider who teaches a farmer and his wife how to fight, but now Shane is transformed from a wounded gunfighter searching for his lost honor into a political man in a lost cause who teaches others how to keep honor alive. (*Naked Dawn*, aptly, was revived by the San Francisco Jewish Film Festival in 2005.)

Jews—Now as Jews

Wartime brought the largest American audiences and the most public acclaim that Hollywood was ever likely to get. Afterward, tax breaks, foreign (and television) sales, and the marketing of feature-related products would prove decisive. For decades into the future, executive giants like Lew Wasserman ("Last of the Moguls") would create strategies to repackage Hollywood products, finding niches the size of elephants (Wasserman personally turned talent agency MCA into a production company for film, but mainly for television), planning film spectaculars and new marketing schemes until ushered out by the 1990s international corporate mergers.

However, for the final era when movies constituted the single central icon of popular culture, consider the fate of some key contemporary Hollywood films tackling in one fashion or another "the Jewish question." Many of them could be described as both patronizing or mere show-biz history and inaccurate history at that. *Mr. Skeffington* (1944), written and produced by twin brothers Julius and Phillip Epstein (best remembered for collaborating on *Casablanca*) has Gentile beauty Bette Davis marry aptly named Wall Streeter "Job" (played by Claude Rains), bear him a son (who is killed in the War), cheat on him repeatedly, and then realize that he is her one true love. *Easter Parade* (1948) was almost a literal parade of tunes by Irving Berlin with a sketchy plot about a pair of dancers played by Judy Garland and Fred Astaire back in the 1910s–1920s.

Rhapsody in Blue (1945) stands, with *The Jazz Singer*, as the most signifying Jewish big film in Hollywood history to the time. Written by Howard Koch and Elliott Paul (but with Clifford Odets and Robert Rossen among others contributing dialogue), produced by Jack Warner and directed by Irving Rapper, it moves tunefully through the life of George Gershwin (starring a gentile, Robert Alda, as Gershwin), as we have seen, inventing or ignoring various aspects of private life as suited to the plot. The song of the title, said to be influenced by black melodies—melodramatically broadcast on the radio just as Gershwin's classical music mentor is dying—expresses the inner tension of the film hardly seen as tension at the time.

More vigorous if still more absurd attempts at happy assimilationism were certainly attempted at the same moment. *Abie's Irish Rose* (1946), an update of a schmaltzy 1920s Broadway play and 1929 silent film of the same name, has VE Day just announced in London, and a Jewish soldier (played by Michael Chekhov) in love with an Irish American U.S.O. singer. They are married by an Army chaplain but they keep the wedding secret as each comes home to waiting family. During the second and third, respectively Jewish and Catholic weddings, one side or another is bitterly unhappy with the couple. The situation changes only with the arrival of a son, Patrick Joseph Levy, and a daughter, Rebecca. As everyone on camera seems to cry together, a kindly Irish cop standing by sings first Jewish, then Irish lullabies, and the families reconcile. The thoroughly Jewish *Variety* called it a "topical misfit" of screaming minorities that cannot get along, and a radio show based on the film was cancelled after listener complaints. With Bing Crosby's imprimateur (his company produced it) and the film was accepted by the equally conservative Catholic Legion of Decency and the Anti-Defamation League, *Abie's Irish Rose* made money without ever erasing the memory of studio embarrassment.

By 1958, Hollywood rendered Herman Wouk's *Marjorie Morningstar* what might be called the still-Jewish melodrama of middle-class life after a brief sojourn in bohemian circles. The mere introduction of the Jewish gangster, after *King of the Roaring Twenties, The Story of Arnold Rothstein* (1961), and of the Jewish madam in *A House Is Not a Home* (1964) in a sense completed filmic assimilation to multicultural society, if it ever could be completed. Recovering Jews, Jewish mobsters, and whores could all be real Americans.

To the considerable surprise of Hollywood itself, a frontal attack on anti-Semitism had meanwhile suddenly proved to be a good business—even if it led to very dramatic HUAC assaults on the writers and directors of the hits. *Crossfire* (1947), one of the most prestigious of the postwar socially relevant melodramas, produced, and directed by two (Gentile) future members of the Hollywood 10, offers a violent contrast. It has a prejudiced and distraught war veteran brilliantly played by Robert Ryan beat an amiable Jewish host (a civilian played by Sam Levene, as a civilian who meets several GIs in a bar and invites them back to his place for a drink) to death. The action in the film comes with the pursuit of the killer by a humanistic detective, and without the Jewish theme it would have remained a mere police drama. However, *Crossfire*, released a few months before the more prestigious *Gentleman's Agreement*, had been prepared as a social shocker, prescreened to representatives of religious groups who had already been carefully polled prior to production about the subject matter.

Hollywood, eager to test its new subject matter before deciding on heavy investments in promotion, had shrewdly gone for gold. Audiences would not have known that novelist Richard Brooks's work, *The Brick Foxhole*, was about a homosexual beaten to death by a veteran with pretty much the same intent and ferocity. In Hollywood, a shift of plot device ("motivation") was perfectly normal. And in this case lucrative: it cost less than $600,000 to make and proved to be RKO's biggest film of the year, earning back millions.

Still, the theme of prejudice offered no guarantee of success. Most others seeking room to discuss anti-Semitism did not do nearly as well, and no small part of the problem remained studio sabotage. *The Vicious Circle* (1949) was an independent production intended to dramatize the historical background to the Holocaust. Its plot revolves around a Czech liberal lawyer in late nineteenth-century Budapest fighting for the rights of Jewish citizens. Just a year after the film's limited release, it was recut, retitled *The Woman in Brown*, and shorn of all references to Jews or even to Europe! Miraculously, in what must have been an interchangeable society of whites' folks in that century, these European-looking people were actually Americans living out an unstated and evidently unpolitical populist grievance. Historical dramas had been generally bad enough box office, and as receipts fell throughout the industry, the theme of Jewish persecution was (at least for a decade or so) considered still worse.

A raft of little films, a mere handful still in Yiddish but most in English, tackled issues that Hollywood continued to avoid. Thus *Open Secret* (1948), a low-budget melodrama scripted by future blacklistee Henry Blankford and future television dramatist-savant Max Wilk of early anthology series, has a murder plot against a crusading Jewish journalist, organized by a rightwing veteran determined to revive the nativist movement. Perhaps such second-bill features might have had a chance, even in the Jewish neighborhoods amid the throes of highway construction and outward-bound mobility—if their political connections were not suddenly so unpopular.

Jews, or rather the Jewish presence and image, usually did better on the sidebars of the story, like the sincere second lead, no dashing hero or devastating heroine, who nevertheless moves the story along and helps the main character get the girl or the guy. The familiar pattern of the 1930s, where known Jewish stars like Paul Muni, Melvyn Douglas, or John Garfield signified Jewishness to in-the-know viewers, held on most amazingly.

However, a (usually) lone Jewish face was also needed in many a GI adventure, like the stunningly realistic *A Walk in the Sun* (1946) where "Jake Friedman" (played by George Tyne) is the native Brooklynite among the embattled platoon, and who has some of the best lines. Sam Levene is likewise the proletarian hero in *Action in the North Atlantic* (1944). Evidently an autodidact, he explains why democracy is worth fighting for; the same year, Jewish-labeled Levene also played the unofficial lawyer for himself and his fellow captured airmen in *The Purple Heart* (1944), abused in a frame-up trial and later executed by the Japanese. John Garfield, another supporting star in *Action* and also Jewish largely by virtue a neighborhood-ish identification, was the best cast in a half a dozen other 1940s films, including *Destination Tokyo* (1944, an ordinary seaman, behind Captain Cary Grant) and *Gentleman's Agreement* where, unlike faux-Jew Gregory Peck, he is the *real* thing who rejects condescension toward the "poor little Jew" and demands justice for all.

Just as Jewish were some filmic expressions of American democracy winning out at home, hardly at the center of the plot but useful to make necessary points. *Till the End of Time* (1946, directed by Edward Dmytryk and produced by Dore Schary, the new liberal boy-wonder on the scene) has GIs striving to find their lives back amid their trauma, not only refusing to join a veterans' group openly prejudiced against Jews (also against Catholics and African Americans) but also personally punching out the bigots. In fact, the resulting bar brawl restores the sense of vitality to one of the three GIs, and sends another to the hospital, from where he can reunite with his family: all in all, a unifying experience. Now a better America can move on.

This set of images was successor to what might be called the victim film, with its roots in the earliest antifascist movies that the studios, fearful of lost European profits, actually permitted to be produced. *So Ends Our Night* (1941), based on a popular novel by Erich Maria Remarque, has a German Jewish refugee (played by Fredric March) denied entry into Austria, sharing a prison cell (for illegal entry) with the unwanted of various countries, then continuing a miserable adventure across Europe seeking personal safety. It was the first screen credit for a young Jewish production assistant headed for great things: Stanley Kramer. *Tomorrow the World* (1943), adapted from a highly regarded Broadway drama, has a propagandized German orphan boy brought into an American home, learning to his horror that his father was Jewish and repelled at the Jews (and "Jew-lovers") around him. After denial and violent rejection of America as well of his true self, he sees the light.

That orphan may in fact represent the ultimate divided state of the 1940s filmic Jew. In Europe, dramatized best in the low-budget classic *The Search* (1947) directed by Fred Zinnemann, where the orphan is discovered (at more or less the last moment) to be Jewish, an escapee fleeing not so much from prejudice but from extermination. Back in America by contrast, the main risk, apart from a return to 1930s Depression's economic conditions, was undoubtedly neurosis. It could be uncharitably suggested the Jewish types needed headshrinking by their kinsmen because they were so frequently the most visible screen neurotics. Oscar Levant was only the most famous, playing himself more or less in a handful of films, while actually one of the highest-paid concert pianists on the planet. *Humoresque* (1946), seemingly a prewar relic previously first made in silent days and based on a Fannie Hurst's short story, gained new life as a vehicle for the emotionally torn figure of John Garfield as crypto-Jewish violinist. This project was launched when Odets' script for *Rhapsody in Blue* was rejected, obviously leaving the neurosis-narrative (and deeply if implicitly Jewish) possibilities for the taking. Hollywood was not the place for anxiety about the differences in the emotional lives between a fictionalized composer and a fictional fiddler.

Instead, the new *Humoresque*, updated to the Depression years, has a Lower East Sider burdened by his poor family while offered uplift by a heavy-drinking, heavily neurotic, and definitely *goyishe* socialite played with great tragic effect by Joan Crawford. To realize his art, he must struggle at once against the overwhelming guilt of abandoning his background, and against the temptations of obsessive love with an immoralist. In the end, faced with the fact that she would certainly drag down her lover's career, the thrice-married benefactress drowns herself, precipitating a solution to the artist's own uncertainties by reminding him that art is indeed for art's sake above all. It seems a strange lesson for 1946, but one that many a Jewish musician or devotee doubtless appreciated in a world gone mad.

After the Lower East Sider as soldier or artist, and apart from the continuation of the vaudevillish Jewish "types" on the screen, the psychoanalyst was probably the most identifiable screen Jew. Fictionalized Freud would not make a major appearance until 1962, when Montgomery Clift in *Freud* (at least Clift was psychologically troubled, if not actually Jewish) played the great analyst. But Barry Sullivan, playing Dr. Alexander Brooks in *Lady In the Dark* (1944, based on a musical with book by Moss Hart, music by Kurt Weill, and lyrics by Ira Gershwin), one of the admired films of the time, had famously prescribed a return to femininity for the Manhattan career girl played by Ginger Rogers. Two battling psychologists played by Jose Ferrer (in his dark looks and cerebral talk, almost definitely perceived as Jewish) and Richard Conte (doubtfully so) contrast an unorthodox and an orthodox therapist in *Whirlpool* (1950), a badly botched adaptation (by Ben Hecht) of a novel by Jewish Hollywood Marxist Guy Endore. From the darkest corners of noir angst to the constant mugging of slapstick, where the "Viennese" psychologist probably made the most frequent appearances of all.

At least one other Jewish role of importance remained for the postwar years to explore: the Bronx gamin, gum-chewing, and slangy but wise to the world's tricks. Only a blind person could fail to see the Jewishness of Judy Holliday (1921–1965), a Bronx-born daughter of a piano teacher who had rushed to the hospital for delivery immediately after watching a Fanny Brice live performance. It was kismet, or something similar. A teenage receptionist at the Mercury Theater, one of the group of Left-leaning improvisationists who made the Village Vanguard a hip spot in wartime, Judy had an unsuccessful tour as a bit actress in Hollywood, returned to New York and won the best supporting actress in a hit play that established her persona.

Holliday replaced an ill Jean Arthur in Broadway's *Born Yesterday*, and again in the 1951 hit film. With an IQ established at 172, she had managed to become America's favorite dimwit—but only to those who failed to look carefully. Adopting the same character in her testimony to HUAC, she confounded the red-baiters (and quietly dropped her contacts with progressive organizations), although she was informally blacklisted in film and television for years. Coming back in *The Solid Gold Cadillac* (1956), this time she plays the stockholder who realizes that the corporate types are a bunch of crooks and organizes a campaign to outsmart them. Miraculously, she manages a combination of Katharine Hepburn's self-possession and Shirley MacLaine's playfulness. All in all, Holliday (whose stage name was an almost literal translation of her birth name, Tuvim) offered an example of what clever Jewish comediennes could have done for decades if given the chance, and others, but especially Barbra Streisand, would make in the self-consciously Jewish era to come.

THE BLACKLIST AND THE DECLINE OF THE SOCIAL FILM

Holliday's fate was not unfamiliar. Jews lost most heavily in the McCarthyism and blacklist period to follow in Hollywood, because they not only constituted a majority of those writers, actors, editors, and musicians actually driven from the industry but were also so often the studio executives, producers, and directors deprived of the needed talent. Harry Cohn almost desperately attempted to protect his writers, and Jerry Wald, up-and-coming producer of the 1940s, was to tell oral historians in 1959 that he spent a decade not being permitted to make the films that he wanted. From another standpoint, the certainty of the FBI field office that industry and L.A.-area Jews were hostile to the Bureau suggested how the ascribed qualities of Jewishness still seemed threatening to J. Edgar Hoover, Walt Disney, and the downright anti-Semitic congressmen of HUAC.

Hollywood, successfully cowed, now produced filmic Jews that shrunk down to their 1930s predecessors, either bland or stereotypic but most of all, generally absent. There was something Jewish about John Garfield, even if only New Yorkers seemed to know for sure; there was nothing apparently Jewish, in the era immediately to follow, about Tony Curtis, aka Bernie Schwartz. His ethnicity drained out of him along with the Method Acting that he had imbibed before settling into silly roles (with the marked exception of his "Method" casting in *The Sweet Smell of Success*) amid the

Hollywood mainstream. It was almost as true at the top: Louis B. Mayer was fired by MGM in 1951, two of the three Warners sold their shares in the studio, Harry Cohn died, while David O. Selznick and Samuel Goldwyn made their last films before 1960. The next generation of moguls would be proportionally almost as Jewish, but definitely more corporate, often talent agency executives, with no broken accents.

The most hilariously awful portrayals of Jews by Jews and others were certainly the biblical spectaculars created to outdo television offerings. *The Robe*, easily the best (and the one written by a blacklist victims, albeit without credit: Albert Maltz), puts the Jews into the background as the rebels against Rome whose would-be savior convinces Roman consul Richard Burton finally to martyr himself. *David and Bathsheba*, *The Ten Commandments*, and *Solomon and Sheba* among others placed Jews in supporting roles when they looked too Jewish, reserving the premiere status like Moses for Hollywood Gentiles with a universality that hardly seemed Jewish at all. Perhaps Elizabeth Taylor (a real-life convert) made the best Jewish appearance when as the Egyptian queen *Cleopatra* (1962) she pleaded to save the grand library of Babylon from destruction by knowledge-hating barbarians. It was an all-time studio money loser.

The fire of passion and commitment still burned (or were allowed to burn) in comedy and show-biz nostalgia, along with melodramatic spotlight. Danny Kaye's movies usually looked something like *Me and the Colonel* (1958), with Kaye as the little guy who exhibits great courage when the chips are down, often enough by imitating a pompous gentile, rather as Charlie Chaplin did before him in *The Great Dictator*. *The Eddie Cantor Story* (1953) seems to do as little as possible with the singer-comic's background and the militant unionism, not to mention the burning antifascism that the background spurred—but something of the past remains unavoidable as his character.

Interracialism offered a marker for the real progress toward a transformed Americanism into which Jews might proudly assimilate. While the dark side of the rise of sound films up to the war years was stained in more than one way by *The Jazz Singer* and *Gone With the Wind*, destined to rise further in another decade only with the strenuous efforts of Hollywood Jewish radicals and mainly (if not only) in high-stepping musicals, cabaret had presented another side of Jewish–Black cultural collaborations. Café Society, the Village venue opening in 1937, alone held a remarkable story. Part Weimar, part left-wing fundraiser and stand-up *shtick*, part jazz experimentation, it placed black performers in front of disproportionately Jewish and highly sophisticated audiences week after week. It defined, in its own small way, the New York sophistication of the Popular Front, and its spirit might have remade a corner of Hollywood, given the chance.

If Café Society and the larger milieu had done nothing more than to place lyricist Abel Meeropol's verse in front of the young Billie Holiday, the experiment would have been monumental in American culture. Appearing in the same 1939 as *Gone With the Wind*, "Strange Fruit" defied every expectation of the commercial "lady singer" of the Ella Fitzgerald type, outraged Southern politicians beyond measure, and put leftwing Meeropol onto the FBI's list. The Bronx High School English teacher, composing music in his off hours, had just walked into Café Society with the lyric in hand and coaxed Holiday to sing it. Although the song's success owed much to Danny Mendelsohn's arrangement, she had captured what the lyricist could not have done himself; the *New Masses* called it, anomalously but not entirely so, the "first successful attempt of white men (i.e., the lyricist and composer) to sing the blues."

Abel Meeropol had just one more hit (and one Hollywood success), with circumstances just as unusual. In 1945, living and working in the film capital, he was asked to provide a song holding together a special human rights short vehicle for Frank Sinatra, a supporter of antifascist idealism. Scripted by Albert Maltz, *The House I Live In*, running less than 15 minutes, played in theaters across the country and won a special Academy statuette. It was a spectacular Jewish intervention in redefining "Americanism." Sinatra's character, himself as hit singer stepping out of a studio, came across a poor kid being bullied and threatened by other boys, and fended off the attackers by explaining that democracy was about "all faiths/all religions/that's America to me." He could not say (or sing) about Jews or African Americans, let alone Japanese Americans returning from camps with their worldly possessions purloined. The boy must have been an inexplicable Catholic in a Protestant neighborhood or vice versa. When Sinatra sang it again, as a staunch Reagan Republican late in his life, he did not need to change a word or intoned phrase.

Progress had seemed possible, perhaps just ahead, amid the public mobilization for the great war against fascism. In 1943, *Cabin in the Sky* appeared on stage, a too-folksy fantasy-musical about the soul of one seemingly lost African American male, but containing several crucial songs written by Yip Harburg and sung by the likes of Ethel Waters and Lena Horne. The show, it is said, contained the first integrated theatrical road cast. In 1945, *Stormy Weather* saw the light, with "book" by future blacklistee Hy Kraft (whose previous work, mostly on Broadway, was most notable for the recreation of pre-1920 Yiddish theatrical atmosphere of the coffee houses on Second Avenue), dancing by the Katherine Dunham troupe and showstopping work by Horne and Fats Waller, in his best moments of a disappointing cinematic career.

Things went downhill thereafter. Films about musicians proliferated during wartime and after, but a Negro "problem" never surfaced—any more than any Jewish "problem" that musicians might continue to face within American society would rear its ugly head. In *Rhapsody in Blue*, the young composer's career takes off when he becomes a lyricist for Al Jolson, and his lasting reputation is made when he is taken up by Paul Whiteman, whose all-white band makes jazz (n the band leader's revealing phrase) "into a lady," removing it from its sullied origins. Near the end of his short life, Gershwin writes *Porgy and Bess*, but he is cheated from life's real triumph when he dies before his classically oriented "Concerto in F" is performed (by his friend Oscar Levant, as in real life) on the Manhattan concert stage. Black music is ultimately a kind of domestic folkishness, which Gershwin, like his European counterpart Ravel, can render into "real" music—but still definitely not at a classical level of real art. That Sidney Buchman wrote *The Jolson Story* (with contributions by a leading Hollywood Jewish Communist, John Howard Lawson) and *Jolson Sings Again*, only drove home the contradiction.

New Orleans (1947), written and directed by Herbert Biberman, was a bold attempt to wed classical music to real jazz, in New Orleans were Louis Armstrong (his only notable Hollywood appearance until *Paris Blues* in 1961) and Billie Holiday are sweethearts who successfully tour Europe with black music, helping to make it respectable. The movie was a commercial flop, perhaps because the blacklist was descending on the writer and director. Holiday herself never appeared in another film. (*Lady Sings the Blues*, a 1971 hit directed by Sidney J. Furie and starring Diana Ross, played the contradiction the other way: both Jews and Reds were apparently absent.)

Nor was Jewish-written interracial drama in the Hollywood big time more notably successful. A young Jewish screenwriter from Chicago, Carl Foreman, penned *Home of the Brave* (1948), in which a psychologically broken African American soldier regains use of his body, with the help of a psychiatrist (naturally Jewish, played by Jeff Corey), by understanding that all soldiers are equal beneath the khakis and polished brass. At a historic moment when Jewish teenagers were seen on the cover of *Life* magazine idolizing Dizzy Gillespie, and romantic crossovers (less frequently marriages) across race lines more often united Jews and Blacks than anyone else, it was all so pathetically inadequate. The Cold War's repressive edge in Hollywood and the crash of box office receipts ended hopes for nearly a decade, meantime squeezing Jewish innovation into hiding—like the humanist sentiment delivered by Jewish leftwinger Ned Young working under a front for Oscar-winning *The Defiant Ones* (1958).

However, the boldest television drama had already "done" interracial themes before *The Defiant Ones*, and in the larger sense. Television's success meant that TV writers, directors, and actors would be required to revive the topicality and political energy of Hollywood by the end of the 1950s. In the meantime, the filmic burden of Jewish humanism and experiment with the forms of popular culture was more likely to go under the radar.

That kind of humanistic liberalism, with rare exceptions the outer limit of permissible political expression during the 1950s, was the marker for a generation of mostly younger men and women from lower-class or lower-middle-class backgrounds who had come of age during the war years and found a place for themselves in entertainment. Largely, if by no means exclusively Jewish, these artists were able to find in their Jewishness the deeper source for their ideals and aspirations and to re-express them in a way that the blacklist, despite its intentions, had not been able to extinguish.

FURTHER READING

Buhle, Paul and Dave Wagner. *Hide in Plain Sight: The Hollywood Blacklistees in ilm and Television, 1950–2002.* New York: Palgrave Macmillan, 2003.

Ceplair, Larry and Steven Englund. *The Inquisition in Hollywood: Politics in the Film Community, 1930–1960.* Berkeley: University of California Press, 1979.

Friedrich, Otto. *City of Nets: A Portrait of Hollywood in the 1940s.* New York: Harper & Row, 1986.

McGilligan, Patrick and Paul Buhle. *Tender Comrades: A Backstory of the Hollywood Blacklist.* New York: St. Martin's Press, 1997.

Chapter 5

Jews in Hollywood Musicals
Bernard F. Dick

The phrase "Hollywood musical" conjures up such names as Alice Faye, Betty Grable, Judy Garland, Gene Kelly, Ann Miller, Fred Astaire, Ginger Rogers, Frank Sinatra, Jane Powell, Howard Keel, Ann Blyth, Betty Hutton, Deanna Durbin, Bing Crosby, Bob Hope, and Dorothy Lamour, none of whom were Jews. Al Jolson, Eddie Cantor, Danny Kaye, Bert Lahr, and Barbra Streisand were.

Although Jolson was a box office favorite in the 1930s, he and Cantor were not film icons, but popular entertainers who made a few historically significant films (Jolson in *The Jazz Singer* [1927], Cantor in *Roman Scandals* [1933], and *Kid Millions* [1934]). Although Lahr will always be remembered as the Cowardly Lion in *The Wizard of Oz* (1939), Hollywood made little use of his unique form of speech song, raspy as it was, in which he inflected the lyrics so rhythmically that the songs could almost pass for music. Kaye's films for Samuel Goldwyn, such as *Up in Arms* (1944) and *The Secret Life of Walter Mitty* (1947), were primarily comedies interspersed with musical numbers showing off Kaye's gift for mimicry and tongue-twisting lyrics. The exception was *Hans Christian Andersen* (1952), a traditional musical with a relatively subdued performance by Kaye in the title role and a Broadway-worthy score by composer-lyricist Frank Loesser. (The film was later transformed into a London stage musical.) Streisand's only successful movie musical was the 1968 film version of her 1964 Broadway triumph, *Funny Girl*. If *Yentl* (1983) included musical sequences, it was only because Streisand wrote, coproduced, directed, and starred in it.

The Hollywood musical may have lacked a significant on-screen Jewish presence, although the genre could never have existed were it not for Jewish composers and lyricists and creative producers such as the following:

Harold Arlen (Hymen Arluck)

Arlen's name will forever be linked with "Over the Rainbow" (*The Wizard of Oz*, 1939), yet he left behind an impressive body of work, including a number of highly regarded stage musicals—*Bloomer Girl*, *St. Louis Woman*, *House of Flowers*, and *Jamaica*. Working exclusively as a composer, Arlen relied on songwriters such as Johnny Mercer and "Yip" Harburg to provide him with the right texts. The symbiotic relationship he had with his lyricists resulted in such standards as "That Old Black Magic" (*Star-Spangled Rhythm*, 1942), "Accentuate the Positive " (*Here Come the Waves*, 1944) and "My Shining Hour" (*The Sky's the Limit*, 1943), all with Johnny Mercer; and "Over the Rainbow" and "Happiness Is Just A Thing Called Joe" (*Cabin in the Sky*, 1943) with Harburg. For the musical version of *A Star Is Born* (1954), Arlen teamed up with Ira Gershwin to provide Judy Garland with the definitive torch song, "The Man That Got Away." Although Arlen composed "Get Happy" for a 1930 Broadway revue, it became the perfect finale for another Garland musical, *Summer Stock* (1950).

Irving Berlin (Israel Baline)

Although Berlin had a couple of Broadway hits (notably, *Annie Get Your Gun* and *Call Me Madam*, both of which were filmed—the latter with the original star, Ethel Merman), he was essentially a gifted songwriter whose songs could easily be incorporated into any script with a plot flexible enough to accommodate musical numbers at various intervals. If the songs from the eighteen movies that featured Berlin's music were arranged chronologically, they would constitute the Irving Berlin Songbook. His music worked extremely well in the Fred Astaire–Ginger Rogers musicals, *Top Hat* (1935), *Follow the Fleet* ([1936], "Let's Face The Music And Dance"), and *Carefree* ([1938], "Change Partners"). In "Cheek to Cheek" (*Top Hat*), Astaire and Rogers absorbed the music so naturally that, to paraphrase Yeats, one could barely tell the dancers from the dance. Other classic Berlin moments on film include the composer himself in a deadpan rendition of "Oh, How I Hate to Get Up in the Morning" in *This Is the Army* (1943); the sensuous "It Only Happens When I Dance with You," sung by Fred Astaire as he waltzed Ann Miller around the parlor in *Easter Parade* (1948); and the "Heat Wave" sequence in *Blue Skies* (1946) with Astaire and Olga San Juan, in which the music rises inexorably to a frenetic climax in which Astaire, his balance impaired by drink, falls from a ledge onto the stage. America's all-time favorite, "White Christmas," was introduced in *Holiday Inn* (1942), in which Bing Crosby, accompanying himself at the piano, crooned it to Marjorie Reynolds, as each seemed to be remembering the Christmases of their youth. If "White Christmas" resonated with World War II audiences, it is because they too could recall better—and happier—times when their "days were merry and bright."

Leonard Bernstein

Although Leonard Bernstein, the most famous musical figure of the twentieth century, enjoyed success as a composer, conductor, and educator, only two of his musicals were transferred to the screen: *On the Town* (1949) with a stellar cast—Frank Sinatra, Gene Kelly, Ann Miller, Betty Garrett, and Vera-Ellen; and *West Side Story* (1961) with choreography by Jerome Robbins that tapped into the American psyche in a way that even *Oklahoma!* did not. Of the two, the better was *West Side Story* (1961), which was a faithful recreation of the original. *On the Town* suffered from the omission of two songs from the 1944 stage production—"Lonely Town" and "Some Other Time"—that were filled with a sense of longing and uncertainty that was characteristic of so much popular music of the World War II era and would have clashed with the buoyant optimism of the movie version, released four years after the end of the war. Columbia Pictures was interested in Bernstein's *Wonderful Town* (1953), the musical version of *My Sister Eileen* that marked Rosalind Russell's return to Broadway, but balked at the cost and instead produced its own *My Sister Eileen* (1955) with a serviceable but unmemorable score by Jule Styne, but a brilliant performance by Betty Garrett in the Rosalind Russell part. What many consider Bernstein's greatest piece of musical theater and his most inventive score, *Candide*, is too much of a connoisseur's work for popular consumption.

Irving (Isidor) Caesar

"Swanee" usually evokes the name of Al Jolson, although it was George Gershwin who wrote the music; and Caesar, the words. Jolson's version, lip-synched by Larry Parks in *The Jolson Story* (1946), may be definitive, but Judy Garland's in *A Star Is Born* (1954) is the one that most moviegoers remember. Caesar also wrote the lyrics for the Vincent Youmans musical, *No, No, Nanette*, which included "Tea for Two" and "I Want to Be Happy." *Nanette* was filmed twice—in 1930 and 1940; the Doris Day movie, *Tea for Two* (1952) is an extremely free reworking of the original.

Sammy Cahn (Samuel Cohen)

Although Cahn was a lyricist, his songs were so popular, both on- and off-screen, that he was often mistaken for their composer, particularly after he appeared in his one-person show, *Words and Music* (1974), which ran on Broadway for one hundred and twenty-seven performances. Since his career spanned four decades (from 1941 to 1982), it is impossible to list his entire output. Among his best-known songs are "I'll Walk Alone" (sung by Dinah Shore in *Follow the Boys*, 1944), "I Fall In Love Too Easily" (sung by Frank Sinatra in *Anchors Aweigh*, 1945), "Time after Time" (sung by Sinatra in

It Happened in Brooklyn, 1947), "Be My Love" (sung by Mario Lanza in *The Toast of New Orleans,* 1950), "Three Coins in the Fountain" (from the 1954 film of the same name), and "I'll Never Stop Loving You" (sung by Doris Day in *Love Me or Leave Me,* 1955).

Betty Comden and Adolph Green

Comden and Green were two of the greatest wordsmiths in the annals of Broadway and Hollywood. They were not only lyricists, but also screenwriters responsible for what is generally considered the greatest American movie musical, *Singin' in the Rain* (1952). Recognized more for their contributions to the musical theater (e.g., the Mary Martin *Peter Pan, On the Twentieth Century, The Will Rogers Follies*) than for the movies, they only saw two of their stage successes turned into films: *On the Town* (1949) and *Bells Are Ringing* (1960). Still, their film work is impressive; their screenplay for *Good News* enlivened what would otherwise have been a routine college life musical, for which they also wrote the witty lyrics for "The French Lesson," in which June Allyson attempts to tutor Peter Lawford, who turns out to be a fast learner. They wrote both the screenplay and lyrics for *It's Always Fair Weather* (1955), an anti-*On the Town,* in which three World War II buddies meet for a reunion, only to discover that their camaraderie ended with the war.

Vernon Duke (Vladimir Dukelsky)

Except for *Cabin in the Sky* (1940), which became a memorable 1943 MGM film with Ethel Waters and Lena Horne, the Russian-born and classically trained Duke was only moderately successful as a Broadway composer. He did, however, enrich the great American Song Book with such classics as "Taking a Chance on Love" from *Cabin in the Sky;* "April in Paris," heard in the 1952 film of the same name; and "Autumn in New York," which subtly conveyed a sense of loss without sounding like a lament and was never featured in a movie musical, but only in Bertrand Tavernier's tribute to jazz musicians, *'Round Midnight* (1986).

Sammy Fain (Samuel Feinberg)

For 30 years, 1930–59, Fain composed songs for Hollywood musicals such as *Foootlight Parade* (1933), in which Dick Powell and Ruby Keeler sang "By a Waterfall"; *Calamity Jane* (1953), with Doris Day's peerless rendition of "Secret Love"; *April Love* (1957), in which Pat Boone introduced the title song; and the title song from *Love Is a Many-Splendored Thing* (1956).

Dorothy Fields

A lyricist who was a poet at heart and one of the first women in a male-dominated profession to achieve prominence, Fields contributed the words to two songs that were added to the score of the movie version of Jerome Kern's *Roberta* (1935), "I Won't Dance" and "Lovely to Look At." She also worked with Kern on the Astaire-Rogers musical, *Swing Time* (1936), which included such standards as "Pick Yourself Up" and "A Fine Romance." Other composers for whom Fields provided lyrics were Jimmy Mc Hugh ("I'm in the Mood for Love" and "I Feel a Song Coming On" in *Every Night at Eight* [1935], which was so popular that it was heard in other films as well), and Cy Coleman (*Sweet Charity*, 1968). Fields' second collaboration with Coleman marked the end of her career: *Seesaw* (1973), a stage musical with a grand score that included the popular "It's Not How You Start, It's How You Finish," was never filmed. She died a year after *Seesaw*'s premiere.

Arthur Freed

Had it not been for the protestations of producer Arthur Freed, head of MGM's musicals division known as the Freed Unit, "Over the Rainbow" would have been cut from *The Wizard of Oz*. The Freed Unit was responsible for such classics as *Cabin in the Sky* (1943), *Meet Me in St. Louis* (1944), *The Harvey Girls* (1946), *Easter Parade* (1948), *On the Town* (1949), *An American in Paris* (1951), *Royal Wedding* (1951), *Singin' in the Rain* (1952), *The Band Wagon* (1953), *Brigadoon* (1954), and *Gigi* (1958).

George and Ira Gershwin

Together they gave the movie musical more classics than, arguably, another composer and lyricist team. For Astaire and Rogers, they wrote "They All Laughed," "They Can't Take That Away from Me" (*Shall We Dance*, 1937); for Astaire without Rogers in *Damsel in Distress* (1947), "A Foggy Day" and "Nice Work If You Can Get It"; for *The MGM Follies* (1938), which was released a year after George Gershwin's death, "Love Is Here to Stay" and "Love Walked In." Even after George's death, the Gershwin legacy continued as the team's music and lyrics were heard in *Girl Crazy* (1943). *The Shocking Miss Pilgrim* ([1947], "For You, For Me, For Evermore"), *An American in Paris* ([1951], "Embraceable You," "I Got Rhythm," "S' Wonderful"), and *Funny Face* ([1957], "How Long Has This Been Going On?" "He Loves and She Loves"). George received the usual Hollywood treatment in the biopic, *Rhapsody in Blue* (1946), with Robert Alda (Alan's father) as the composer. His masterpiece, *Porgy and Bess* finally arrived on the screen in 1959, two decades after its premiere in an unusually faithful version directed by Otto Preminger. Although neither the Porgy (Sidney Poitier) nor the Bess (Dorothy Dandridge) did his or her own singing, the result was still an electric piece of musical cinema.

E.Y. "Yip" Harburg (Isidore Hochburg)

It is difficult to say whether "Over the Rainbow" owes its greatness to Harold Arlen's music or Harburg's words. Rather, the music and the lyrics were mutually complementary. "Rainbow" may not have been Arlen's best music, or Harburg's greatest lyric, but in combination it achieved a universality that few movie songs did. The equally well-known "Brother, Can You Spare a Dime?" (music by Jay Gorney) was not heard in the movies but came from a 1932 Broadway revue. Broadway, in fact, was Harburg's natural habitat: *Bloomer Girl* (1944) and *Jamaica* (1957) with Arlen; *Finian's Rainbow* (1947) with Burton Lane; *Flahooley* (1951) with Sammy Fain, an artistic failure with a subtle political subtext dealing with McCarthyism; and *Darling of the Day* (1968) with Jule Styne. A political activist to the end of his life, Harburg invested his lyrics with a deep compassion for the marginalized and underprivilegd, giving racists their due in *Finian's Rainbow* and satirizing right-wingers in *Flahooley*. One wishes he had worked more in Hollywood.

John Kander and Fred Ebb

Kander and Ebb may never rival Rodgers and Hart or Rodgers and Hammerstein in popularity, yet they created two Broadway musicals, *Cabaret* and *Chicago*, which became Oscar-winning films in 1972 and 2002, respectively. Although not all of Kander's *Cabaret* score reached the screen, the opening number in which the epicene master of ceremonies (Joel Grey) promises the audience a haven from the outside world (a soon-to-be Nazi Germany) caught the mockingly cynical mood of the original, as did Ebb's lyrics in the title song, in which Sally Bowles (Liza Minnelli) delights in living for the moment even if it means dying of pills and liquor. The team also gave Minnelli a showstopper for her concerts (and New York its own anthem): the title song from *New York, New York* (1977). Ignored in its day, *New York, New York* has now become a cult musical.

Jerome Kern

Jerome Kern was a major Broadway composer before Hollywood benefited from his prodigious talent. Although several of his musicals were filmed, notably *ShowBoat* three times (the second, in 1936, being the most faithful), he augmented the Great American Song book with "The Folks Who Live on the Hill" (with Dorothy Fields), which Irene Dunne sang so tenderly in *High, Wide, and Handsome* (1937) and is now a cabaret standard; and the songs for two Rita Hayworth musicals, *You Were Never Lovelier* (1942), with Fred Asatire; and the even more impressive *Cover Girl* (1944), with Gene Kelly. The former included the title song and "Dearly Beloved"; the latter, a World War II favorite, "Long Ago and Far Away," a lushly romantic ballad that crystallized the longings of a war-weary

America. Although the 1941 movie version of the George and Ira Gershwin's 1924 musical *Lady Be Good* retained only a few songs from the original to which it bore little resemblance, the score included one number that was especially meaningful at the time of its release, "The Last Time I Saw Paris," which Kern wrote with Oscar Hammerstein II in 1940 after the fall of France and which Ann Sothern sang poignantly in the film. Since "The Last Time I Saw Paris" was not composed expressly for the movie, there was some criticism when it won the Oscar for best song, even though it was superior to the other nominees. MGM made an attempt to immortalize Kern in *Till the Clouds Roll By* (1946), but succeeded only in showcasing its stars, including Frank Sinatra in a ghastly version of "Ol' Man River."

Burton Lane (Burton Levy)

Although Lane is chiefly known as a Broadway composer (e.g., *Finian's Rainbow, On a Clear Day You Can See Forever*, neither of which fared well on the screen), he collaborated with Alan Jay Lerner on the score for MGM's *Royal Wedding* (1954), in which Fred Astaire and Jane Powell performed a number that may have had the longest title on record: "How Could You Believe Me When I Said I Loved You When You Know I've Been a Liar All My Life?" Lane's most popular song, "Everything I Have Is Yours," was first heard in *Dancing Lady* (1933), but rendered more expressively by Ezio Pinza in *Strictly Dishonorable* (1951).

Frank Loesser

One of Broadway's greatest composer-lyricists, Loesser did not tackle the stage musical until *Where's Charley?* (1946), followed by one of the theater's greatest musicals, *Guys and Dolls* (1950), and the Pulitzer Prize–winning *How to Succeed in Business Without Really Trying* (1960), all of which were filmed, and except for *Where's Charley?*, did well at the box office. Until 1945, Loesser was based in Hollywood, writing the lyrics for such memorable songs as "The Lady's in Love with You" (*Some Like It Hot* [1939], not to be confused with the Billy Wilder film), "I Don't Want to Walk Without You, Baby" (*Sweater Girl*, 1942), and "They're Either Too Young or Too Old," sung by a jaded Bette Davis in *Thank Your Lucky Stars* (1943) as she bemoaned the lack of eligible males during World War II. In 1944, Loesser began composing, and the rest is musical history. In *Christmas Holiday* (1944), a blond Deanna Durbin, playing a hooker (but only for those in the know) introduced his classic, "Spring Will Be a Little Late This Year," investing it with kind of wistful resignation that the lyrics demanded. Although Betty Hutton, labeled "The Blonde Bombshell," could tear into a song as if it were an object of attack, Loesser gave her the opportunity to reveal her more lyrical side in "I Wish I Didn't Love You So" (*The Perils of*

Pauline [1947]). Once Loesser realized his metier was the musical stage, he made a few return visits to Hollywood, picking up an Oscar for "Baby, It's Cold Outside" (*Neptune's Daughter*, 1949) and composing the score for the *Hans Christian Andersen*. Because of *Guys and Dolls* and *How to Succeed*, Loesser's name will always evoke Broadway, but he would never have become the composer of two such legendary musicals had he not learned his craft in Hollywood.

Frederick Loewe and Alan Jay Lerner

The musically gifted Loewe and the Harvard-educated Lerner pooled their respective talents to provide Broadway audiences with a succession of masterpieces, two of which were faithfully recreated on the screen: *Brigadoon* (1954) and their biggest hit, *My Fair Lady* (1964). Two others, *Paint Your Wagon* and *Camelot*, were cinematic disasters. Their original movie musical, *Gigi* (1958), was the cinematic equal of *My Fair Lady*, delighting audiences with such memorable numbers as the spirited "The Night They Invented Champagne," the sunset duet between Maurice Chevalier and Hermione Gingold ("I Remember It Well") in which Gingold delicately reminded Chevalier that his memory is not what it was; Chevalier extolling the joys of the golden years ("I'm Glad I'm Not Young Anymore"); and the rhapsodic title song performed with romantic ardor by Louis Jourdan. When Loewe soured on Broadway after *Camelot*, which underwent enormous changes en route to New York, Lerner approached Burton Lane, and the two came up with *On a Clear Day You Can See Forever* (1965). The subject matter (reincarnation) baffled the critics, although the score was Lane's best since *Finian's Rainbow*. The 1970 movie was too overproduced to baffle anyone. Although the stage version could boast of excellent singing by John Cullum, his film counterpart, Yves Montand, could not handle the music, leaving the real singing to Barbra Streisand, who could.

Joe Pasternak (Szilagy Somlyo)

The Hungarian-born Pasternak first worked as a producer at Universal, where he helped shape the career of soprano Deanna Durbin, who, after her debut in *Three Smart Girls* (1937), in which she captivated audiences with her rendition of "Someone to Care for Me," became an instant star—but only for a decade. After making her last movie in 1948, she retired from the movies to live in France. Pasternak left Universal seven years before Durbin did, relocating at MGM, where he produced musicals that were not in the same league as Arthur Freed's, but were still quite respectable—e.g., the Judy Garland vehicles, *Presenting Lily Mars* (1943), *In the Good Old Summertime* (1949), and *Summer Stock* (1950). Pasternak did for Mario Lanza what he did for Durbin: he made the tenor into a star, albeit a short-lived one, beginning with his film debut in *That Midnight Kiss* (1949), followed by *The Toast of New Orleans* (1950), in which he sang "Be My Love" with music by Nicholas Brodszky and lyrics by Sammy Cahn; and Lanza's greatest success, *The Great Caruso* (1951). Pasternak's later films were far from mediocre, but only a few of them—e.g., *The Student Prince* (1954), *Love Me or Leave Me* (1955), and *Jumbo* (1962)—were truly distinctive.

André Previn

Like Bernstein, Previn was a composer and conductor—fields in which he was more successful than he was in film. When he composed the music for *It's Always Fair Weather*, the movie musical was on the verge of becoming moribund. *Inside Daisy Clover* (1958) was not a musical, but "You're Gonna Hear from Me," belted out by Natalie Wood (with a voice double), is an indication of what Previn could have written if the movie musical were in its pride of place.

Richard Rodgers and Lorenz (Larry) Hart

Unfortunately, Rodgers and Hart's greatest musical, *Pal Joey* (1940), was never filmed when it should have been, reaching the screen in 1957 with an overaged and slightly dissipated Frank Sinatra as Joey, sanitized lyrics, and a happy ending. Virtually all the film versions of Rodgers and Hart's musicals are disappointing, largely because Hart's ultrasophisticated and frequently risqué lyrics would not have appealed to a mass audience. However, the team did write original material for Ernst Lubitsch's *Love Me Tonight* (1932), which included Maurice Chevalier's signature song, "Mimi," as well as "Isn't It Romantic?"; the forgettable *The Phantom President* (1932); and the Great Depression curio, Lewis Milestone's *Hallelujah, I'm a Bum* (1933), remembered more for its rhyming dialogue than its score. The biopic, *Words and Music* (1948), should be seen for the *Slaughter on Tenth Avenue* ballet, danced to perfection by Gene Kelly and Vera-Ellen, not for its shallow portrait of Hart (Mickey Rooney), whose main problem seems to have been shortness of height, not homosexuality which, admittedly, could not have been depicted at the time.

Richard Rodgers and Oscar Hammerstein II

Even before Larry Hart died in November 1943, his alcoholism (suggested in *Words and Music*) forced Rodgers to look for another collaborator, finding his alter ego in Oscar Hammerstein II, who substituted simplicity and humanity for Hart's wit and cynicism. Rodgers and Hammerstein were the ideal combination for wartime and postwar America as they created a succession of extraordinary musicals: *Oklahoma!*, *Carousel*, *South Pacific*, *The King and I*, and *The Sound of Music*, all of which reached the screen relatively intact. Although they only wrote one original movie musical, *State*

Fair (1945), the result was the Oscar-winning song, "It Might As Well Be Spring." Like *Hans Christian Andersen*, *State Fair* was also transformed into a stage musical but never rivaled the original.

Sigmund Romberg

The composer of such operettas as *The Student Prince*, *New Moon*, and *The Desert Song* (all of which were filmed—the first two twice, the third three times) also collaborated with Dorothy Fields on a Broadway show that was as much musical comedy as operetta: *Up in Central Park*, filmed in black-and-white in 1948 with Deanna Durbin, minus the exquisite "Close as Pages in a Book." One of his best loved songs, "When I Grow Too Old To Dream," was exquisitely sung by Evelyn Laye in *The Night Is Young* (1935). His life was given the usual Hollywood treatment in *Deep in My Heart* (1954) with José Ferrer as Romberg.

Harry Ruby (Rubinstein) and Bert Kalmar

Although Ruby worked with other lyricists, his chief collaborator was Kalmar. MGM told the story of their journey from vaudeville to Broadway in *Three Little Words* (1950), with Fred Astaire as Kalmar and Red Skelton as Ruby, which included a sampling of some of their work, including the title song and "I Love You So Much." "A Kiss to Build a Dream On," their most popular song, never appeared in a musical but in a melodrama, *The Strip* (1951), in which Louis "Satchmo" Armstrong personalized it, so that it became the standard against which other renditions are measured. "Kiss" was also nominated for an Oscar, losing to "In the Cool, Cool, Cool of the Evening."

Arthur Schwartz

He collaborated with several outstanding lyricists, including Howard Dietz ("Dancing in the Dark," heard in the 1949 film of the same name and "I Guess I'll Have to Change My Mind" from *The Band Wagon*, 1953), but his best work was for the theater, especially the scores for *Stars in Your Eyes* (1939), *A Tree Grows in Brooklyn* (1951), and *By the Beautiful Sea* (1954) with that impeccable lyricist, Dorothy Fields; and *Revenge with Music* (1934) and *Inside U.S.A.* (1948) with Howard Dietz.

Stephen Sondheim

Admired for his intricate rhyming lyrics and scores hovering between opera and operetta, Sondheim is only represented on film by *A Funny Thing Happened on the Way to the Forum* (1969) and *A Little Night Music* (1975), neither of which gave any indication as to why the originals ran so long on Broadway. Sondheim's greatest musicals—*Follies*, *Sweeney Todd*, *Passion*, *Pacific Overtures*—are too intellectually demanding, and require absolute concentration, particularly on the lyrics, to appeal to nontheatergoers. Sondheim's lyrics for Bernstein's *West Side Story* and Jule Styne's *Gypsy*, filmed in 1961 and 1959, respectively, are more in keeping with the traditional musical form and thus are more accessible to mass audiences.

Jule Styne (Jules Kerwin Stein)

Best known as a Broadway composer, whose hit shows (*Gentlemen Prefer Blondes*, *Bells Are Ringing*, *Gypsy*, and *Funny Girl*) translated into hit movies, Styne began his career in Hollywood, where he enriched several otherwise pedestrian movies with his music. His frequent collaboration with Sammy Cahn resulted in "I've Heard That Song Before" (*Youth on Parade* [1942]), "I Fall In Love Too Easily" (*Anchors Aweigh* [1945]), "I'll Walk Alone" (*Follow the Boys* [1944]), "Time after Time" (*It Happened in Brooklyn* [1947]), and "It's Magic" (*Romance on the High Seas* [1948]). Styne's greatest achievement, *Gypsy*, with lyrics by Stephen Sondheim, resulted in the quintessence of musical theater. The 1962 screen version, with Rosalind Russell in the role created by Ethel Merman, includes the entire score, but one would have to go to the original cast recording to savor its greatness.

Harry Warren (Salvatore Guaragna) and Al Dubin

Composer Warren, a Christian, and lyricist Dubin, a Jew, together recreated the essence of Tin Pan Alley in a number of Warner Bros. musicals, the most famous being *42nd Street* (the title song, "Shuffle Off to Buffalo," "You're Getting to be a Habit with Me"). They also provided the shattering climax to *Gold Diggers of 1933*, "Remember My Forgotten Man," a dirge to the World War I veterans who received less than a hero's welcome on their return to civilian life. The "Lullaby of Broadway" sequence in *Gold Diggers of 1935* is equally dark, dramatizing the fate of a "Broadway baby" who pays with her life for a night on the town.

Kurt Weill

Once the German born Weill and his wife Lotte Lenya came to America, Weill, a serious composer in his own right, turned his sights on Broadway. Three of his musicals were adapted for the screen—*Knickerbocker Holiday* (1944), *Lady in the Dark* (1944), and *One Touch of Venus* (1948), the last two falling woefully short of the originals. "My Ship," the ballad so essential to the plot of *Lady in the Dark*, disappeared from the garish movie version, but at least *Knickerbocker Holiday* retained the classic "September Song"; and *One Touch of Venus*, "Speak Low." Weill and Ira Gershwin provided the songs for *Where Do We Go from Here?* (1945), a time travel musical that included the rousing "The Nina, the Pinta, the Santa Maria."

Jews may not have invented the movie musical, but they certainly enriched it.

FURTHER READING

Green, Stanley. *Encyclopedia of the Musical Film*. New York: Oxford University Press, 1981, 27.
"Jewish Songwriters and Composers." "Jewish-Composed Broadway & Hollywood Musicals." *Jews in Music*. http://jinfo.org.
Kendrick, John. *Who's Who in Musicals*. http://www.musicals101.com/whoswho.htm.

Chapter 6

Making a Scene: Jews, Stooges, and Censors in Pre-War Hollywood
Dan M. Bronstein

Relief for the Jews! How about Relief from the Jews?
—Harry Cohn

We specialize in the upsetting of dignity.
—Moe Howard

"Most children watching 'The Three Stooges' didn't realize it," notes journalist William Grimes, "but an understanding of Yiddish was required to get a lot of their jokes." The Yiddish language—still not dead—is nevertheless, most certainly not the *lingua franca* of today's youth although mangling the English language and peppering dialogue with Yiddish is an American Jewish comedy tradition passed down to Sid Caesar's *Your Show of Shows* through the films of Mel Brooks and beyond. At least for American Jews in the 1930s and the 1940s, Moe, Larry, and Curly's persistent usage of Yiddishisms like "*chazeri*," or the greeting of "*Shalom Aleichem*," were just a few examples of Stooges' explicit display of Jewishness. Who else but Jews would peddle less than fresh fish on the street singing "... Sword Fish, Whitefish, Herring and Gefilte Fish, *and that ain't all*!" "Jewishness" has always been an elusive concept, repelling easy definition. However, an understanding of the three Stooges' Jewishness was required to "get" them in their full glory. In the years before America's entry into World War II and the beginning of the *Shoah*, showing one's Jewishness or "making a scene," comedic or otherwise, was actually a counter-cultural statement. The Stooges did not script their own films, but their routines and spontaneous moves "rewrote" their films, including the crypto-political content.

In the early decades of the twentieth century, Jews in America, immigrants and children of immigrants were Americanizing, not simply from external pressure, but also from forces within. They in turn began their pivotal role in the creation of a new American mass culture. American Jews, or more accurately in many cases, Americans who happened to be Jewish, were impacting popular culture in areas as widespread as film, the comic book industry, the visual arts, music, the written word, and theater. "Old" America had been undergoing radical change for decades: urbanization, a changing economy, and changing mores. Hollywood movies were reflective of these changes even as films were among the primary cultural and industrial instigators of transformation of American popular culture. Perhaps the most visible manifestation of the growing prominence of Jews in American cultural life was the Hollywood film industry. Concurrently, American anti-Semitism grew to historic proportions in the 1930s, peaking, according to David Wyman, in 1944.

John Murray Cuddihy has argued that post-Emancipation ideologies like Marxism, Freudianism, *Haskalah*, and Reform Judaism have a "double audience"; on the one hand, each ideology seeks to remake Jews themselves, while on the other hand, each one of these ideologies endeavors to explain Jews to the majority culture. Moreover, Cuddihy argues, "secular Jewish intellectual ideologies are exercises in antidefamation."

The Three Stooges were neither intellectuals nor prophets of any particular ideology, but they did have a double audience, and many of their films served the cause of antidefamation. Their movies defended working-class Americans even while they mocked the working-class experience. In their defense of the marginalized of American society, the Stooges films were also among the first, and most explicit attacks, albeit via humor, on the Nazis, and were produced well before it was popular or "safe" to do so. For various minorities, Jews, and others, comedy has been one venue of critiquing general society even while making fun of one's own cultural niche. Although paradoxical, comedy provided American Jews with the format for asserting themselves through a parody of the other. In the face of the rise of Fascism in the old world and rising anti-Semitism in the new world, such loaded comedy was no simple or safe endeavor.

One might question whether there was there anything funny whatsoever about 1930s anti-Semitism, but to a great extent Hollywood's main response was to take a stance of silence. In the 1930s and 1940s, many a Jew and Gentile alike argued that it was in the interest of the Jewish people not to "make a scene" against the Third Reich; better to use quiet diplomacy in dealing with the Nazis than openly protest. All the more so, it was believed that the use of humor, mockery, and satire would inflame anti-Semitism and bring further disaster on Jews in Germany and throughout the world. Until Japan's attack on Pearl Harbor, many in Hollywood opposed using films, comedic or otherwise, to confront Hitler. Particularly at a time when the movie industry, although ostensibly under Jewish "control" produced largely *Judenrein* films, the Stooges constituted explicit expressions of defiance against those who would defame the Jewish people.

In the 1930s, the so-called Jewish "movie moguls" were themselves anxious lest the movie industry be viewed as "too Jewish," and attempted to manage the Jewish image in mass culture, mostly by closeting the explicit expressions of Jewishness in Hollywood films. As film historian Patricia Brett Erens and others have noted, the popularity of Jewish performers like the Marx Brothers and Eddie Cantor fell in the 1930s, as did general Jewish subject matter in the American motion picture industry. Moreover, as Neal Gabler writes, "Hollywood was itself a means of avoiding Judaism," for the movie moguls, "not celebrating it."

Gabler and others have chronicled how the Jews "invented Hollywood." However, the ancillary canard of Jews "controlling" Hollywood became a serious manifestation of a more complex, popular American anti-Semitism. Both Roman Catholics and Protestant Americans found occasion to accuse filmmakers of committing blasphemy while producing pornography. The attack came from a variety of religious groups and political strains. Some of the most notorious attacks came from the ostensible exemplar of "Old America," Henry Ford. Mincing no words, Ford used his broadsheet, the *Dearborn Independent*, as early as 1921 to claim that it is the "genius of that race to create problems of a moral character in whatever business they achieve a majority." Another example was the Reverend Gerald L.K. Smith who tapped both the religious and political sources of anti-Semitism, and in 1944 used his broadsheet, *The Cross and the Flag*, to decry the "Rape of America by Hollywood." On and off screen, Hollywood and its denizens became emblematic of moral and material decadence.

The significant and recurring protests of segments of the American public to films and to various Hollywood "scandals" had generated earlier efforts by the movie industry toward self-censorship. The "Production Code Administration" (PCA) was instituted in 1934. Headed by Joseph L. Breen, the PCA was charged with enforcing the rules of the "Production Code," a system laying down the moral rules for all films produced in Hollywood.

Many of the non-Jews charged with monitoring Hollywood morals were not exactly *Judeophiles* or particularly enthralled with the American Jewish experience. Breen once characterized Jews as "vile people" and "scum of the earth," who "seem to think of nothing but money making and sexual indulgence." However, to be fair, the moral pressure exerted on Hollywood as well as its own project of self-censorship was an ecumenical venture. As historian Felicia Herman has documented, some members of the American rabbinate also sought to contain the dissemination of material they also viewed as offensive or as embarrassing to American Jewry as a whole. When edits were requested by PCA they were usually implemented. Simon Louvish has detailed how even the Brothers Marx—whose films serve as the "skeleton key" to American Jewish comedy—were subject to such bowdlerization. Nevertheless, some comedic material, dismissed as "lowbrow," succeeded in evading censorship.

In the years immediately preceding Pearl Harbor, among the most sensitive topics in the film industry was the portrayal of the war unfolding in Europe. Reacting to a 1933 anti-Hitler film project, *The Mad Dog of Europe*, Breen warned agent Al Rosen that there was a "strong pro-German and anti-Semitic feeling in this country and because of the large number of Jews active in the motion picture industry, the charge is certain to be made that the Jews, as a class, are using the entertainment screen for their own personal propaganda purposes." Even by 1942, Breen was still arguing against anti-Axis films, arguing that the "function of the code is not to be patriotic; it is to be moral."

One of the most virulent expressions of anti-Semitism of the era was the canard that Jews, for the sake of personal profit, were dragging the United States into another European war and likewise that American Jews were evading military service. One anti-Semitic ditty circulating around American military bases during the war asserted:

I'll work like hell and never stop
I'll stay right here until I drop
I'll piss in my pants and shit in my shoes
I'll save the world for the god dammed Jews

The obvious delicacy of treating or dealing with such popular perceptions was not lost to the movie industry executives who also happened to be Jewish. Warner Brothers was among the first Studios to break Hollywood's silence with *Confessions of a Nazi Spy* in 1939. And Groucho Marx, no less, praised the Warners for the "only studio with any guts" for actually confronting Nazism. While other such films followed, so did reaction from congressional isolationists and anti-Semites such as North Dakota's Senator Gerald Nye who convened a Senate investigation into "Moving Picture Screen and Radio Propaganda" only weeks before the attack on Pearl Harbor.

Well remembered for its pioneering role in satirizing the Nazis, Charlie Chaplin's *The Great Dictator* appeared in 1940, long thought to have been the first anti-Nazi comedy. Indeed, at the time it generated a great deal of controversy and at least in part contributed to congressional investigations into "warmongering" in Hollywood. (Later, Chaplin suggested that had he known the full scale of Hitler's genocidal polices he might not have even made it.) Unlike many of the other films, including comedies of the era, *The Great Dictator* directly confronts the oppression of Jews, albeit in the form of slapstick found in Chaplin's silent works. At the same time, the villains of the film are not Nazis, but rather a mildly euphemized version. Referencing anti-Semitic *pogroms* and the infamous *Kristallnacht*, Jewish homes and businesses are trashed, while the then loaded word "Jude" is smeared onto broken windowpanes. In one particularly poignant scene, after being beaten up by stormtroopers, Chaplin, playing a simple Jewish barber, does a cartoonlike dance in front of the store wreckage while "Jude" flashes several times across the screen.

Satiric slogans like "kill the Jews and wipe out the brunettes" are chanted while military officers openly discuss using anti-Semitism as a societal safety valve and dissidents are sent to concentration camps.

The Great Dictator is also a comedy of errors, in which the Jewish barber and the Hitler stand-in "Adenoid Hynkel" are both played by Chaplin. Still, the Great Dictator is a mixed bag, at points playing like a Keystone Kops film—with stormtroopers as the kops—while at other times *The Great Dictator* aspires to profundity. In one scene, Chaplin the Jew and a rebellious military officer are slapstickishly marched into a concentration camp. And yet, at the close of the film, Chaplin the Jew disguised as Hynkel the dictator gives an impassioned and messianic speech: "Jew, gentile, black and white, in this world there's room for everyone," he intones, blaming "greed" and "intolerance" for fascism. Instead, preaching universal brotherhood and invoking the Gospel of Saint Luke, Chaplin instructs the audience that "we're coming into a new world, a kindlier world." Unfortunately, that world was far from actualizing Luke's dreams.

Along with *The Great Dictator*, the other comedy usually mentioned in the same breath is Ernst Lubitsch's *To Be or Not To Be* released two years later. The latter, even with its generally mild humor, as embodied by Jack Benny, was at the time considered controversial. For one thing, as the film historian Thomas Doherty, writes, the Nazis are "miscast" as "sustained comic foils in a literal theater of war," and unlike Chaplin, Lubitsch does not portray the Nazis euphemistically. However, with one important exception, Poles rather than Jews serve as symbols of the downtrodden. *To Be or Not To Be* also involves playacting and confused identities, as Polish actors pretend to be Nazis including Hitler himself. Mockery comes to the fore with Hitler described as the "man with the little mustache," and the actor playing Hitler stating "Heil myself." And it is a theater that is mocked up as the headquarters of the Gestapo in Warsaw even while concentration camps are referenced. However, this is also a Hollywood love story with Hollywood melodrama, not sure of whether to be silly or serious. On the latter end of the spectrum, the character of Greenberg, another Polish actor, recites Shylock's assertion of humanity—"Hath not a Jew eyes?"—from the *Merchant of Venice* in the film's most impassioned moment. At the very same time, the Nazis are portrayed as idiotic lunkheads, not unlike the Germans of *Hogan's Heroes*. Ultimately, a critical *New York Times* review of the film from early March 1942 in part still rings true today. And while in the post–Mel Brooks "Producers" era of American Jewish comedy we might argue with the reviewer Bosley Crowther's belief that the film needed a "little more taste," we might still agree with his desire for a greater "unity of mood" to the film.

Descending from the artful heights of Chaplin and respectability of Jack Benny, we sink to the level of low-culture stalwarts, the three Stooges. Regardless of personal taste, it is irrefutable that the Stooges are almost universally recognizable icons of popular culture. In various forms and configurations, on the big screen and small, the Stooges have been part of American culture for around three-quarters of a century. For many fans, the "classic" era of the Stooges ran from 1933 to 1946, when the team was made up of brothers Moses and Jerome Horowitz, aka Moe and Curly Howard, and Larry Feinberg, or Fine, the former from Bensonhurst, Brooklyn, the latter Philadelphia. Each and every one of them had entered into comedy via different routes, but all honed their skills on the Vaudeville circuit. In fact, it was another Horowitz brother, Samuel or "Shemp," who had founded the team with Moe—along with their exploitive leader and "straight man" Ted Healy—before Jerome was old enough to join his brothers in show business.

The story of the Stooges actually begins with Moe, the fourth of five children born to Solomon and Jennie Gorvitz—their name apparently changed to Horowitz during the naturalization process—two second cousins who had immigrated to the United States from Lithuania. While the two oldest sons, Irving and Benjamin, took a more conventional route going into the business of insurance, Shemp, Moe, and Curly, born respectively in 1891, 1893, and 1903, of course chose the more radical path into show business. Moe, was the first to work in the entertainment industry. Even in childhood, Moe was developing his own particular *shtick*. Jennie Horowitz had decided that Moe should wear his hair in curls, but Moses, repeatedly beaten up at school for such an effeminate look took matters into his own hands, sculpting his hair into its familiar bowl form. Dropping out of high school in 1914 at the age of fifteen, Moe joined an acting troupe, which sailed up and down the Mississippi River, performing a variety of genres, from Shakespeare to more populist fare.

Influenced by his younger brother, Shemp joined forces with Moe on his return to Brooklyn in 1916, performing a variety of acts in various neighborhoods and at the Coney Island boardwalk. Their first big break was joining forces with former neighbor and upcoming Vaudevillian, Ted Healy. Although the exact details have been lost, the brothers Howard joined Healy's act around 1924, becoming his "Stooges." Moe and Shemp became the literal targets of Healy's jokes and his slaps. Like other Vaudeville acts, Healy and his Stooges featured song, dance, and humor, but the specialty was what Stooges biographer Michael Fleming termed as Ted Healy's "orchestrated mayhem" of slaps, pokes to the eyes, and various other beatings administered against the Stooges. The team was not complete until the arrival of the bushy-haired Larry Fein in 1925.

Arriving in America in about 1900, Larry's parents, Joseph and Fanny Feinberg, settled in Philadelphia. In 1902, Larry, then Louis or Louie, was born. At an early age, Larry was the family performer and comedian, skilled at singing, and playing the violin. However, unbeknownst to his parents, he made his first impact as a teen boxer. On learning of his son's secret life, Joseph Feinberg literally dragged Larry out of the boxing ring and unknowingly thrust him into the world of Vaudeville, where Larry's personal *shtick* was playing violin while doing a Russian-style dance. After Healy saw the bushy-haired, tuxedo-tails bedecked Fein doing a jig while playing a fiddle, he knew he had found a third stooge. Making the move from Vaudeville to Broadway, Healy and his Stooges were featured in then popular stage reviews *A Night in Spain* (1928) and *A Night in Venice*. However, all was not well; Shemp periodically left the group to pursue his own acting career, and more importantly, Healy was not a good boss. A violent alcoholic, Ted Healy also controlled the finances and persistently exploited his Stooges. However, because of Healy's fame, the Stooges joined him in moving to Hollywood, making the film *From Soup to Nuts* in 1930 for the Fox studios. While hardly a comedy classic, and most certainly a critical failure, the Stooges themselves were singled out for praise. Although their movie career did not fully take off until four years later, the Stooges managed to find continual work on the local theater circuit. In the early 1930s, two critical events changed Stooge history. The group began an extended and litigious split from Healy in 1930 and Shemp left the group to go solo in 1933; the result was the addition of perhaps the best-known Stooge of them all, Curly, and by 1934 a film career at Harry Cohn's Columbia pictures, producing films into the 1960s.

Throughout their films, each Stooge had his own particular hairstyle and persona. Moe, with his bowl hair cut, was the group leader, who, although only barely more intelligent than the others, ruled through fear and violence. Larry with the bushy hair was the hapless comedic foil to both Moe and Curly, and later Shemp, one step above Curly in status, but still under Moe's thumb. Curly, the youngest brother at the bottom of the Stooge hierarchy, was also the star. In his youth, Curly, or Jerome, was an athlete and briefly a trained dancer, sporting a full head of hair, and a mustache. However, as a Stooge, Curly became known as the bald, "fat" one, who, while always the target of various physical blows, likewise seemed to be physically indestructible. Although often the purveyor of ridiculous puns and terrible singing, Curly's genius was his extraordinary physical comedy. Unlike his screen persona, he became increasingly withdrawn offscreen, suffering a series of unsuccessful marriages, and enjoying the company of dogs over other people. Alternatively, Larry was apparently the partier of the group, while Moe was the Stooges' staid business manager. For almost ten years, from the mid-1930s to the late 1940s, the "classic" Stooges team offered an endless stream of movies. Nevertheless, following Curly's stroke in 1946—he died in 1952—Shemp replaced his younger brother until his own death three years later. Although fans may argue over which among the four was the funniest stooge, there is no disagreement that Shemp's replacements, Joe Besser and Curly Joe DeRita, could never fill the shoes of Curly or Shemp. Nevertheless, even after almost two hundred film shorts and decades of television syndication, the Stooges' own anti-Nazi films remained under the radar screen of film historians, Jewish and otherwise.

Only many decades after its production has the Stooges' short film *You Nazty Spy*, also 1940, been acknowledged as having predated the *Great Dictator*. Yet at the time, it seemed to completely escape the attention of Hollywood critics, the Isolationists of Congress, religious rabble-rousers, and corporate boardroom anti-Semites.

Like the Stooges, Chaplin had intended to "make fun of the homicidal insanity of the Nazis." But, where Chaplin was artful the Stooges were blunt. Chaplin had joked that Hitler had actually stolen the mustache from him, but it is "You Nazty Spy" that inaugurates the tradition of Jews play-acting as Nazis and Adolf Hitler himself. Strangely enough, the Stooges introduce themselves in *You Nazty Spy* with the simultaneous declaration "*Shalom Alechiem*!" However, soon they morph into the Nazis themselves, although instead of the twisted crosses of the swastika, their armbands are emblazoned with twisted snakes.

Moe Howard himself plays Hitler in the guise of "Moe Hailstone" dictator of Germany stand-in "Moronica." Along with Larry Fine playing Minister of Propaganda, "Pebble" Curly is Field Marshall "Gallstone," a sort of combination of Mussolini and Goering. Referencing geopolitical events—the Danzig Corridor is referred to as "*Double Crossia*" corridor, xenophobia—"your minorities are overcoming our majorities, until our majorities become the minorities"—and most starkly shows a simple farmer with an unauthorized chicken being sent to a "concentrated camp." Serving educational purposes, the short also defines concepts such as dictatorship, while discussing book burnings. Unlike Chaplin, Jews are not explicitly mentioned but are present via Brooklynese Yiddish. And in the very Jewish fantasy that is *You Nazty Spy*, the dictatorial leaders of Moronica are in the end devoured by lions, a poignant fantasy when so much suffering was yet to come. Even so, Moe Hailstone's death was arguably more reflective of American Jewry's feelings toward the Nazis than Chaplin's speech or Lubitsch's love story. As one cast member, (an actress playing the role of "Mata Herring") later noted, up until *You Nazty Spy* "none of the studios had done that kind of thing at that time." In fact, behind the scenes, it was one of the favorite films of the Stooges and their longtime producer and director, Jules Weiss, aka Jules White.

Also unique to *You Nazty Spy* is that is followed by a sequel—written and produced by the same crew—*I'll Never Heil Again*, probably the only sequel among the almost two hundred movie shorts making up the Stooges repertoire. Although Hailstone, Pebble, and Gallstone had been devoured by lions in *You Nazty Spy*, they returned for *I'll Never Heil Again*, released in the summer of 1941.

In this instance, Fascist Italy, Imperial Japan, and what appears to be Stalinist Russia also take hits from Hailstone, Pebble, and Gallstone. (It is also revealed that Hailstone's mustache is removable and that the dictator refers to it as his "personality.") However, in this case, the three stand-ins for

Hitler, Goebbels, and Goering end up with their heads mounted on the wall next to other animals. This was nothing less than revolutionary given the internal pressures mitigating against anti-Nazi productions in Hollywood. Even before the appearance of *You Nazty Spy*, the Stooges were skewering anti-Semitism in its American and German manifestations.

One of the more notable examples was the 1936 short *Ants in the Pantry*. The Stooges' bellicose German boss, exterminator "A. Mouser," threatens to fire them, demanding that they "drum up business" by deliberating spreading vermin in people's houses: "You give them ants, *und* mice and moths, all through the houses, you *Dumkopfs*!" Crashing a pre-fox hunting party, the Stooges find themselves in a familiar position. As Moses Horowitz, aka Moe Howard, later explained, the "three of us always went into an area of life which we were not supposed to understand . . . we would take a man with a high hat, a monocle and spats, and smash him in the nose with a pie, thus bringing him down to our level." A stunning counterpart to archaic anti-Semitic stereotypes of Jews releasing vermin on gentiles, *Ants in the Pantry* eerily parallels medieval anti-Semitism and the propaganda of the Third Reich. The Stooges later returned to the role of exterminators in "Termites of 1938."

Likewise, *All the World's a Stooge*, released in the spring of 1941, shows once again how the Stooges, as hapless *schlemiels*, are unable of keeping a job. In this instance, they are recruited to act like war "refugees" by the wealthy "Ajax Bullion," whose morally oblivious wife, "Lotta Bullion" demands the acquisition of her own set of refugee waifs. Lotta, unaware of where the war is taking place or which country was producing refugees, is introduced to the Stooges by their singing of a Stooge version of Al Jolson's "Mammy" and tackling their new mother. After setting Lotta on fire with one of Ajax's cigars, the Stooges once again manage to completely ruin their own "coming out party" held by Lotta.

Undoubtedly, these shorts were also a channeling of profound class anger; the allusions to anti-Semitism and the Third Reich are unmistakable. Although the Stooges developed a series of wartime propaganda–type films, aimed at the Japanese, such as the brutal *The Yolk's on Me* and *No Dough, Boys*, (both 1944), most of their explicit World War II efforts were directed against Nazi Germany. In 1943's *Higher Than a Kite*, the Stooges disguised as Nazis greet other German officers with "Hang Hitler" and the film ends as a photograph of Hitler stuck to Curly's backside is bit by a bulldog dressed in U.S. Marine Corps regalia. Ironically, the Stooges accomplished this feat with the apparent acquiescence of their patron—and financial exploiter—Harry Cohn.

Cohn was infamous for a self-loathing of his own Jewishness—in a town full of less than proud Jews—to the point of being accused of being an anti-Semite himself. A hardball businessman, it was also believed that in the early thirties in admiration of Mussolini he had modeled his Hollywood office after that of Il Duce's. And yet, as Gabler argues, Cohn, like other Jewish Hollywood moguls, whose "class, lack of education," not to mention religion, "had all conspired to make a great hurt—the hurt of the outsider," never played the role of the "sha sha Jew," and moreover, surrounded himself with other typical "New York"—read loud, vulgar, and ostentatious—Jews. Even while he might have, as Gabler writes, "exhibited active contempt" towards Judaism, he still managed to produce and distribute some of the most potent and explicit anti-Nazi satires of the era.

Although perhaps the most indiscreet, the Stooges were not the only comedy troupe to confront German anti-Semitism. Noting the decreasing number of Jewish references in the films of the Marx Brothers, Lawrence J. Epstein argues that the Brothers' "retreats" in Jewishness made their work an "incomplete revolution." Some Jewish references appear in 1929's *Coconuts*, but perhaps the best example of the brothers' confrontation of Jewishness, or rather Jewish self-hate, was Chico and Harpo's outing of wealthy socialite "Roscoe W. Chandler" (a character based on the self-hating financer Otto Kahn) as the former peddler "Abie the Fishman" in 1930's *Animal Crackers*. However, in a clandestine fashion, anti-German sentiment also appears in other Marx Brothers films of the 1930s and 1940s.

In these films, the very embodiment of everything wrong with Germans was the actor Sigfried Rumann, who likewise played an idiotic Nazi in *To Be or Not to Be*. Rumann makes his first appearance as the insufferably arrogant and uptight opera manager Herman Gottlieb in *A Night at the Opera*, and by the time of the release of the postwar *A Night in Casablanca* plays his Germanness explicitly as a fugitive Nazi officer Heinrich Stubbel. At least for Harpo, who had traveled through Nazifying Germany in 1933 and who had quietly contributed funds to the Irgun, the Germans were more than simply buffoons. Still, the censors gave far more scrutiny to the uptown Marx Brothers than to their Brooklyn/Philadelphia cohorts the Stooges.

Given the endless stream of Three Stooges movie shorts, and even a few full-length films, from the 1930s to the 1960s, and given their wide distribution to thousands of theaters throughout the United States, this lack of attention from the censors is deserving of attention in the twenty-first century. It was perhaps their low class status that permitted the Stooges to pioneer explicitly anti-Nazi material. The far more common Hollywood tactic in combating anti-Semitism was through combating "ignorance" and promoting ethnic diversity as a virtue, if not conflating it with Patriotism. Thus, by educating Americans about ethnic diversity, Hollywood believed that anti-Semitism could be defeated in a safe and patriotic fashion. Doherty notes the blossoming of an entire World War II film genre of morality plays through the narrative of combat movies. Unlike the anti-Semitic canards about Jewish "goldbricking" their patriotic duty making the rounds of American military bases, Hollywood endeavored to demonstrate that all Americans, regardless of religion or ethnicity, were on the same side in the struggle to preserve liberty.

This was no small change, and Doherty goes as far as to argue that the "nature of the contract between Hollywood and American culture was rewritten between 1941–1945." Anti-Semitism or not, the war transformed American movies from being "mere entertainment," to serious works of art serving particular educational and ideological purposes.

In so many films American combat units were portrayed as being made up of an ethnically diverse group of fighting man, often including Irish, Italians, Jews, northerners as well as southerners, Catholics, Protestants, and Jews. In later decades, the clichéd ethnically diverse groups of fighting men were viewed as a sappy if not excessively nostalgic and romanticized view of the Second World War. However, at the time, the Jews of Hollywood, who worked directly with the U.S. government in making these films, believed that their work was a form of defense against anti-Semitism. Doherty traces this "ecumenism" to the classic film *Guadalcanal Diary* in which an apparently Protestant service, whose participants include the son of a *Hazzen*, is led by a Catholic priest. Many other examples of religious ecumenicism and ethnic pluralism appeared throughout the 1940s. Even John Wayne, perhaps the most "all-American" actor of all time, jumped onto the bandwagon of pluralism. By the time his World War II classic *Sands of Iwo Jima* appeared in 1949 there seemed to be nothing unusual about showing a dying Marine recite the *Sh'ma*, even in one of the "Duke's" films.

In contrast to the subterranean humor of the Stooges, the mainline Hollywood response of affirming pluralism was not threatened by censorship because it was tied into government propaganda activities. Even so, hatred against the Axis and its principles, as Doherty discusses, was to be "properly directed," and the explicitly violent and angry lampooning of the Nazis was sidelined to the low-culture cartoons or comedy shorts. Low culture or not, cartoons and comedy shorts, especially those of the Stooges, were mass-produced, to be found stuffed in between full-length feature films in theaters across the United States. Besides which, as Doherty points out, real war can never be fully portrayed on the screen. Yet, beneath the noses of Hollywood censors and self-conscious studio heads, it was the greatest lowbrow comedy team of the era, the Stooges, who were able to take on the Nazis.

Ironically, perhaps the only time the Stooges faced censorship was in 1948's *Heavenly Daze*. Production stills show Moe playing his namesake Moses, holding the tablets of the Ten Commandments in what appears to be heaven. However, at the request of the PCA, this scene was cut and has since been lost. Likewise, in 1938's *Mutts to You*, one scene featuring the Stooges as Yiddish-speaking Chinese, is one of the few "classic" Stooges films unavailable on VHS or DVD, while *The Yolk's on Me*, while still available to the public has periodically been banned from television on account of its portrayal of the Japanese. However, their anti-Nazi films have never been subject to such restrictions.

Even before America's entry into the war, the films of the Stooges referenced concentration camps, Fascist coups, ethnic strife, starvation, and war. With the Stooges, hatred and anger and acts of violence were not simply "properly" directed at the Nazi, but rather openly directed, as Hitler, Goering, and Goebbles are devoured by beasts and beheaded, their heads posted to a wall like trophies. In addition, perhaps of greatest significance, the Stooges' *oeuvre* reached a far larger audience than Lubitsch or Chaplin could have hoped for. Historian Stephen Whitfield rightly notes that many of Hollywood's Jews were not particularly observant Jews or even committed to Jewish communal concerns. Indeed, those American Jews actively engaged in Jewish communal affairs had never elected the movie moguls to lead American Jewry. Nonetheless, the Hollywood Jews, as "non-Jewish" Jews as they may have been were, perhaps the most visible examples of "Jewishness" and for better or worse, viewed as purveyors of Modernity via new technologies and new morality. To act out against the archenemies of the Jewish people, albeit through comedy, and to do so through mass media reaching every corner of America's heartland, was truly to "make a scene."

FURTHER READING

Carr, Steven Alan. *The Hollywood Question: America and the Belief in Jewish Control Over Motion Pictures Before 1941*. Ph.D. Dissertation. University of Texas, Austin, 1994.

Doherty, Thomas. *Projections of War: Hollywood, American Culture, and World War II*. New York: Columbia University Press, 1993.

Epstein, Lawrence J. *The Haunted Smile: The Story of Jewish Comedians in America*. New York: Public Affairs, 2001.

Erens, Patricia. *The Jew in American Cinema*. Bloomington, IN: Indiana University Press, 1984.

Fleming, Michael. *The Three Stooges: Amalgamated Morons to American Icons*. New York: Doubleday, 1999.

Gabler, Neal. *An Empire of their Own: How the Jews Invented Hollywood*. New York: Doubleday, 1988.

Herman, Felicia. "The Effort to Reform Motion Pictures." *American Jewish Archives*, Vol. LIII, Numbers 1 & 2 (2001).

Hoberman, J. and Jeffrey Shandler. *Entertaining America: Jews, Movies and Broadcasting*. New York: Princeton University Press and the Jewish Museum, 2003.

Maurer, Joan Howard, Greg Lenburg, Jeff Lenburg. *The Three Stooges Scrapbook*. Secaucus, NJ: Citadel Press, 1982.

Chapter 7

Animation
Tom Sito

American animated cartoons are known and loved around the world. The imaginative antics of characters created by Walt Disney, Hanna & Barbera, Pixar, and other artists are more than entertainment; they are lifelong memories for generations. In 1941, when the U.S. State Department asked the leaders of several Latin American countries what they would want to stay out of the coming World War II, among other things they asked for was Donald Duck. In a 2001 *TV Guide* poll, two of the most recognizable faces around the globe were Bugs Bunny and Scooby Doo. In one hundred years, the medium has expanded beyond cartoons to influence live action film and television. The same technique that made Woody Woodpecker jump moved armies of Orcs in *The Lord of the Rings* or demonstrated to a skeptical public how NASA planned to fly a space probe through the rings of Saturn. Animation artists continue to extend mankind's ability to visualize our wildest dreams. Americans of Jewish heritage are a big part of the Toontown *miszpoche*. This chapter will attempt to briefly sketch the achievements of Jews in American mainstream animation, paying particular attention to four studios in which Jews played significant roles: Max Fleischer, Leon Schlesinger, UPA, and DreamWorks SKG.

As with many modern popular entertainments, cartoon animation was created at the dawn of the twentieth century. In 1900, Brooklyn Eagle cartoonist James Stewart Blackton went to New Jersey to interview inventor Thomas Edison at his Menlo Park laboratory. English-born Blackton was a cartoonist who, between newspaper gigs, did a lightning-sketch act on stage. A lightning-sketch act was just that; the artist lectured to the audience while he drew very quickly on a large pad and easel. Blackton's act used the crude racist humor of the period. He would draw a stereotype face formed from the words Coon (black man), Kelly (Irish man) and Cohen (Jewish man). Sometimes he did the routine in a dress and called himself Mademoiselle Stewart.

Drawing of a 1930s-era animation desk. (Illustration by the author.)

As Blackton and Edison discussed his invention of motion pictures, he drew his portrait. Then, Thomas Edison touched on the possibilities of animated trickfilms. Animation toys like zoetropes and flipbooks had been around for years. Perhaps they could photograph flipbook cartoons onto George Eastman's new celluloid roll film and run them just like a live action movie? After consulting photography pioneer Eadweard Muybridge, J. Stuart Blackton drew a series of images in a sequential order to simulate movement. When filmed, they seemed to the eye to spring to life (in Latin "animas," to give life). J. Stewart Blackton created *The Enchanted Drawing* (1900), the first American animated cartoon. It was a very simple trick where the artist in live action would draw a face on a pad on an easel. Then the face magically came to life, laughing and puffing on a cigar.

J. Stewart Blackton went on to create more animated films that ran in Vaudeville shows along with his lightning-sketch act. Soon, other top cartoonists like Winsor McCay, George McManus, and Bud Fisher became interested in the new idea. Artists in France, England, and Russia began making trickfilms. French artist Emile Cohl was the first to call animation a new medium of artistic expression. Cocteau, Dalí, and Picasso expressed interest.

The difference was in most countries the chief exponent of animation was an atelier of artists experimenting with conceptual ideas. While, in America, it was newspaper barons, like William Randolph Hearst and Joseph Pulitzer, who first saw their commercial potential. Animated films could bring their comic pages to life for paying theater audiences. In 1900, for people too poor to attend a show or opera, the mass entertainment was the newspapers. For many new immigrants who were not yet facile in English, the comic strips and the Sunday Funnies provided a relief from the loom and the assembly line. In comics like *The Yellow Kid* and *The Katzenjammer Kids*, big city newspaper comics celebrated the urban ethnic experience. Cartoonists like Rube Goldberg and Milt Gross reflected the Jewish take on getting used to life in this strange new country called America.

At this time most of America was going to theater variety shows collectively known as Vaudeville. For a nickel you saw a procession of jugglers, singers, magicians, and cartoonists lecturing about their popular cartoon creations. Creating an animated version of the comic strip to run in vaudeville theaters would boost interest in the characters and so increase sales of newspapers. So American animated cartoons from their inception were tied to the newspaper, theater, and advertising industries. The earliest recurring series of animated cartoons were of characters already popular comic strips like *Little Nemo, Mutt & Jeff, Bringing Up Father,* and *The Captain and the Kids*.

Many young would-be cartoonists first dreamt of having their own comic strip in a newspaper, but that kind of work, being pretty exclusive, was about as likely as becoming a movie star. So they found refuge in the burgeoning cartoon flicker business. These pioneering artists found you could make a decent living at this, despite the worried glances of their parents: "From *this* you are making a living?"

The increasing demand for animated cartoons in recurring series of six to ten shorts soon made it hard for one artist to draw it all himself. While trying to honor a contract with Pathé for several shorts, cartoonist John Randolph Bray came up with the idea of utilizing the new assembly line technique of Frederick Taylor, then being used with great success by Henry Ford to build automobiles. In 1913, for his *Colonel Heeza Liar* series, Bray set up a regular cartoon factory north of the Bronx in New York. One artist "animated," that is, drew the movement of the character, another painted backgrounds, another inked the characters onto transparent celluloid acetates frames, and another colored them in. Instead of one artist with an assistant grueling away for weeks to create a few brief minutes of animation, regular assembly lines could turn out a short in a few weeks.

More animation companies appeared using Bray's production model. They wanted to move beyond being a fiefdom to newspaper companies. In 1916, William Randolph Hearst paid top dollar to set up a studio of animators called IFS. However, by 1919, he was tired of his movie and cartoon studios and got rid of them. Bud Fisher, the print cartoonist owner of the Mutt & Jeff Studio, who did not animate himself, managed to squander most of his operations profits on his girlfriends and fast lifestyle. Then Otto Messmer, working for the Pat Sullivan Studio, created Felix the Cat, the first animation star not beholden to any newspaper comic strip. Felix was a hit with the public, beloved by everyone from Charles Lindbergh to Groucho Marx. The fledgling little animation studios saw a way to bypass the newspaper conglomerates and offer their shorts directly to theaters nationwide. They could accomplish this by making deals with the rising new independent motion picture production companies like Samuel Goldwyn or the Fox Company. However, to reach them, the animators needed producers and agents to represent their business interests.

It was a small leap from theatrical agent and theater producer to representing theatrical cartoon makers. Like many who caught the entrepreneurial spirit of the age, a number of Jewish business people joined the new medium. The first animation executives like Amadee Van Beuren and Charles Mintz were distributors who needed a steady supply of cartoon flickers to distribute to vaudeville theaters.

Margaret Winkler, the "Great Live Wire Saleslady of Warner Bros.," was a former assistant to movie boss Jack Warner who went out on her own in 1917. She became one of the first producer-agents for cartoon shorts. Margaret brokered the deals whereby Max Fleischer and Pat Sullivan could launch their own independent studios. She enabled twenty-two-year-old Walt Disney to start his studio doing the *Alice in Cartoonland* series. At one time she represented, or as they say "repped," the two most successful cartoon series of the 1920s: Sullivan's *Felix the Cat* and Fleischer's *Out of the Inkwell*. Her brother, George Winkler, was also an animation executive. In 1924, Margaret Winkler married another film producer, Charles Mintz.

Margaret Winkler at age 93. (Courtesy of the John Canemaker Collection.)

Mintz was the distributor whose contractual machinations outmaneuvered Oswald the Lucky Rabbit away from Walt Disney, forcing him to come up with something else: Mickey Mouse. Mintz's studio produced shorts throughout the 1930s. Had Margaret Winkler-Mintz remained active, her example might have helped women gain early importance in the upper levels of animated production. However, as was the custom of the time, she stepped back from her career to be a full-time wife and mother. Animation management in America remained mostly male-dominated until the late 1970s.

As the Roaring Twenties began, members of the animation community began to follow the live action studios in their westward migration to a little California town called Hollywood. In 1923, Walt Disney had moved out from Kansas City and established the first Hollywood animation studio. Mintz and Walter Lantz followed and the growing major movie studios set up their own in-house cartoon studios as part of their short subject departments.

The pioneer animators like Winsor McCay, J. Stewart Blackton, J.R. Bray, and Emile Cohl were not Jewish. However, many Jews did join the crews of the early New York animation studios: Isadore "Izzy" Klein and his brother Phil, Sid Marcus, Arthur Davis, J.F. Leventhal, Manny Gould, and Ben Sharpsteen. Frank Goldman was credited with inventing the three-hole peg system, replacing the two-peg system of Canadian Raoul Barre, to keep animation drawings registered in place. In 1901, while at the Brooklyn Daily Eagle, J.R. Bray made the acquaintance of two brothers, Max and Dave Fleischer. They were the children of prosperous Austrian Jews who

Izzy Klein and his wife Ann Klein on May 22, 1977. (Courtesy of the John Canemaker Collection.)

had immigrated to New York in the 1880s. A few years later Bray gave them jobs in his animation factory.

Max Fleischer was a gentleman with a Charlie Chaplin mustache and a broad smile. His brother Dave, the taller of the two, always dressed well: tailored suits and spats. The Fleischers enjoyed dabbling with inventions. Their family had already achieved some small success by inventing simple gadgets: a hook-and-eye fastener for garments and brass buttons for policemen's uniforms that snapped off for polishing. Charles Fleischer, their oldest brother, created a type of coin-operated, claw-digger machine like the ones still found in arcades today.

The Fleischer brothers first tried jobs as ushers, stage managers, and newspaper errand boys. For a while, Max was an art editor for *Popular Science Monthly*. Now they got jobs working for J.R. Bray, but they still indulged their interest in inventions. In 1915, they patented the Rotoscope. It was a process of tracing a cartoon character over live action. In 1919, Max and Dave, after a stint in the Army during World War I, created a series called *Out of the Inkwell*. It starred a new character called Koko the Clown. Dave pranced about in a clown suit made by his mother, Amalia. Then Max drew over the blown-up live action frames to create realistically fluid human movement. Dave joked that he kept the clown costume around because if their fortunes did not improve he could effect a quick career change. The Rotoscope technique was used widely by a number of studios. In future years, it provided the concept for the digital motion capture used in films like *Titanic* and the *Lord of the Rings* trilogy. J.R. Bray told Max and Dave that if they wanted to strike out on their own with their *Out of the Inkwell* characters they were welcome to do so. With the deal negotiated by Margaret Winkler, the Fleischers left Bray's studio and set up for themselves on Manhattan's 45th Street and Lexington Avenue, later moving to 1600 Broadway at 49th Street.

The *Out of the Inkwell* series (1921–1929) proved to be a hit with audiences. It was soon followed by other successes like naughty little flapper Betty Boop and the bouncing ball sing-a-longs called *Song Car-Tunes*. By 1929, after trying their own distribution arm, Red Seal Pictures, the Fleischers' output was distributed exclusively through Paramount Pictures. When sound became all the rage, the Fleischer's convenient Broadway location enabled them to take advantage of many of the famous musical stars of Broadway and vaudeville. Because they worked the clubs at night, Paramount contract stars like Louis Armstrong, the Mills Brothers, and Cab Calloway could spare a few hours in the afternoon to drop in and record a cartoon voice track. After trying several earlier singers, the voice of Betty Boop was done by Jewish American actress Mae Questel. In the short *Betty Boop's Rise to Fame* (1934) Betty is called on to do an impersonation of popular stage comedienne Fanny Brice. She sings about being an American Indian in Brice's unmistakable Hester Street brogue, "Voops I'm an Indian,

Max and Dave Fleischer. (Illustration by the author.)

Oij! I'm an Indienne. On mein feetz is a moccasin-shoes, on mein hed iz a fedda of a goose, on mein beck iz a liddle papoose!"

While other cartoon studios were still struggling to find an audience, Max Fleischer's output gave the Walt Disney Studio its most serious challenge. In 1932, the Fleischers signed a deal with King Features Syndicate to develop E.C. Segar's *Thimble Theatres* character, Popeye. King Features, in turn, could create a Betty Boop comic strip. Vaudeville entertainer, Red Pepper Sam originated Popeye's unique voice. However, when he asked for too much money, Max replaced him with Jack Mercer. He had heard the assistant animator doing a versatile impression of the spinach-eating sailor. Mercer remained the voice of Popeye until his death in 1977. Mercer was so amazed at his luck being the exclusive voice of Popeye, he was loath to ever ask for a raise. This was noted with sometime annoyance by Mae and Jackson Beck, the voice of Bluto, when they wanted to form a common front when asking for more money. Besides Betty Boop, Mae Questel created the voice of the sailor's love interest, Ms. Olive Oyl. She styled her as an impersonation of Jewish actress, Zasu Pitts. Animator and historian Howard Beckerman joked, "People called Max Fleischer the Jewish Walt Disney. I prefer to think of Walt Disney as the *Goy* Max Fleischer." While not intentional, Max Fleischer's studio used a preponderance of Jewish artists: Izzy Sparber, Jack Ozark, Edith Vernick, Eli Brucker, Dave Tendlar, Bill Deneroff, Lou Zukor, and Myron Waldman. In 1935, he promoted the first woman animator in American cartoons, Lillian Friedman-Astor. They brought a lot of the spirit of the city streets, say *Yiddishkeit*, to their cartoons. The top-grade musical talent combined with the New York urban-centric settings gave Fleischer cartoons an early sophistication that set them apart from the California cartoons' more rustic barnyard settings. While Disney cartoons were about farm and small town life, Popeye and Betty Boop looked like they lived in a rough waterfront ghetto. By 1935, Popeye had surpassed Mickey Mouse, for a time, as the most popular character in America.

In the short *Betty Boop's Ups and Downs* (1932), the Moon is an auctioneer trying to sell off the Earth as the other planets gather around. Mars bids, then Venus bids, and then Saturn enters the scene with his signature rings morphed into an orthodox fur *schmalka* hat straight out of Crown Heights. He wins the Earth for a lower bid than Venus put in:

Saturn: I bid tventy! (*Moon awards him the Earth*) I got 'em, I got 'em, the whole voild! (*mutters*)
Moon: Gimme, Gimme!
Saturn: Oh, the munuh, the munuh, huh?
Moon: Pay Cash!
Saturn: Here, here, you goliph(?) you—
Moon: Thank You!
Saturn: (looking at "For Sale" sign) So vat is vat is here vats? I'll pull gravity out of the oith and see vhat happins!
Cartoon mayhem results with buildings and people flying through the air.
Saturn: (circling the earth) Oiy, Oiy (muttering) I knew I got shtuck! Yeah, yeah.

The Fleischer Studio thrived during the Great Depression, but as the staff grew the growing tides of industrial union organizing was soon knocking at Max Fleischer's door.

After the 1929 stock market crash, a club of politically active artists formed and called itself the Unemployed Artists Association (UAA). When President Franklin D. Roosevelt's NRA regulations were passed, the UAA changed its name to the Artist's Union, with an offshoot called the Commercial Artists and Designers Union (CADU). In late 1934, they, in turn, set up an animation committee called the Animated Motion Picture Workers Union (AMPWU). They targeted the New York animation industry as an area ripe for unionization. They declared, "We must first explore all possibilities of shop organization, find those large numbers of workers such as fashion sketchers, art services, textile designers and animated cartoonists who are the most exploited." Jewish animator Phil Klein was an early member of the Artist's Union.

Max Fleischer was not a bad boss. His artists called him the Last Victorian Gentleman. During the depths of the Depression, he gave his artists cash bonuses and big holiday parties. He said, "My employees could always come to me with their problems." Max preferred ruling his crew like a family, with himself as the loving, yet all-knowing Papa. Nevertheless, New York was a city where the inequities of class privilege clashed head on with progressive and radical politics. The problems of the Great Depression greeted every artist on their way to work: breadlines, children picking through trash for food, radical speakers on every corner, and unemployed workers' riots. These same artists were raised by their immigrant parents to distrust the ruling class and stick to their Yiddish Socialist organizations. Bosses meant the aristocrats, the Czar, and his Cossacks. No one can protect you like your own kind. Mr. Hitler in Berlin and Mr. Mussolini, who hate Jews, also hate unions. Your Uncle Bubbie read the *Daily Worker* or the Yiddish daily *Forward*, often wrapped in the *Wall Street Journal* for protection. Of course, Max Fleischer was not a blueblood Romanov or Fascist but a self-made immigrant himself. He and his brothers worked hard to get where they were. However, to many of his staff, he was still a boss.

By 1937, the Max Fleischer animators were clamoring for their own union. After Max refused the union any recognition and fired selected troublemakers, the Fleischer workers went out on strike in May 1937. What had been a happy family was now the scene of picketlines and fistfights on the street in front of 1600 Broadway. Stink bombs were thrown at Dave Fleischer's home and sit-down strikes disrupted Paramount movie theaters showing Fleischer cartoons. After a brutal couple of weeks, their distributor, Paramount Pictures, compelled Max and Dave Fleischer to sign a contract recognizing the animators' union.

However, Max and Dave had one more trick up their sleeves. Max's sister, Edith, had been scouting out properties in Miami, Florida, a right-to-work state, where Governor Fred Cone boasted, "all the labor organizers here are hanging from trees!" Just a few months after the strike ended, Fleischer relocated their entire operation down to Florida.

Even though the new studio was state-of-the-art and air-conditioned, the Miami of 1938 was not the cosmopolitan metropolis it is today. It was still a sleepy Southern backwater town with mandatory curfews for African Americans. Artists would take their break by strolling across the street from the studio and watch Seminole Indians wrestle alligators for money. Some local stores posted signs that they refused to serve Jews, and a visit by vacationing Cab Calloway got Lou Fleischer an angry note from the local Ku Klux Klan.

With no film community in place, everything had to be shipped in special. All film stock was processed back in New York City. A number of employees, like Mae Questel and Lillian Friedman, refused to relocate. Their places had to be filled only by paying top dollar. All this was ruinously expensive. At the same time Paramount was asking for high quality shorts based on the new popular comic book hero Superman. Max warned Paramount that the budget would be three times the normal rate for a short film. They made ten shorts, then blamed the budget overruns on Max. Finally, when the studios last big effort, a feature film called *Hoppity Goes to Town* (1941) lost money, Paramount pulled the plug. The Fleischer Brothers were out, the Miami studio abandoned, and the studios reorganized back in New York City. Under animators Seymour Knietel and Izzy Sparber, it was renamed Famous Studios. This was for Famous Players-Lasky, the old name of Paramount Studios. Once settled back in New York, production head Sam Buchwald wanted no further trouble and immediately signed a labor contract with the union.

The Fleischers tried several lawsuits but never recouped much. Famous Studios, later, simply Paramount Studios, continued to make theatrical shorts. In addition to the *Popeye* series, they added a series called Harveytoons. The more famous characters of Harveytoons included Casper, Little Audrey, and Baby Huey.

In all the annals of animation, among artists, Leon Schlesinger is considered one of the more popular of animation producers. Stocky, affecting white suits, cigarettes, and a futile comb-over, Leon started the title and graphic firm Pacific Art & Title. He helped the struggling Warner Brothers get the funds to create their hit film *The Jazz Singer* (1928). In return, the Warner Bros. granted Schlesinger exclusive rights to create cartoon shorts to go out attached to their films. Leon called them *Looney Tunes* and *Merrie Melodies* in impersonation of Walt Disney's successful *Silly Symphonies* label. Leon Schlesinger was well known for his frugality. Animator Bill Melendez said no one could fake a heart attack better than Leon when you came to ask for a raise. Leon housed his crew in a funky old building on Van Ness Blvd., which the animators dubbed "Termite Terrace." It was outfitted with old furniture from neighborhood garage sales and had creaking floors. If an artist wanted to discard his empty Coke bottle but did not want to get up from his desk, he simply punched a hole in the wall and dropped the bottle in. Yet despite all this, Leon was beloved.

What made Leon Schlesinger ideal was that, as an executive, he understood the separation needed between the creative and financial ends of animation. He focused on budgets and schedules and otherwise left the artists alone. He also shielded his crew from meddling executives higher up. Studio mogul Jack Warner was reputed to have said to the Bugs Bunny creators: "I don't know what the f**k you cartoon guys do. All I know is we make Mickey Mouse." The animators made up a mock storyboard for a Bugs Bunny cartoon they never intended to produce. They would leave it out whenever Leon had to take some Warner Bros. VIPs on a tour. Leon had rehearsed on it well enough that he could sound very knowledgeable on the animation process. This further helped insulate the artists from the prying eyes of upper echelons. And, most important, while some executives were notorious for their lack of a sense of humor, Leon had a great one. When the artists created Daffy Duck, they had Mel Blanc conceive Daffy's voice as an

Friz Freleng, drawn by Chuck Jones in 1976. (Courtesy of the John Canemaker Collection.)

imitation of Leon's well-known lisp. When they nervously screened the first cartoon, Leon stood up and said, "Gee guysth, that ducksth' voice sthure iths fffunny!" Another time he interjected into a discussion on art direction: "Put more purple in. Purple ith a funny color!"

The Looney Tunes of Leon Schlesinger reflected the ethnic mix of the new American urban dweller. That same heady ethnic soup boiling in the New York tenements that created a Groucho Marx and a George Gershwin was also the origin of a character like Bugs Bunny. Mickey Mouse mirrors the Midwestern farm persona of his creator, Walt Disney. One of the reasons Bugs Bunny never seems to need updating is that he is modern urban man, a child of the streets, with attitude to spare. He reflected perfectly the way America in the Swing Era saw itself. He also reflected the image America had of itself after the Pearl Harbor attack. In every cartoon, Bugs Bunny just wants to be left alone. However, when Elmer or other aggressors disturb his peace, he pays them back in spades. "Of course you know this means war!" was his signal for retribution. Even though of Bugs' four fathers—Friz Freleng, Tex Avery, Bob Clampett, and Chuck Jones—only Friz was Jewish; the story artists Warren Foster, Ted Pierce and Michael Maltese were New Yorkers. There is consensus on the origins of the grey rabbit. Film critics called Bugs Bunny the first *schnorrer* in cartoons.

Many of the artists responsible for the Looney Tunes manic energy were Jews. Isadore 'Friz' Freleng was from Kansas City; he came out to Hollywood when Walt Disney set up his studio but he accepted a better offer to move to Charles Mintz Studio in 1930. When Mintz's operation restructured, Freleng led his crew over to Leon Schlesinger's camp to be the early backbone of his operation, frequently acting as the unofficial representative for the artists on the staff.

With his first directorial efforts, with no cartoon stars yet, Friz Freleng experimented with some Jewish *shtick*. In Freleng's early short, *Shuffle Off to Buffalo* (1933) Old Father Time runs a warehouse providing babies for the stork to bring. Each ethnic group (Italians, Eskimos, etc.) sends in a shipping order to be filled. When he gets a note printed in Hebrew, on cue, the orchestra starts wailing the song "*Mazeltov*." Father Time produces a cute, curly black-haired moppet. "Wo bisd du?" he says to the child, then inkstamps his tuckus with the Kosher-Pareve symbol and sends him on his way.

Mel Blanc was a radio performer and vaudevillian whose first impersonations were Yiddish accents he heard over the radio while growing up in Portland, Oregon. He became a mainstay at Warner Bros., at times doing all the voices of a cartoon, even the characters impersonating other characters, like Bugs Bunny doing Jerry Colonna and so on.

The Schlesinger Looney Tunes crew excelled at lampooning modern issues and shamelessly imitated modern stars, including many Jewish stars like Eddie Cantor, Jack Benny, Benny Goodman, and Edward G. Robinson. Jewish artist Ben Shenckman designed the distinctive caricatures of these celebrities. It is a tribute to the Looney Tunes quality that even though their humor was very topical to the swing era, the cartoons never seem to date. They are just as popular now as in when they were created. Other Jewish artists at Warner's included Sid Marcus, Lee Guttman, Florence Finklehore, Bernie Gruber, and Ray Katz. Martha Goldman-Sigall was a painter and inker there from 1936 to 1943. Long after, during her retirement she and her husband Sol became dosons of the Warner Bros. Museum. Martha's prodigious memory makes her a rare resource to writers and historians of the Golden Age of Hollywood. She wrote her memoirs *Living Life Between the Lines* in 2004.

After Leon Schlesinger sold his Looney Tunes/Merry Melodies Company to Warner Bros. outright and retired in 1944, Eddie Selzer was sent to manage the cartoonists. Eddie had been a low-level Warner's *apparatchik* who arranged publicity reviews with long-legged showgirls. Gone was Leon's broad smile. Eddie uttered an infamous but immortal comment when he interrupted a raucous artist's gag session: "I don't understand what all this laughter has to do with making cartoons." Mel Blanc recalled that within a few months most of the animators were begging Leon to come back out of retirement.

Chuck Jones sparred frequently with Eddie when trying to make creative decisions. In 1947, when Chuck wanted to introduce a new character named Pepé Le Pew, Eddie snapped, "Absolutely not! No skunks!" Chuck said later, "If Eddie said no, we knew we just had to do it!" When Eddie saw the final film, *For Scentimental Reasons*, he walked out of the screening room muttering, "No one is going to laugh at that shit!" The short not only was a hit and made Pepé Le Pew a major Warner's star, it won an Oscar as well. As producer, Eddie was the only one to go up on stage and collect the Oscar, which he then took home.

MGM used a number of Jewish artists, including Irv Spence, Harry and Ed Love, Ray Abrams, Lew Irwin, and Ruth Miller. When Jerry the mouse danced a rousing number with Gene Kelly in the film *Anchors Aweigh* (1944), Ken Muses's animation was ably assisted by Jewish artist, Barney Posner. In 1937, great cartoonist Milt Gross came to Culver City to direct. He did two shorts for MGM using his characters Count Screwloose and J.R. the Wonderdog. They used his wild, anarchic sense of humor that could make even Charlie Chaplin giggle. However, he clashed with the MGM producers. His services were discontinued because it was felt the short's raucous humor was too *déclassé* for the rarified heights of MGM.

Of course, no discussion of animation would be complete without Walt Disney. Starting in 1923, Walt Disney built his little Kansas City cartoon company into one of the largest entertainment corporations in the world. His influence is enormous: sound cartoons, Technicolor, feature films, television, and theme parks. The very concept of entertainment "synergy." However, for our current needs, we must restrict ourselves to the topic at hand.

Walt Disney Studios employed many Jews: Oscar Fischinger, an avant-garde artist who fled Hitler and created the distinctive look of the Bach *Toccata and Fugue* sequence for *Fantasia*. Maurice Rapf, a Jewish socialist writer, wrote an early draft of the controversial film *Song of the South*. The great composers, Richard and Robert Sherman, who created the music for *Mary Poppins* and *Jungle Book*. Art Babbitt, born in Omaha of mixed Russian Jewish parents (the original family name was Babbittski), went on to create the character Goofy, the Wicked Queen in *Snow White*, and Geppetto in *Pinocchio*. In the 1950s, even when conservative current ran high in America, when choosing a director for his big budget live action production *Twenty Thousand Leagues under the Sea* (1954), Walt Disney hired Richard Fleischer, the son of his old competitor, Max Fleischer.

Character designer and writer Joe Grant was originally on track to be a syndicated newspaper caricaturist when he caught Walt's attention. Joe Grant's original family name was Gomelinski. When his grandfather moved them from Russia in the 1880s, he declared, "No more Russian names; we now need American names. Who is the most famous American alive? General Grant!" So Grant it became. With his friend, Bronx-born Dick Heumer, Joe cocreated such classics as *Dumbo*, *Fantasia*, and *Lady and the Tramp*. Other Jews included Ferdinand Horvath and Jules Engel, Hungarian immigrant designers. Also, David Hilberman, Zack Schwartz, Margaret Selby, and Bernie Wolf. Marty Sklar oversaw the construction and running of Disneyland for over fifty years.

A charge that emerged in film circles was that Walt Disney himself was anti-Semitic. Richard Schickel first leveled the accusation in his 1967 book

The Disney Version. The charge was elaborated on by Marc Eliot in his 1995 biography *Walt Disney: Hollywood's Dark Prince*.

Some cite the infamous scene cut from the 1933 Oscar-winning short *The Three Little Pigs*. In it, the Big Bad Wolf tries to gain entrance to the Pigs' house by disguising himself in what looks like an Orthodox Jewish peddler's black outfit, cooing, "I'm givink free semples . . ." Others mention the villain in *Pinocchio*, Stromboli, as being an ethnic slur on Jews. However, the character may have been more an impersonation of the exaggerated gesticulation of the then-dictator of Italy, Benito Mussolini. The animator of that scene, Bill Tytla, was a close personal friend of Art Babbitt, which also makes such a charge unlikely. Eliot's book claimed that Disney attended Nazi American Bund meetings. This last charge has been discredited by Art Babbitt, who had become Walt's enemy. The feisty Babbitt himself snuck into Bund meetings to report their activities to the FBI.

Marc Davis was one of Disney's crew of animators known as the Nine Old Men. Marc was raised by a Jewish father and Scottish mother. He created such memorable characters as Cruella De Vil and Maleficent. He also designed the Disneyland ride Pirates of the Caribbean. Marc maintained, passionately, his entire life, that Walt Disney was never prejudiced. This view was shared by Joe Grant, who wielded great influence in the studio, until he formed his own graphics company in 1949. "Walt, Anti-Semitic? Hogwash! What am I?" Joe would often say. Maurice Rapf noted how Disney donated to Jewish war orphanages after the Holocaust. Walt hired Rapf knowing he was a well-known Jewish radical socialist who was eventually blacklisted. The Sherman Brothers and director Ben Sharpsteen are equally passionate in Walt's defense.

By 1941, most of the Hollywood backlot studio workers had unionized and gone to a forty-hour week down from forty-six. The live-action movie directors, writers, and actors had accomplished much to win recognition of their guilds. Now the animators of Hollywood wanted the same. After some wrangling, by May all the Hollywood "toon" factories were under a Screen Cartoonist Guild contract, except the Walt Disney Studio. The Disney animators now desired their own union and, like Max Fleischer before him, Walt Disney saw unions as just a bunch of Communist troublemakers. Walt Disney's chief attorney, Gunther Lessing, was an old Texan who viewed unions as an East Coast, un-American thing.

From May to October, the Walt Disney Studio was wracked with a bitter labor strike by the animators, film editors, and screen publicists. After bitter weeks of pickets and nationwide boycotts by the American Federation of Labor, the strike was settled by federal mediation. Nevertheless, many hard feelings remained and Walt Disney remained personally hurt. He maintained a lifelong grudge against many of its leaders. A number, but not all, of the Disney strike leaders, like Art Babbitt, Margaret Selby, Dave Hilberman, Bill Hurtz, and Zack Schwartz just happened to be Jewish. Years later, some

Animation

The Disney Strike of 1941. (Illustration by the author.)

of them felt that any anti-Semitism Walt might have had toward them was aggravated by the strike. But other Jews, like Joe Grant, Marc Davis, and Ben Sharpsteen sided with Walt and stayed at their desks.

So was Walt anti-Semitic or not? Walt Disney was a man of his time, raised with the same early-twentieth-century values of America as Henry Ford. Like many people of his time, he sometimes resorted to ethnicity to quickly label people. Walt's contemporaries, Jewish Hollywood moguls like L.B. Mayer and David O. Selznick, were constantly referring to each other in derogatory terms as kikes and *yids*. Being a minor player and one of the few gentiles in this crowd, meant, at times, you had to talk the talk. To modern eyes, focused through political correctness, we look on these crude ethnic labels as degrading. However, to many at the time, an ethnic label was a badge of honor.

Walt Disney grew into a leading Hollywood conservative, while many Jewish American animators were politically progressive, supporting Franklin Roosevelt and his New Deal policies. He was a founder of the Society for the Preservation of American Ideals, an entertainment industry lobby also backed by Louis B. Mayer of MGM. When the House Committee on Un-American Activities began investigating Communist subversion in the entertainment industry in 1947, Mayer and Walt Disney were among the first friendly witnesses to testify. The HUAC investigations and studio blacklist damaged the careers of many notable animators like Dave Hilberman, Bernyce Prolifka, Eugene Fleury, Phil Eastman, and Zack Schwartz.

United Productions of America (UPA) was a studio formed in 1944 by renegade Disney and Warner Bros. union activists who wanted to explore new artistic styles. Animation artists like Zack Schwartz, Jules Engel, Dave Hilberman, Bill Hurtz, Abe Levitow, Ade Woolery, Alan Zashlove, Bob Dranko, and Gentiles Steve Bousutow and John Hubley soon joined the Industrial Film & Poster Service, started by Jewish artist Herb Klynn. They first considered naming their studio Union Productions because their first big client was the United Auto Workers. The UAW commissioned a short to promote the reelection of President Franklin Roosevelt in 1944. Called *Hell Bent for Election*, it announced to the world the distinct UPA style. Distributing their films through Columbia, UPA created some brilliant cartoons: *A Unicorn in the Garden* (1953), *Rooty-Toot-Toot* (1952), *The Telltale Heart* (1953), *Gerald McBoing-Boing* (1951), *Madeleine* (1952), and many more. Animators, tired of endless, cutesy cat-chases-the-rat cartoons, flocked to UPA. Animators there talked about Søren Kierkegaard, the Bauhaus, new trends in art like the work of Piet Mondrian and Jackson Pollock. The revolutionary styles and subject matter of UPA broke new ground and influenced animation studios around the world, most notably in Eastern Europe. Their ideas also extended out to advertising and into the new format of television production. Arguably, no other studio since Walt Disney exerted such a great influence. Director Gene Deitch wrote: "UPA was born at a time before cynicism set in to our culture. We all really *believed*." Small wonder Warner Bros. director Friz Freleng joked, "When I die, I don't want to go to Heaven, I want to go to UPA."

The Hollywood Blacklist invaded UPA's happy home. Columbia Studios held a controlling interest in UPA and was its exclusive distributor. They sent producer Steve Bosustow a list of artists to be fired for being politically suspect. These included many of the former Disney activists like Hilberman, Hurtz, and Hubley.

As the 1950s wound into the 1960s, the situation in the animation world mirrored events affecting the live-action film community: the decline and break-up of the large Hollywood Studio system and the rise of television. As major studios like Warner Bros., Paramount, and MGM shut down their animation units, new studios like Jay Ward, Hanna & Barbera, and Depatie-Freleng rose to take their place. Independent productions flourished the way they could not have during the monopoly of the old Hollywood movie moguls.

As box office for theatrical cartoons slumped and the cartoon short all but disappeared, the rising new field of advertising offered new opportunities for artists. When animators now spoke of innovations, instead of *Fantasia* or Droopy, they spoke of Markey Maypo or the Murial Cigar ads on TV. New artists of Jewish heritage here included Eddie Rehberg, Lee Mishkin, Howard Beckerman, Howard Basis, Phil Kimmelman, and Hal Silverman; as well as Terrytoons' producer Bill Weiss. Lou Hertz created a major advertising firm in Atlanta. Gene Deitch was responsible for the Terrytoons Renaissance, introduced new styles into the studios, like that of designer Jules Feiffer. He created popular shows like *Sick Sidney*; Sidney was a neurotic elephant with a style of humor popular with the 1950s–1960s mania for analysis, used by Jewish comics like Mort Sahl and Woody Allen. Later, Deitch moved to Prague, where he created the little *meeshkayt,* Nudnik. Hal Seeger developed shows like *Milton the Monster* and *Batfink*; Ernie Pintoff won Oscars for his shorts *The Critic* (1963) and the *Violinist* (1959) using the voice talents of Mel Brooks and Carl Reiner. Pintoff created another neurotic character named Flebus (1959). Abe Levitow directed the first animated TV special, *Magoo's Christmas Carol* in 1961. This program utilized the music of Broadway composer Jule Styne, another Jewish American. UPA veteran, Leo Salkin, directed Brooks and Reiner again in the TV special *The 2000 Year Old Man* (1975). Speaking of voice talents, television enabled a number of talented Jewish actors to also create characters for animation. Alan Reed (born Ted Bergman) created the voice of Fred Flintstone; Wally Cox was the voice of Underdog and Paul Frees (Solomon Hersch Frees) was the voice of Boris Badenov on *Rocky & Bullwinkle*.

In the late 1960s, animator Lou Scheimer started a company with Norm Prescott and Hal Sutherland called Filmation. They started with the Larry Harman franchise for Bozo the Clown and expanded to become one of the bigger producers in animation. In 1983, they scored a major hit with *He-Man and the Masters of the Universe.* Many Jewish artists lent their talents to this effort, including Ed Friedman, Lou Kachivas, Sheldon Bornstein, David Teague, Gary Goldstein, and old Max Fleischer veterans, Lou Zukor and Jack Ozark. In 1973, writer/director Bob Kurtz set up his studio Kurtz & Friends, which became an award-winning commercial producer for the next thirty years. More women entered the ranks of animator in the 1970s. In the footsteps of Selby Kelly and Lillian Friedman came Nancy Beiman and Lorna Cook.

Ralph Bakshi was a child of the New York slums like the tenement dwellers of an earlier era. He was of mixed Jewish and Italian ancestry. Beginning at CBS's Terrytoons, he set up his own production with producer Steve Krantz to bring the popular underground comic *Fritz the Cat* to the big screen. It was the first X-rated cartoon. *Fritz the Cat* (1972) was a hit, followed up by films like *Heavy Traffic* (1973), *Coonskin* (1974), and *The Lord of the Rings* (1977).

Meanwhile, animation branched out to effect live-action filmmaking. In the 1950s, former Disney/UPA animator Les Novros set up a company called Graphic Films to explore the possibilities of animated movie effects.

Howard and Iris Beckerman in their studio, 1972. (Courtesy of Howard Beckerman.)

He directed the film *Universe* (1964), which melded animation tricks into NASA space images so successfully that viewers could not believe they were not seeing genuine close-ups of distant stars and galaxies. Jewish-born Novros also was a creative force in the films *2001: A Space Odyssey* (1968) and *COSMOS* (1974). His early experimentation with computer imaging helped set the stage for the revolution in digital filmmaking in the 1990s. Cosmos was a watershed in the development of the virtual environment. Host Carl Sagan strolled through a computer-generated mock-up of the Great Library of Alexandria, destroyed two thousand years ago.

The labor-activist tradition of Jewish artists lived on in the person of Morris "Moe" Gollub. Moe, an artist at Disney and Hanna-Barbera, was also an illustrator of paperback book covers like Louis L'Amour westerns and adventures stories like *Turok: Son of Stone*. Moe was one of the first Disney animators to sign with the cartoonists' union back in 1941. As president of the Motion Picture Screen Cartoonists Local 839 Hollywood, he led the animation community in two major industry-wide strikes. These were to try to create a runaway clause in studio contracts. This would halt losing local jobs to the overseas market, which provided cheap foreign labor. The strikes met with mixed success and could not stem the tide toward globalization.

Famed live-action movie director Steven Spielberg is also a longtime producer of animated films. Ever since he first put a cameo of Daffy Duck's *Duck Dodgers* on a television behind Richard Dreyfuss in his film *Close Encounters of the Third Kind* (1978), he has supported animated projects. He was a producer of the 1988 Oscar-winning hit *Who Framed Roger Rabbit*. In 1986, he teamed with animator Don Bluth and *Star Wars* producer David Kirshner to do the films *An American Tail* (1986) and *The Land Before Time* (1989). He later started an international animation team in London named Amblimation that created the films *American Tail: Fievel Goes West* (1991) and *We're Back! A Dinosaur's Story* (1993). Meanwhile, for the small screen, Spielberg created the Warner Bros. hit TV shows *Tiny Toon Adventures* (1990) and *Animaniacs* (1993). He also coproduced the TV series *Amazing Stories* which, in 1993, did an all-animated episode called *Family Dog*, directed by Brad Bird (*The Incredibles* and *The Iron Giant*). David Kirshner, who coproduced with Spielberg, went on to produce more animated feature films like *The Pagemaster* (1994), *Cats Don't Dance* (1997), and *Curious George* (2006).

Jeffrey Katzenberg was an executive brought over with Michael Eisner from Paramount when Roy Disney and Frank Wells took over the Walt Disney Studio in 1984. Under the regime of Eisner and Katzenberg, Disney Animation had a new golden age of animation success: *The Little Mermaid* (1989), *Beauty and the Beast* (1991), *Aladdin* (1992), *The Lion King* (1994), and *Tarzan* (1999). In television, Disney produced hit shows like *Gummi Bears, Goof Troop*, and *Kim Possible*. They created the market for direct-to-video films like *A Goofy Movie* (1995) and *The Return of Jafar* (1994). They brought into animation production new blood from the Broadway stage, many of whom were of Jewish ancestry: Peter Schneider, Tom Schumacher, Gary Krisel, Jim Pentecost, Charlie Fink, composers Steven Schwartz (*Godspell, Wicked*), the team of Howard Ashman and Alan Menken (*Little Mermaid, Beauty and the Beast*).

Some old-timers grumbled at the overhaul, but the success spoke for itself. Whereas in 1961, 56 percent of the total income of the Walt Disney Company was from theme park revenue and real estate, in 1991, 51 percent of total revenue was generated by animation and supporting products. In 1984, Walt Disney was sixteenth in total box office, and by 1988 they were number one. The animated film *The Lion King* (1994) alone, brought in billions in profit and was spun into a successful Broadway musical.

A second generation of Jewish artists was brought up by the Golden Age animators to contribute to this Disney Renaissance. In the 1970s, Art Babbitt lectured at the Richard Williams Studio in London. One listener was a gifted young man from Cherry Hill, New Jersey, named Eric Goldberg. Eric went on to work with New York–based animator Tissa David on the Joe Raposo musical *Raggedy Ann & Andy* (1977). He then owned his own West End animation studio. In 1990, at the behest of Charlie Fink (who had also brought Joe Grant back out of retirement) Goldberg came to Walt Disney, where he created the distinct look and performance of Robin Williams Genie in the film *Aladdin* (1992). Eric Goldberg then codirected the musical *Pocahontas* (1995) and directed the Al Hirschfeld–inspired sequence for *Fantasia 2000*. Later, at Warner Bros., Goldberg directed the animation of Bugs and Daffy for the Joe Dante film *Looney Tunes: Back in Action* (2003). In this, he was joined by animator Bert Klein, who went on to direct the animated titles for the film *Fat Albert* (2004). Steve Goldberg (no relation to Eric), a digital artist who pioneered the technique of morphing movement with his 1990 film *Locomotion*, became a mainstay of the Disney feature computer animation department. Steve Segal, another CGI (computer generated imaging) pioneer, made independent films and worked at George Lucas' Industrial Light and Magic. His animation contributed to the Pixar classics *Toy Story* (1995) and *A Bug's Life* (1998). Doug Frankel came from New Jersey to contribute his skills to Disney's *The Lion King* (1994) and *The Emperor's New Groove* (2000), as well as *Fern Gully: the Last Rainforest* (1992). Then he went on to Pixar to animate on *The Incredibles*. On the film *The Iron Giant*, Jewish American art director Alan Bodner created the critically acclaimed look. At the same time, Arna Selznick was the first woman to direct an animated feature since German Lotte Reiniger of the silent era. She did *The Care Bears Movie* (1985), followed by Yvette Kaplan in Mike Judge's *Beavis & Butt-Head Do America* (1996). Yvette was also the head story artist on the 20th Century Fox hit *Ice Age* (2002) and the director of Disney's *Arthur*.

Alex Kupershmidt emigrated from Russia to become an animator at the Disney Florida Studio. His talents contributed to the films *Mulan* (1998), *Lilo and Stitch* (2002), and *Chicken Little* (2005). By now, animation had enough history to spawn an industry of historians and analysts writing critically of the medium. The People of the Word are well represented in these ranks: Leonard Maltin, Charles Solomon, Jerry Beck, Maureen Furniss, Karl Cohen, Howard Beckerman, and Dr. Harvey Deneroff.

In television, Fred Seibert produced a short films program for Ted Turner that gave birth to the hit TV series *Dexter's Lab, Johnny Bravo*, and *Powerpuff Girls*. On a smaller scale, Caroline Leaf created *The Street*, an independent film based on a short story by Jewish Canadian author Mordecai Richer. The Fox Network started a revolution in TV animation with

The Simpsons. In 1987, producer James L. Brooks hired *LA Weekly* underground cartoonist Matt Groening to develop animated interstitials for Fox's *The Tracey Ullman Show*. At first, Fox wanted Groening to use his trademark Binky Rabbit from his regular *Life in Hell* comic strip, but Groening was reluctant to lose control of his bread-and-butter character. Instead, he developed a dysfunctional family sitcom he called *The Simpsons*. Rather than use typically low-paid TV animation writers, Brooks went into the world of big-time sitcoms and assembled a team of top writers. Groening relied on a team of brash young directors: David Silverman, Wes Archer, and Jim Reardon, anchored by Disney Brad Bird. *The Simpsons* became one of the most successful shows in TV history, earning multiple Emmy awards. The adventures of Bart and his hapless dad Homer are as popular in 2005 as when the show debuted in 1988.

In 1994, personal and creative differences caused the Michael Eisner—Jeffrey Katzenberg team to split. Jeffrey Katzenberg took his leave from Disney. He teamed with longtime friends Steven Spielberg and music producer David Geffen to form DreamWorks SKG. Among their announced plans for film and television production was animation. They combined Spielberg's old Amblimation crew brought over from London with expatriates from Disney.

Lorna Cook had been one of the first to help Katzenberg and Spielberg set up DreamWorks. She had been one of the first women to break into the mostly male world of Disney animators in the early 1970s. She worked on films like *The Lion King, Mulan*, Don Bluth's *The Secret of Nimh*, and *The Land Before Time*. At DreamWorks she codirected an animated feature, *Spirit: Stallion of the Cimarron* (2003). Long-time colleagues of Jeffrey Katzenberg, Sandra Rabins and Penny Finkleman-Cox, also produced *The Prince of Egypt*. They both later moved on to start the feature animation department of Sony Animation. They were joined by Sony Imageworks head Barry Weiss. Under Weiss' aegis, Sony excelled at groundbreaking digital animation on live action hit films like *Stuart Little* (1999) and *Spider-Man* (2002). Sony Imageworks also did the animation for the Robert Zemeckis' Christmas feature *The Polar Express* (2004), based on the book by Chris Van Allsburg, a convert to Judaism.

DreamWorks' first big release was *The Prince of Egypt*, nicknamed in the industry as *The Zion King*. Knowing *The Prince of Egypt* would be dealing with, at times, controversial interpretations of the Bible, DreamWorks went out of its way to do its research. The artists attended lectures by Steven Spielberg's favorite rabbi. Effects animator Esther Barr teased, "If I'm going back to Yeshiva classes, I hope I get a set of Cross Pens when the film is done!" All kidding aside, despite reaching out to major religious leaders, they encountered initial resistance to the film. One Georgia televangelist referred to *The Prince of Egypt* as "their" version (meaning the Jew's version) of the Moses story, and emphasized the "berg" part of the names Spielberg and Katzenberg. (Spielberg was also executive producer of *Who Framed Roger*

Rabbit and *The Land Before Time*.) The film was screened at the Vatican before the Sacred College of Cardinals. The first reports were that "they were amazed." DreamWorks recruiting director Debbie Goldstein joked: "Are they amazed that they liked it, or amazed that they never saw so many Jews in one movie?" After *The Prince of Egypt* (1998) DreamWorks moved on to create the films *The Road to El Dorado* (2000) *Antz* (1998) *Sinbad: Legend of the Seven Seas* (2003), and *Madagascar* (2005). They also bought the rights to a small children's book by illustrator William Steig titled *Shrek*. DreamWorks made *Shrek* (2001) into a major franchise spawning sequels and merchandising amounting to billions of dollars.

At the same time, Jewish American comedian Adam Sandler produced an animated film entitled *Eight Crazy Nights* (2002). Based on Sandler's popular "The Hanukkah Song," the story was of a cynical young man, who learns the true meaning of Hanukkah from an old *alter kocker* in a lonely shopping mall. Comedian Jerry Seinfeld is writing and directing an animated feature at DreamWorks, about bees called *Bee Movie*, due to come out in fall 2007.

As animation passed its hundred-year anniversary, traditional hand-drawn and painted cartoons had yielded to digital technology. Pixels replaced pencils. New studios like Pixar, Blue Sky, and Cartoon Network became the hitmakers. In all these studios as well as in television and interactive media, artists of Jewish ancestry continue to contribute their unique sensibilities to the mix. Animation's global reach now means that by 2006 several companies plan to start animation feature production in Israel itself.

Meanwhile Joe Grant, who had begun with Walt Disney in 1933 on the *Three Little Pigs*, continued at the studio. His refined storytelling skills contributed to such contemporary hit films as *The Lion King* and *Aladdin*. Joe was the only artist to have worked on both *Fantasia*'s, the one in 1940 and the one in 2000. Grant became an important factor at Pixar studio, training artists, and lending ideas to their hit films *Toy Story, A Bug's Life, Finding Nemo*, and *The Incredibles*. He renamed *The Scary Monsters Project—Monsters Inc.* and it became one of Pixar's biggest hits. Beloved and respected by the entire animation *miszpoche*, in 2005, just shy of his 97th birthday, Joe Grant died. He was at his table, drawing.

ACKNOWLEDGMENT

Special thanks to Roberta Street, Martha Sigall, Eric Goldberg, and Mark Mayerson and Jerry Beck.

FURTHER READING

Adamson, Joe. *The Walter Lantz Story*. New York: Putnam, 1985.
Barrier, Michael. *Hollywood Cartoons*. New York: Oxford University Press, 1999.

Beckerman, Howard. *Animation. The Whole Story*. New York: Amereon House, 2001.
Carbaga, Leslie. *The Fleischer Story*. New York: De Capo Press, 1988.
Cohen, Karl. *Forbidden Animation*. Jefferson, NC: McFarland, 1997.
Crafton, Donald. *Before Mickey, American Animation. 1898–1928*. Cambridge, MA: MIT Press, 1987.
Fleischer, Richard. *Out of the Inkwell*. Lexington, KY: University Press of Kentucky, 2005.
Lawson, Tim and Alissa Persons. *The Magic Behind the Voices*. Jackson, MS: University of Mississippi Press, 2005.
Maltin Leonard. *Of Mice and Magic*. New York: McGraw Hill, 1980.
Schickel, Richard. *The Disney Version*. New York: Avon Books, 1967.
Scott, Keith. *The Moose That Roared*. New York: St. Martin's Press, 2000.
Solomon, Charles. *Enchanted Drawings, The History of Animation*. New York: Knopf, 1989.
Thomas, Bob. *Building a Company*. New York: Hyperion, 1998.

Chapter 8

The Jewish Film Festival
Deborah Kaufman and Janis Plotkin

By the 1970s and the 1980s an entire generation of post–World War II Jewish Americans had grown up in an atmosphere characterized by increased assimilation into mainstream American culture. This generation held connections to the immigrant experience through their grandparents and parents, but was firmly planted in the new world. With the decline of American anti-Semitism after World War II, and the establishment of the state of Israel, this generation felt a decidedly new sense of entitlement. Jewish identity continued to be based on various forms of ever-attenuated religious observance, but secular modes of Jewish identity were becoming more pronounced, most particularly, Jewish efforts in education and in activities focusing on the Holocaust and on Israel. Influenced in part by the counterculture, supported by an expanding economy and upward mobility, and with this new sense of entitlement as American Jews, many in this post-1960s generation began experimenting with alternative modes of secular Jewish expression outside of the mainstream Jewish establishment. Although the establishment was predominantly characterized by Jewish Federation bureaucracies, fundraising drives for Israel, and social service delivery, the younger upstarts were forging a different path. New literary and political publications, experimental theaters, and *klezmer* and avant-garde music groups were sprouting across the country. Young Jewish filmmakers outside of Hollywood were using the medium of film to begin to express themselves about contemporary Jewish identity.

Much of the cultural product of this era reflected a degree of alienation from the Jewish establishment and ambivalence about American society in general. However, there was also a positive expression of something entirely new and somewhat inchoate. The new generation of independent filmmakers were decidedly outside of the Hollywood system with its stereotypes, sentimentality, and saccharine endings, and their work reflected the sense of an alternative Jewish reality based on lived experience, but often without references to religion, the Holocaust, or Israel—the standard iconography of mainstream Jewish life. There was no *Fiddler on the Roof* or *Exodus* in this new world of Jewish film. These young artists were reflecting on their lives, challenging norms, creating new tropes, and about to have a major impact on Jewish identity in the United States.

In this context, the first Jewish Film Festival was conceived and founded in 1980 by Deborah Kaufman, a recent law school graduate and political activist who had sought and found sponsorship for what she thought was going to be a one time event from Seymour Fromer, the visionary and iconoclastic founder of the Judah Magnes Museum in Berkeley, California. The intention was to use independent Jewish cinema to spark a new and open discussion of politics and culture inside the Jewish community, and to challenge Hollywood stereotypes of Jews in the public at large. Three institutions—the Judah Magnes Museum, the American Film Institute in Washington, D.C., and the UCLA Film Archives—supported the first Jewish Film Festival, which consisted of independently produced documentary and fiction films from around the world and played in Los Angeles at the UCLA Film Archives, in San Francisco at the Roxie Cinema, and in New York at the 92nd Street YMHA in 1981.

The Festival was an immediate hit, movies for a new generation bred on mass media but sick of Hollywood, alternative points of view for those who did not affiliate with the increasingly conservative and bourgeois Jewish establishment, and a safe entryway into Jewish culture for anyone else who would pay the price of admission. The Festival was a critical success and thoroughly sold-out in its first year. National tours and international presentations were to follow. Kaufman brought in Janis Plotkin, a community organizer with a track record of work in the Jewish community, to expand the Festival, which became an independent nonprofit outside of the sponsorship of the Magnes Museum.

The programming emphasized alternatives to mainstream Jewish religious observance, to the increasingly commercialized and sanctimonious Holocaust memorialization, which foregrounded Jewish "victim" status, and to the established Jewish community's uncritical support for Israel. History, secular culture, and hybrid identities were given central focus with films like Marlene Booth's *The Forward*, Alan Berliner's *Intimate Stranger*, and Josh Waletzky's *Image Before My Eyes*, which, in particular, mirrored the identity of the new Jewish Film Festival more than anything else. Here was a portrait of Jews in pre-Holocaust Poland—another time and place, but thoroughly recognizable—a world of incredible diversity, revolutionary impulse, and internal conflict—Socialists, Zionists, Bundists, the secular and the Orthodox, the affluent and the indigent, a rich but turbulent cauldron of culture reacting to the challenges of modernity, quintessential outsiders on the edge of history.

Janis Plotkin, filmmaker Rex Bloomstein, and Deborah Kaufman, 1984. (Courtesy of the San Francisco Jewish Film Festival.)

The Festival pioneered midnight screenings of silent classics like *The Golem* accompanied by a specially produced avant-garde musical soundtrack. It produced groundbreaking panel discussions on stereotypes of women and images of Palestinians in Jewish films, and hosted edgy parties in warehouses and art studios that brought together filmmakers, students, academics, artists, political activists, the gay and lesbian community, and the non-Jewish film-goers who together were the core support for the Festival from the beginning.

During the early years, from the early 1980s into the early 1990s, the Bay Area based Jewish Film Festival produced thirty-eight Festivals and presented two hundred and fifty new, independent films to audiences in eighteen American cities. Its annual summer showcase event in San Francisco and Berkeley drew tens of thousands of people. The nonprofit American Film

Sold-out audience at the 1,400-seat Castro Theatre in San Francisco. (Courtesy of the San Francisco Jewish Film Festival.)

Institute sponsored the Festival's first national tour and the commercial Landmark Theatre chain sponsored two later national tours. These early tours planted seeds for future festivals around the country. There was an optimism, idealism, and sense of fun about the Festival that was hard to imagine in this more cynical time of beleaguered and institutionalized arts organizations struggling to survive.

As the Festival garnered media attention and awards, it became a launching pad for independent filmmakers from around the world. It developed a growing and fiercely loyal audience of many thousands that were eager for provocative programming and for discussion and debate with the ever-growing number of Festival guest filmmakers, speakers, and luminaries. Functioning both as a political intervention and also as the creator of new communities, the Festival affirmed that secular culture could play a significant role in defining Jewish identity. Festival films were having a growing impact as they not only reflected culture and identity but also shaped it for an increasing number of viewers.

In these years before the Internet, the Festival pioneered grassroots outreach through cross-promotional strategies and community organizing, and years before Sundance and Miramax, the Festival created an audience for independent cinema, outside and in opposition to Hollywood. The Festival played at independent repertory theaters before the installation of 70-mm and video projection, when reels still ran on projectors run by people, not machines. It was the era when film festivals were not sponsored by banks and blue jeans, when branding was for cattle, and when audiences were forgiving when a film arrived from Bulgaria without subtitles. In the years before corporate underwriting of international film festivals, there was more spontaneity and adventure both for programmers and for audiences. Visiting filmmakers, especially from abroad, were like rock stars and became the catalyst for a Jewish/Bundist/PostModernist version of sex, drugs, and rock and roll. The most repeated line about the Festival became "It's my favorite Jewish holiday!" People were advertising in the personals columns of the alternative weekly papers, "Meet me at the Jewish Film Festival." They did not know what to expect when they came for a screening of *Republic of Dreams*, a surreal German film about the mysterious and apocalyptic Polish writer Bruno Schulz, but they knew it was going to be exciting.

There were major obstacles along the way. Some were financial—all nonprofit arts organizations struggle to survive in America. Other obstacles were political. The Jewish establishment consistently pounded the Festival for challenging the status quo, particularly on the Middle East. At the time, the Jewish mainstream, supporting Israeli hardliners, banned all public contacts between its associated agencies and Palestinian leaders. The Festival opposed this quarantine. In 1988, during the first Palestinian *Intifada*, the Festival screened Mira Hammermesh's documentary *Talking with the Enemy*, and invited noted Palestinian peace activist Mubarak Awad as a guest speaker with the film. Amid threats from mainstream funders, the Festival stood firm in its promotion of free association and dialogue, the event was sold-out, and Award was warmly received with a standing ovation. The political pressure and subsequent funding cuts backfired. Open-minded and dialogue-oriented Bay Area Jews, mostly unaffiliated with the mainstream, gave even more financial support to the Festival, more than replacing funds that had been cut.

Coming up on the Festival's tenth anniversary in 1990, the Jewish establishment criticized the Festival's approach to the world-shaking transformation underway in the former Soviet Union. Representing Israeli government thinking, American Jewish officials advocated getting Soviet Jews quickly out and airlifting them to Israel. The Festival approach, on the other hand, emphasized strengthening continued Jewish life, culture, and resistance in one of the cradles of modern Jewish culture. The Festival's vision was to produce a Jewish Film Festival in Moscow, a cultural event that would challenge Communist suppression of ethnic cultures and encourage international artistic exchange. It was the most complicated and unique production of the Festival up to that time, with advance trips to Moscow by special delegations to negotiate contracts, the production of bilingual materials, and difficult visa negotiations (particularly for the Israeli filmmakers).

Deborah Kaufman, Aviva Kemper (founder of the Washington, D.C. Jewish Film Festival and filmmaker), Josh Waletsky (filmmaker), and Janis Plotkin in front of Pagoda Palace Theatre, San Francisco 1986. (Courtesy of the San Francisco Jewish Film Festival.)

Linking up with a Soviet cosponsor during the period of "Glasnost" and "Perestroika," the Festival joined with its Soviet counterpart, the American-Soviet Film Initiative, to form a thoroughly unprecedented joint venture. The American Soviet Film Initiative was led at the time by Rustam Ibragimbekov, a member of the Congress of Peoples' Deputies, a Muslim from Azerbaijan, a supporter of Jewish rights, and a firm advocate for radical change in oppressive Soviet society.

Perhaps a Jewish Film Festival in Moscow was pushing the envelope a bit too much for the Soviet *apparatchiks*. Things did not go smoothly. The anti-Semitic mayor of Moscow shut the event down three weeks before the

Audience at the first Madrid Jewish Film Festival, October 1992. (Courtesy of the San Francisco Jewish Film Festival.)

opening, claiming there were too many Jewish events in Moscow (there were in fact none taking place at the time). Films and one ton of printed materials were suddenly "lost" in the cargo warehouse of the airport. The tiny, underfunded Jewish Film Festival and its Soviet film counterparts had to appeal to the highest levels of the Soviet government and Communist Party to get the Festival back on track.

The Jewish community in Moscow was on pins and needles, and an international delegation of film directors and guests waited in Moscow for a decision. Finally, with cultural diplomacy in full gear and the international press exposing the authorities' fraudulent excuses, the mayor of Moscow was overruled, reportedly by officials in the Politburo itself, much to everyone's surprise and delight. The Festival opened as scheduled in March 1990 in four Moscow theaters, drawing 50,000 astounded and appreciative people of all backgrounds and ages. It was the largest Jewish event in the history of the Soviet Union.

The success of the Moscow venture led the Jewish Film Festival to a second international foray, this time to Spain. That year, 1992, was to be the quincentennial of the Columbus voyage from Spain to the "new world." For Jews, it was also a quincentennial that triggered different memories—of a Golden Age that had been wiped out in what was to be the prototype of "ethnic cleansing." In an attempt to highlight Jewish Arab cooperation in medieval Spain and to put a spotlight on *Sephardic* and *Mizrachi* Jewish

Delegation of guest filmmakers and journalists at the first Moscow Jewish Film Festival, March 1990. (Courtesy of the San Francisco Jewish Film Festival.)

culture that had been marginalized by *Ashkenazi* and Eastern European Jewish elites, the Festival went to Madrid in 1992 for the 500th anniversary of Columbus's voyage, and the 500th anniversary of the Inquisition and the expulsion of Spanish Jews and Muslims.

The Jewish Film Festival linked up with the state-sponsored Filmoteca in Madrid to produce an international Film Festival focusing on Sephardic and Mizrachi representation. It was to be another completely unprecedented cultural phenomenon. The Festival reached sold-out audiences, mostly students in their twenties and thirties, who stayed on for electrifying postfilm discussions about the meaning of multiculturalism, at a time when a bloody, new war in the former Yugoslavia was creating its own short-hand for genocide—yet again using the language of "ethnic cleansing."

Back in America, the Festival published the first *Catalog of Independent Jewish Cinema* (which has since been updated in a 4th Edition), distributed international Jewish subject films through Atara Releasing, programmed films for local public television station KQED, and consulted with an ever-growing population of Jewish filmmakers. Although not an *auteur*-based Festival, important new film directors, including Dani Levy, Jean Pierre, and Luc Dardenne from Europe, and American documentarians such as Aviva Kempner and Judith Helfand, were cultivated and showcased. The Festival was also an important international forum for new Israeli cinema,

The Jewish Film Festival

Filmmakers and festival directors in front of Surf Theatre, San Francisco, 1983. (Courtesy of the San Francisco Jewish Film Festival.)

exposing audiences to the groundbreaking works of Amos Gitai, Eytan Fox, and Avi Mograbi. Major non-Jewish filmmakers whose works dealt with Jewish themes, including Michael Verhoeven, Michel Khleifi, and Aleksandr Askoldov, were honored guests.

In the 1990s, film submissions shifted from 35mm and 16mm urban, secular explorations of immigration, resistance, and progressive politics to videotaped personal diary films and movies that focused on the suburban experience and the search for new forms of spirituality. Assimilated Jews continued to search for identity by looking into the past but giving new meanings to tradition. For example, Greg Bordowitz's *Fast Trip*, *Long Drop* mines Jewish ethics to face the loss and despair caused by the AIDS epidemic. Another shift took place: Jewish subject cinema was being recognized in the mainstream Jewish community, and Hollywood. It was clearly not a fad, but a phenomenon that was here to stay.

While the Festival flourished, the mainstream Jewish establishment was pondering a series of challenges about the continued assimilation of American Jews. Every survey conducted at this time underlined a continuing shift in demographics and cultural identity. The majority of American Jews identified themselves as "unaffiliated" with the mainstream Jewish community and its established institutions. Whatever the political implications—and they were open to interpretation—the demographic facts were incontrovertible. What was to be the response to intermarriage and lower Jewish birth rates? To what degree should gay and lesbian Jews be welcomed and recruited into communal life and positions of leadership? How do we accommodate and support the growing number of nonwhite Jews with meaningful programs and services? Surveys indicated the Festival was identifying and reaching these people who identified as "cultural Jews," and the marginally affiliated and nonaffiliated Jewish community, as well as the public at large, with meaningful programs, entertainment and education. The mainstream suddenly recognized that the Jewish Film Festival was a model to be emulated, and if possible, co-opted.

By the late 1980s, other Jewish Film Festivals were springing up around the world, first in metropolitan areas such as Boston, London, Washington, D.C., and then expanding into less likely areas and more far-flung regions. In each location, the Festival reflected the needs, priorities, and tastes of the local community. The Boston Festival took advantage of the academic community and produced program guides with essays by local scholars. In London, the Festival was sponsored by the British Film Institute at the National Film Theatre and was an instant success among film aficionados. In Washington, the Festival was sponsored by the Jewish Community Center, and became a model for a growing number of "sponsored" festivals, that worked closely with the local Jewish establishment and with the Israel Embassy.

The Festivals that remained independent of sponsorship, including the San Francisco Jewish Film Festival, struggled for funds from foundations, donors, and public agencies whose budgets were being slashed by government cutbacks and a growing cultural conservatism. Box office income never could subsidize the costs of these year-round arts organizations. The sponsored Festivals, on the other hand, often had an advantage in terms of their funding support, but this in many cases complicated or compromised their curatorial freedom and ability to program more far-out fare. Would, for instance, a Jewish community center or synagogue-sponsored Festival be willing or able to show a film like *Treyf*, a documentary diary about American lesbians who challenge the Israeli occupation of Palestine? Or a film like *Trembling Before G-D*, a film exploring the lives of gay Orthodox Jews?

The special problems generated by questions of sponsorship and financial underwriting remained a challenge, especially in an era characterized by increasing levels of corporate underwriting. While the very essence of an arts organization is the presentation of material that challenges audiences, "rocks the boat" and indeed makes audiences uncomfortable. Funders and sponsors usually want their names associated with programs that celebrate, uplift, and provide inspiration. It is a contradiction that is still being fought out in the culture at large.

By the 1990s, there was a veritable explosion of Jewish Film Festivals, both independent and sponsored. In New York, the Festival was launched by the Jewish Museum, screened at Lincoln Center, and curated by a committee of film advisors. Toronto emerged as another major Festival site, seed-funded entirely by one farsighted Jewish philanthropist. Festivals emerged in Sydney, San Diego, Rio de Janeiro, and, in Berlin, Germany, after fifty years of World War II. There are now scores of firmly established Jewish Film Festivals throughout the world, programming a diverse range of films, each with unique curatorial vision.

As popular Jewish Film Festivals proliferated, so did the production of Jewish films. In the early years of Festival programming, perhaps a few dozen films were submitted to the Festival for consideration. Twenty-five years into the movement, literally hundreds of films are submitted for review to Festivals worldwide, some with tiny budgets, and others with budgets well over one million dollars. The degree of success of the Festivals and of independent Jewish cinema in general was reflected in the establishment in the 1990s of the National Foundation For Jewish Culture's Fund for Jewish Documentary Cinema, funded by a major grant from Steven Spielberg's Righteous Persons Foundation. This Fund has continued to be an impetus for the production of new independent Jewish cinema.

Because of its involvement with funding, the National Foundation for Jewish Culture recognized the growing importance of the Festival movement as a bridge between filmmakers and audiences. It began to play a role in networking and mentoring new Festivals, organizing, and convening a National Conference of Jewish Film Festivals, which meets every eighteen months in the U.S., drawing representatives from dozens of Jewish Film Festivals.

By the mid-1990s, the San Francisco Jewish Film Festival was at a turning point. It had laid the foundation for a successful international movement and was now focused on institutional and program growth, building an infrastructure that would sustain the Festival into the future. Several new paths were forged. The Festival began to reach out to a new and younger generation with the New Jewish Filmmaker Project, an annual program that trains teenagers how to write, shoot, and edit their own Jewish subject films, which are then premiered at the annual Film Festival. The San Francisco Jewish Film Festival also expanded its main summer event to include screenings to the south in Silicon Valley's high-tech capital and the home of Stanford University, Stanford, and to the north in suburban Marin County.

The Festival continued to reap rich rewards from screening challenging films rather than programming to the lowest common denominator. During the height of the second Palestinian Intifada in 2001, the Festival showcased the Academy Award–nominated film, *Promises*, about the lives of Israeli and Palestinian children. The program drew a sold-out audience at its urban venues, but most surprising was an audience of 1,100 people at a suburban theater, after which Israelis, Palestinians, and American Jewish audiences sat together and had a thoughtful and respectful discussion with the filmmakers about the failed peace process and the future of the Middle

East. This and other similar proactive interventions for dialogue, led to ongoing collaborative programming with the San Francisco Arab Film Festival.

Meanwhile, the Festival also grew by programming monthly screenings at a new downtown multicultural arts center, serving residents of the city. With this, the San Francisco Jewish Festival began to present films year-round.

In the new millennium, independent cinema was finally a recognized part of the culture, and even the commercial success of documentary films was on the horizon. The Internet revolutionized communication with audiences, other film programmers and anyone interested in Jewish films. Film programming was enhanced by access to information from other international film festivals. The San Francisco Festival pioneered this medium building a website that showcased an online archive and library of independent Jewish films. The Festival also experimented with Festival web blogs and enhanced site interactivity. In the new frontiers of digital communication, The San Francisco Jewish Film Festival continued to break new ground.

The Festival's artistic program also grew with the intent of showcasing artists working in other mediums. Some of these special programs included the a cappella drag queen beauty shop quartet, The Kinsey Sicks, singing *shtick* and Yiddish songs from the theater stage, and Fat Chance Belly Dance, jiggling to DJ Cheb I Sabah's Middle Eastern music mix. In 2002, making a recognizably oppositional statement to the drive towards war on Iraq, the Festival arranged with Yoko Ono to play a rare clip from the film *The Bed-In*, and audiences sang along with John and Yoko's "Give Peace a Chance."

The twentieth anniversary of the Jewish Film Festival was notable for its focus on film and music to enrich the overall cultural experience. The Festival commissioned a score by American composer and violinist Daniel Hoffman for a reprised screening of the silent classic *The Golem*, as well as a production of a live opera accompanying the screening of the experimental video homage to pre-war Hungary, *Free Fall* by Peter Forgaczs. Finally, the Festival staged a live performance from the Kurt Weill opera *Street Scenes*, preceding the reprise of Film Festival audience favorite *Septembers Songs: The Music of Kurt Weill*. Continuing its efforts to bridge many mediums, the Festival also produced a museum quality exhibit exploring the history of the Jewish Film Festival.

In 2003, the Festival joined with other arts and media communities by buying and moving into a permanent building space, a center of film culture and cultures, in central San Francisco. This move opened up the doors for new collaborations and opportunities that would secure the Festival's future.

Though the Festival movement as a whole has matured and become established, Jewish filmmakers are still exploring identity and culture in fresh and original ways, reflecting the diversity that is Jewish life around the world. Although institutional challenges in the form of funding, sponsorship issues, or corporate influence confront each Jewish Film Festival, new and ever broader audiences continue to be reached by this cultural phenomenon that has planted firm roots into the Jewish landscape and will continue to grow into the next generation.

Chapter 9

A Brief Introduction to Jewish American Radio

Henry Sapoznik

> My mother listened to WEVD from morning until night. It was very special for all those immigrant people that we knew. That was their connection with America. It was the station that spoke their language.
> —Doris Cohen, child singer on Jewish radio programs

> We were doing our Yiddish Swing program on Sunday. We had a tremendous audience. We did the show from the Capitol Hotel, and we had blacks and Spanish people who didn't understand Yiddish. It was the most fabulous reception you'd ever want to see a show receive!
> —Claire Barry, of the singing duo the Barry Sisters

Coming hard on the heels of restrictive and xenophobic anti-immigration laws, radio emerged in the 1920s as a new mass medium for the acculturation of millions of newly arrived immigrants from around the world.

By the mid-1920s, thousands of Yiddish-speaking Eastern European Jews had established themselves economically and culturally, most in large urban centers like New York City, Chicago, Detroit, Philadelphia, and Boston. In New York, a second generation was already deserting the crowded tenements of the Lower East Side for more modern, middle-class neighborhoods in the Bronx and Brooklyn. As the community became more diffuse, it nonetheless continued to maintain a broad network of specifically Jewish social and cultural institutions such as Yiddish theaters and newspapers, Jewish trade unions and *landmanshaftn*, and religious and secular educational institutions. Like those established by other immigrant groups, these Jewish institutions helped ease the way into American life, but at the same time, played a role in strengthening ethnicity by expressing the American Jewish identities of the new and not-so-new immigrants.

With the advent of radio, another forum for ethnic identity and Americanization was added to the list of immigrant cultural institutions. The earliest known broadcast aimed directly at American Jews was a Yiddish-language variety show sponsored by the Libby Hotel on New York station WHN in 1926. This show is but one example of the sorts of radio programs that catered to various ethnic groups from the very beginning of American broadcast history. Broadcaster Donald Flamm claims to have been the first to offer multilingual programming in 1925 over WMCA, the radio station he then owned:

Let's put a program on each day, a different language each hour—we'll have an announcer who speaks that language but we also will have everything interpreted so we don't lose our audience . . . Monday night was German night. Tuesday night was French night. Wednesday night was Jewish night.

There were few stations that broadcast exclusively in one particular foreign language. Rather, ethnic and foreign-language programs tended to share time on one nonnetwork radio station. A day's broadcasting in the late 1920s or early 1930s, on WBNX, for example, might include such offerings as:

Aileen O'Reilly, Quaint Irish Cities: Dublin
Rathy Hungarian Trio
La Rivista Italiana
Polish Radio Folks Ensemble
Neste Club Colored Art Hour
German Recipes for Housewives
Jewish Events of the Week

Often these groups shared studio space, announcers, and even performers. On of our interviewees, Shirley Pahl, a pianist at WBNX, remembers:

First you had the preachers on at 6:00 in the morning and I played the organ then, background music. And then you would have the Spanish, the Irish, whatever came in. It was ethnic music and I picked it all up.

By the 1930s, there were numerous stations that aired Jewish or Yiddish and other ethnic programs, bringing news, advertising, advice, and entertainment to listeners across the United States. During the heyday of Jewish broadcasting in the 1930s–1940s, listeners in New York could turn the dial and hear several hours of Jewish programming every day. Even in smaller places like Sioux City, Iowa, a Yiddish-speaking Jew could turn on *Der*

Tog's weekly radio show on WABC affiliate KSCJ in 1929 and hear an operetta called *A Shabes in Shtetl* (A Real Sabbath in the Home Town), with music performed by actors from the Yiddish theater, a *klezmer* band, and a children's chorus from a *Talmud Torah* (religious school).

Listeners in New York in 1945 could catch fifteen minutes of "Yiddish Swing" on the *The American Jewish Hour*, a program broadcast on WHN every Sunday. In 1955, even as Yiddish and Jewish radio programming was diminishing, Yiddish-speakers could tune in to WEVD and hear the advice-dispensing Jewish Philosopher.

Jewish and Yiddish radio began to decline in the mid-1950s due to continuing Jewish assimilation, the decline of radio and the rise of television, and the cold war's emphasis on Americanism. However, before it faded, it served its listeners by reflecting and helping to shape an emergent American Jewish culture. Today, new waves of immigrants, including Jewish immigrants from the former Soviet Union, are utilizing radio and new forums such as cable television to mediate the experience of Americanization.

A CHRONOLOGY OF JEWISH AND YIDDISH BROADCASTING

Shtetl on the Air

Jewish radio reflected and helped to define American Jewish immigrant culture by simultaneously borrowing from popular American entertainment and drawing on Jewish tradition.

Our series will show that when Jewish radio borrowed directly from the mainstream media, the material was often *faryidisht* (yiddishized) and transformed to fit the sensibilities of the Jewish immigrant audience. Jewish radio producer Sholom Rubinstein remembers:

> WEVD grew so that at its heyday, we had 65 quarter-hours of advertising a week, and it became a rather big business. We had 2 Yiddish copywriters whose sole job was translating English commercials into Yiddish and giving them a little Yiddish *kvetch*—a Talmudic saying. The Talmud was a great source of opening lines for our commercials.

We will explore how, in a sense, Jewish radio duplicated aspects of traditional Jewish society, mimicking the communal functions of *yeshiva, besmedresh* (synagogue), *tsedoke* (alms), *rebbe*, wall newspaper, and storyteller by translating these institutions into the quiz show, on-air synagogue service, charity appeal, advice show, announcement, and literary reading.

The quiz show, a popular genre on mainstream radio, was a particular favorite among Jewish listeners, who tended to idealize learning and intellectualism. Surviving examples from the 1940s include *What Do You Know?*, sponsored by the B. Manischewitz Company, in which contestants were asked questions about the Bible in between interludes when a live orchestra played such tunes as "Riffin' the FREYLAKHS." *Sharfe kepelakh* (Sharp Little Minds) was broadcast from in *yeshivoth* in the New York area and mimicked the Old World tradition of once-a-week examination of schoolboys by their elders.

In the postwar period, the *Daf Hashevua* (The Weekly Talmud Page) show, provided an opportunity for listeners to study *Torah* every Saturday night with Orthodox rabbis who were beamed into their living rooms via WEVD. On the second anniversary of the program in 1952, Rabbi Meyer Bunim suggested in Yiddish that history would record not only the great *yeshivas* of yore in Babylon but also "the *yeshiva* called WEVD, 1330 on your dial," with its "tens of thousands of students." Switching to English, Rabbi Bunim addressed "our English friends who are listening in" and suggested that listening to *Daf Hashevua* could help to counteract the dangers of "foreign influences entering the home.... For the home with *Torah*, everything is holy ... even the radio becomes holy."

If *Daf Hashevua* mimicked the ambience of synagogues in Pinsk or Rovne, *Der Yidishe Filosof* (The Jewish Philosopher) replicated on WEVD the role of both the local *rebbe* and matchmaker. Troubled listeners would write in to Israel Lutsky describing their problems, and the "sage," or Jewish Philosopher, would tell them how to untangle their lives. As Beatrice Goldsmith, a researcher for the WPA in the mid-1930s, cynically noted, the Jewish Philosopher "expanded into the matrimonial business" by inviting listeners

to his place where, for an admission of fifty cents they can be entertained, dance, listen to one of his very own lectures, drink punch and meet intelligent, marriageable folk of the opposite sex with enough cold cash on hand to make family life possible (and profitable). He calls this market the "Jewish Philosopher's Institute" and it seems to be going great guns.

There were clones of the *Jewish Philosopher* program on other stations, who often imitated their competitors. WMCA had *Problemen bilder* (*Problem Scenes*), whose star, Jennie Goldstein, capitalized on the fame she had won in the Yiddish theater as "the prima donna of weeping." WEVD's version of the advice show was a dramatization of *The Jewish Daily Forward*'s popular newspaper advice column, *A bintl briv* (A bundle of letters). Episodes dramatized in 1932 included: "A Husband Loses His Wages Playing Cards," "A Victim of Prosperity," "Love Shmove," and "A Revolution Against Father."

This show was later followed by another dramatized advice show, *Tsures Balaytn* (People's Problems), sponsored by a Brooklyn Hospital. Actress Rita Karin will give our audience some sense of the show's flavor:

Every script, of course, had to end with a stroke or some kind of misfortune. So when [the writer, Nuhem Stutchkoff] invited me to audition he asked, "*Kenst di shrayen?*" ("Can you yell?") Because I play a daughter or a wife or neighbor and misfortune befalls me. The first thing I shout is "AHHHHHH *GEVALT*!" If you couldn't yell, you could not qualify to play in Stutchkoff's show.

Jewish oral tradition found a particularly comfortable niche on the air. Readings of poems and literary works by radio personalities were regular fare. For example, in the 1940s, The Story of General Gershelman, a Yiddish novel by A. Buchstein, was serialized and read on the air by Yiddish actor Victor Packer. Another Yiddish actor, Zvee Scooler, known as "Der Grammayster" (The Rhyme Master), continued the tradition of the *badkhn* (wedding jester) by offering commentary on current events and philosophical quandaries in (often humorous) rhyme.

JEWISH AND YIDDISH RADIO AS A COMMUNAL AFFAIR: STRENGTHENING THE BONDS OF ETHNICITY

> My father Chiam had one dear friend who had a store open on Sunday mornings. And if Esterl was singing, the customers could be standing in line waiting for their belly lox and he'd say, "Khayim's Ester zingt [Chaim's Esther is singing] and you are all going to wait."
> —Esther Deutsch, child performer

As Lizabeth Cohen has noted in *Making a New Deal: Industrial Workers in Chicago, 1919–1939*, radio was originally a "grassroots" medium, improvisational and intimate. As the earliest radio stations broadcast with very low wattage over no more than a fifteen-mile radius, audiences and sponsors tended to be local. Cohen writes:

From the start, nonprofit ethnic, religious, and labor groups put radio to their service. In 1925, almost a third of the 571 radio stations nationwide were owned by educational institutions and churches, less than 4 percent by commercial broadcasting companies. Even when newspapers, department stores, and radio shops sponsored stations, as they frequently did, they ran them as public services, not as commercial operations [. . .] The local orientation of these sponsoring organizations coupled with the limitations of radio technology and an excessive demand for access to the airwaves gave radio broadcasting in the early years a strong local character, even in a major center of radio broadcasting like Chicago.

Radio station schedules published in Yiddish newspapers in 1932 indicate that a fair number of Jewish community organizations in New York ran regular radio shows. For example, the Brooklyn Jewish Charity Federation had a slot on Wednesday nights at 10:30 on WLTH; the Women's League of the United Synagogue broadcast on WINS on Thursday at 1:30; the Jewish Butchers' Guild sponsored a program on WLTH on Wednesdays and

Fridays at 3:00; and the Israel Orphan Asylum featured a variety show on WMCA on Tuesday at 10:00 P.M.

Non-network radio stations like WLTH, WEVD, WBBC, and WARD provided local businesses and organizations with unique points of access to potential customers and supporters. Producer Sholom Rubinstein noted that early ethnic radio was run much like public access television today, inasmuch as anyone could come in off the street and purchase fifteen minutes of airtime for a charitable appeal for a *yeshiva* or for a musical program laced with commercials for a local clothing store.

Locally produced Jewish radio programs were often run on a shoestring, and sometimes as a "Mom & Pop" business, with many tasks performed by family members. Rubinstein reports getting his start in radio as a teenager when he would do research at the public library for his father's program on "Great Jewish Composers." Another interviewee, Betty Perlov, remembers serving as an unpaid child extra in her father's radio plays.

Jewish radio might be produced as a nuclear family affair, but it catered to an extended family. Listening to the radio could be a participatory communal event, an experience rather different from today's passive consumption of television. As Cohen notes, early listening practices tended to promote and strengthen "ethnic, religious, and working-class affiliations rather than undermining them."

For example, *Der Tog* reported that many listeners tuned into its show at "Jewish restaurants, where there are radios" and in Jewish hospitals and sanatoriums. *The Jewish Daily Forward* noted that many families without radios went to the houses of friends to listen to the *The Forwards Hour*: "After the first program, Mr. Fertig of Brownsville called to say that several families had attended a party at his home to listen to the show."

The content of the programs themselves tended to strengthen ethnic identification. Jacques Ferrand of the Common Council for American Unity (CCAU), an advocacy group for ethnic radio, noted that

Foreign language broadcasts have a special appeal also to many young Americans of foreign parentage who cannot read with ease, or at all, their parents' language, but who understand it when it is spoken. For these younger people, the foreign-language programs help to bridge the gap between the generations. Hearing folksongs, music, and stories of their parents' country of origin, these young people often gain a more sympathetic understanding of family attitudes and backgrounds.

Like other ethnic radio programs, Jewish shows often catered to listeners' nostalgia for the Old Country, such as *Der Tog's* 1929 musical *revue*, "Purim in Shtetl," or WRNY's 1932 broadcast of the *Boiberiker Kapelye*, which performed "Jewish melodies and wedding dances in the old style of the small-town *klezmer* in the Old Country long, long ago." (Though not many of these shows have survived, vintage recordings of many of the tunes played on Jewish radio are available, and will be used in our documentary.)

Ethnic broadcasters reminded listeners of their European roots, but they also dwelt on the very subject of Americanization with humor programs, which poked fun at the dissonance between Old Country culture and the American environment, by encouraging immigrants to laugh at their own difficult early experiences in the New World. The long-running serial, *The Brownsville Zeyde*, which starred Baruch Lumet (the father of film director Sidney Lumet) focused on the mishaps of an Old World grandfather transplanted into the home of his Americanized children. Comic sketches such as one broadcast on WEVD in 1932 about a presser who "had done so well in America that his friends made a benefit to send him to a sanatorium" were also common fare on Yiddish-language frequencies.

Betty Perlov's mother, Vera Rosanka achieved renown as a character called the "*Yidishe Shikse*" (The Jewish Gentile), who spoke with a Russian accent, making comic mistakes in both Yiddish and English. Perlov remarks: "People loved to hear these English mistakes. So their English wasn't great, but they loved to laugh at someone else." Good-natured poking of fun at American culture might take the form of Yiddish parodies of American popular songs, such as a spoof of the "Syncopated Clock," sung by Seymour Rexite.

In fact, Jewish radio provided its listeners with a counterpoint to the narrow ethnic stereotypes that were perpetuated by mainstream radio. Unlike mainstream shows, in which Jews were usually portrayed as comically malapropistic outsiders or, alternatively, philosophically wise lower-middle class shopkeepers, Jewish radio programs provided a wide range of Jewish characters, including doctors, lawyers, and policemen.

Radio, in the age of live studio audiences, was a highly participatory medium, drawing on earlier traditions of vaudeville and theater. Betty Perlov remembers an extreme example of an audience's conflation of home, family, community, and radio program:

My father had a program, which was called *Mentshn on oygn* (*Men Without Eyes*) . . . It was the story of a young woman, Bettele, who was me, who was in a terrible fire and her face got horribly scarred and she was very disfigured and falls in love with someone who is blind. . . . Anyway there was a scene where there was a wedding and my father just took a hazardous guess and said "why don't you come to the station and see the wedding scene?" He had no idea that hundreds of people would show up, which made him have to hire the Broadway Central [Hotel] and which permitted 3,000 people to come in at a quarter a head to see the wedding scene of Betty and her blind husband. And everyone seemed to bring a present. We had loads of chocolate cakes and tablecloths and sheets, some of them still unused, that was divided among the company who in those perilous depression times were able to use everything they were given.

"SEND DOWN FOR A CREAM-CHEESEL": ADVERTISING AND JEWISH RADIO

> The sponsor was Dr. Julius Lumenfeld. He was a dentist. His office began at the corner of Orchard and Delancey. By the time the show was over three years later, his office, with thousands of little Jewish dentists working for him like little gnomes poking away at people's cavities, ran the full length of Delancey.
> —Sidney Lumet, child performer on Yiddish radio

> There was a commercial for King Solomon Cemetery and what broke me up on that was "*yeder kever iz arumgeringlt mit an asfalt vok.*" Every plot is surrounded with an asphalt walk. I wanted to add, which I never did, that the corpses can come out and take a seat on the bench for awhile and then go back again. It was pretty rough selling cemeteries on the air.
> —David Opatashu, actor and radio announcer

Ethnic radio helped speed the Americanization of immigrants by introducing them to American products in the intimacy of their own homes and native languages. As Andrew Heinze concludes in Adapting to Abundance: Jewish Immigrants, Mass Consumption, and the Search for American Identity, immigrants were able to create "elements of a new cultural identity with consumer goods." Heinze suggests that, through consumption, Jews transformed their traditional attitudes toward luxury items, previously used primarily in religious observance as objects, which delineated the holy from the mundane by "elevating the dignity of the ordinary Jew as a partner in the divine covenant." In the New World, "luxury items," or consumer products, became "emblems of secular adjustment and progress in America" and expressions of a distinctive *American Jewish* identity. Yiddish newspaper and broadcast advertising were reflections of and agents in what Heinze calls the "reconciliation of traditional Jewish attitudes with the values and images promoted by American advertisers."

When people are asked what they remember most about Jewish and Yiddish radio, they often respond by reminiscing about their favorite commercials. These most memorable commercials were in and of themselves entertainment, offering much more than the endlessly repeated radio jingles of today. As Sholom Rubinstein notes, in the 1920s–1940s, Yiddish copywriters "turned out reams of copy because in those days, nobody ever dreamed of repeating a commercial. A commercial was done, gone, and a new set for next week."

Jewish radio married advertising to the Yiddish theater, sometimes couching sponsors' appeals in the form of a dramatic sketch or musical *revue*. This interweaving of advertising and entertainment was not unique to Jewish radio. As Roland Marchand writes in *Advertising the American Dream*, during the 1930s, "no inviolate line between 'editorial content' and advertising characterized radio in the years following 1928." "Interweaving" was the norm. However, Jewish radio gave the dramatized commercial an ethnic twist. Sholom Rubinstein remembers:

... the marvelous commercials of Nahum Stutchkoff who wrote the little vignettes for Breakstone's Cream Cheese. It sold but it certainly entertained a lot of people because he had these characters in the grocery store and all kinds of reasons why people had to send down for a "cream-cheesel."

In fact, Jewish radio, like all other ethnic broadcasts, was driven by the selling of airtime to sponsors. As Rudolf Arnheim and Martha Collins Bayne noted in a study of "Foreign Language Broadcasts Over Local American Stations" published in *Radio Research* in 1941, the most prevalent advertisements on Yiddish radio were for foods and medicines. Sponsors of specifically Jewish food products included *Rokeach, Horowitz Margareten, Wolff's Kasha*.

But mainstream advertisers were sometimes also drawn to the ethnic airwaves, recognizing that they could broaden their market by appealing to consumers in their native languages. Large advertisers included Baker's Chocolate, Postum, Diamond Crystal Salt, and Maxwell House. The Carnation Milk Company was so pleased with Israel Lutsky, "The Jewish Philosopher," whose show ran on WEVD for many years, that they awarded him a pension when he retired in 1963.

An undated WLTH promotional circular aims at enticing non-Jewish sponsors by touting the benefits of advertising on Yiddish radio (emphasis in the original):

What portion of the New York market shows the greatest concentration of CONSUMERS, of RETAIL STORES, of BUYING and SELLING activity? — THE JEWISH RESIDENTIAL NEIGHBORHOODS! ... A COMPLETE SELLING JOB IN NEW YORK MUST INCLUDE THE VAST JEWISH FIELD. Jewish radio programs have powerful appeal for the Jewish people. Usually of a national or folk nature, with characteristic music, WLTH's Jewish progams are listened to with undivided attention rarely witnessed among the usual radio tuners-in. ...

The heart of any effort to secure or hold the Jewish trade is continuity. Continuity is more than a mere matter of language. To be really Jewish, it must be conceived with a deep and intimate understanding of the Jewish mind ... It must be written in the living idiom of this colorful language known as "Yiddish."

The Continuity men at WLTH are graduates of the one and only school where all the resources of this highly idiomatic language may be learned—the Jewish Theater. They have at their command every trick and turn of appeal to impress the Jewish mentality.

Ethnic radio station managers developed innovative strategies for securing sponsored airtime. One of our interviewees, Miriam Leifer, remembers helping her boss, station manager Victor Packer, develop a WLTH Grocers Association, which placed posters for the Brooklyn-based station in local grocery stores, in exchange for easy access to tickets to live shows for their customers. Packer and Leifer also conducted "pantry surveys" of Jewish homes, which enabled them to go to advertisers with the message: "Look, so and so is getting all the activity. We want to push your product. We can do it. These are our people." After World War II, the "store" broadcast, which presented musical programs in grocery stores before live audiences, became a popular genre of program on WBBC and WEVD. Those who came to the store for the recording session, also received gifts of the sponsors' products.

Ethnic broadcasters' need to compete with mainstream stations and the networks for sponsors had a major influence on the quality of programming. Foreign-language broadcasters depended on local and small businesses for advertising revenue rather than on big national advertisers. Because small advertisers were unable to purchase large blocks of airtime, ethnic station managers were obliged to fund the broadcast day with a proliferation of "spots," for a large number of small advertisers. Program content was sometimes all but eclipsed by advertisements.

The emphasis on advertising on Yiddish radio stations irritated Beatrice Goldsmith, a researcher for the WPA:

On the smaller stations, which operate on a shoe-string, entertainment has been all but wiped out. There are dozens of announcements to one record of a "Galician Wedding Dance" or a song by a diabetic soprano. We counted a: Furniture Store, Mineral Water Company, Shoe Store, Delicatessen Store, Photographer Shop (artistic wedding photos), Gift Shop Clearance, Men's Suit Special, and Wedding Temple—all sponsors of two numbers (vocal) by a child with a passion for getting ahead of the piano. Sometimes the pianist will play two bars of a song and stop, never to continue, while the announcer calmly reels off another sale.

Ethnic radio commercials sometimes also had a crossover appeal to members outside the group, thereby providing ethnic advertisers with wider markets for their wares. As Donald Flamm, owner of the multilingual station WMCA notes, not only Jews listened to Jewish programs, Germans to German shows, or Italians to the Italian music hour. Multiethnic listenership offered products like Stuhmer's bread and Breakstone's sour cream the opportunity to reach out to diverse consumers. The 1940s commercials for the "Joe and Paul" clothing store, whose comical jingle, written by Sholom Secunda, mingled Yiddish and English, is a good example of how an ethnic commercial could transcend the boundaries of its target Jewish audience. By the late 1940s (when the store itself no longer existed), the jingle had spawned a number of parodies, including one recorded by the Pupi Campo salsa band.

AROUND THE FAMILY TABLE: DRAMA AND MUSIC ON THE JEWISH DIAL

Ethnic radio served a particular dual economic purpose: it was a forum for advertisers (both immigrant entrepreneurs and mainstream sponsors), but also a provider of jobs for immigrants who found themselves locked out of mainstream radio, to which few ethnic actors successfully made the transition from the foreign-language stage, and where non-Anglo-Saxon roles tended to be restricted to stereotypes.

Yiddish-language radio became a particular haven for Jewish performers during the Depression when the Yiddish theater began its decline. Performers were able to eke out the season by taking on day jobs as radio announcers, as characters in on-the-air soap operas or dramatized commercials, or as musicians in the station orchestra.

In fact, Jewish and Yiddish radio not only substituted for live theater but also stimulated the production of "spin-off" plays and revues. Betty Perlov relates:

Many of the radio sketches were transformed into plays. They would take a program that had gone on for several months like the "Yiddishe Mama." The stars of these programs would work towards the culmination by putting on a play of the radio program, and the people who listened to them could come and actually see the characters—they really believed in them!

Popular examples of theatrical spin-offs from radio included Nchum Stutchkoff's *Bei Tate Mames Tish* (Around the Family Table) and *The Brownsville Zeyde*. Sidney Lumet, whose father Baruch played the "Brownsville Zeyde" on WLTH, recalls:

He would take ten episodes or eight episodes and string them together and make a play out of it, and then he would rent a theater like the Hopkinson or a Second Avenue house. And he'd put out all the dough himself and if we did business, he'd make some money and if we didn't, he'd lose a lot.

Jewish radio helped to create celebrities, who parleyed the fame they had achieved for characters developed on the airwaves into furthering their careers on the theater stage. Vera Rosanka ("The Yidishe Shikse"), Zvee Scooler ("Der Grammeister"), and cantors Leybele Waldman and Moishe Oysher are all examples of talented performers whose work in radio helped them attain stardom.

Yiddish radio drew heavily from Yiddish theater fare, reflecting popular trends or catering to the nostalgia of audiences. As J. Hoberman has noted in *Bridge of Light: Yiddish Film Between Two Worlds*, even the titles of Yiddish movies and plays tend "invoke blood ties and family relationships." Indeed, Yiddish radio plays were frequently family dramas. (Statistics cited in Arnheim's and Bayne's 1941 study of foreign-language radio broadcasts indicate that Yiddish radio had a higher proportion of family dramatizations than the broadcasts of other ethnic groups, accounting for 35 percent of the dramatizations on the Yiddish airwaves as opposed to 19 percent in the total of the sample.)

A typical example of Yiddish radio "family" drama was the long-running *Bei Tate Mames Tish* (Around the Family Table), broadcast once a week on

WEVD in the 1930s. An episode aired in 1939 featured the character of Devorah, an immigrant grandmother, who is deeply troubled by her rude and assimilated granddaughter Reyzele. Reyzele forces her "lower-class" grandmother into an old age home and does not invite her to her wedding. Grandma nobly gives her Americanized descendant her blessing, but dies three weeks after the latter's wedding.

Musical *revues* were heavily favored by sponsors and listeners of ethnic radio and Jewish radio was no exception. The first *Der Tog* program on September 30, 1928 is reported to have starred Molly Picon, Joseph Rumshinsky, Sam Kestin, and "the entire chorus" of the Second Avenue Theater. According to a newspaper account, the show included a medley of Yiddish melodies, starting with *Kol Nidre* and ending with something identified only as a *lebediker melodie* (lively tune). Presented by Z.H. Rubinstein, the newspaper's news editor, the program also included a musical *revue* of various operetta songs "from Goldfaden to Rumshinsky." The report noted that "the biggest hit was naturally made by Molly Picon. She sang, declaimed, laughed, and cried, and made a wonderful impression."

Musical programs could also be eclectic, as was a *Der Tog* program, broadcast on February 10, 1929, which featured cantors singing Yiddish melodies and vaudeville stars (accompanied by children on violin and piano).

Musical programs continued their popularity throughout Jewish radio's heyday. In the early 1940s, *The Hammer's Beverage Program* on WLTH featured the vocal talents of "Raisele and Shaindele—The Gay Twins," who regaled listeners with Yiddish swing and folk songs. The *Hammer's Beverage Program's* competitor, *The American Jewish Hour*, sponsored by the B. Manischewitz Company and other advertisers, offered a quarter hour of Yiddish swing every Sunday on WHN. Featured regulars included the Barry Sisters (billed as "The Dairy Maids" when Edelstein's Tuxedo Brand Cheese was the sponsor), the well-known clarinetist Dave Tarras, and tenor Jan Bart.

Jewish radio served not only as entertainment but also as a forum for their artistic aspirations for their children. As Andrew Heinze notes in *Adapting to Abundance*,

> Although the basic musical instrument of the *shtetl* was probably the fiddle . . . the piano became the pride and joy of Jewish homes in America . . . Meeting a number of needs, the piano emerged in many Jewish homes as a means of satisfying the group's extraordinary interest in American popular music, which turned into a medium of cultural adaptation, as an instrument for refining Jewish children and raising the social status of the household . . .

Variety shows featuring child stars and amateur hours were common offerings on the Yiddish dial. As cynic Goldsmith reports:

Fetter Nochem's ["Uncle" Nochem Stutchkoff's] children's hour became famous a few years ago and since then there are many "uncles" who are none other than the regular station announcers themselves who run "*Kinder winklen*" [children's corners]. Kids from Folk *Shuls* (Arbeter Ring, Sholem Aleichem, etc.) were the first to be drawn into these broadcasts because they learn Yiddish songs as part of their curriculum and every two-by-four Folk *Schul* has a chorus and singing teacher. But these brats who perform on the minor Bronx and Brooklyn stations are of the genus "Hopkinson Theater"—products of a little Second Avenue theatrical training. They sing folk songs now and then but in the main stick to *Scholem Secunda*. And they generally dedicate each song to someone whose birthday it is or who was ambitious enough to request it.

HIGH CULTURE AND SOCIALISM: WEVD AND *THE JEWISH DAILY FORWARD*

> If we ever have pogroms in America, they will be because of Jewish shows. Every nothing, every ignoramus who does not know how to put two words together so that they make sense becomes an announcer . . . When they sold you the radio, they promised you that you would hear all kinds of special things—symphonies, operas, famous artists, famous speakers—the best and the finest would be brought to you on the radio. They do, in fact, give a little of the finer sort of music, but only a little. . . .
> —Yosef Rakhlin, "The Boring Songs and the Played-Out Witticisms on the Radio Programs—One Seldom Hears a Fresh Melody or a New Joke—The Miserable Yiddish Shows," *The Jewish Daily Forward,* August 10, 1932

Musical *revues* and amateur hours provided fertile ground for critics of "*shund*" (Yiddish for "trash") who, like Goldsmith, expected radio to civilize the masses rather than cater to their "vulgar" tastes.

The high-low culture debate replicated similar controversies within both mainstream radio and other areas of Yiddish culture. As Roland Marchand writes in *Advertising the American Dream*, the developers of early radio thought of it as "a civilizing force," which would be "debased" if commercial considerations were allowed to determine program content.

Yiddish newspapers in the United States were never free of *feuilletons*, which condemned "*shund*" and prescribed higher artistic standards for Yiddish performers. Indeed, by the 1920s, Yiddish "art" theaters like the eponymous Yiddish Art Theater, Jewish Art Theater, and the ARTEF had emerged with serious repertoires and European stage techniques that were considered even more avant-garde than those of mainstream American theater. On the other hand, *shund* continued to thrive in other theaters as popular entertainment.

Some Yiddish-language broadcasters were self-conscious about Yiddish radio's poor image. For instance, when the prestigious, socialist, Yiddish newspaper *The Jewish Daily Forward*, began broadcasting its own program in 1932 over WEVD, it bragged about the high cultural standards it would set for the Yiddish broadcasting field:

The Forward radio program has elevated the spirit of Yiddish broadcasting. It proves that the Forward radio program will play a similar role as the Forward does as a newspaper. It is said that Ab. Cahan turned out to be the editor, in a sense, not only of the Forward, but of all Yiddish newspapers, because they all learned, and were forced to institute, things which the Forward had introduced. The Forward Yiddish program will force many radio programs to become more respectable and worthy if they are to imitate use.

WEVD was reorganized in late 1931 with substantial financial backing from the *Forward*. For four years, the station had been unsuccessfully run by the Socialist Party as a noncommerical enterprise and had gotten into trouble with the FRC over various regulatory violations. The *Forward* and the Socialist Part had a long history of mutual interests and ties, which included both ideological affinities (the *Forward* espoused a moderate socialism) and corporate connections (the newspaper's publisher Abraham Cahan, and its general manager, B. Charney Vladeck, were members of the Board of Directors of WEVD's licensee, the Debs Memorial Fund).

WEVD was not the first newspaper to sponsor a radio broadcast: in 1928, the *Der Tog* (The Day) variety show program, sponsored by the New York Yiddish daily newspaper, began to air on WABC. (In 1930, WABC was purchased by William Paley and became the flagship station of the then fledgling CBS network. Unfortunately, no examples of the *Der Tog* program, which continued until 1932, are known to have survived.)

By the end of the 1930s, the *Forward* had fully taken over the reins of the WEVD, although it retained its call letters (Eugene V. Debs's initials). The *Forward* also honored WEVD's high-minded public service agenda by reserving evening hours for noncommercial English language discussion programs on political, social, and educational topics. The station alloted programming time to the Socialist Party, which gradually diminished over the course of the next decade.

At the opening of the station's new state-of-the-art facilities at the Hotel Claridge in fall 1932, WEVD pledged to provide listeners with high-quality programming while maintaining its commitment to radicalism. Speakers included John Dewey, Morris Hillquit, and the editor of *The Nation*, Heywood Broun. Articles in the *Forward* claimed that WEVD was the only radio station in the country which presents the free voice of America, the voice of the worker, of the oppressed people, the voice of the liberal and Socialist spirit, the voice of protest . . . the only station on whose microphones capitalism has yet to lay its brutal paw.

However, despite its anticapitalist rhetoric, the *Forward* intended to make a profit from their new venture. WEVD's new owners agressively sought purchasers for the commercial time slots on its daytime schedule and relentlessly publicized its own regular program, *The Forwards Hour*, in the pages of its daily. Reportedly, Socialist leader Norman Thomas soon found it easier to obtain airtime on NBC's station WJZ than on WEVD, the station named for Eugene Debs. Moreover, notwithstanding defiance against "millionaire" broadcasting networks such as CBS and NBC, WEVD's new manager Vladeck maintained very friendly relations with David Sarnoff, NBC's founder. In 1923, Vladeck and Sarnoff exchanged several cordial letters about Valdeck's interest in erecting a radio transmitter atop the *Forward* building. In 1929, Vladeck was in touch with NBC about purchasing time for a *Forward* show on some of its affiliate stations. Apparently, nothing came of these ventures.

WEVD did not start regularly broadcasting in Yiddish until the fall season of 1932 (though it had broadcast Jewish programs prior to its stewardship by the *Forward*). Its first program, *The Forward Radio Hour*, followed the newspaper's tried and true formula of mixing the serious with the entertaining (and imitated the by-then defunct radio program of its competitor newspaper, *Der Tog*), by offering "high quality" music from the orchestra of Joseph Rumshinsky and other well-known performers from the Yiddish theater; humorous sketches; and occasional speeches by Socialist candidates. (One of the earliest programs on September 25, 1932, featured a speech by gubernatorial candidate Louis Waldman who gave what was billed as "the first speech in Yiddish by a candidate for governor" in New York history. On one occasion, Vladeck went on the air to instruct new voters on how to use the voting machines.)

WEVD was soon a popular station, offering a variety of commercial and noncommercial programming produced by itself as well as independent broadcasters. Some of its programs were even simulcast over other New York stations, such as WJZ (on NBC's Blue Network). In 1937, it claimed that its own program, *The Forward Hour*, commanded the largest audience for a non-English program in the United States. In the same year, *Variety* cited the station as the outstanding station in the field of social service. The station maintained its "high culture" standards when it came to Yiddish programming, eventually serving as one forum for the prestigious (but short-lived) broadcasts of the Yiddish wing of the WPA's Theater division (which featured the members of ARTEF Workers Theater Group).

YIDDISH RADIO DURING WORLD WAR II

> [The news in Yiddish] was delivered by my father, Z.H. Rubinstein. Dad was born in Lemberg, Poland and I remember the day he reported the fall of that city to the Nazis. His voice on the air was steady but the tears rolled down his cheeks as he spoke of the fate of his hometown.
>
> —Sholom Rubinstein

Like other foreign-language radio stations, WEVD provided immigrants with news in their own languages, thereby providing people who were hampered by lack of proficiency to English with access to information. However, these news programs did more than just translate wire dispatches into Yiddish or Italian—they provided their own slant on current events and gave more news about "the old country" than the mainstream media offered.

As Arnheim and Bayne's 1941 report on foreign-language broadcasting noted:

[Foreign-language news broadcasts] contain about four times as many foreign as domestic items. . . . This shows that the foreign language news bulletins, rather than giving regular information on American affairs to people who prefer to hear it in their own language, complement American news fare with a greater supply of items from foreign sources.

The report found that Yiddish-language programs had the highest percentage of foreign news: 92.9 percent, as opposed to the 84.2 percent of Italian broadcasts or the 76.1 percent of Polish programs.

On the eve of America's entry into World War II, the researchers found that unlike mainstream news programs, the news on Yiddish radio had a strongly interventionist flavor:

Yiddish news announcers and commentators . . . show themselves eager to stress the importance of British victories and United States help: they express repugnance for the Nazi terror and refer to the anti-American spirit of Hitler sympathizers in this country. They are anti-German and pro-Roosevelt.

As Americans became increasingly polarized about isolationism vs. intervention in foreign affairs, foreign-language radio was charged not only with having poor programming and too many commercials, but also with being un-American. Groups like HUAC raised suspicions that sedition was being broadcast over the foreign-language airwaves and that the Americanization of immigrants was being retarded by the ethnic radio programs. Although German and Italian stations found themselves particularly scrutinized, Yiddish-language broadcasters were also subject to the scrutiny of other Congressional committees, as well as social scientists preoccupied with "solving the social problem of foreign-language groups."

In response to these attacks, liberal organizations such as the American Civil Liberties Union and the American Council for Unity conducted studies of foreign-language radio and testified in court on behalf of beleaguered ethnic broadcasters. The FCC gave serious thought to the idea of banning foreign-language broadcasts altogether and then decided that American security interests would be better served by regulating ethnic stations. In an address delivered before the American Civil Liberties Union on February 12, 1941, FCC Chairman James Lawrence Fly stated:

Current world conditions have also raised special problems—for example, the question of foreign language broadcasts by some of our domestic stations. Many who hear these programs without understanding them—and few of us can understand all of the 31 languages spoken over U.S. stations last year—are concerned lest, because the language is not English, the thoughts expressed must be un-American. . . . To discontinue foreign-language broadcasts, especially at a time when so many influences are competing for the allegiance of our foreign-born citizens and residents [would] tend to cut the off from the democratic influence of well-managed radio stations, broadcasting to them in the languages they best understand and to which they are most responsive. . . .

Indeed, even after America's entry into the war, foreign-language broadcasting was permitted to continue. Foreign-language broadcasters, like the mainstream media, were required to operate according to a system of self-censorship. Following the lead of the Office for War Information (OWI), the mainstream stations downplayed news of the Nazis' implementation of a "Final Solution" against European Jewry, preferring to speak in general terms about "victims of Hitlerism." In an era in which many Americans admitted to harboring anti-Semitic feelings, OWI research revealed that emphasizing the Jewish identities of victims alienated audiences, while reports of persecution which mentioned no ethnicity brought forth sympathy and indignation. Although information about the death camps was available to the American media as early as 1943, journalists feared arousing the public's skepticism.

Very little in the way of Yiddish or Jewish newscasting from the 1940s has survived. Interviews with radio personnel have revealed that while some news about the Holocaust was broadcast, more comprehensive reportage and commentary were reserved for the pages of the Yiddish press. Mass protest events and memorial gatherings, however, were often broadcast over local radio stations. One surviving example is a WNYC broadcast of the 1944 commemoration of the first anniversary of the Warsaw Ghetto Uprising on the steps of New York's City Hall, which includes a speech by Mayor Fiorello LaGuardia to a crowd of 25,000.

REFUGEES ON THE AIR

The plight of refugees from Hitler's Germany and later, Nazi-occupied Europe, provided a new focus for American Jews and Jewish broadcasters. Discussions on the air on stations like WEVD and WLTH explored the merits of various schemes to rescue European Jewry. As American Jewish leaders became more convinced that the lifting of British restrictions on Jewish immigration to Palestine offered a solution to the refugee crisis and as American Jews became increasingly more Zionist, the airwaves reverberated with talks and speeches by representatives of the various factions of the Zionist movement.

Aid organizations like the Joint Distribution Committee (JDC) and philanthropic agencies such as the newly formed United Jewish Appeal (UJA) used radio as a forum for raising public consciousness about refugees and for drumming up financial support for their work. One example of such programming is the 1943 "The Line Moves Slowly," a prose poem written by Robert Nathan chronicling the suffering of an individual refugee. The recitation of the poem by well-known actor Fredric March was followed by a speech by JDC Chairman Edward Warburg about the agency's activities in Europe.

Refugee actors and actresses found a venue on *Refugee Theater of the Air*, a dramatic series broadcast in Yiddish over WMCA in 1938, in which the performers acted out what might have been scenes from their own lives. Skits in the first episode included one in which a vaudeville troupe hears the news about the Austrian Anschluss, and another in which the performers agree to cut sad material from their acts "because there are a lot of Americans in the audience."

With the raised awareness about refugees, even mainstream radio began to feature sympathetic stories. CBS shows like *Columbia Workshop* presented Frank Lovejoy in "Mr. Cohen Takes a Walk" (1939), about a kind and humble Jewish merchant who secretly helps an anti-Semitic neighbor in trouble. Novelist Edna Ferber penned a radio drama in 1941 titled "A Cable from Lisbon," which took the form of a letter from a Polish Jewish refugee in a prison hospital.

After the war, the Hebrew Immigrant Aid Society (HIAS), United Service for New Americans (USNA), JDC, and other refugee advocacy groups used radio programs to campaign for the admittance of increased numbers of what were now called "displaced persons" (or "DPs") into the United States. These radio programs were produced by the organizations, sent out to radio stations, and broadcast in various cities.

USNA was one of the most prolific producers of pro-DP propaganda, broadcasting dozens of English-language radio programs over local radio networks. Their program formats included docudrama radio plays; talk shows in which government officials discussed the plight of refugees and the desirability of permitting their mass immigration to the United States; broadcasts of pro-DP speeches by government officials and Jewish leaders on the same theme; and a "This Is Your Life"–type studio program titled *Reunion* on which survivors were reunited with loved ones and related the horrors of their wartime experiences before a live audience.

USNA's radio plays continued in Jewish radio's tradition of preferring family dramas. The organization's radio plays reduce the political issues surrounding immigration policy to the level of family dramas. Surviving examples include "This Is New Jersey" (date unknown) in which the refugee Schneider family settles on a chicken farm and are given a helping hand by their neighbors, "the people of New Jersey"; and *The Golden Door* series (ca. 1947), which featured dramatized human-interest stories about DPs.

In *Reunion*, onstage reunions (complete with heartrending shrieks and hysterical crying) between Holocaust survivors and family members who had managed to immigrate to the United States before the war, were sandwiched in between less traumatic reunions between American high school buddies and girlhood friends, all taking place in front of a studio audience.

Hardly any pro-DP radio writer could resist using the Statue of Liberty as a motif—many of the radio dramas contain a climax in which arriving immigrants encounter the Statue in New York Harbor. American icons offered the American Jewish organizations an apt symbol for the conflation of American and Jewish history. In fact, the organizations made other attempts to recast postwar Jewish immigration to the U.S. in the mold of American history by likening the refugees to the pilgrims of the Mayflower and even, in one episode of *The Eternal Light* (a program initiated by David Sarnoff, and coproduced by NBC and the Jewish Theological Seminary) to Native Americans who crossed the Bering Strait!

THE DECLINE OF JEWISH RADIO

> We had 12 different languages on the station: we had Greek, we had Italian, we had Yiddish, we had Japanese, we had Chinese—like we had a League of Nations. So it was 'the station that speaks your language' but not anymore! The Italian disappeared, the Greek disappeared, I'm slowly disappearing. . . .
> —Art Raymond, host of a Jewish music radio program

Within a decade after the end of World War II, Jewish radio—and all foreign-language broadcasting was on the decline in the United States. A 1949 CCAU report on foreign-language broadcasting noted that even while there was a "boom" in American broadcasting as a whole, foreign language broadcasting was decreasing:

While about one-sixth of the U.S. local stations carried foreign-language programs in 1944, less than one twelfth did so in January 1948. Moreover, in the past six years the total "time on air" of foreign-language programs have been discontinued. Twenty-six stations have cancelled their entire foreign-language schedule.

The reasons for the decline of Jewish and other ethnic radio are not entirely clear. Many factors pointed to the survival of Jewish, and even Yiddish radio. The postwar influx of Jewish Holocaust survivors provided new potential listeners for Jewish programs. Moreover, surveys and other studies showed that many second-generation American Jews listened regularly to

Jewish and Yiddish radio. Commercially, foreign-language stations were doing well. As the CCCAU report pointed out:

The curious fact is that foreign language programs, such as they are, continue to be very profitable.... Another paradox is that foreign language programs are being dropped at a time when they have again demonstrated their capacity to hold reliable audiences. As a matter of fact, a number of stations and programs have noted an increase in their audiences since the war—WOV, for instance . . . and WFOX's "Jewish Morning Hour" (Milwaukee, Wisconsin).

The creation of the State of Israel and the new support for Zionism within the established American Jewish community might have led to a new sense of Jewish pride, which could have manifested itself on the radio airwaves. Even in the early years of the Cold War, when "100 Percent Americanism" was stressed, foreign-language radio might have been utilized as a medium for patriotic propaganda (as it had been during the war). The CCCAU suggested just such a role for ethnic radio:

In national and international terms, the existence of foreign language radio in this country, with a potential audience the size of the total French audience . . . is one of the most powerful illustrations of American democracy at work, and a clear demonstration of the truth that people of many different origins, keeping their own customs and languages, can live and work together in peace. . . . No other country has so many personal contacts with so many different peoples, and such a potential army of propagandists for peace.

Supporters of ethnic radio also had answers to the old charge that foreign-language radio hampered the Americanization of new immigrants. They were able to point to ways in which such programs could "give some information of value for the adjustment of the foreign born to the American way of life." (One ethnic station, WHOM in New York, even expanded their public service profile by offering a program called "Operation Naturalization," an Americanization evening class which was conducted at their studios.) However, these feeble attempts to make ethnicity seem downright American were not strong enough to counter the assimilatory pressures of the era.

In the late 1940s and the early 1950s, station after station cancelled foreign-language broadcasting and announced decisions to broadcast only English-language programs. Sometimes the cancellation of ethnic time slots resulted in lawsuits by foreign-language broadcasters who claimed that the stations were violating the principle of free speech and working against the public interest. The stations were often able to get judges to dismiss the suits on the grounds that occasional "religious programming" fulfilled their mandate of providing a public service.

Moreover, stations that switched to "All-American" formats were able to cite the "poor quality" of many foreign-language programs. Non-network radio had never really divested itself of its low-culture image. Even its supporters acknowledged that the content of many ethnic programs left much to be desired, blaming the "time-broker" system on which many ethnic broadcasters depended:

The "time-broker" system and the necessity of relying on many different sponsors ... acts as a straight jacket [sic] on the foreign-language broadcaster ... the overdose of commercial spots disrupts his program and makes intelligent programming virtually impossible.... He has no time to think of anything other than "giving the sponsors what they pay for"....

Some ethnic broadcasters and their supporters noted that the average foreign-language programmer operated as an "isolated unit," making it "extremely difficult for him to defend his rights and his position." There were attempts to form foreign-language broadcast associations, and local ethnic broadcasters might pool their efforts in lawsuits against stations that cancelled their programs, but overall, little came of these efforts.

Jewish radio programming became increasingly stagnant after World War II. Television stole away the audiences of even mainstream radio. Its national, rather than local nature, helped perpetuate the notion that there could be a homogenous "American" culture.

The discouragement of ethnicity was felt in all areas of Jewish culture. The Yiddish theater was on the wane and assimilation on the rise. Jewish musicians, writers, and artists were crossing over to the mainstream and identifying as American, rather than Jewish or Yiddish artists. Little was being created in the way of new Yiddish music, theater, or literature. Art Raymond, the host of a Jewish music show on WEVD, remembers coming to the station for the first time in the late 1950s:

There was so little Jewish music available on records at that time, so the staff announcers were playing old records, and mostly they were playing cantors. All the guys who were dead ... and so before and after every record practically that they played it was *olev hasholom* [rest in peace]. ... "We're going to listen to Yosele Rosenblatt, *olev hasholom*...." To me it was the Undertakers' Network.

The rise of Hebrew and the popularity of Zionism helped redirect Jews to Israel as a source of culture and pride. American Jewish children moved to the suburbs away from daily contact with Yiddish-speaking extended family and went to Hebrew school in the afternoons. New Jewish music played on the radio was apt to come from Israel: the Hebrew folk and pop songs might inspire, but they were not relevant to everyday American life in the way that the old Yiddish songs had been.

Even as they were helping a Jewish immigrant class assimilate into American mainstream culture, Jewish broadcasters were sowing the seeds of their own demise. Yet today, Yiddish radio is can be periodically heard in New York and other cities as one of many ethnic voices on the airwaves, on stations that are preserving an important tradition by giving new immigrant communities access to their own cultures within the larger American experience.

FURTHER READING

Sapoznik, Henry. *Klezmer! Jewish Music From Old World to Our World*. New York: Schirmer Books, 1999.
The Yiddish Radio Project website www.yiddishradioproject.org.

Chapter 10

Jews on the Radio, 1920–1953
Ari Y. Kelman

Between 1920 and 1953, radio was the dominant medium in the United States and, arguably, in the world. Every major performer from stage and screen appeared on radio, and nearly everyone who wrote or performed anything dramatic, musical, or literary either made guest appearances or offered their work for on-air adaptations. In some respects, radio seemed like an extension of the stage, screen, and page, and given the prominence of Jews in American popular music and performance, their presence on the airwaves is a function of their involvement in entertainment more broadly.

This chapter will focus on Jews who were involved in radio from the medium's popularization during the early 1920s through 1953. I offer two reasons for this periodization. The first reason is the rise of the popularization of television, which exploded in 1953, turning it from a novelty into a near necessity and a replacement for radio at the center of the domestic entertainment industry. American audiences who formerly listened to prime-time radio broadcasts now gathered around their televisions, and sponsors and corporate interests that previously backed radio shows followed their audience to the new medium. Ironically, television featured many of the same performers as radio had only a year earlier. The second reason follows from the first. With attention focused on television, the radio industry responded by expanding the number of available radio licenses during the early 1950s, in the hopes of reinvigorating radio as listening opportunities also expanded. In addition to opening up the airwaves, the postwar economic boom supported suburbanization, which, in turn, led to increased commuting time and the creation of "drive time" radio. The invention of the transistor made radios cheaper and more portable than before, and the sound of radio shifted from that of serials and soap operas to news stations and disc jockeys.

This chapter is divided into two sections: "Behind the Scenes," which focuses on the roles of people, like David Sarnoff, the president of RCA and founder of NBC, William Paley, CBS president, and writer/producer/performer Gertrude Berg, in the development and growth of the radio industry. The radio industry is virtually unimaginable without the efforts—for better and for worse—of these individuals behind the scenes. The section "On the Air," addresses the persona—both real and fictional—of Jewish radio performers. Gertrude Berg figures significantly here as well, alongside performers like Al Jolson, Eddie Cantor, Mel Blanc, and others, who left their deepest impression on the medium through their performances on the air.

BEHIND THE SCENES

Born in 1891 in the *shtetl* of Uzlian, a small town southeast of Minsk, David Sarnoff was arguably the most influential figure in American radio. As a youngster, he was schooled in *kheder* (traditional religious school for boys), before leaving with his family to join his father who had already settled in New York. Sarnoff, like most immigrants his age, attended public school and studied at the Educational Alliance, a Lower East Side institution intended to help Jewish immigrants develop the skills to succeed in America. And, like most immigrants, his family struggled and young Sarnoff tried to help out, beginning with a job as a newsboy selling the Yiddish daily *Tageblatt*, before moving up to open a delivery service, catering to local newsstands.

His career in radio began as a telegraph operator for the Marconi Company, where the myth has it that he helped relay the message that the Titanic had sunk. By 1915—still five years before the first recognized radio broadcast—the enterprising young Sarnoff had developed the idea of the "radio music box," the precursor to today's radio receivers. When General Electric bought the American arm of the Marconi Company to create the Radio Corporation of America, Sarnoff was in position to become President, an office he assumed in 1930. Initially a producer of radio receivers, RCA was to spin-off the National Broadcast Company and, under Sarnoff's direction, become one of the most lucrative and influential forces in radio. Sarnoff fought hard for commercial broadcasting and, in 1926, arranged the first coast-to-coast broadcast by stringing together individual stations telephone cables leased from AT&T, thus creating the first national broadcast network.

While Sarnoff was growing NBC, he developed relationships with a handful of Jewish leaders on the Lower East Side, including Barch Charney Vladeck, who turned to Sarnoff for advice about building a radio tower for the *Jewish Daily Forward* in 1923.

Sarnoff's chief rival in network radio was William S. Paley, who began his memoir by stating, "I was the child of immigrants." Born in Chicago to a middle-class family in 1901, Paley observed that his family "lived in unquestioned consciousness of being Jews," but added that he found Jewish ritual "worse than boring," and recalled that he memorized the Torah portion he was to read for confirmation phonetically, "and did not understand a single word." However, his life as a youngster in Chicago appeared Jewish enough, moving as a small child from "west of the loop" to the large Jewish neighborhood in Rogers Park. After a stint in Western Military Academy in Allton, Illinois, Paley returned to Chicago, enrolled in the University of Chicago and joined the Jewish fraternity, *Zeta Beta Tau*.

Later, Paley and his father relocated to Philadelphia and took over partial responsibility for the family's cigar business, a Jewish industry during the early 1920s. Socially, Paley traveled in primarily Jewish circles and fondly recalled an episode with noted Philadelphia gangster Max "Boo Boo" Hoff and his friendship with Ben Gimbel of the Gimbel's department store family.

His first foray into radio was as the sponsor of *The La Palina Smoker*, a thirty-minute variety-type program on WCAU, a local Philadelphia station owned by Isaac and Leon Levy. At the time, WCAU was a member of the United Independent Broadcasters, a fledgling network that had recently teamed up with the Columbia Phonograph Broadcasting System to expand the number of affiliates to sixteen. By 1927, the UIB was in trouble and Paley orchestrated a buyout, assuming ownership of the enterprise. Two years later, CBS had forty-nine stations in forty-two cities in its network. Paley actively promoted himself and his network as the rival to NBC, hiring stars like Paul Whiteman and Will Rogers to give his network a little star power, working out a deal with the New York Metropolitan Opera, and signing crooner Bing Crosby, whom he put opposite NBC's most popular program, *Amos 'n' Andy*.

Paley recalled canceling Father Coughlin for his "messages of hate and extreme political views," but did not mention Father Coughlin's penchant for anti-Semitism, focusing instead on the growth of his network, which soon challenged NBC for radio dominance. Part of Paley's strategy for taking the lead on radio included raiding NBC for talent and signing away some of Sarnoff's most popular and lucrative names.

While Paley and Sarnoff worked entirely behind the scenes, Gertrude Berg created them, becoming, along with Freeman Gosden and Charles Correll (the writers and performers of *Amos 'n' Andy*), one of the most powerful figures in early radio and becoming at least partially responsible for establishing its viability as an entertainment source and an industry. Berg, who began her career writing short skits for the guests at Fleischmann's, the Catskills resort owned by her parents, launched *The Rise of the Goldbergs* in 1929 on NBC without a sponsor (Fleischmann's, incidentally, was founded and first owned by the family of the same name who earned a fortune selling yeast and became Rudy Vallee's [not Jewish] first sponsor). While Berg's role as a performer will be discussed below, as a producer and writer she helped establish the financial viability of radio by achieving nationwide popularity which, according to NBC, was "not limited to any one section or to the audience of several stations." As the writer and principal performer on the program, Berg pioneered product tie-ins with her sponsors and used her character's popularity to produce a collection of short stories "translated" from the show's first season (with an introduction by Eddie Cantor), a number of stage plays, a feature film, and a cookbook. Berg parlayed her matronly character into a virtual media machine in its own right, and used the confusion between herself and her on-air persona to stimulate interest and pathos.

One person who had little sympathy for Berg was radio producer Himan Brown, who later became a successful director of classic radio programs like *Adventures of the Thin Man, The Affairs of Peter Salem, Dick Tracy, Grand Central Station*, and *Inner Sanctum*, which takes credit for turning the creaky door from a nuisance to a horror-genre standard. Born in Brooklyn, Brown recalled his first exposure to radio, "I was in knee pants, and a shop teacher at Boys High School said, 'There's a new thing now, radio,' . . . .You bring in a Quaker Oats box and wrap copper wire around it and you heard WLW in Cincinnati. What a revelation that was right here in Brooklyn." Not quite 18 years old, he started on radio with a series of poetic readings called *Hi-Brow Readings,* before debuting a program that featured him reading Milt Gross' cartoon *Nize Baby* in its trademark Jewish dialect (Milt Gross himself had been on radio, too, appearing alongside comedian Harry Hirschfeld, Jimmy Hussey, and animator Max Fleischer, creator of Betty Boop and Popeye, in a 1926 show called *The Jewish Poker Game* on New York's WGBS).

Brown recalled meeting Berg. "One morning a lady called. She said she was living in the Bronx—her name was Gertrude Berg and she had a series called *The Rise of Molly Goldberg* [sic] and would I come and talk to her because I could play Jake with her. She enjoyed my Jewish dialect." Brown agreed, and played Jake for six months, after which Berg, he recalled, "told me to get lost." After that, he teamed up with Julie Birns on a program called *The Bronx Marriage Bureau* and an Italian knockoff of *The Goldbergs* called *Little Italy*, where he, again played the father. Later in his career, Brown went on to produce numerous television programs and promotional materials for the Jewish Federation of New York.

In a more explicitly Jewish format, writer Morton Wischengrad specialized in melodrama, and had many opportunities to display his dramatic skills as the head writer for *The Eternal Light*, a program underwritten by the Jewish Theological Seminary that depicted American Jewish life. The Eternal light debuted in 1944 and aired for nearly twenty years on NBC, and Wischengrad went on to win the Peabody award in 1948 for the patriotic program, "Communism, US Brand." Wischengrad's involvement in radio and television made him one of the most prominent Jewish voices in postwar American media.

Far from the radio studio, agent Abe Lastfogel represented some of the biggest stars in radio including Jimmy Durante, Eddie Cantor, George Burns, Gracie Allen, director Fred Zinneman, Danny Thomas, Dick Powell, David Niven, Fanny Brice, Frank Sinatra, Katharine Hepburn, Spencer Tracy, Lana Turner, Rita Hayworth, Walter Matthau, Al Jolson, Mae West, Edward G. Robinson, James Cagney, Will Rogers, and Elvis Presley. Lastfogel worked for the William Morris Agency, where he began his career in the mailroom before becoming the head of WMA's Los Angeles office, at which time, Lastfogel, a Jewish immigrant, had become one of the most powerful agents in entertainment.

On a much smaller scale, Morris Novick, who immigrated from Russia as a young child, served as the program director at WEVD, where he practically defined public interest radio, earning widespread praise for his cultivation of relevant and highly intellectual English-language programs. Under Novick's direction, WEVD launched programs like the *University of the Air*, and helped make the station one of the leading sources of political and intellectual programming. Interestingly, Novick, who began his career as the program director for Unity House, the ILGWU's summer resort in the Catskills, avoided responsibility for the station's Yiddish programs that, ironically, bear a more prominent legacy.

Many more hosted local radio programs on the margins of the radio world: in New York, Meyer Horowitz, who hosted the Village Grove Nut Club, from the Village Grove Restaurant on Sheridan Square three times a week from 23:00 P.M. until 2:00 A.M.; still others, like Hugo Gernsback, who coined the term "science fiction;" and small-time businessmen like Sidney Baruch, Sam Gellard, Rabbi Aaron Kronenberg, and Herman Lubinsky—who went on to found the influential jazz label, Savoy Records—owned some of the smaller, independent radio stations that dotted New York's radio landscape.

In academia, Theodor Adorno became one of the most prominent observers and commentators on the cultural phenomena around radio. Born in Germany, Adorno came to the United States in 1938, with his friend and colleague Max Horkheimer to work with sociologist Paul Lazarsfeld at the Princeton Radio Project at Princeton University. The Radio Project was the first academic institute dedicated to the study of radio, and despite his role as the Project's "music director," Adorno butted heads with Lazarsfeld and left for Los Angeles in 1941.

ON THE AIR

Coming from the stages of vaudeville and Broadway, Jewish performers like Al Jolson, Fanny Brice, and Sophie Tucker had established themselves in popular media long before radio. Thus, radio sponsors were quick to capitalize on both the conventions of performance and recognition of performers.

Consequently, many radio performers rooted their success, as well, in already lucrative careers off the air, and the roster of early Jewish radio stars almost parallels that of the stage.

Sophie Tucker (born 1884) already had become a nationally recognized star by the time radio became a national phenomenon. Tucker, known as the "last of the red-hot mommas" came out of vaudeville and began appearing regularly on radio in 1926, on a program called *Theater Magazine*. Capitalizing on her fame, Tucker earned her own program, *The Sophie Tucker Playhouse Program* and later led *The Sophie Tucker Orchestra* in 1936.

Similarly, Fanny Brice played her success off the air into a career on it. Brice had long since become one of America's most popular comediennes before she earned a regular place on radio. During her vaudeville days, she created a character called Baby Snooks, a whiny toddler that always played to big laughs. In 1936, she performed Baby Snooks for the Ziegfeld Follies radio show, and the character became a regular on the vaudeville program *Good News*, where her character played until 1948. By the mid-1940s, Snooks had become so popular that she earned her own show, behind the writing strength of Dave Freedman and Phil Rapp, who also wrote for Eddie Cantor, among other performers.

Al Jolson traced a similar career path to the radio, with a reputation as America's most popular singer and having starred in *The Jazz Singer* (1927), the first movie with synchronized sound. The following year, he began performing on radio and finally earned his own program on NBC, as the host of *Presenting Al Jolson* in 1932. Despite his fame, the program failed, but Jolson proved too promising a vehicle for investors and in 1934, he was back on the air as the host of *The Kraft Music Hall* before moving in as the host of *The Shell Chateau*, a 60-minute Saturday night variety program. In 1936, he moved again, leaving NBC for *The Lifebuoy Program* on CBS, where he would end his radio career having earned only modest success.

Unlike Jolson, Eddie Cantor found even greater fame on radio than he knew as a star of the stage. Cantor was raised by his grandmother on the Lower East Side, where he attended the Educational Alliance and Surprise Lake camp, where he began performing. To earn extra income, Cantor also worked for the Isaac Gellis sausage factory (which later became an early sponsor of Yiddish radio). As a young man, Cantor performed widely with George Jessel, singing Irving Berlin songs and winning Jewish fans by speaking "not with a Yiddish accent, but with Yiddish inflections." After a few guest appearances on Rudy Vallee's *Fleishmann's Hour*, Chase and Sandborn invited him to host their eponymous radio program, for which he hired writer David Freedman, while still working on stage *revues* with Jessel, George Burns, and Gracie Allen and others, whose careers he helped launch by inviting them to perform on his program. Cantor was instrumental in helping George Jessel find his place on radio, although Jessel ultimately became much better known for producing films.

Cantor quickly became one of the most popular performers on radio and, unlike most other Jewish performers of his stature, remained deeply involved in Jewish organizations and concerns. In 1932, he took the presidency of the Jewish Theatrical Guild, a position he held for the next thirty years. Cantor used his fame to establish philanthropies for Surprise Lake and Hebrew University, and raise money for numerous other Jewish causes. Although known as a comic, Cantor also earned a reputation for his outspoken stances against anti-Semitism, Henry Ford, and Father Charles Coughlin, and for his support of the WPA Federal Arts Project, for which his sponsor, R.J. Reynolds, dropped him.

George Jessel introduced Arthur Tracy to Eddy Cantor when Tracy was still living in Philadelphia. With his new connections, Tracy moved to New York and began performing in Yiddish theater before being discovered by Broadway producers, Lee, Jake, and Sam Shubert, who also claim to have given Al Jolson his first break on Broadway. The Shuberts promoted his stage and recording careers, which he bolstered by cultivating a dedicated radio audience through his performances as the mysterious "Street Singer." Among the first to turn the disembodied voice of radio performers into a marketing ploy, The mystery lasted only a few months, but by then, Tracy had developed a significant following and began appearing as himself on radio and off it.

George Burns also benefited from his association with Eddie Cantor. Burns' father was a part-time cantor and got his start singing in the Peewee Quartet, a vocal group of Jewish boys, before touring with the "Fourth of July Kids," where he met both Cantor and Jessel. In 1922, Burns teamed up with Gracie Allen, and after almost ten years of continuous touring, they became regular guests on Cantor's radio program before earning their own program and their own fans.

Burns and Allen settled in Beverly Hills, where they quickly became best friends with Jack Benny and his family. Benny was born into to a "conventional, warmhearted Jewish family," began his career playing violin in the pit orchestra of a vaudeville theater in his hometown of Waukegan, Illinois. He eventually met his wife Sadie Marks at a *Passover seder* in Vancouver in 1921, to which he was brought by Zeppo Marx, a distant relative of the hosts. Benny began his career with a guest spot on the Ed Sullivan show before earning his own program with the sponsorship of Canada Dry, General Tires, and General Foods. By 1937, *The Jack Benny Show* had become the most popular program on radio. His wife Sadie played his on-air spouse so well that they had her name legally changed to Mary Livingstone—the character's name. Benny played a well-intentioned but congenitally foolish character who became the butt of almost every joke on the show. Benny wrote, "I was as much the fall guy for Rochester (his African-American butler played by Eddie Anderson) as I was for Phil Harris or Mary Livingstone." Benny also featured a fictional Jewish character named *Mister Kitzel*, played by dialect comedian

Artie Auebach, and explained the source of the character in the following way. "Don't ask me why this became funny when we translated it into Jewish dialect—but it did." Once, a joke about Southern Methodist University provoked letters of response from the two Jewish fraternities at the school and an invitation to Mr. Kitzel's son to pledge ZBT. During World War II, Benny did his part to support the war effort and joined the USO, noting, "but for the grace of God and my father's emigration, I could have been one of the victims of Dachau or Buchenwald or Auschwitz."

Jack Benny's on-air rival was the non-Jewish Fred Allen, for whom novelist Herman Wouk worked as a writer for a time. Benny's distant cousins, Groucho, and Chico Marx hosted a short-lived show called "*Flywheel, Shyster and Flywheel*," which was but one failure among many for Groucho's radio career. Groucho, despite his wide success on stage and screen could not find a suitable radio vehicle until promoter John Guedel invited him to ad lib as the host of *You Bet Your Life* in 1947.

Benny also gave vocal comedian Mel Blanc his start on radio. Blanc, known as the "man of a thousand voices," and the genius behind the animated characters Tweety Bird, Sylvester the Cat, and Bugs Bunny, began on radio in 1935, playing a duck on the Joe Penner Show. Sometimes, he worked more than twenty different shows each week, as a one-man sound effect, appearing as Jack Benny's beleaguered car and Judy Canova's Mexican handyman, Pedro. Eventually he earned his own program on CBS in the mid-1940s. Blanc recalled his first radio character, which eventually grew into Porky Pig: "Leon called me in and asked me if I could do a pig—a fine thing to ask a Jewish kid." Blanc, who remained friendly with Benny, frequently told of his desire to buy a Rolls Royce and have "KMIT" on the license plate—*Kish Mir Im Tuchas*, "kiss my ass" in Yiddish.

Yiddish frequently snuck onto radio surreptitiously, and found more expressions in accent than outright in Yiddish words. One of the most popular Yiddish dialect performers was Gertrude Berg, the brains behind *The Rise of the Goldbergs*. Born in East Harlem, Berg became a national figure with the success of her radio program and her signature "Yoo Hoo! Mrs. Bloom!" became something of a national phenomenon. She wrote and performed her scripts in Jewish dialect, because, she claimed, she was "trying to be authentic" and make her program about "ordinary people." For her character Molly Goldberg, "next to the constitution of the United States, the ten commandments came first." After beginning without a sponsor, she quickly earned the support of Pepsodent and became the nation's second most popular program. Berg hired Yiddish theater comedian Menasha Skulnik to play Uncle David, and actor Phillip Loeb to play Jake. Loeb eventually was named in the HUAC anticommunist purge of the early 1950s, which drove him to commit suicide in 1955, despite Berg's defense of him.

Like Gertrude Berg, comedian Ed Wynn straddled the line between production and performance. Wynn made his radio debut in 1922, when he played "the perfect fool" on WJZ in Newark. On this program, Wynn's producers first introduced the "live studio adueince" to radio, and Wynn became one of the first performers to integrate humor into broadcast advertising. By 1932, Wynn had signed on with Texaco to play "the fire chief," a comical character with an infectious high-pitched laugh, which became his signature role. Always looking for an angle, Wynn invested in the Amalgamated Broadcasting System, which he hoped would compete with NBC and CBS for a national audience. Wynn turned New York station WBNX—a popular station for non-English-language programs through the 1940s—into the nascent network's anchor, and celebrated his new endeavor with a feast of hot dogs, pastrami, and salami sandwiches. The network, however, proved less memorable than the feast, and it quickly disappeared, along with a substantial portion of Wynn's investment.

Jewish bandleaders Benny Goodman and Jule Styne led their own musical programs during the 1930s. In December of 1934, the Goodman Orchestra was one of three bands hired for NBC's new three-hour music program *Let's Dance*, an important vehicle in the popularization of swing music among white Americans.

One of the most beloved and famous voices in all of radio belonged to Mel Allen. Allen began his career on radio after entering the Army in 1943 where he served on *The Army Hour* and other Armed Forces Service radio programs. Allen was one of 500,000 Jews to serve in the American military during World War II, and one of many to turn his experience there into a career in the years following when he became a popular sports announcer.

CONCLUSION

The role of Jews in the radio business between 1920 and 1953 speaks to a few parallel phenomena from which it cannot be isolated. The great immigration of Jews of eastern European descent that began around 1880 and ended decisively in 1924 found 2.5 million Jewish immigrants living in American cities seeking entertainment and employment. Performance seemed to provide, for those with the appropriate talents, an opportunity for both. For those with other talents, the upsurge in activity and creativity in American urban centers fostered numerous other opportunities for people to take advantage of emergent economies and industries.

Radio grew out of vaudeville and out of the press. It owed debts to both businessmen with big dreams and local appliance dealers who turned their storefronts into broadcast studios. Jewish immigrants (and members of other immigrant groups, too) stood poised to take advantage of these opportunities when they presented themselves, and thus create the phenomenon of Jews on American radio.

FURTHER READING

Berg, Gertrude. *Molly and Me*. New York: McGraw Hill, 1961.
Fein, Irving. *Jack Benny: An Intimate Biography*. New York: Putnam, 1976.
Goldman, Herbert. *Banjo Eyes: Eddie Cantor and the Birth of Modern Stardom*. New York: Oxford University Press, 1997.
Hoberman, J. and Jeff Shandler. eds. *Entertaining America: Jews, Movies, and Broadcasting*. Princeton and New York: Princeton University Press and the Jewish Museum, 2003.
Kelman, A. Y. *Station Identification: A Cultural History of Yiddish Radio in America*. Berkeley, CA: University of California Press, forthcoming, 2007.
MacDonald, Fred J. *Don't Touch that Dial! Radio Programming in American Life from 1920–1960*. Chicago: Nelson-Hall, 1979.

Chapter 11

Jewish Talk Radio: Programming in Our Time and Place

Ariana Green

In an age when Christian talk radio generates buzz and a mass audience, Jewish talk radio is understudied and not well known. It encompasses more than one might think. When the words "Jewish" and "talk radio" are paired together, perhaps Al Franken or Howard Stern, or maybe a liberal host on National Public Radio (NPR) or a Jewish station owner come to mind? Only a rare breed—mostly very observant Jews residing in, say, New York—will conjure images of a talk radio program that deals with Jewish social and political issues from a Jewish perspective, one that might mix in some Cantorial music and kosher restaurant advertisements for good measure. These radio shows exist in the United States, and Jews and non-Jews alike tune in— increasingly so now that the Internet is redefining radio, making it both worldwide and cheap to disseminate.

This chapter presents a picture of U.S. Jewish talk radio at the beginning of the twenty-first century. In November of 2005, the author interviewed many of the prominent personalities in Jewish talk radio, and their perspectives are shared in the coming pages. These individuals are first introduced in "the cast of characters" section, in which they comment on Jewish programming. Later in the chapter, they tell of their career trajectories. To the best of the editor's knowledge, this chapter is the first scholarly work that sets the stories of the major Jewish talk programmers side by side, documenting and comparing their journeys and visions.

It becomes clear in this examination that most hosts of Jewish programming per se are men, and that those men are by in large politically right of center, which, it should be noted, contrasts with the predominant view of talk radio Jews as left-wingers. One of the few women in Jewish radio, Marilyn Kleinberg Neimark of the Pacifica Network affiliate WBAI's show

"Beyond the Pale: Radical Jewish Culture and Politics," argues that Jewish radio's association with political and religious conservatism is precisely what keeps it marginal, even among Jews. Her show, the only self-declared left-wing Jewish show broadcasting nationally in 2005, has a small, loyal liberal following in New York. However, she is far outnumbered by conservative male hosts throughout the country.

Rife with a unique set of challenges and opportunities, Jewish talk radio's development is intertwined with the rise of niche programming and innovative technology. Yet despite new frontiers for Jewish radio, funding and mass listenership remain hard to attract.

A HISTORY OF AIR TIME: U.S. JEWISH RADIO THROUGH THE AGES

Although this chapter focuses on contemporary programmers, Jewish radio is not new. It is, however, poorly documented. Radio historian Donna Halper, one of the few scholars who has studied Jewish radio's history, penned a seminal piece in the *Encyclopedia of Radio*, to which readers are directed for further information.

Halper asserts that Jewish radio goes as far back as the 1920s. A synagogue service from Baltimore was broadcast via a ham radio in 1921, and on February 12, 1922, KDKA broadcast a service from Pittsburgh's Temple Rodef Shalom, where Rabbi Solomon Goldenson spoke.

Soon, Jewish radio moved beyond just recording of religious services. New York's WRNY broadcast a Jewish wedding—bride Winnie Gordon and groom Julius Goldberg, as well as Rabbi Josef Hoffman, got airtime for the celebration in March 1926.

Jewish radio was used to advance causes. Rabbi Stephen S. Wise, a well-known New York City rabbi quoted in *The New York Times* and *Time* magazine stories, urged radio listeners to donate to European Jewish refugees in 1922.

In late August 1923, New York's WEAF began airing a weekly Jewish show that included Jewish folk and liturgical music in Yiddish and Hebrew, along with discussions of Jewish holidays and conversations with U.S. Jewish speakers.

The FCC at the time required a percentage of religious and public service programming, and shows like that started by the Hadassah organization helped meet the mandate. Just over a decade after the first Jewish program, major networks also caught on. In 1935, NBC started airing "Message of Israel," featuring famous Reform rabbis, including Boston's Harry Levi.

World War II changed the tone of Jewish shows. Halper writes:

While news of Hitler and the Nazis dominated the newspapers, some Jewish radio programs began providing news and information that the network newscasts were still not saying much about. Rabbi Stephen Wise took to the airwaves to condemn the prejudice of Father Charles Coughlin, the anti-Semitic radio priest. The chairmen and women of many Jewish organizations decried the persecution of Jews in Europe and tried to raise funds to help them. But Jewish programs were usually short and seldom on the air more than once a week; while they did call attention to the problems Jews faced, they could not compensate for the lack of coverage the rest of the week.

In October 1944, the Jewish Theological Seminary put "The Eternal Light" on air, a show developed by Seminary president Louis Finkelstein. It included radio dramas about biblical personalities, as well as famous Jews. "It often presented thought-provoking stories with ethical dimensions, and it was still on the air (having moved to TV) in the late 1970s," Halper writes.

Jewish celebrities have dabbled in Jewish radio. Parodist and comedian Mickey Katz did a show in the 1950s in Los Angeles, while actor and folksinger Theodore Bikel created "Thedore Bikel at Home," which aired on FM stations in New York, Chicago and Los Angeles in the 1960s. Zvi Scooler, an actor in Yiddish theater, did commentary on New York's WEVD for four decades.

As researchers investigate what has been left out of Jewish radio's record, it is this author's hope that the quotations and interviews collected from living Jewish radio programmers for this chapter will spur interest in the topic. The stories of Jewish radio must be read in the context of their time and place. They can in turn provide a more complete picture of these times and our places.

THE CAST OF CHARACTERS: COMMENTING ON U.S. JEWISH RADIO

Zev Brenner

"One of the biggest challenges is getting more mainstream companies to advertise to the Jewish marketplace," said Zev Brenner, president and executive producer of Talkline Communications Network, which he founded in 1981. An ordained rabbi turned pioneer of Jewish radio, Brenner hosts his own show, "Talkline with Zev Brenner," and also buys time for Jewish radio on stations throughout the country. He is heard online at http://talklinecommunications.com. "I would say I also face challenges in terms of programming," he continued. "There are people who won't advertise with us because they think we're too controversial, and since we refuse to shy away and aren't afraid of saying things different from what the choir wants to hear, our programming decisions can affect us [financially]."

Brenner, a former optician, has made his living for the past twenty-four years from Jewish radio. Although he identifies as a politically conservative Orthodox Jew, he said he makes a point to interview diverse guests on his show—among them Al Sharpton, Bill Clinton, and Mikhail Gorbachev. One of the best-known Jewish radio protagonists, Brenner said he is committed to making Jewish talk more accessible.

"We're on the Internet, and we're also launching a 24-hour-per-day Jewish satellite radio channel," he said. "We're hoping to feed iPods and cell phones soon. I spoke to a manufacturer that would make radio Sabbath combatable. If you're cooking, you would be able to listen through the oven, which is really cutting edge [and would not violate Sabbath laws]."

Brenner said he hopes to broaden his impact on the Jewish community. "I'm most proud that we give the Jewish community a voice, especially with elected officials," he said. "We make known what the average [Jewish] person is thinking, and we let people hear different perspectives."

B'nai B'rith

The Jewish organization B'nai B'rith, founded in 1883, began a radio program in 2005. At this writing, the programming is just online, but staff said station time is on the horizon.

B'nai B'rith describes itself as "an international Jewish organization committed to the security and continuity of the Jewish people and the State of Israel, defending human rights, combating anti-Semitism, bigotry and ignorance, and providing service to the community on the broadest principles of humanity." A radio program, it is thought, could advance the mission.

Longtime staff member Harvey Berk, who was involved in spearheading the radio project, said that unlike most of the other Jewish radio programs in existence, B'nai B'rith's does not approach issues from a right-of-center, Orthodox perspective. "Most of those existing models [of Jewish talk radio] have a very limited focus," said Berk. "We're looking for something that really creates a different sort of model, that says you don't have to be involved in the Jewish community to care about these issues. For example, we interviewed somebody inducted into the NFL hall of fame, a Jewish football player, but I can't think of other Jewish radio shows that would do something on someone like that who just happens to be Jewish."

Phil Fink

Phil Fink has been in radio since 1963. He began his professional career as a host and producer of a college program and went on to become a jazz disk jockey of a commercial radio station in Cleveland, Ohio. His current show, "Shalom America," airs in Cleveland on WELWAM 1330, Sundays from 7:00 A.M. to 9:00 A.M., and on www.shalomamerica.us. He attributes the paucity of Jewish radio to station owner fears.

"The reason why there is no real Jewish talk radio to the best of my knowledge is that stations are not set up for it, because of liabilities," he said. "Many programs are done where stations don't want the liability of having people calling in who might condemn another religious group. [Jewish programs often] do not have the capability of editing remarks by an anti-Semitic caller. Someone could sue the station even though there may be a disclaimer.

Christian stations are different because they are owned by a Christian company, and their staff people work for the station, [whereas Jewish hosts frequently buy time on a non-Jewish station]. Radio stations today broker their time for programs that are not a part of the format. Jewish programming is almost always brokered. The station sells the time to the host, and he in turn sells the advertising to sponsors to make up the cost.

Larry Gordon

Larry Gordon founded a daily Jewish music and news program on WFMU in New Jersey. His current talk programs and interviews can be heard at www.mesorahradio.com. Today, Gordon publishes and edits the *5 Towns Jewish Time*, a weekly newspaper, but he is still considered part of the Jewish radio community for the maverick work he did.

"It's very similar to what it was when I started in 1975," Gordon says of Jewish radio. "It has always been sorely underdeveloped and has not progressed the way other media—like Spanish media or Christian radio—has expanded to the point where they can buy their own radio stations by the dozen. Any radio station goes up for sale nowadays, and usually a Christian or Spanish broadcasting company will purchase it."

Gordon's view on the challenge of getting advertising is such:

Part of the reason you can't sell a lot of advertising for Jewish radio is because major companies are under the impression that plenty of Jewish issues are broadcast in mainstream media. Israel dominates the news. Everything from peace initiatives in the Middle East to war in Iraq in some way can be traced to Israel. Advertisers are not going to commit major dollars to a religious Jewish broadcast because it's a statistically nonexistent market to the perception of media moguls and advertising providers.

Dov Hikind

New York State assemblyman Dov Hikind has a radio show once per week for an hour. In 2005, he is serving his tenth term as a Democrat representing the 48th Assembly District (Boro Park, Dyker Heights, Kensington and parts of Flatbush), but he at times supports Republican candidates and is considered conservative on many issues. He finds having a show useful to his political career and regrets the lack of Jewish talk programming in general. "My view of Jewish radio is that it is extremely limited," he said. "There's not really that much. In terms of different programs that do serious programs and stuff. I don't think there is all that much."

He is paving the way for other politicians—many of whom are good at expressing themselves vocally—to try radio. "As an elected official, it helps tremendously to have a radio show," Hikind said. "I deal with issues that have nothing to do with my job as assemblyman. We talk about everything—things are very up to do date, things we have not read about, issues that concern people, medical issues. We interview authors of major books, bestsellers in the *New York Times*. We talk about the Holocaust. I stay away almost totally from doing something local. If someone calls with a comment about a specific thing on the block, we tell them to call the office."

Shmuel Kaplan

Rabbi Shmuel Kaplan can be heard, along with co-host Michael Hoffman, in metro Washington on "Awake, Alive and Jewish," which airs every Sunday at 10:00 A.M. on WTOP Radio/Federal News Radio AM 1050.

A leader of the Chabad Lubavitch movement, Kaplan is a Hassidic Jew, whose show mixes music, interviews, educational features, Israeli news and "irreverent banter." He has been the host of his show since 1980.

Kaplan puts the radio cost issue in distinct terms. Although others say it can be pricey and prefer Internet distribution, he points out how much cheaper it is to buy station time than operate a synagogue. "It's so cost effective," he said. "All we pay is pennies in comparison, compared with what any other medium would cost. An hour costs between five and 700 dollars. Our advertisers are car dealerships, gift shop, food shop, restaurants (only kosher). Each hour has about six to eight minutes of ads."

He continues, "I don't think people have really thought through the idea of how effective Jewish radio could be. The average institution thinks of taking care of itself—the synagogue wants membership—and time on the radio won't necessarily increase membership, so why would they do that? We are interested in the community. I have seen that those who have done [Jewish radio] have been individuals. Institutions, [besides B'nai B'rith], I've never seen."

Yaakov Menken

Rabbi Yaakov Menken founded Project Genesis and created many of its sites and programs. Project Genesis aims to use technology in the service of others, and Menken has helped different Jewish organizations advance that aim. A graduate of Princeton University (computer science) and Yeshiva (Rabbinic studies), Menken hosted the radio show "Torah Talk," which can be heard on www.torahmedia.com, and is exploring new ways to disseminate Jewish radio. "If we imagine wireless Internet completely blanketing the country, or if we have a stream of our favorite radio, the whole idea of frequencies could be rendered obsolete," Menken said. "I don't think we've quite gotten there. What's the chance that someone could build a device that sticks in the car and uses a little computer and flips between presets? At that point, it will be realistic to have a fulltime Jewish radio station."

Menken is at the forefront of helping Jewish talk keep up with and make use of innovation. "There is a constant process of exploration," he said. "Not every initiative is going to work. We have a lot of incubating new projects just like in the for-profit world, but we're not going to get five million in venture capital for a new initiative. But since I have a computer science background, we grew to the point that we were called upon to do for-profit consulting, so I have a separate company that does so. It means we're always exploring the latest technology. We keep up with the trade journals and every so often say, 'Hey, we can use that.' If I were devoted fulltime to an Internet business, it would be more lucrative—but the tradeoff is a good one."

Marilyn Kleinberg Neimark

As a liberal accounting professor at City University who cohosts a Jewish radio show, Marilyn Kleinberg Neimark laments the under-representation of liberal and secular perspectives on Jewish radio. Her show on New York's WBAI, "Beyond the Pale: Radical Jewish Culture and Politics," cohosted with Esther Kaplan, deals with art, culture and politics that reflect and affect Jewish life. Her perspective is unabashedly left. "The majority of Jews in New York City are still liberal," she said. "If one limits oneself to reaching Jews who are formally affiliated with Jewish institutions and have synagogue membership, then the audience would appear as if it were more conservative and Orthodox. Whereas I think that if you look at Jews nationally, there are a lot of unaffiliated Jews, many of whom are still strongly Jewish identified who are quite liberal politically."

She sees existing Jewish organizations as limited, and views her show as an outlet for Jews frustrated with this shortcoming. "There are hundreds of thousands of liberal and left Jews, on college campuses in particular," she said. "On many campuses, the only venue for Jews is Hillel. For a kid who wants to question what's happening, especially in Israel and Palestine, they're not going to find a hospitable environment in most Hillels, with few exceptions. I think our program and programs like ours open up opportunities for a broader and more nuanced discourse."

Art Raymond

Many people see Art Raymond as the grandfather of Jewish radio. Although he focused on music, it seems necessary to include him in any essay dealing with Jewish programming. Recently retired, Raymond began working in radio in 1963 as a staff announcer and went on to create the first well-known show featuring Jewish music with English-language hosting and commentary. Raymond thinks the market for Jewish talk radio is out there, and that it just needs to be tapped. "I think Jewish talk radio could increase," he said. "People want someone's explanation of what's going on politically. My experience is that too many amateurs are on the air. If you tune in, you want the guy in charge to be knowledgeable and to express himself professionally so that you aren't embarrassed that the guy sounds like some jerk off the street. There are too many guys who are not experts. That's my beef. They try to sound like an expert. Too many are opinionated. . . . I want to hear from experts on both sides."

Gavriel Sanders

Gavriel Sanders used to work in Christian radio. An evangelical minister turned Jewish, his show can be heard at www.fivetownsradio.com and http://gavrielsanders.com. He does not like that Jewish radio lags behind its Christian counterpart. "Jewish radio is really banal compared with Christian media, which is very sophisticated," he said. "I'm a convert. Before I was a Jew, I was one of those, so I know. I'm active in Jewish radio now, and I see Jews don't have a very aggressive message as compared to say the Christian evangelical enterprise, which is driven by a mission statement to reach the world. There are exceptions to the rule: Chabad has been aggressive in trying to reach people."

Sanders would like to see the quality of Jewish radio improve. "A lot of it is very provincial and not always very exciting," he said. "When I compare it with regular mainstream media, it's kinda mom and pop the way it comes off. There is big room for improvement. No one is really dedicating the bucks to it, though."

Nachum Segal

An Orthodox Jew who knows his music as well as his politics, Nachum Segal is an influential host of Jewish radio. His show, "JM in the AM," has been featured by the New York Times and is heard both in the New York area and at www.jmintheam.org and www.nachumsegal.com. Segal sees assimilation as the reason Jewish programming remains limited. "Even observant Jews are so assimilated that Jewish radio is not everyone's first choice," Segal said. "It's not like Chinese, Spanish or Portuguese communities. We're so intertwined in American society that it's a miracle I have any listeners. It's those who want to be up to date on the Jewish world, whose day is not exciting enough Jewishly, and my show helps them. I think my listenership is mostly Orthodox, but not by such a large majority, probably just over 50 percent. There is a significant portion who are non-observant, and their only real connection to Judaism is my show."

Segal says success must be measured on a distinct scale, for the Jewish market will always remain small. "My website, www.nachumsegal.com, is extremely popular, but in the scope of things, it's a blip, it's nothing. It's in the hundreds of thousands per week, and it just started in March."

Yaakov Spivak

Rabbi Yaakov Spivak was a co-host with Zev Brenner when Talkline (then called Night Rap) began. They were heard on WNYM, the former WEVD 13:30 A.M., which was purchased by Salem Communications for Christian radio. Listeners demanded that some Jewish programming remain on the station after the sale, so Brenner and Spivak became hosts.

In 1987, Spivak went on to ElectroVision Media, though he and Brenner are still good friends and sometimes collaborators. Today, Spivak's radio studio is attached to the synagogue where he is a rabbi in New York. He is heard in Denver on KHNC drive time, on WSNR in the New York area and on WNN in South Florida. His show is also played on international shortwave and can be heard online at www.jewishradionetwork.net. Spivak has been interviewed on MSNBC, Fox, CBS, and ABC.

Spivak, who went to broadcasting school after becoming a rabbi, says his audience is distinct. "I am an Orthodox Rabbi with and conservative politics, out to reform the left. The people who like my views are the rootsy people," he said. "I find that heartland America will relate more to Orthodox thinking than Conservative or Reform because Orthodox is more hardline, and [that part of] America appreciates fundamentalist principles."

PERSONAL PATHS AND WISDOM: THEIR STORIES

Radio personalities capture other people's stories. That is their job. They listen, ask questions, and give opinions. But rarely does a host share details about his or her own background. In select segments of the interviews conducted by the author, below the reader has an opportunity to learn more about where the day's Jewish talk radio hosts come from, and where they may be heading.

Zev Brenner

How do you approach Jewish issues through radio?

My perspective stems number one through a Jewish perspective. If I interview presidents, Al Sharpton, whomever, we're gonna talk [about the Jewish community]. Even when I have these people, they don't have to be Jewish. If they're doing something interesting to the Jewish world, we'll talk about that, because you're not going to hear those issues on ABC radio.

On my show, it's a broad-based program. It's not religious per se, though I will cover religious topics. My show is not a Torah class. I do have someone who does that. I'm overall in charge of programming and business, overseeing sales. Unlike major stations, we have to make sure the programming supports itself.

What sort of responses do you get from listeners?

I find people who are upset with me that I will cover topics that [they think] shouldn't be covered. For example, homosexuality in the Orthodox Jewish community. I had a gay Orthodox rabbi and one who opposed and a filmmaker who made the film "Trembling Before God." The feeling is sometimes, amid segments, that I put on something too controversial and that by talking about it, I give it legitimacy. I say that we need to explain statements, that's why we're here.

We've had black leaders on for dialogue. We had Julius Lester, today a practicing Jew [who was the host of a WBAI show and was charged with anti-Semitism for airing a black girl's "Jew Boy" poem during the Ocean Hill Brownsville Teacher's Strike in 1968], got people upset. People felt he didn't change and was still anti-Semitic. We didn't shy away from the issues. We have been keeping dialogue open.

You say publicly that you are interested in black–Jewish relations. What is your standpoint?

I do believe blacks and Jews should work together, but it has to be done on a different basis than it has been done. There has to be respect both ways. There has to be understanding without compromising our position. I did a program on the Caribbean American parade in Brooklyn, and an African American called in and said Hasidic Jews diss Caribbean culture, because when they march, they turn their backs on women dancing. And I explained, "It's only for religious reasons that they don't want to see scantily clad women."

What was Jewish radio like when you started?

Most Jewish radio shows in the country at the time consisted of older Jewish music. We pioneered doing a call-in talk show with newsmakers and celebrities. In 1981, we went form a one-hour per week to two to three, and at some point, we took over the whole station. We were the largest Jewish block, and today we are the leading Jewish radio and TV network in the U.S. We still do mostly talk today.

How did the dispute over WEVD affect your radio career?

In 1981, there was WEVD, but it was not a full-time Jewish station; it just had a lot of Jewish programming. Prior to my going in, WEVD had sold its AM part and was only going to be FM. There was an outcry [from listeners] because not everyone had FM. We got involved in AM because that was part of the selling agreement: It said there would have to be some Jewish radio to satisfy the public outcry at the time.

From where do you get financial support?

Ads are very strong in the local community, local merchants. We work with companies, banks, movies, something that wants to meet Jewish people. It's been a struggle to get ads, but I think the advent of cable is making it easier because niche became "in." All of a sudden, there's a channel for children, women, golf lovers—that has helped.

I also work with the ethnic market. I tell agencies, "When you advertise in the *New York Times* in general, [that's not as targeted]. The pitch has to be different if you want to reach Jews." Then they'll say, 'Wow, they're interested in me.'"

Who are your listeners?

There's a misconception that it's only conservative listeners. Thirty to 40 percent of our audience is Orthodox, and they're very vocal. A lot of them don't have TVs, so they learn things about the outside world through our program. I'm on the lecture circuit, I go to conservative and Reform places, and they tell me they listen [to my show], though they don't call in. There's also a nice following in the Christian community. We deal with black–Jewish relations, and we'll get black feedback.

Listenership numbers are hard to say because there's been no scientific study. A phone company did a survey of our audience. We pulled in 18,773 phone calls [during the time block], rivaling big stations in how many people responded. We pulled more than ABC radio on certain days. Right now, I'm [heard] in the Florida area every night, and also on a Satellite network in addition to our own. New York is our biggest market.

My show is at 9 P.M. Monday to Thursday and Saturday at midnight. We're on WSNR 620 AM now. On Saturday we're on Christian radio, WMCA. We produce about 10 hours per week of Jewish radio and are in the process of starting a cable network.

Why isn't there more Jewish radio in the United States?

The truth is the Jewish community, we are a people of the book and haven't really embraced TV and technology in the way Christians have. In New York right now, we have three different radio stations running Russian, yet we don't have a full-time Jewish station. The Jewish community hasn't been very supportive of these programs. We don't get a lot of advertising from big Jewish organizations. They don't do a lot. To a certain degree, big Jewish companies take Jewish media foregranted. They're there for interviews, but are not [financially] supportive.

B'nai B'rith

The author conducted a joint interview with Studio J Producer Janet Rathner, long-time B'nai B'rith staffer Harvey Berk, and Director of Communications Debbie Auerbach-Deutsch.

BERK: The guy that created B'nai B'rith radio is no longer on staff. Jay Garfinkle was a radio and TV broadcast veteran. His idea was that because the organization, more than any other organization in the Jewish world, cuts across the whole spectrum from observant to secular, from big city to small town, B'nai B'rith was the best organization to create a vehicle that is like a Jewish version of "All Things Considered." A lot of people have radio shows that talk about so and so uncle going to be giving a lecture, or here's this organization, that organization. But the idea here is to present a show that focuses on everything Jewish—sports, culture, books, TV, current events. All of that information. Very little of it is academic, very little of it is organizational news. I'd be lying if I didn't tell you there is an agenda. Where there is an area where B'nai B'rith has expertise, we will use that expertise. For what's happening in the United Nations, it made sense to interview the director of B'nai B'rith about world affairs. We interview on issues instead of about what B'nai B'rith is doing.

AUERBACH-DEUTSCH: From the standpoint of what this means for us, we got involved initially because we thought, "Okay, the Internet is a fabulous medium and reaches a lot, but not everyone, but radio is a terrific medium." The growth of Satellite and Internet radio mean there's an opportunity to provide 24-7 Jewish music like we have on our website, to get our message and information out. That means not only what is special about our organization, but also about what is special about being a Jew in this world. We continue to be an organization of all Jews. How much money you make does not matter.

BERK: Now we're weekly over Sirius channel 140 WRN Sundays. The eventual goal is we're looking for funding so we can get to communities across the country, syndicating, and we would buy an hour's worth of time in big and little communities so people don't have to use the Internet or satellite radio. The Internet is a tremendous vehicle, but a lot of people don't like to sit in front of the computer [to listen]. We're also looking to do podcasting. Right now, it's just Janet. In a week, there will be two people. There's a part-time contract engineer who does technical work. It's not a major commitment—only one hour per week, but that's available 24-7 via the web, and one can access back segments. Every show consists of six or seven segments. There's hired talent and commentary every week. Most of the time, it's the executive vice president or associate vice president.

We know that in order to get significant penetration in the marketplace, we need to get on radio stations throughout the country. What we are doing currently is to prove what can be done while we try to find a philanthropist who believes in the value of this kind of a model. We think it's unique in that there are few projects that could be active overnight and could work equally well in the biggest and smallest communities. That to us is our selling point.

In one week, our radio show had tips on how to look for housing for grandparents, a feature on Israeli hip hop violinists and a football player. All the topics have something to do with Jewish issues. None can be construed as religiously Jewish.

Phil Fink

How did your radio career progress over time?

I have been doing radio since 1963. I started when I was 20, and I became the host of the Jewish radio program quite by accident. I was working for a radio station in Cleveland, much like WEVD. It was a foreign language station, and I was the only one who spoke English without an accent. I produced commercials and read the news, so they hired me as an engineer and announcer. There was an older gentleman who did a program in English, Yiddish and Hebrew. I became his engineer . . . and then I took over the show [because the gentleman asked for more money]. . . . I used the knowledge that I had. I can speak Yiddish and Hebrew. My grandparents lived with us, so I learned Yiddish from them. I was schooled in Cleveland at the Hebrew Academy of Cleveland. I am observant. I don't like to use the word Orthodox. [Today] I have guests that are recorded. I don't edit, but I don't feel I can get someone in at 7:30 A.M. on Sunday. Still, I always do live shows. My program is done live for spontaneity and to accept calls from listeners. However, it's not a talk show; it is a mixture of Jewish music of all genres and what is new from Israel, as well as guests.

How is your show distinct from other Jewish radio shows?

Most programs on the radio today are aimed at a particular group. They program to a small niche listenership. Many [intended for] the Orthodox community just look at the Orthodox community. I don't. I program for everybody. Cleveland has a Jewish community of eighty thousand, so just to program for a segment of the audience is counter-productive. I also have a non-Jewish audience, and I promote Judaism as a positive part of Jewish lives. I've had Christians say to me, "We didn't know that's how you celebrate." Over the years, I've done over 15,000 interviews. When I first started, it was like pulling teeth to find people to interview. Now I get books by the hundreds, calls from organizations, people who want to be on the program. . . . I'm not a rabbi, so I would be remiss in giving advice to people. I do know Jewish law, and there are a lot of interpretations of Jewish law. I believe in dialogue with people, and that is why I have rabbis of all denominations and priests who have appeared on the program. If there is something in the news that needs a definition, I will call a rabbi. There are some who are regulars on the show, and they are called in to add their expertise . . . . Mine is the only Jewish radio program in the world that reads the Book of Esther in Hebrew from start to finish on the radio, with the permission of a rabbi who has since passed away—one of the most respected rabbis in the world. In order to hear the Book of Esther, you have to hear it in person, in order to be considered a part of the mitzvah. There are people, elderly, sick, new mothers, who can't go out. So I asked the rabbi and said, "If we do no commercials and read it from start to finish and state at the beginning that it is only for elderly etc., is that okay?" We are going into the 32nd year. . . .

Where would you place yourself in the history of Jewish radio?

I'm 61, so other than Art Raymond, I'm really one of the oldest living Jewish radio people. Here's a history lesson: Jewish programming 70 years ago was mostly done in "Yinglish," a mixture of English and Yiddish. Much of the programming was done for immigrants. There was no TV then. Immigrants that came over wanted a touch of home from people they could understand. Many didn't speak English. Jewish radio filled a void; it brought back memories of Europe and of time gone by. It also brought the listeners news of the day and a drama or comedy or two.

Will Jewish radio be around in 40 years?

Good question. Don't forget, most of the Jewish community is assimilated. We listen to all types of radio. Only if something is good will they listen to us. We are a conduit not just to the past, but also to the future. If you put a Jewish program in Iowa, it will last one week. If it's in California, Miami Beach, Cleveland, Boston, then it's a different story.

You are an observant Jew, but you differentiate yourself from that group. Why?

The Orthodox community has become conservative politically. I have not. My interpretation is that the Orthodox community has become more right wing as time has gone on. I saw the switch coming at the end of Bill Clinton's presidency. "The man was not a moral man," people said. Yes, he did have sex with that woman. And George Bush campaigned on his religiousness.

Orthodox Jews have become more powerful. They have more day schools, more schools of higher learning, they're financially more powerful, they wield power in Washington through certain organizations.

I like to think for myself within the confines of Jewish law. I have taught my children to do the same. If I have a question on Jewish law, I look up the law, and if I still need guidance, I ask a competent rabbi.

Larry Gordon

What was the content of your radio show at the beginning?

I started out doing music, largely from Israel. I was about 20, and I was learning with the audience. The talk aspect developed with time, between 1975 and 1985. It seemed modern, but you're talking barely 30 years after people came from the experience of the Holocaust, [so I was talking to] many survivors. We broadcast a Holocaust remembrance day with panels of survivors. . . . We had religious leaders, programs with psychiatrists and psychologists.

That program was on a college radio station, which was non-commercial. It was on 7 to 9 A.M., Monday to Friday. It was an odd thing. It was 1977; we were 22 or 23 and wanted to do a program during morning drive time. We wanted to find a radio station to do it on, and we went through the phone book in New York and New Jersey and called all the stations. We had a lot of energy. We asked, "Do you have a 24-hour broadcast license, and do you broadcast 24 hours a day?"

We found FMU in Jersey, part of a Lutheran Church. . . . Then the administration of the college, people a little higher up in the hierarchy [than those who hired us], discovered after three months that there was a Jewish radio program on the station. It was a 1500-watt broadcast to most of New York and a good part of Jersey. They wanted to get rid of us, but by that time, we had such popular support that they couldn't.

From there, I left because of disputes with the college over money. . . . Someone got in touch with me from WEVD, and I became in charge of the 8 P.M. to 3 A.M. slot. . . . The content of those shows was talk on different subjects, panel discussions, politics, political candidates, Israel. All kinds, all under the rubric of Jewish interest. We had Conservative, Reform, Orthodox rabbis. We presented differences of opinions on abortion, gay rights. Leaders of pro-abortion and gay rights are Jews, probably not affiliated Jews. . . . Then I was having kids, 4 kids in 5 years. I was not making enough money, and I had to get another job. I drifted away from radio. I stopped doing radio in 1989. I think I left commercial radio WEVD in 1986, then I was working until 1989 at WMPA, and that station was eventually bought by the same company that bought WEVD, Salem Media, which does Christian programming.

Are you still involved with radio at all today?

I'm going to Washington tomorrow with managers of XM Satellite. They want to do a Jewish radio channel. They want to hear about the ideas. No programmer, especially if he is Jewish, thinks there is a need for Jewish programming, because [they think] all programming is Jewish. You put on the TV at night, and you'll hear Yiddishisms like *chutzpah* because these are writers, producers who are Jewish. The average guy will think there is such an inordinate amount of Jewish content.

I don't believe they understand what it is. It's not just a market of six million Jews in the U.S. Half can't even identify as conscious Jews. It's not 10 percent, which is Orthodox, which is a few hundred thousand people. But it's an audience that is larger. Kosher organizations did a study and found that 30 percent of the American population looks for kosher food—because of the Muslim population and the idea that kosher is cleaner and healthier. As a result of that, one agency certifies over 300,000 products. Look at Hershey's and others that weren't kosher for a long time. [They realized kosher eaters] are a loyal, upwardly mobile market. That's the same with the market that would go for programming that has at its core Jewish guidance, not just religious, looking at Israel. There are over 200 countries in the world, and yet the *New York Times* can't go a day without a story about microscopic Israel, which involves the American Jewish community and the relationship with Israel. It's unbelievable the amount of various topics that could be done.

I think Jew and non-Jew, anybody with minimal intelligence and any kind of orientation, is interesting in what is happening in Israel, with the war in Iraq—which to many is an outgrowth of Israel-Arab conflict.

Dov Hikind

What is the purpose of your show?

We do very serious programming. We do all kinds of stuff. I think we do a great program. It's only an hour. It's a program that a hell of a lot of people listen to everywhere. It's very professional.

It's therapy for me. It's an unbelievable opportunity. Radio is a very powerful medium. I've always known that. It's an unbelievable opportunity to go out there every week and speak with a great number of people. It's informative. It helps get a message out.

All our shows are live. In the past five to six years, I've never done a taped program. I use radio every week to highlight, talk about and mobilize the community.

Who are your listeners?

I would say a great number of my listeners are observant. There are all kinds. We have a huge following from Orthodox and Hasidic communities. When we do a lot of phone calls—it's hard to believe—but in an hour, we've done shows where we did 37 phone calls in one evening after we presented an issue. Our lines light up nonstop when we take phone calls. They come from Great Neck, Connecticut, parts of New Jersey, New York. And from non-Jews. Maybe 15 to 20 percent will identify themselves as non-Jews, even though we don't ask them if they're Jewish; people will say, "I'm not Jewish." People listen to my show, unquestionably, from a variety of backgrounds. They tell me.

How did you get started in radio?

I was first into radio in terms of a regular show five to six years ago. But forever as an elected official, I've been on radio numerous times over the years. I have a Ph.D. in political science. I spent years teaching at Baruch. Radio is not my profession. I love it. I think it's fabulous. I would love to have a radio show on ABC or WOR. We've even talked about the possibility that after I finish being in elective office, they're interested. For now, as an elected official, it's just an extra thing that I can do to get out to a lot of people in the tri-state area.

What are your goals, personally and for the show?

My goal every week is just to give people a great show. And to do things as effectively as possible and be as informative as possible. There are no real goals beyond that. What I do is very limited because it's only an hour a week. Our show has become very successful financially from ads. We make good money, which is amazing, it's nuts. I'm talking after expenses. The cost of doing radio is probably the greatest disadvantage [for others]. It really limits you in terms of being out there. Zev Brenner, as you know, makes his livlihood from Jewish radio. For me, if I didn't make a cent, I'd still do it. It's purely a side thing.

How do your personal politics figure into your program?

Most radio shows, the successful radio shows, on a regular basis get monotonous because nothing changes. If Rush Limbaugh loves Bush and hates the Democrats, [you know what to expect]. And Republicans can't do wrong, and Democrats can't do right. I'm not that way. I'm definitely very opinionated, but I wouldn't play that role, nor would I be the guy on the left. I think I'm a bit right of center, others would say so. I don't consider myself one way or another. Some things, yes, some things not. That's what's tough about defining people. It works on some things. My voting record in Albany is that 99 percent of stuff is no different from how the black or Puerto Rican Caucus votes.

I have my opinions on things. The war in Iraq for instance. The reform movement is contemplating coming out with a resolution against the war. I'd be critical of that on the radio. But it depends on which issue. There are a lot of ways to look at things.

What type of feedback have you heard regarding your show?

I hear a lot more of the positive, to be honest. I love the negative. The calls I enjoy the most are those who are critical. They're the most fun calls. People tell me nobody can talk [in the household] at 11 P.M. because everyone is sitting around and listening to my show. A 10-year-old called one night, and I said, "Where are your parents?" He said, "Oh, they're listening to your show."

Who advertises on your show?

The Maimonides medical center in Brooklyn is a huge supporter of our show. Other supporters on a regular basis who have spent are everyone from Con Edison to Do All Travel, one of the largest wholesale travel agencies in the Jewish community. Also Metropolitan Geriatrics and political candidates advertise, not only Jewish ones. Bloomberg spent a lot of money advertising. All kinds of political people during June, July, August, September and October.

Shmuel Kaplan

Why did you start a radio show?

My show has been on for over 25 years. We started because we were looking for a cost effective way to communicate with the largest possible audience, and I felt radio fit that bill. If you take all of the synagogues in the area and calculate how many attend Shabbat services on an average Shabbat, you'll have, say, seven to nine thousand people, maybe. If you figure in the cost of maintaining 20 or 30 buildings that host the Shabbat services and compare the cost and the number of people we reach per hour, you'll see what I mean.

Our goal is to educate people in an entertaining way, so they don't realize they're being educated. The non-Jewish staff of the radio station where we're on always enjoys the program. They say it's so different from anything they are familiar with.

We have always had at least two people hosting, so there is banter between two. It's irreverent banter. It's funny, if you will. I'm not the rabbi, and they're not who they are. We tease each other. I think it is a successful format. I have had one main co-host. We never talk for more than five minutes in a row; it's an hour which moves well.

How far is your reach today?

We haven't been able to get accurate figures on how many listen because the Arbitron ratings don't take into consideration our demographics; the ratings are lumped in areas where there are no Jews, so there are other ways we're trying to gauge our reach. For example, we try to see how quickly the switchboards light up. We think that somewhere between five and 10 thousand people listen to the show.

We know we have listeners across the board. We have non-Jewish listeners as well. They happen to chance upon the show because it's a station they set their radio to. They like the music and to learn about Judaism. We have very few Hassidic listeners because there aren't many in the area—that's not our audience.

The advantage of radio is that people can pick it up wherever they are. There is an audience of people carpooling kids to Hebrew school, and they turn us on when they're in the car. The advantage is that radio lets you be mobile, and you can still listen.

Where do you fit into the Chabad Lubavitch movement?

My title is the regional representative of the Lubavitch movement. I was appointed. I've been in that for 30 years. I'm a rabbi with Lubavitch. There are quite a number of Chabad shows. We are part of the Hasidic movement.

In a typical show, we open up with commentary on some topical issue—it could be something on the calendar, it could be a holiday event, it could be an event happening in the community. Then we intersperse that with music. Then we come back with some editorial comments about things in the community or news in the last couple weeks, giving a torah perspective on issues, or that this is what the Jewish law and history would say about events.

What stance do you take on issues of the day?

The abortion debate is one thing, but in Israel, there is an organization that helps people overcome their desire for an abortion; it supports women and children, somewhat, financially. [We did a show on them.] I make my views clear: I'm against abortion, though there are conditions where it is justified. I'm Hasidic, that's understood. I'm politically conservative—usually, not always.

An example of an issue we covered: during an election, what are our obligations to participate? There is a torah perspective. It says there is an obligation to be concerned with the welfare of the country in which we live and influence people among which we live. The Torah requires we take a stand on issues.

Yaakov Menken

What are some of the limits of radio?

Because the radio show only enabled us to reach people in the Baltimore region, whereas a weblog is worldwide, I started a weblog, and it has proven to be a better communication medium for the people we are trying to reach. The weblog has a different set of promotion issues as it were. We've exceeded in readership what we had as projected listenership. The problem with doing a radio show to a niche market is that in an era of superstations, they are looking for a very large audience share. And it is difficult to justify financially the amount of money they want out of someone doing something niche oriented. Unless you're dealing with public broadcasting, they'll be looking for financial return.

How is new technology changing the way radio is distributed? Who is at the forefront?

Most of the new technology is coming from Aish, Chabad, Torah.org, weblogs—basically from the Orthodox community. I think there are more people at this point in the Orthodox community who are making Judaism a central focus of their lives, through writing, creating podcasts or radio programming.

We have been doing podcasting, the newest form of distributing a radio show to people around the world without a station. At this time I am between outlets. The podcasting is imminent—it's something our organization is looking to do for a series of rabbis, so that people will be able to say, "I'd like a weekly class from such and such rabbi." They'll be like "Torah Talk," which I hosted before. With Project Genesis, we are always trying to do things taking advantage of new technology. We saw the potential of a radio show as part of the web, but it only went so far because of the cost of delivery on a station.

Why did you start a radio program?

The idea of the radio program was to introduce people to various types of Jewish education and resources, and to speak to various experts in the field about what they were doing and why. We hoped it would be beneficial to reach both the Orthodox community, who wanted something interesting that spoke to them, and also to catch other Jews and non-Jews. We had a full show dedicated to interviewing. We were doing the show in the fall and winter of last year [2004], broadcasting on a Baltimore station that did sports mostly. It was one hour, once per week, on Sunday. People would have to specifically think about it and tune in. We were 8 to 9 P.M. We would look at, well, we wouldn't say it was political, but it wasn't a class in

Judaism. On the contrary, we had interviews with interesting people, like the engineer who is helping modify modern ovens so that they meet the needs of the Sabbath-observant, the head of a company serving Noachides [non-Jews observing the Seven Laws of Noah] and a senior editor of the Artscroll Talmud. It was a diverse mix.

What are challenges you face in getting to broad segments of the population?

Explaining the advantages of this approach is hard. The community that is most active on the Internet is a younger set. The donor base who can make programs happen are an older set. We're neither an established Jewish organization, nor are we doing things in the established way. We have to try to explain to people who we are in order to be able to financially support the projects. Right now, those who support us are local Baltimore federations, as well as federations all across the country, foundations and an awful lot of individual Jews, from Reform to Orthodox.

Marilyn Kleinberg Neimark

Tell me about your program?

We aren't strictly talk radio. We are basically a magazine format. We focus on radical Jewish culture and politics. We're very catholic with a small "c" about what we consider Jewish. In the political realm for sure, anything involving New York City, education, labor, civil liberties, immigration, judicial appointments are all issues that we cover. We've a very broad understanding of what we think are the issues that people who are Jewish ought to be concerned about and that Jewish institutions often fail to weigh in on, or at least in the way we hope they will. . . . We cover Israel and Palestine. We talk to cultural artists, writers, filmmakers who are Jewish or in some way express Judaism in the work they do. We air on Sundays from 12 to 1 P.M. on WBAI, and we're streamed live and archived online. We're in the process of launching our own website where the archives will stay up for longer. We've been on the air for 10 years. The weekend of the 13th of November, 2005, we had a two-hour live broadcast, with an audience, at the Center for Jewish History, celebrating our 10th year. I've been involved almost the entire time. I started about three months into it with my co-host Esther Kaplan. The shows are usually live, occasionally prerecorded. Not a big percentage is music.

What are the pros and cons of working on a listener-sponsored radio station?

We're listener-supported, so we can sort of measure how we have been doing. The station has had financial difficulties in recent years. But our show's contribution during fundraisers has been increasing, which suggests that we're holding up against the trend at WBAI.

I'm not sure about listener statistics. Around five to eight years ago, Arbitron found that we had 10 to 12 thousand listeners. My sense is that the listenership has been growing, and it's not just a Jewish audience. We have a large non-Jewish listenership, and our listeners range from relatively young people to a lot of seniors. Some of our listeners get very angry with our coverage of Israel and Palestine. We have on the show Israelis and Palestinians who are strong advocates of Israeli withdrawal from the occupied territories. We talk frankly with people on right of return issues, about the question of the role of Israel in the dispossession of the Palestinians. We tend to ally ourselves with people in Israel who are on the left and in the peace movement.

What is your radio and religious background?

I'm a professor at Baruch, part of City University, and I teach accounting. In many respects, my job is unrelated—in most respects. Radio is my avocation. I love it as a form. Before this, I co-hosted a show on WBAI called Econonews, a leftwing take on business. Esther, my co-host on Beyond the Pale, is a journalist, who has worked for the Village Voice, the Nation and other publications. And she produces another radio program on labor issues. She's the author of a new book, *With God on Their Side,* which looks critically at fundamentalist Christianity's influence on American government and public policy.

In terms of Judaism, I have in the past been synagogue-affiliated and attended services with some regularity We are now High Holiday Jews. But I've gotten less and less so interested in going. That has to do with finally deciding I'm not comfortable with all the talk about God both because I'm not a believer and because of the reluctance of the Jewish community to grapple with the liturgy, the God part and the patriarchal part.

Esther feels the same way, I think. For many years, I belonged to B'nai Jeshurun in Manhattan and worked closely with the rabbis and the synagogue on a lot of political issues. We are still close personally to the current rabbis. But that particular community has gotten more conservative.

I feel very connected culturally to Judaism. I think, yes, there is space for more shows like ours. I think we are more in tune with the zeitgest of contemporary American Jews than conservatives. The Reform movement just voted against this administration's Iraq policies, which is quite a fantastic thing. Jewish organizations have been very reluctant to criticize this administration for fear it would adversely impact policy on Israel.

WBAI has historically had many Jewish employees and listeners. Is this still the case?

Historically, yes, but these days, I would say the leadership is predominantly African American, and a lot of programming is geared to that community. Still, quite a few co-hosts are Jews, as are many listeners and supporters. At the same time, the station has had a reputation as anti-Semitic, not totally earned, but not unearned either. The station has had a troubled relationship with the Jewish community over the years. Sometimes WBAI has been a little tone deaf about what is or isn't anti-Semitic. Esther and I confront anti-Semitism when it does rear its head at the station, and I think that along with others at the station, we play a productive role.

Art Raymond

How did you get your start in radio?

I started back in 1963. I originally got into radio at 21. To sum up my situation, I am an American DJ who spent 10 years in radio doing everything but sports. I did news, classical music, whatever. After 10 years of being a staff announcer and doing interviews, public service, anything except sports, I found my calling in Jewish music and then went to that and specialized in it for the rest of my radio career and was very successful in Philadelphia, New York City and Florida. Being in New York, I was heard in parts of Connecticut and New Jersey. . . . I got interested in doing a Jewish music show because there was a large Jewish audience in Philadelphia. I did a three-hour Jewish music program every Sunday. . . . I went to New York City and made a deal with WEVD AM to do a one-hour show every day, five days a week. I was doing a show on Sundays in Philadelphia. And then five days out of the week in New York. I commuted. After a while, I moved back to New York and lived there, my hometown, and on Sundays, I drove to Philadelphia to do the Sunday show in person, live. After about 12 years, I gave up the Philadelphia show. My show in New York expanded to four hours per day, six days per week. I continued to do my program on WEVD for 35 years. Before I finished on WEVD, I moved to Florida, about three or four years before the show ended in New York. I was doing a two-hour Sunday program in Florida and had my own studio, and I [shipped] my programs to New York until 1998.

How did your religious views affect your show?

I'm semi-observant and conservative. It had nothing to do with religion, my program. One thing I tried to do: I did not teach or preach. I was there to entertain. I was very successful at it. I was paid more than anyone else in any Jewish radio. Any Jewish guy who did a Jewish program any place in America. I was very successful. I had many sponsors, advertisers and went on many years.

Gavriel Sanders

What is the purpose of your show?

The sense of mission I had as a Christian minister, I still have it—focused on the Jewish community. The format of the show began with a focus on the

Five Towns, an area of Long Island, New York. The program quickly moved beyond just local because we do a lot on Israel. I try to expose people to information that leads to transformation.

I want people to do something. I don't want to just give data; I want to lead to make a difference. Say there's a political issue that needs a response to put pressure on representative authorities or people putting pressure on the press to release information, to raise awareness on a particular issue. I bring in guests who have solutions. What do you do? It's outcome oriented. That's how I think. I don't want to just push air. How many people will participate? Fewer than I want, more than I know. It's a matter of providing an appropriate format that is casual, but honest and meaningful—no hiding and nobody is preaching.

What have you heard back from listeners?

Most are observant Jews, but not all, and not all are Jewish. People like the music on the station. People tell me they feel refreshed, challenged and appreciate the candor. They like the variety of guests and that it's not commercially driven. People always criticize me on my use of Hebrew. I use Israeli Hebrew. Others want something more traditional. Mostly I speak in English, but I'll throw in certain terms. I've never done a whole show in Hebrew.

What are the benefits of operating exclusively online?

I produce a one-hour show per week, sometimes longer. Because it's on the Internet, I know when people are listening. People listen throughout the week. It used to be that 500 or 600 people would be listening online at any given time, mostly from New York and Israel. Now the show comes on at a particular time, then it's posted, then it goes to archives. There are three stages.

Five Towns has never been affiliated with a terrestrial station, because that is very expensive, not to mention the whole issue of FCC licensing and regulations, maintenance and tower issues and hearings. It's cheaper to lease time. Zev Brenner is all about leasing; he has allocated time people can lease. Five Towns has talked about it, but I doubt that will happen. There is some sponsorship on the website.

I do see a newer generation. I think that the ease by which people can now enter in individualized broadcasting through using the net gets people inspired. It's easier to evolve from a primitive beginning than it was to get though the door and beurocracy of a radio station. Someone with talent can find a place. It's parallel with the "indies" in the music industry who can bypass traditional distribution systems. I think the same thing is true here. It's possible to establish a presence.

How does your radio career as a Jew differ from your Christian radio career?

I've been in radio at different times. This is my third iteration. This stretch has been almost three years. The first two were Christian radio. My personality is basically the same. The outcome and expectation is different. Before it was a matter of trying to evangelize the world, whereas in this case, I just want to make a difference, motivate individuals to provide a diversion.

I didn't become a liberal when I converted. I've always been reasonably conservative. My experience with liberals is that say one thing and do another. It makes for good theory, but I just try to look at the bottom line in terms of people.... I call NPR [National Public Radio] National "People's" Radio because they are basically socialists. A lot of the Jews involved are very liberal, and they get caught up in socialism. It bothers me that people associate Jews and radio with liberalism. There is a huge constituency of Jews who are not that way.

Nachum Segal

What drew you to radio?

I began when I was 20 years old. The show was an extension of what I was doing in college radio. It started with a lot of community announcements; the growth has been its influence. People now want to be on my show—Jewish organizations and government people want to be featured.

In September of 1983, I was hired to host a show at 91.1 fm WFMU. It was a not-for-profit, listener-supported show. In 1992, I started an evening commercial show with Jewish news, music and information at night with listeners in New York and New Jersey. The show in the evening was heard in a lot of places online. [In 2000], the *New York Times* said we had 54,000 listeners. We have never done anything to measure—that was based on an independent survey.

How has your show changed over time?

The show has matured as I've matured. I'm married with kids, so I have a different perspective on life now. The show has become consumer friendly, music and news-wise. There's Hasidic, yeshivish, klezmer and Israeli music. There has been a continued growth of the show. There was a time when I was begging people to come on as guests, whereas now it's about turning people down because it's hard to find time to interview everyone.

It's rare that a show is more than 50 percent talk. The first 90 minutes out of 180 minutes are music. Then there's usually a guest or two.

How hard is it to get advertisers?

We have no problem finding clients. The problem is what price can you agree on. We have advertisers from wine companies, Judaica stores, car leasing in Jewish neighborhoods, kosher companies, events that are prominent.

How do listener preferences guide your program?

I have a folder of feedback. People have told me how my program has brought them closer to Judaism, has caused their family to move to Israel. Because of all the time we spend talking about Israel, it has encouraged people to visit Israel. I think that my listeners run the gamut from the Hassidic man for whom the show is nothing more than a little entertainment to a Jewish person who would not even remember that he was Jewish if it weren't for listening to my show.

People give me negative responses if I play something that's out of their specific taste—too rock 'n' roll or too old fashion. Politically I'm considered sympathetic with the Zionist camp in Israel. It depends who you are. I have gotten comments like, "I love your show but hate your politics" hundreds of time.

Do you have plans to change or expand your show?

What I've done over the last couple years is a major expansion. I was complaining about the numbers problem. Now the fact that I'm accessible around world has given me hope. I get emails from Israel, England, France, Venezuela, Beijing, all over the United States and Canada. That has been an incredible injection of spirit. I would think, ideally, since the web is cost effective in that you can present 24 hours of programming and not become bankrupt, my goal is a 24-hour live format on the web. Other hosts would participate. I think my strength is in programming. Now I need vehicle to use that. I think there is a method and genius behind putting together a show that can appeal to a vast number of people. There has to be someone driving that truck who has to figure out what the average listener wants to hear, to keep them all tuned in. I'm anticipating that soon people will listen in their car, from their cell phone and on the web. I'm open to everything, joining forces. I don't know that I've met anybody appropriate yet.

What are your politics like?

I don't think they've changed, except that as I got older, I have greater appreciation for the "other side." I think I've gone from being knee-jerk to trying to understand what is going through other people's minds and thinking about the opposing side. I think I'm much more patient and mature. And I try to think more.

I invite people to the show, some from Israel, who are very left [even though I'm considered Conservative politically].

What will the next generation of Jewish radio look like?

I have a substitute staff that takes over when I'm away. I would argue that I've brought in interesting young personalities and continue to do so. To cover the Yeshiva league's sports, I had an 18-year-old doing it.

Yaakov Spivak

You are a rabbi with master's degrees in education, a diploma in broadcast journalism and a license to teach social studies. Is radio the dream synthesizer?

I always had an affinity for media. That's why I went to broadcasting school. I got classic training in radio. I'm a licensed ham radio operator. I have a license to broadcast with a transmitter on shortwave. I'm professionally trained—both in the technical and journalistic aspects of the industry. Plus, being a rabbi, I can bring into it the rabbinic and Talmudic history and philosophy. And I'm a licensed social studies teacher for high school. As I'm getting older, I'm into [radio] a lot more. I do talk shows. I'm on the air three to four hours a day, between the morning drive and my shortwave programs.

What do you think of talk radio today?

I like Rush Limbaugh and Bob Grant in New York. Political and philosophical lines have been drawn. On the one hand it's horrible, but it's democracy, so it's beautiful. What I like is that Limbaugh will say what he is. Some networks say, "We are doing this in the name of journalism," but they're really not so journalistic—they have their issues, too. That goes for both sides, whereas with [Sean] Hannity and Limbaugh, what you see is what you get. That's not fair when hosts say they're unbiased when using public airways. In broadcast, using airwaves, you have the responsibility to tell people where you are coming from. I enjoy Fox News, but they say "fair and balanced," which isn't always so. My criticism goes across the board, right and left.

I tell people, "I'm a Republican, I'm Yaakov Spivak, and I support the president in many things, except leaving the door open for all illegals. I support the president's foreign policy, and this is who I am. If you're a caller, I will be happy to let you on. As long as you are decent, you can express your point of view." You know who I am. About 40 percent of my callers disagree with me. I love it.

Walk me through the strategy that goes into coming up with a show segment.

Let's say I will start a program like this: I will start with the story of King Saul, who is told to execute Agag, King of Amalek, but doesn't. The Talmud says he who is merciful to cruel will one day be cruel to the merciful. In other words, that you will be cruel to the merciful if you let a killer go. So I start with a passage from the Bible, then to Talmud, then I'll go to history and say what happened in 1938, when Hitler could have been crushed by the allies. Here was a situation where the allies could have crushed him in a second, but they said, "No, let us be merciful." So there was a cruel guy, and you are merciful to him, and you sell out. Then the comparison goes back to Saul where a city was destroyed, indicating that Saul was cruel to the merciful. This then leads to the story of Purim. Fast forwarding, I point out how Chamberlain sells out to Hitler in Munich, waves a piece of paper of peace, then London is bombed.... Then I'd move the conversation to France and current events, and how France says, "Let us tell you how to handle the Muslim population." The Muslim population promises kids 72 virgins if they carry the skulls of a Zionist bus driver to the gates of Paradise. Israel is tough on them. But the French say, "We are very liberal with them," and now they are burning down French towns. In such cases, you have to decide which people you can save. He who is merciful to the cruel will one day be cruel to the merciful.

No one does things in a style similar to mine. People broadcast Torah or political commentary. No one does both. There are not that many people around with my combination of degrees.

[In my show I try to counter] a social phenomenon that I see: the dumbing down of America. People don't know who the vice president is. It's a dangerous situation. Originally, the founding fathers only wanted landowners to vote, which sounds elitist. But the fact is that so many people in the world out there are ignorant beyond ignorant. People come here not bothering to learn the language. My favorite line is: "If you want to be a hairdresser or a plumber, you have to pass a test in order to get a license. Yet you don't need a license to raise a kid, sit on a jury or decide who will be president. All you have to be is 18."

JEWISH RADIO INTO THE FUTURE

The future of Jewish radio spells promise and problems. On the one hand, numerous interview subjects attested to the new possibilities available with the Internet, satellite radio, and technology. On the other hand, there is a consensus among Jewish radio hosts that not enough advertisers are interested in supporting the programming and that not enough people listen.

The question then becomes: Will Jewish radio broaden its appeal? And if so, how? If a show becomes less focused on Hasidic perspectives, it could lose its core audience who want Orthodox interpretations. Yet if a host hones in on a very specific aspect of Jewish life, listeners could get bored. The hosts interviewed above are grappling with these quandaries and coming up with unique solutions.

Some point to the need for better distribution channels—not relying exclusively on station time or the Internet, perhaps expanding to podcasts and even "ovencasts" (see Zev Brenner's section). Others argue that audiences must be cultivated through publicity and outreach—that once people listen a few times, they will realize how good Jewish shows are and tune back in.

It is the author's hope that some questions about Jewish radio's past, present, and future have been answered in this compilation of interviews. Jewish talk programming remains understudied, and this chapter is one step toward bringing it the attention it merits.

Chapter 12

Television Drama of the Golden Age
Judith Smith

Television was the transformative medium for the postwar generation, and its development was marked by its emergence at a crucial point in American culture, just as World War II was ending, and the possibilities of the new postwar world were taking shape. How and in what terms would wartime promises of an expanded postwar democracy be fulfilled, and how might television as a medium address these promises? World War II redefined the public sphere, and the public unity required for a successful war against fascism encouraged multiethnic cooperation in the platoon, on the shop floor and on the city block. Families were separated and scattered; and young men and women in the military and on the homefront encountered against each other outside of former local, ethnic, and racial networks. The needs of the wartime mobilization encouraged the social insurgencies of labor organizing and civil rights challenges to segregation, and the interactions with different people and places during the war years encouraged people to rethink parochial assumptions of ethnic and racial difference and to imagine postwar society as the beginning of something new. FDR's "soak the rich" income tax policies, full employment, the expanding number of workers protected by social security and union contracts and later the GI Bill and highway building expanded the number of people who could move from the working class to the middle class, buy homes, and take advantage of new educational and professional opportunities. However, the Depression experience of scarcity was vivid in people's minds, large pockets of poverty persisted, and Americans benefited unevenly from this economic growth, making the new gains seem at the same time within reach and precarious. Television's broadcast scope from the national into the living room had enormous potential to reshape public life and private experience.

These years were also a turning point in American Jewish culture. Many American Jews were now one and two generational experiences away from the greenhorn mentality of immigrant forebears. During the war, American Jews stationed overseas and on the home front struggled to comprehend the horrible fate of European Jews under Nazism, and to know what to do about an increasing number of verbal and physical attacks on Jews in communities across the country. Most mainstream Jewish organizations eschewed public discussion of anti-Semitism, Nazism, or the death camps, because it seemed too dangerous to call attention to Jewish victimization. They responded to the news of mass killings of Jews with generous attempts to care for survivors, stressing their American loyalties and condemning prejudice and bigotry generically rather than anti-Semitism in particular. Especially after the war, the murder of European Jews was commonly seen as one among many Nazi atrocities, and Jewish organizations played a leading role in many postwar campaigns to oppose all forms of ethnic, racial, and religious intolerance. Alternatively, some left-wingers, Jews among them, saw the wartime discrediting of Nazi racialization as presenting a special opportunity to discredit fascist racialization in general, and they seized the moment to challenge racial boundaries of all kinds and to publicly expose and critique varieties of American anti-Semitism and assumptions of racial inequality. What kinds of public discussions of these issues would leave their imprint on television?

Live drama was an important and prominent feature of television production from 1949 to 1960. It was largely shaped by the generation born in the 1920s, touched by the traumas and hopes of the 1930s, seared by their experience of war, and excited about the new possibilities television represented. In these early years, television provided an extraordinary new venue for writers to explore a wide range of social issues with a broad audience. When the exceptional broadcast struck a chord with viewers, its characters and themes entered the popular imagination and provided a shared reference point for a whole generation. When television dramas were remade as movies, and many of their directors and scriptwriters migrated from New York to Los Angeles, their subjects and their visual styles influenced Hollywood filmmaking.

When production for the new medium of television began in earnest at the end of the war, live drama was one of the initial formats to be tried. Early experiments in live drama appeared as part of the first broadcast schedules in 1944. In April 1945, NBC's *Television Theater* made its Sunday night debut with an adaptation of a popular late 1930s play, Robert Sherwood's *Abe Lincoln in Illinois*. Broadcasting from New York, the theater capital of the country, television producers assumed they had abundant dramatic properties from which to draw, and by the fall of 1948, there were six drama anthology shows on television, including CBS's *Studio One*, and NBC's renamed *Philco Playhouse*; eleven more would go on the air by the fall of 1950. Drama became a staple for the television's developing audiences, ranked as the highest rated programming in the early audience surveys. The number of television sets increased from 10,000 to 12 million between 1946 and 1951. By 1951, the coaxial cable linking the east and West Coast meant that shows like *Philco Playhouse*, originally limited to NBC's seven East Coast stations, could now be broadcast in major cities across the nation via sixty-one network stations. By the end of the decades hundreds and hundreds of plays had been broadcast; for example, *Kraft Theatre*, the first hour-long series, produced 650 plays between 1947 and 1958.

Writers and directors from Jewish backgrounds played a central role in television drama because they were part of the New York theater world from which it drew, especially the left-wing theatrical milieu of the 1930s and 1940s. The idea of bringing classical and socially conscious drama to new audiences through television was inspired by the rich experimentation in popular theater in the 1930s, ranging from productions of New York's Group Theater to the government-sponsored regional Federal Theater Project production, and innovative theater on radio, such as Orson Welles' "Mercury Theatre on the Air." The more familiar vaudeville and minstrely stereotypes, and the most frequently performed classics began to give way as new kinds of ethnic and working class characters populating new kinds of plays dramatizing pro-labor and anti-fascist themes appeared on stage and on the air. During the war, popular theater was utilized as a key vehicle for maintaining military and domestic morale. Some soldiers with theater experience found themselves transferred to special performing units, supported by the military to tour defense plants and military bases. Jews and non-Jews had worked closely with each other in the left-wing theatrical world of the 1930s, and many of them fought together in World War II. Together they would create the production styles and themes of live TV drama. The earliest TV producers, such as NBC's Fred Coe and CBS's Worthington Miner, came from mainline Protestant backgrounds but they had been drawn to theater's bohemian culture and touched by the drama of the popular front left. Coe's high school Presbyterian theater group performed Clifford Odets' play *Waiting for Lefty*; Coe acted in the Nashville Community Playhouse production of Maxwell Anderson's Sacco and Vanzetti play, *Winterset*, and in the summer of 1939, he directed its production of a modern dress anti-fascist version of *Julius Caesar*, assisted by Vanderbilt student Delbert Mann. Coe turned to popular fiction by writers on the left for some of his early adaptations, such as a December 1947 production of Tennessee Williams' short story "The Last of the Solid Gold Watches" and an April, 1949 version of Budd Schulberg's controversial portrait of an ambitious Jewish Hollywood producer, *What Makes Sammy Run*. Miner had been part of New York's left theater in the 1930s, directing social protest plays by Albert Bein, Paul Green, and Irwin Shaw. Minor's first *Studio One* season in 1948 included his version of a modern dress *Julius Caesar*, with Roman legions costumed to suggest Nazis. During the 1949 season, the Yiddish film actor

David Opatoshu helped Minor adapt a short story by the popular Jewish writer Ben Hecht for broadcast on *Studio One*.

Connections from Yale Drama School helped a number of early staffers to find their way to live television. Coe and Delbert Mann had attended Yale Drama School and they hired other Yale graduates to work with them at NBC, including the director William Corrigan and the writers Tad Mosel and J.P. Miller. Max Wilk, whose father worked for Warner Brothers and who wrote for Goodyear-Playhouse as well as other television shows, trained at Yale, as did Herbert Brodkin. During the war Brodkin had made films with the Army Signal Corps; after the war, he moved from being a set designer for Broadway productions to working as a set designer for CBS, eventually producing several drama anthologies, including *Goodyear Playhouse*, *Alcoa Hour*, *Studio One*, *Playhouse 90*, and the *Studio One* spin-off series, *The Defenders*. Brodkin would later produce several of the important television dramas dealing with the Nazi final solution for European Jews.

The early goal of television drama, to bring Broadway to the people, meant that initially it did not stray far from conventional Broadway theatricality. Although Miner explored new camera technique for the plays and short stories he personally adapted for television in the first several years of *Studio One*, he stayed within what he thought to be the theatrical norm, rotating drama, comedy, murder mysteries, and adaptations of classics. As he later described his conception, "It was black tie. There were no dark alleys or kitchen sinks on *Studio One*. There were evil souls and dangerous people, but they dressed for dinner. If they were raped, it was in satin." The successful genres of drama on radio provided the frameworks for the majority of early television plays: police reporter and crime drama, courtroom drama, documentary drama based on newspaper headlines, romance foiled and then revived by twists of fate, and small town girls confronting family obstacles to true love. Early television followed the racially and ethnically exclusionary practices of Broadway and radio drama, assuming a norm of Main Street whiteness, and favoring characters with a "clean American look," unmarked by ethnic, race, class, or regional particularity. In 1952, the African American actor Frederick O'Neal estimated that less than four tenths of one percent of the actors appearing on television were black.

Experimentation with the medium, discovering the style and subject matter most suitable to television's special capabilities, provided the openings for the new kinds of acting and writing departing from the "clean American look" that would come to characterize live TV drama. Walter Bernstein, the grandson of Russian Jewish immigrants, was a writer for *The New Yorker* whose army years were spent working on soldier musical touring shows, including *This Is the Army* and writing for the soldiers' weekly magazine, *Yank*. He retrospectively described the process of discovery of the early years in television: "Television was new. Television was exciting . . . television was this wonderful electronic *tabula rasa* that everyone was rushing to write on. Is it film? Is it theater? It's television! The fact that it was shot live brought it closer to theater. On the other hand, you did shoot it with a camera. Nobody knew anything. It was unique. You could not stop a show once it started. There were no retakes. You could not edit what you shot...."

New York's 1930s left wing theater world shaped early television drama directly when the Actor's Studio, progeny of the Group Theatre, with a membership including many Jews, produced an early television drama anthology from the fall of 1948 through the fall of 1950. *Actors Studio* TV broke out of a rigid Broadway format and away from conventional standards of glamour, presenting one act plays adapted from short fiction. *Actors Studio* TV's weekly productions introduced a whole generation of Method-trained directors, including Martin Ritt, Daniel Mann, and Yul Brynner, and actors such as Martin Balsam, Lee Grant, Julie Harris, Kim Hunter, Cloris Leachman, Nehemiah Persoff, Eva Marie Saint, Maureen Stapleton, Jo Van Fleet, and Eli Wallach, to expand TV drama's psychological and visual range beyond the "clean American look."

The popular theater imprint on early television, especially its encouragement to explore the social concerns of the day, collided with the rising political power of anticommunism, which created roadblocks in subject matter and limits on personnel. *Counterattack*'s *Red Channels* published broadcast listings in June 1950, providing the means for regularizing a mechanism to blacklist the left-wing actors and writers who had been central to so much popular theater throughout the 1940s. Sponsors, already sparring with network management over control of program content, responded to the threat of conservative-activated consumer boycotts by institutionalizing censorship machinery. Eventually the networks themselves took over this regulatory function, and made it fully effective. Blacklisting mechanisms multiplied when HUAC resumed its broadcasting industry hearings in 1951 and 1952, amplified by the American Legion's additional investigations and publication of *Firing Line*. Sponsorship rules for television drama replicated the segregationist dynamic of radio, with industry norms dictated by Southern prohibition on any presentations of race outside of minstrelsy humor and domestic service. These limits formed the implicit boundaries shaping the sense of what was possible on network television drama.

In 1950, Martin Ritt began to work for CBS. The son of Jewish immigrants, Ritt had gotten involved in theater in the 1930s, participating in the Federal Theater Project, the radical Theatre of Action, and the Group Theatre in the late 1930s. He had acted in and directed plays during the war in a special Army Air Forces Unit. Moving to television, he directed and produced shows on *Danger, Somerset Maugham Theatre, Celanese Theatre,* and *Starlight Theatre,* often alternating with his friend, Yul Brynner, Michael Chekhov's protégé, and sometimes drawing on scripts written by another friend, Walter Bernstein. Ritt did what he could to take advantage of the freedom to experiment and improvise in TV drama until he was abruptly fired from CBS shortly after he and *Danger* were named in *Counterattack* in May and September 1952.

It was Yul Brynner who brought his friend Sidney Lumet, also connected to the popular front theatrical left, to CBS in 1950 as his assistant director, offering this invitation: "Listen, come on in, nobody knows what the hell they're doing." Lumet was the son of the Warsaw-trained Yiddish actor director Baruch Lumet, and he had begun to act in Yiddish productions on stage and on the radio in the 1930s, appearing in Federal Theatre and Group Theatre productions in the late 1930s. Lumet served in the Army Signal Corps for five years, and then after a disagreement with the Actor's Studio, formed an alternative Actor's Workshop in 1947. He described his turn to directing as "being at the right age when TV came along." Lumet took over as director of *Danger* in 1951 when Brynner moved on to play the lead in the Broadway musical *The King and I*, directing more than 500 television drama productions for *Play of the Week*, *Best of Broadway*, *Goodyear Playhouse*, *Playhouse 90*, and *Studio One*.

In his position, Lumet was able to bring along others who would become important television drama writers. He bought the first script written by the then-advertising writer Reginald Rose, "Bus to Nowhere," for a CBS drama show *Out There* in 1951. The aspiring dramatist Paddy Chayefsky sold his first two television play scripts to *Danger* in the spring of 1952. In 1953, when Lumet directed the television version of the radio history docudrama

Television writer Paddy Chayefsky at his typewriter. Photographed by Walter Albertin for the *New York World Telegraph*, 1958.

show *You Are There*, he employed as writers his friend Walter Bernstein, by this point publicly blacklisted from television, and Bernstein's partners, the blacklisted left-wing Jewish Hollywood screenwriters Arnold Manoff and Abraham Polonsky. *You Are There* offered Lumet and the blacklisted writers an unusual opportunity for dramatizing historical incidents that paralleled contemporary social concerns about conservative and anticommunist threats to civil liberties, civil rights, and freedom of dissent.

New representations of Jewishness appeared on live television drama after the turn to using original plays. These original plays were written by a cohort of television playwrights who collaborated in turning away from satin and towards the kitchen sink by creating the "drama of ordinary life" most characteristically identified with television drama. Writers' original scripts began to be used on *Philco Television Playhouse* in the fall of 1950, becoming its mainstay by the spring of 1951. A few original scripts appeared on *Studio One* in 1951 and 1952, becoming the norm after 1953.

The turn to original drama resulted from the technological limitations and liabilities of filming Broadway theater, and the insatiable demand for fresh dramatic properties for weekly productions. Contemporary psychological dramas were eminently well suited to television technologies of production and viewing. Live drama designed for television could turn technical limitations—less flexibility with focus, lighting, and depth of field, minimal sets, modest costuming—into virtues. Television's claustrophobic settings and shot compositions, over the shoulder close-ups, more dollying than in film to compensate for fewer camera setups, and predominantly close and medium shots encouraged writing interior, intimate drama. Television's placement in the home also encouraged the turn to psychological drama, the "drama of introspection." Because viewers watched TV in private rather than as part of a public audience, its success depended on its ability to suggest "intimacy and immediacy," to give viewers the illusion of "prying into the private lives of your fellows." One early television dramatist, Tad Mosel, characterized the television plays as "personal drama," describing the playwright as going into "other people's houses and tells what he sees there," proposing that "the life may be an unimportant one, but it implies a community, which in tern implies the world." The turn to the ordinary was itself a challenge to norms of theatricality, glamour, and artifice, and potentially an unstable setting for enhancing sponsors' products.

Paddy Chayefsky was the first and most important writer from a Jewish background to understand the special possibilities of televisual intimacy for popularizing generic white ethnic characters, and for including recognizable but not stereotypical Jews as inhabiting the world of everyday people. Chayefsky, the American-born son of Jewish immigrant parents, was drafted into the army right before his graduation from City College in 1943. There he abandoned his given name of Sidney in favor of his chosen name of Paddy, writing the military melting pot into his own signature. After being wounded, he got reassigned to a Special Services division in London, where he met Garson Kanin and the infantryman–stage manager Arthur Penn, also a protégé of Michael Chekhov and later a director on *Philco-Goodyear*. Chayefsky joined David Swift, Robert Alan Aurthur, Horton Foote, David Shaw, Tad Mosel, Gore Vidal, and J.P. Miller as part of the group of writers associated with Fred Coe's *Philco-Goodyear Playhouse*. Horton Foote's evocation of region in his early one act plays exploring frustrated lives and lost loves in small-town southeastern coastal Texas helped to create the prototype for character studies in other locales. In 1952, Chayefsky was trying to support himself and his wife as a writer by adapting books and plays for radio and television when Fred Coe invited him to adapt a *Reader's Digest* article, "It Happened on the Brooklyn Subway."

Chayefsky's adaptation, "Holiday Song," broadcast on September 14, 1952, offered a strikingly new representation of Jewishness. The play introduced two survivors of Nazi death camps, miraculously united by a Long Island cantor struggling with a loss of faith. These two were among the first characters to represent European Jewish wartime experience on television. All the Jewish characters in the play, the cantor, his niece, the rabbi, the congregants, are conveyed as living in a contemporary but self-enclosed Jewish world. They represent a significant departure from the modern passing Jew favored by a film like the 1947 *Gentleman's Agreement*, the unmarked everyman characters created by Arthur Miller in *All My Sons* (1947) and *Death of a Salesman* (1949), and the original *Reader's Digest* account of a reunion of WWII refugees not explicitly identified as Jewish. In the play, rock-throwers breaking the synagogue's window motivated the cantor's crisis of faith and made the connection to the much more powerful anti-Semitism of Auschwitz that had brutally separated the young family who would be reunited through the cantor's intervention.

Chayefsky's Jewish framing was very unusual in 1952; it was apparently "too Jewish" for David Susskind, the Harvard educated Jewish head of the talent agency and production company associated with *Philco-Goodyear*, who suggested removing it. However, Fred Coe supported Chayefsky's conception and even expanded it, broadcasting the play on September 14, 1952, four days before Rosh Hashanah, and casting as the cantor the famous Yiddish actor Joseph Buloff. (Just three years earlier, the Jewish lead character in Coe's adaptation of *What Makes Sammy Run* had been played by Puerto Rican–born actor José Ferrer.) The show got a terrific response from viewers, with Buloff receiving "something like four thousand letters" and it was repeated the next year, also starring Buloff, also scheduled to highlight the celebration of the Jewish New Year. Chayefsky explained his choices to rewrite a news story and postwar suburban location as setting for a "charming folk tale about a small Jewish community" as based on the precedents created by the 1938 European art film Marcel Pagnol's *The Baker's Wife* and the work of Yiddish writer Sholom Aleichem, kept in circulation by the Yiddish theater in New York. The sensibility of "Holiday Song," especially its generational struggle to mediate between old world folkways and modern common sense, was quite distinct from the publicly stated concerns of postwar American and religiously defined Judaism.

Chayefsky's second television play, and his first original credit, "The Reluctant Citizen," broadcast February 8, 1953, revolved around another Nazi concentration camp survivor, whose brutal experiences left him fearful and dependent on his children until a sympathetic social worker at the Educational Alliance helped him aspire to become a "useful and productive citizen." Although only about one fourth of the "Displaced Persons" who entered the U.S. were Jewish, Chayefsky intentionally wrote this character as Jewish, and Coe again chose Buloff to play the role.

After creating these initial Jewish characters, Chayefsky turned to other urban ethnic characters to represent the world of the ordinary. In his next television play, "Printer's Measure," broadcast April 26, 1953, he changed the ethnicity of the characters, who had been based on the Jewish printers he met while working in his uncle's print shop, to Irish. Perhaps, as the Philco-Goodyear television director, Delbert Mann, later speculated, he wanted to avoid being typed "only" as a Jewish writer. He created an Italian butcher as the lovelorn, perhaps autobiographical, character in his next play "Marty," broadcast May 24, 1953, an ethnic representation reinforced by casting Marty's mother, aunt, and Italian customer with actresses from New York's Italian theater. The main character in his 1954 play "The Mother" was an Irish garment worker; his 1954 play "In the Middle of the Night" featured a Jewish garment manufacturer in love with a younger non-Jewish employee. When interviewed, Chayefsky boasted that his neighborhood insider expertise enabled him to create believable ethnic character across ethnic lines. He insisted that he had grown up with Jewish, Italian, and Irish families and that he observed "a distinct similarity between their homes—very close families ties among emotionally volatile people." Television critics at the time noted that Chayefsky's Jewish characters became ordinary by being indistinguishable from other urban working people: "sometimes they are Irish, sometimes Italian, sometimes Jewish, but it doesn't matter. . . . All the major characters are first and second generation Americans; all must work to earn their living." Chayefsky's plays *included* Jews as part of a created ethnic world where drama derived from juxtaposing economic and emotional dependence against autonomy. None of films made from his television plays—*Marty* (1955), *The Catered Affair* (1956), *The Bachelor Party* (1957), or *Middle of the Night* (1959)—featured ordinary characters marked as Jewish.

The television writers Reginald Rose, Rod Serling, and Ernest Kinoy, also from Jewish backgrounds, specialized in a different genre of original drama. Many of their plays experimented with how to best present social justice themes illuminating broadly defined norms of exclusion and discrimination. With political and social sensibilities shaped in crucible of popular antifascism in the late 1930s and 1940s, they hoped to warn of the dangers of fascist racialization and loss of democratic liberties, and to critique conformity as an implicit challenge to McCarthyism. They wrote some of the best-known and most enduring original dramas on television. However, operating within the constraints of commercial sponsorship, segregation, and anti-communist censorship on television required subterfuge and dramatic substitutions. Censorship generally made it impossible to show American anti-Semitism or racism directly. Sometimes, more provocative themes "got through," especially to audiences who recognized these limits.

Reginald Rose is perhaps the writer most closely connected with dramatizing social injustice in television drama. Rose spent a year at City College, three years in the Quartermaster Corps in the army, and five years working as a clerk, publicity writer and advertising copywriter in the late 1940s and early 1950s before he sold his first script to CBS. A number of Rose's most well known plays appeared in 1954 and 1955 on *Studio One*, produced by the anti-fascist German emigree writer Felix Jackson and Herbert Brodkin. After learning to write for television on fiction adaptations and cops and robbers dramas, Rose wanted write an hour-long original play that could express "indignation at mankind's sometimes terrifying irresponsibility and disregard for the basic needs and rights of people." He was thinking about "genocide, pogroms, lynchings, wars" when he figured out an acceptable framework for television drama: using a preventable death of a child in a generic small town school room to lead the grown-ups to acknowledge their own responsibility for what happened. This play, "The Remarkable Incident at Carson's Corner," was broadcast on January 11, 1954.

In his next play, "Thunder on Sycamore Street" (March 15, 1954), Rose tried to go directly to the most pressing social justice issue in the late 1940s and 1950s, the embattled struggles for desegregation. He hoped to probe the white resistance to the 1953 challenge to housing segregation in Cicero, Illinois ("people stoning Negroes in front of their apartments . . . women in the mob, some of them actually holding small children by the hand as they hurled rocks at their neighbors"). The story editor for *Studio One* thought the drama was great, but insisted that "we can't do a Negro," or a Jew or a Catholic. The compromise was an ex-convict homeowner and his family facing a neighborhood mobilized to drive them away. Experienced viewers attempted to decode the censorship tactic: "It was variously felt by viewers with whom I discussed the show that Joseph Blake [the ex-convict] was meant to symbolize a Negro, a Jew, a Catholic, a Puerto Rican, a Communist or fellow traveler, a Japanese or Chinese, a Russian an anarchist, or an avowed atheist. Not one single person I spoke to felt he was actually meant to be an ex-convict." However, the prohibition on direct representations of black resistance or white backlash and political dissent seriously limited the reach of television drama. The practice of substitutions blurred different forms of discrimination, which were not socially and morally equivalent.

Appearing on a late night talk show in 1958, Paddy Chayefsky revealed the logic by which television drama made these substitutions for race, repeatedly. "Suppose... Rod Serling... wanted to write such a simple matter as the Little Rock story. You'd have to make [the character in the play] a Hungarian immigrant coming in from the other country, and the reason they didn't like him was because he looked dirty... Let's face it, you can't write the Little Rock thing..."

Rose continued to encourage audiences to question the politically complacent and conformist crowd and to stand-up for the underdog, in "Twelve Angry Men" (September 20, 1954), "An Almanac of Liberty" (November 8, 1954), on *Studio One* and in "Crime in the Streets" (March 8, 1955) on *Elgin Hour*. His "Tragedy in a Temporary Town" depicted the threatened lynching of a Mexican migrant worker, on *Alcoa Hour* (February 19, 1956). He expanded the courtroom as a format for exploring how class and racialized assumptions shape the criminal justice system in his two-part play "The Defender" on *Studio One*, which later became the basis for the TV series in 1961. Immigrant radicals were center stage when Rose's play about Sacco and Vanzetti appeared on NBC's Sunday Showcase in 1959. Rose was responsible for two accounts of Jewish resistance to Nazi anti-Semitism on television: the 1959 half-hour play, "The Final Ingredient," broadcast on a Sunday program sponsored by the Jewish Theological Seminary, showing inmates at Bergen-Belsen defying camp regulations and risking death to celebrate Passover; and the 1987 TV miniseries "Escape from Sobibor," dramatizing one of the historically documented large-scale Jewish escapes from a Nazi death camp.

Rod Serling was another prolific television dramatist from a Jewish background whose work often explored themes of exclusion and difference. Serling had been a paratrooper in the Philippines during World War II, receiving a purple heart for war wounds. Writing for radio while attending Antioch College on the GI Bill, he began to sell scripts to the drama anthologies after moving to New York. His *Kraft Theatre* play "Patterns" (January 12, 1955) exposed ruthless corporate politics so powerfully that viewers requested a second broadcast, the first broadcast repeated because of popular demand. But Serling faced heavy censorship when he wanted to dramatize community tensions related to the August 1955 lynching of Chicago fourteen-year-old Emmett Till on a summer visit to relatives in a town in the Mississippi Delta and the subsequent acquittal of his abductors. Serling had already been advised that the conflict could not be depicted as black against white, so his initial script redrew the central event as the killing of an elderly Jewish pawnbroker by a miserable town malcontent in an unspecified southern location. The malcontent was tried and released by his own neighbors, as Serling described it, "The story of a town protecting its own on a 'he's a bastard but he's our kind of bastard' basis. Thus, the town itself was the real killer." Press reporting of Serling's offhand comment that the revised play was originally inspired by the Till case mobilized extensive white segregationist protest. Subsequent sponsor pressure required the locale to move to New England, the victim to be a foreigner of unspecified national origins, the killer to be a decent American boy "momentarily gone wrong" before "Noon on Doomsday" was broadcast on *US Steel Hour* (April 25, 1956). Of course the word "lynch" was absolutely forbidden. Serling acknowledged that censorship made "Noon on Doomsday" a "lukewarm, emasculated, vitiated kind of a show," but he remembered "thinking in a strange, oblique, philosophical way, 'Better say something than nothing.'" Serling became a master of indirect analogy, exploring of issues of inclusion and exclusion, false accusation, and scapegoating through using science fiction conventions of time travel and alternative universes in his series, *The Twilight Zone*.

Towards the end of the 1950s, references to wartime anti-Semitism related to Nazism became more frequent. Ernest Kinoy, a radio and later television writer who was a Jewish prisoner of war in a labor camp in Berga, Germany during World War II, wrote "Walk Down the Hill" for *Studio One* (March 18, 1957). This play, the first television drama set in a concentration camp, used the German demand for Jewish prisoners to be identified and separated from other POWs as the starting point for exploring Jewish identity as defined externally or internally. In the early 1960s, Kinoy's scripts insistently invaded the territory previously forbidden on television, writing prize-winning episodes for Rose's series, *The Defenders*, exposing the workings of anticommunism on television in "Blacklist" and spotlighting southern black resistance to segregation in "Non-Violent." He would also go on to write episodes of the African American history epic *Roots* in 1977 and the television play *Skokie* in 1981, dramatizing the confrontation in a Midwestern community between American survivors of Nazism and American neo-Nazis.

The last important venue for original television drama was *Playhouse 90*, broadcast from Los Angeles rather than New York beginning in 1956, and abandoning live for filmed production in 1957. Many of the important producers, directors, and writers for the drama anthologies had credits on *Playhouse 90*, including Fred Coe, Herbert Brodkin, Arthur Penn, Delbert Mann, Robert Mulligan, John Frankenheimer, Franklin Schaffner, Reginald Rose, Rod Serling, Ernest Kinoy, J.P. Miller, Tad Mosel, Horton Foote, and David Shaw. It was *Playhouse 90* that produced one of the most widely circulating accounts of Nazi war crimes, Abby Mann's documentary drama, "Judgment at Nuremberg," broadcast April 16, 1959. Mann, the son of Jewish immigrants, had begun to write scripts for the anthology dramas in the early 1950s but his most notable television work from this period was this play's dramatization of issues of justice and moral responsibility in the war trials. Mann's television play utilized documentary footage. It included the footage of the concentration camps introduced at the actual trial, in combination with scenes shot on a Hollywood sound stage, and it surfaced the tension between Cold War political interests and the prosecution of former Nazis, although the network famously insisted on blanking out several mentions of the word "gas" in deference to program sponsors. "Judgment at Nuremberg," later produced as a Hollywood film written by Mann, provided a central reference point for American viewers trying to comprehend the significance of the Nazi final solution. Sympathy for outsiders, the working poor and racial minorities who find themselves trapped in a social system and denied rights would thread through Mann's later films and made for television movies.

The last original drama which appeared on *Playhouse 90* was a play by Rod Serling about the most important Jewish resistance to Nazism, the Warsaw ghetto uprising. Although Serling was apparently concerned about being narrowly categorized as a Jewish writer, he fought for the play, despite script rejections and sponsor objections. "In the Presence of Mine Enemies" was broadcast on May 18, 1960, apparently because a strike by the Writers Guild of America left the series without an alternative. The play balanced heroes, villains and victims among the German (George Macready and Robert Redford), Polish (Oscar Homolka), and Jewish characters (Charles Laughton, Arthur Kennedy, and Susan Kohner), and explored ethnic, national and religious identities as parochial and arbitrary.

During the decade, the increasing control of sponsors over programming, illuminated by their power to enforce an anticommunist blacklist, narrowed the parameters for live drama content, especially as new filmed television experiments offered themselves as new more commercially popular prototypes. The innovatively filmed *I Love Lucy*, first broadcast in October 1951, demonstrated the powerful appeal of continuing characters and self-reflexive humor interposing show business and everyday life, and filmed westerns, like *Gunsmoke*, premiering in April 1952, also offered continuing characters that captivated an adult audience. Lowered ratings for drama anthologies followed the increase from 12 million viewers in 1951 to 32 million in 1955, and the regional and class diversification of the expanded television audience. The ties with the New York theatrical innovation weakened as television production moved from New York to Hollywood, and the abandonment of kinescopes in favor of videotape for television transmission enabled editing that allowed taped shows to be more like movies. Although it was not immediately apparent, original television drama anthologies, ever more filmlike, were no longer able to compete with the more popular elaborate adaptations and television spectaculars that attracted advertising sponsorship.

At the same time, the dissonance between the social world of the ordinary and consumer celebration of the advertising meant that original drama was becoming less acceptable as a setting for sponsors. As early as March 1954, sponsor directives urged Fred Coe to produce more "conventional boy-meets-girl type of light presentation," rather than the realist troubles of the *Playhouse* dramas. According to *Time*, the ad agency explicitly complained of the "lack of upbeat endings," with one unnamed adverting executive dismissing even its modest alternatives to the conventional as themselves formulaic: "One week there'd be a story about a blind old lady in Texas, and the next week, a story about a blind young lady in Texas." Anticommunist interest in tightening the parameters of "the ordinary" was revealed in the comments of one viewer, writing to the president of Philco after the broadcast of Horton Foote's "The Midnight Caller" that "not one person in the cast was a normal American. They were all neurotics for one reason or another. It is a shame with so many fine stories available such trash is forced on the public." Coe tried to shield writers and plays from interference with sponsors, but by August 1954, Coe himself was fired from the *Philco-Goodyear Playhouse*, and the writing was on the wall for the kind of dramatic writing he had encouraged. When Worthington Minor formed a production unit with Franklin Schaffner, Fielder Cook, and George Roy Hill to produce television drama for Kaiser Aluminum Hour in the fall of 1956, he found his projects censored as too controversial, including one adapting an old Galsworthy play about anti-Semitism in Britain. Minor quit in protest, and within three months, the others, failing to get the green light for original scripts by Rose and Robert Alan Aurthur, were themselves fired for refusing to produce the noncontroversial and more "Americana-oriented" plays preferred by the sponsors and the networks. The demise of *Playhouse 90* in 1961 marked the end of the era.

The drama of ordinary life and the drama of social injustice created by the Jewish television playwrights would continue to circulate after the era of live television in the plays that moved from television to film (Chayefsky's *Marty, The Catered Affair, The Bachelor Party*, and *The Middle of the Night;* Serling's *Patterns* and *Requiem for a Heavyweight*; Rose's *Twelve Angry Men* and *Crime in the Streets*; Abby Mann's *Judgment at Nuremberg* and *A Child Is Waiting*); in the later series, mini-series and made-for-television movies associated with the writers and producers; and through the visual styles of the television directors who moved into film, such as Martin Ritt, Sidney Lumet, and Arthur Penn. Original television drama in the golden era played a key role in expanding the visual and dramatic possibilities for representing Jewishness, Jewish concerns for social justice, and Nazism's racialization of Jews in the mid-twentieth century.

FURTHER READING

Bernstein, Walter. *Inside Out: A Memoir of the Blacklist*. New York: Da Capo Press, 2000.
Boyer, Jay. *Sidney Lumet*. New York: Twayne, 1993.
Buhle, Paul and Dave Wagner. *Hide in Plain Sight: The Hollywood Blacklistees in Film and Television, 1950–2002*. New York: Palgrave, 2003.
Castleman, Harry and Walter J. Podrazik. *Watching TV: Six Decades of American Television*. Syracuse: Syracuse University Press, 2003.

Considine, Shaun. *Mad as Hell: The Life and Work of Paddy Chayefsky.* New York: Random House, 1994.
Cunningham, Frank. *Sidney Lumet: Film and Literary Vision.* Lexington: University Press of Kentucky, 2001.
Jackson, Carlton. *Picking up the Tab: The Life and Movies of Martin Ritt.* Bowling Green: Bowling Green State University Press, 1994.
Kim, Erwin. *Franklin J Schaffner.* Metuchen: Scarecrow Press, 1985.
Kindem, Gorham. *The Live Television Generation of Hollywood Film Directors: Interviews with Seven Directors.* Jefferson County, NC: McFarland and Company, 1994.
Kisselloff, Jeff. *The Box: An Oral History of Television, 1920–1961.* New York: Penguin, 1997.
Krampner, Jon. *The Man in the Shadows: Fred Coe and the Golden Age of Television.* New Brunswick: Rutgers University Press, 1997.
Miller, Gabriel. *The Films of Martin Ritt: Fanfare for the Common Man.* Jackson: University Press of Mississippi, 200.
Novick, Peter. *The Holocaust in American Life.* Boston: Houghton Mifflin, 1999.
Rose, Reginald. *Undelivered Mail: A Memoir.* Xlibris: 2000.
Schaffner, Franklin. *Worthington Minor: A Directors Guild of America Oral History.* Metuchen, NJ: Scarecrow press, 1985.
Shandler, Jeffrey. *While America Watches: Televising the Holocaust.* New York: Oxford University Press, 1999.
Smith, Judith. *Visions of Belonging: Family Stories, Popular Culture, and Postwar Democracy, 1940–1960.* New York: Columbia University Press, 2004.
Sturcken, Frank. *Live Television: The Golden Age of 1946–1958 in New York.* Jefferson, NC: McFarland and Company, 1990.
Svonkin, Stuart. *Jews Against Prejudice: American Jews and the Fight for Civil Liberties.* New York: Columbia University Press, 1997.
Wilk, Max. *The Golden Age of Television: Notes from the Survivors.* Chicago: Silver Spring Press, 1999.

Chapter 13

Intellectual Pogrom: How the Blacklist Purged Political and Cultural Discourse in Early Television
Steven W. Bowie

Any history of Jewish popular culture in the twentieth century must contend with the anticommunist witch hunts that forced hundreds of artists out of the mass entertainment industry during the 1950s. A majority of the artists who were blacklisted, as well as many studio executives who acceded to their persecution and many ex-radicals who named names, were Jewish. The most prominent actors affected by the blacklist—John Garfield, Judy Holliday, Lee J. Cobb—were all among the handful of Jews who had become major movie stars. Whether Jews were a covert target of the blacklist or whether they merely seemed to be disproportionately affected because the film industry itself (and in particular its progressive wing) was dominated by Jews remains a matter of debate. Regardless of the extent to which anti-Semitism was a motivating force, though, the results were indisputable: the blacklist interrupted or even destroyed the careers of many of the most prominent Jews in the American arts.

Most studies of the blacklist examine its impact on various media as a whole, or neglect to differentiate between them in their discussion of the "Hollywood blacklist." However, the mechanism of the blacklist operated differently in each industry: by innuendo and denial in the movies, partially and unpredictably in the theater, and as a complex and corrupt bureaucracy in television. It is in the latter realm that the blacklist operated most visibly and, one can argue, most cruelly, and yet the specifics of the blacklist's impact on the "Golden Age" of television have rarely been scrutinized in detail.

To its misfortune, the American television industry emerged at precisely the same time as the postwar anticommunist scare and subsequent blacklisting of many left-wing artists. The House Un-American Activities Committee's (HUAC) widely publicized hearings on alleged communism within the film industry took place in 1947, only a year before the first organized slate of prime-time television programming debuted. The late fifties, when the blacklist began to fade, was also the period when the independent, New York-based era of television was subsumed into the more commercial production entities of the movie studios in Los Angeles. The timing was devastating, and perhaps not entirely coincidental.

Because most successful film and radio artists saw no future in the primitive electronic box, television out of necessity recruited a fresh crop of struggling New York writers, actors, and directors who defined the aesthetics of the medium as they went along. In particular, a group of fledgling "television playwrights" were drawn to topical material that reflected the period of disorientation and uncertainty following World War II. Rod Serling attacked fascism in *A Town Has Turned to Dust*; Reginald Rose explored bigotry in *Thunder on Sycamore Street* and human rights in *An Almanac of Liberty*. Less confrontational writers still focused on simple poor people (as in Horton Foote's *The Trip to Bountiful*) or ethnic minorities (Paddy Chayefsky's *Holiday Song* and *Marty*) that were rarely seen, at least in a positive light, on the silver screen.

Ironically, this new group of television progressives owed its political awakening in part to the work of artists who were just then being cast out of the movie industry. If the Hollywood blacklistees were radicalized by the economic crisis of the Great Depression, then this younger generation had been the teens who grew up under the influence of the left-wing literature, theater, and music of the thirties. In many ways, they resembled the Hollywood radicals of the preceding generation. A majority of them were Jewish, and many were the children of European immigrants who had come to America to escape ethnic persecution. Just as the Hollywood Jews were among the first in the United States to understand the danger of Hitler, many of the TV generation—in their teens or early twenties when war broke out—enlisted eagerly in the armed forces to fight the violent anti-Semitism that they often took personally. This ideological motive for joining the war effort persisted in peacetime, when cleaning up social injustice in American society seemed a logical follow-up to the liberation of Europe. These artists were, if not radicalized, at least energized by the bonanza of a new and as yet unrestricted medium in which to explore fresh ideas.

At first, it seemed to many in television that the blacklist would pass them by, just as it had never fully clamped down on the New York theater. After all, the House Un-American Activities Committee's interest in routing Hollywood communists was widely seen as political opportunism: branding a movie star as a Red meant big headlines. Television had no stars as yet.

However, a collision with McCarthyism was inevitable as television rapidly became a mass medium. The search for communists in radio and the movies began to peter out just as television viewership exploded in the United States: Americans owned three million television sets in 1951 and twenty-three million only two years later. By 1953, Lucille Ball was a bigger star, and a more attractive target, than anyone who had been forced out of the movies for his or her political beliefs. And what about those writers and their "kitchen sink dramas"—what sort of political activities were they concealing? Liberals like Rose and Serling were safe, but their contemporaries with a more radical political history would not have the opportunity to become celebrity writers. For those who controlled the ideas disseminated across the airwaves, the blacklist had the desirable if perhaps tangential effect of silencing (or at least driving into hiding) the most radical voices that might influence the content of television.

THE BLACKLIST INDUSTRY

Perhaps the crucial distinction between the movie industry blacklist and the television blacklist is the way in which the latter became institutionalized. Hollywood operated as a company town. Power was concentrated in the hands of a handful of studio executives and top producers, all of whom agreed in 1948 to end the employment of suspected communists. Word of mouth was the only tool needed to deny someone work all over town. Once someone was named as a communist, he or she had little recourse but to seek employment abroad or in another line of work.

The television industry was larger and less centralized. Power was divided between the networks and the advertising agencies, while much TV production was outsourced to independent production companies that had no direct equivalent in Hollywood. Talent was numerous and largely unknown, and therefore harder to monitor. Those who were blacklisted had more opportunities to work in secret, and those who wished to keep them out of the industry had to work harder. What evolved was an intricate system of give-and-take between blacklisters and resisters, one that turned the lives of the participants into equal parts Shakespearean tragedy, Beckett-style farce, and Kafkaesque crisis of identity.

Many of film and radio's suspected communists were outed publicly in congressional testimony. Because the television blacklist came later and involved less established artists, it developed largely out of the private sector—the cottage industry of right-wing publications and "clearance" brokerages whose motives and methods were even murkier and more impure than HUAC's. Walter Bernstein's experience was typical: though he was then and remains one of the best-known blacklistees, Bernstein was never named as a communist in congressional testimony. Like most who landed on television's blacklist, Bernstein was first smeared in the pages of *Counterattack* and *Red Channels*.

Counterattack: The Newsletter of Facts on Communism was a monthly manifesto issued by three ex-FBI agents who hit upon the idea of compiling back issues of the *Daily Worker*, *New Masses*, and any other pamphlet or document associated with the left. Names culled from this morgue would be vividly fomented against in *Counterattack*, which was so popular that in June 1951 it spawned a book, *Red Channels: The Report of Communist Influence in Radio and Television*. The subtitle made it clear that the magazine's publishers had found a more responsive audience in the broadcasting world than in other entertainment media. *Red Channels* named 151 "suspected communists" in the performing arts, and asserted that the American Communist Party and its allies "now rely more on radio and TV than on the press and motion pictures as 'belts' to transmit pro-Sovietism to the American public." A new battleground had been declared.

Counterattack and *Red Channels* quickly cut a swath through the TV industry. Ed Sullivan, embarrassed by an outcry over the appearance of Red-baited dancer Paul Draper on his show *Toast of the Town*, conveyed legitimacy on *Counterattack* by vowing to clear future guests through one of its three FBI agent founders, Theodore Kirkpatrick. In the fall following its publication, *Red Channels* claimed two prominent victims from the ranks of new television shows. Jean Muir, cast as the mother to all-American teen Henry Aldrich, was booted off *The Aldrich Family* despite her protests that most of what *Red Channels* reported about her political past were lies. *The Goldbergs* was canceled by Sanka after the show's star/producer Gertude Berg refused to fire *Red Channels*-named cast member Philip Loeb; conveniently, the series re-emerged the following season with a new actor in the role of Jake Goldberg. Loeb, a suicide in 1955, became one of the blacklist's martyrs. He and Muir were well-known performers whose terminations signaled that television, like the film industry, would embrace a policy of capitulation.

Kirkpatrick and company's literary output became not merely a handbook for blacklisting, but also a visual symbol that companies could cite as due diligence in the fight against communism. Ad agency executives were instructed to display *Red Channels* on their desks. High-ranking CBS personnel were signed up for subscriptions to *Counterattack*, whether they wanted it or not.

Counterattack and its imitators acquired their influence by staging persuasive demonstrations of how Red-baiting could directly impact the financial bottom line of advertisers. Although today's television networks have the final word on program content, that power rested squarely with ad buyers until about 1960. Most TV shows were sponsored by one or two large corporations that routinely dictated changes in scripts and set decorations. Anecdotes about how pioneers could not "ford a dam" on a Chrysler-sponsored series, or how only the good guys could smoke on a show funded by a cigarette maker, were common. When the Red scare arrived, it was natural for sponsors' authority to extend into decisions about political content and, more devastatingly, personnel.

In 1953, a pressure group called Aware, Inc. emerged and launched a crafty, aggressive campaign against the live television industry. One of its founders was Laurence Johnson, a Syracuse grocer and an officer in something called the National Association of Supermarkets. Johnson refined the technique of the boycott threat into its most potent form. Suspecting that the CBS anthology *Danger* continued to harbor Reds even after its initial producer Martin Ritt was blacklisted, Johnson contacted its sponsor, the Block Drug Company, with this proposition: what if Block's product, Ammident toothpaste, were to reside in all of the stores under his control beneath a sign exposing *Danger*'s Stalinist infiltrators? Meanwhile, Ammident's chief competitor, Chlorodent, would be displayed nearby under a sign attesting to its manufacturer's patriotism. It was an insidious deployment of social pressure—who would want to be seen dropping the Commie toothpaste into his shopping cart—that naturally impelled ad buyers to cave in to the blacklist.

Johnson's tactics were so effective that he became the era's ultimate emperor with no clothes. He pressed CBS executives into sending him prospective cast lists. Network executives listened when Johnson saw a name he did not like. Johnson and his family were even invited in to watch rehearsals and offer input. Johnson was an elderly, speechifying fellow who under calmer circumstances might have been taken as something of a rube. But, as *Danger* writer Walter Bernstein observed, "everyone in the room accepted his right to determine who and what went on the air."

Although Laurence Johnson was himself an ideologue, Aware, Inc., was in fact a thinly disguised blackmail racket motivated more by greed than politics. It sold networks and ad agencies gossip about prospective employees, at the same time offering blacklistees opportunities to buy their way back to work. Aware or similar agencies would charge the networks $5 to $25 per name for "research"—a fee that might escalate into a payoff that would ensure a clean bill of health for the actor being inquired about. Actress Kim Hunter wrote to Aware cofounder Vincent Hartnett requesting an explanation for her blacklisting. Hartnett replied that for $200 she could purchase a breakdown of what her political "problems" were. Harvey Matusow, an opportunistic informer for the FBI whose congressional testimony had made him something of a celebrity, acted as a consultant for Aware and later denounced the clearance process as an elaborate scam. Matusow admitted accepting payoffs from talent agents to clear their clients, bribing conservative columnists to turn up the heat on suspected Reds, and putting on an actorly sales routine in Madison Avenue visits to rev up executives' fear of political fallout.

Eventually it became more convenient for the networks and ad agencies to internalize the tracking of subversives. Each compiled its own record of alleged communists, a top-secret index that constituted more of an actual written blacklist than existed in Hollywood. Of the agencies, Young & Rubicam was especially odious. It had been the executioner when its client, General Foods, panicked over a handful of viewer letters and dropped the axe on Jean Muir in 1950. A few years later, producer Fred Coe collided with Y&R when his groundbreaking dramatic anthology split its sponsorship, becoming the *Philco* and the *Goodyear Television Playhouse* on alternating weeks. Coe found that Y&R, which represented Goodyear, vetted artists' names far more aggressively than Philco's ad agency—and so he made a concerted effort to schedule blacklisted talent to work on Philco's weeks.

Procter & Gamble employed John Neil Reagan, brother of Screen Actors Guild president Ronald Reagan, as its hatchet man. Reagan would arrive at a network executive's office and read aloud a list of names, instructing the executive not to use any of them on a P&G-sponsored program. The ritual was choreographed to keep blacklisted actors' names from appearing on any piece of paper bearing a Procter & Gamble letterhead.

Throughout the industry, a paper trail was avoided. Most of the dirty work was done by phone. Casting supervisors would call a secret number, read off the names of actors they hoped to hire, and hear a "yes" or "no" without explanation or opportunity to appeal. At CBS, the ominous phrase was, "Sorry, we can't clear."

Of the networks, CBS was the most rabid in its adherence to the blacklist, ironically because its history of producing progressive dramas on radio had tagged it as "the liberal network." It was the only network to implement, in imitation of some government agencies and universities, a loyalty oath for its employees. Its internal clearance department was the most draconian, headed by rabid right-winger Daniel O'Shea, a former lackey to David O. Selznick whose relish for his new job earned him the nickname "vice president in charge of treason." In early 1951, CBS hired a former FBI agent named Alfred Berry to investigate all its employees for possible communist ties, even sending him to Washington to track down "leads." *Studio One* director David Pressman became a typical victim of these invasive background checks. CBS offered him a lucrative long-term contract in 1952, but an eleventh-hour vetting of Pressman's past got the director summoned to the office of network lawyer Joseph Ream. The aptly named Ream confronted Pressman with evidence of his Party membership (inaccurate in its specifics, as it happened) and informed him that CBS would not sign the contract. Pressman was blacklisted.

STRATEGIES OF RESISTANCE

Testimony before HUAC, however bilious or craven, had the dubious advantage of a certain accuracy. The Committee knew that its public support would erode if verifiable inaccuracies made it into the record, so friendly witnesses were allowed to give names only after investigators had found at least two independent sources to identify every alleged communist. Not only were *Counterattack*'s data more suspect but the fractured nature of the industry—with each ad agency and network working independently—also turned the clearance process into a deranged game of telephone. Mistakes and inconsistencies were the norm, not the exception. ABC's *Treasury Men in Action* worked from a reverse "white list" of cleared talent available for hire. One actor became unemployable simply because his name was misprinted on the list. The sponsors of *Armstrong Circle Theatre* refused to clear an actor named Rex Thompson, who turned out to be ten years old (and was eventually permitted on the show). Even this sort of dark joke had its tragic counterpart, though: producer David Susskind was refused permission to employ an eight-year-old girl because her father was politically troublesome.

After a certain point, this kind of insanity began to work in favor of the oppressed. Producers sympathetic to those on the blacklist realized that they could turn clearance departments' ineptitude and secrecy to their advantage, and a quiet counterinsurgency began. Producers submitted the same names repeatedly, hoping that a clerical error would allow an actor to work (and running up the networks' research bills as a side benefit). CBS casting director Ethel Winant exploited a twenty-four hour deadline imposed on clearances by noting the exact time a name was submitted; if a response was not received by the same time the next day, the person was hired.

Personal manipulation of the blacklist's enforcers was another strategy. When Winant came up against Max Vanzoff, a conservative but fair Armstrong Tile executive who insisted that no one on the blacklist was innocent, she challenged him to investigate each case himself. Vanzoff agreed. If the charges against an artist seemed bogus, Vanzoff would authorize his or her hiring, and the *Armstrong Circle Theatre* became a haven for certain blacklistees. Famously, blacklisted movie star Judy Holliday did a *Goodyear Television Playhouse* segment in 1954. Her casting came about after producer Fred Coe got the show's ad agency representative drunk at his retirement luncheon and asked for a favor. With nothing to lose, the outgoing Young & Rubicam executive let Holliday do the show.

Although Coe—the most influential producer of live dramas—would fight on behalf of artists deprived of work, he stopped short of employing them without approval. Only a handful of producers were willing to take that risk. The most controversial of them was David Susskind, a former agent who ran the independent production company Talent Associates. Throughout the blacklist era, Talent Associates routinely tried to clear blacklisted talent or hire them under the table whenever possible. Walter Bernstein, for instance, wrote for TA's prestigious *Play of the Week*, and Susskind managed to get Martin Ritt off the blacklist when he hired Ritt to direct the film version of a TA television play, the *Philco Television Playhouse*'s "A Man Is

Ten Feet Tall." However, Susskind was so adept at network politics and, by most accounts, so personally abrasive that many were reluctant to accept him as a sincere foe of the blacklist. The prickly writer Arnold Manoff worked for Susskind once and found that he preferred unemployment. Susskind submitted director David Pressman's name to the networks every year for more than a decade, but would never tell Pressman exactly who was blackballing him (information that could have been ammunition for a lawsuit). Some wondered if Susskind's true motive was getting cheap talent (a blacklisted writer usually commanded a far lower price than he would if allowed to pursue a career under his own name), or suspected that Susskind himself was politically indifferent and his underlings—especially partner Al Levy—were the ones pushing to help unemployed left-wingers.

A unique operation emerged in England, where blacklisted American publicist Hannah Weinstein bought an abandoned movie studio and began producing action programs—*Colonel March of Scotland Yard*, *Sword of Freedom* and notably *The Adventures of Robin Hood*—for U.S. television. A key strategy in setting up her company was Weinstein's access to top writing talent that would be unavailable if not for the blacklist. Weinstein's "story department" consisted of young American ex-reporter Albert Ruben, who commissioned scripts by airmail from the communities of blacklistees in Europe, Los Angeles, and New York. Almost all of the writing credits on *Robin Hood* and the other shows were pseudonymous, and even the company's correspondence hid the writers' true identities: Ring Lardner and Ian McLellan Hunter signed their letters to Ruben as "Will Scarlet" and "Friar Tuck." Because of Weinstein's geographical remoteness, the writers in her employ were never exposed, and when Weinstein shut down operations toward the end of the blacklist era, it was for personal and financial reasons rather than political ones.

Remarkably, one CBS staff producer managed to set up a stable of covert blacklisted talent right in the lion's den. Charles Russell, who replaced Martin Ritt as the producer of *Danger* in 1952, was an aristocratic, apolitical WASP whose movie-star looks had earned him a brief stint as a Fox contract player in the forties. For reasons no one quite understood, Russell risked his career by employing a trio of ex-movie writers who had fled to New York—Walter Bernstein, Arnold Manoff, and Abraham Polonsky—on *Danger*. A year later, Russell took on a new anthology drama, *You Are There*, and had the chutzpah to allow it to be entirely staff-written by blacklistees. At first, Bernstein and the others submitted their scripts under pseudonyms, but eventually CBS uncovered this ploy and ordered it stopped. Russell and his writers responded by engaging politically untainted impostors who would pose as writers for the benefit of snooping executives. These "fronts" were usually either sympathetic unblacklisted writers, or civilians from outside the industry who were prepared to spice up their lives with a little cloak and dagger.

Predictably, such melodramatic tactics often led to farcical outcomes. Writers who worked steadily under a pseudonym lost track of who knew their true identities. A writer might visit a studio and be called different names by different people, or complete a pseudonymous assignment without ever being sure if the show's producer knew he or she had actually used a blacklisted writer. Joan Scott once dived behind a potted plant to avoid being spotted in company that would have revealed her identity to a producer for whom she was writing under the name "Joanne Court." In most cases, once a writer established a pseudonym, he or she was stuck with it until the end of his or her career. *Ben Casey*'s Howard Dimsdale ("Arthur Dales"), *The Ghost and Mrs. Muir*'s Alfred and Helen Levitt ("Tom and Helen August"), and others never reclaimed their true names professionally, simply because it was easier for a writer (even a fictitious one) with recent credits to get jobs than it was for a writer who had not officially worked in a decade.

Similar crises of identity went on in the lives of fronts and the writers who worked under their skirts. When a front was required to put in an appearance at a network, he might find himself asked to comment intelligently on a script he had not read, let alone written—or to write out a new ending while the director looked over his shoulder. If a front were himself a writer, delicate clashes of ego would result from the two writers' varying abilities. Walter Bernstein lost his front Howard Rodman because Rodman felt that Bernstein's work was not up to his standard; conversely, Abram Ginnes parted company with a front who was embarrassed that the Ginnes scripts he put his name on were getting better reviews than his own work. Little wonder that when Bernstein turned his blacklist experiences into a screenplay, the film that resulted (Martin Ritt's *The Front*) was a comedy.

RETURN FROM EXILE

In the film industry, a widely publicized event, that is, the appearance of blacklistee Dalton Trumbo's name in the credits of two major 1960 releases (*Exodus* and *Spartacus*), signaled the end of the blacklist. No comparable watershed moment occurred in television. There, the blacklist trailed off into an inconsistent and often infuriating anticlimax. Many writers and actors, particularly those actually named before HUAC, found themselves unable to work even after the blacklist was supposed to be over. The complicated machinery established by the networks to clear talent ground on with no one at the controls. Artists who had never been named publicly as communists often did not know what authority to ask for permission to go back to work. Actress Lee Grant's employability was restored simply because a member of HUAC owed her lawyer a favor. Irving Brecher, the creator of *The Life of Riley*, escaped by writing a letter to Ward Bond, a right-wing actor who had clout as a kind of self-appointed clearance zealot.

Others less fortunate were required to go through some public *mea culpa*, usually a specific act that would generate a morsel of political capital for a clearance agency or newspaper columnist. Kim Hunter published a letter offering qualified support to Aware, Inc., at that organization's urging. Radio actor Henry Morgan made a speech before AFTRA urging that it not take a stand in defense of Philip Loeb. Such acts were morally dubious but not as heinous as naming names, leaving holdouts on the blacklist unsure about whether to judge them as betrayals or as acceptable concessions to pragmatism.

In 1963, Reginald Rose received the okay from CBS to produce a segment about a blacklisted actor for *The Defenders*, an issues-oriented legal drama he had created two years earlier. Rose was astonished. He had actually pitched the idea to get out of a script commitment, assuming the blacklist was one subject the network would always pass on. Once the script was assigned to writer Ernest Kinoy, the banana-peel logic of the blacklist returned. The show's producer Bob Markell and story editor David Shaw were summoned to the network and told that the main character would have to be a movie actor, because "there is no blacklist in television." Shaw and Markell were aware that *The Defenders*' casting director had just that morning submitted a list of names for clearance. Oblivious to irony, CBS refused to clear David Pressman to direct the episode; he would have to wait two more years before working on *The Defenders*. Stuart Rosenberg, who got the assignment in his place, won an Emmy for it.

Another Emmy victor for "Blacklist" was Ernest Kinoy, not himself a victim of the Red scare. Ironically, Kinoy defeated two blacklistees, Arnold Perl and Allan E. Sloane (a "late friendly" witness who gave names to HUAC after three years on the blacklist). However, the Television Academy would soon begin to recognize of the work of artists returning from the blacklist. In 1966, writer Millard Lampell won an Emmy for a *Hallmark Hall of Fame* play. Lampell's speech, which included the oft-quoted remark, "I think I ought to mention I was blacklisted for ten years," drew considerable press attention and made it permissible for many in the industry to acknowledge a shame that was rarely discussed. Not that everyone got the memo: CBS chairman William Paley and Sylvester "Pat" Weaver, the head of NBC television during the blacklist era, denied the existence of the blacklist (at least at their own networks) until the end of their lives.

A less publicized but more viscerally satisfying Emmy victory occurred the same evening when blacklisted actress Lee Grant won for her work on the prime-time serial *Peyton Place*. In August 1965, Grant joined the cast of ABC's runaway hit as Stella Chernak, a woman who returns to the show's titular small town following a mysterious exile in Los Angeles. Grant's take on this character was revelatory and uncompromising: seething with minute variations of rage and resentment, Grant never let a note of sentiment or forgiveness creep in as the sullen Stella (clearly identified as an ethnic minority from the poor side of town) plotted revenge against the rich WASP prudes who had driven her out. *Peyton Place* was a savvier show than it has been given credit for, but Grant stormed through it with a fury that seemed to overflow the boundaries of gentility the series set for itself. Although the writers drew no obvious parallel, one could not help but see the blacklist as the subtext of Grant's electrifying performance. Here was a case not just of an artist being recognized after a long absence, but of the art itself thrusting an accusing finger toward injustice.

Among writers, a fortunate few had found pseudonymous outlets for their passion even before the blacklist ended for them. *You Are There* restaged a different historical milestone each week, and segments on Galileo, Dreyfus and the Scopes trial allowed the show's writers to champion covertly (in Walter Bernstein's words) "civil liberties, civil rights, artistic freedom, and the Bill of Rights." The *Robin Hood* team made much of the fact that their hero was, in fact, an early practitioner of the radical redistribution of capital. Robert Lees (as J.E. Selby) wrote a number of *Lassie* episodes in the late fifties, each an opportunity to showcase a "lesson or moral" for the show's mostly juvenile audience. Like many of the ostensibly propagandistic films written by Hollywood communists, Lees' *Lassie* scripts espoused a utopian humanism that was not a challenge but a paean to traditional American values.

By the early sixties, Lees and many others were able to reenter the industry openly. Dozens of former blacklistees found work on the most important television shows of the day. Writing as "David Adler," Frank Tarloff was the only writer to make major contributions to both of the best sitcoms of the early sixties, *The Dick Van Dyke Show* and *The Andy Griffith Show*. Arnold Manoff, under the name "Joel Carpenter," wrote a series of offbeat comedies for *Naked City* and *The Defenders* before his untimely death in 1965. Arnold Perl also died young, in 1971, but his final contributions to the medium, two deliriously strange plays for the *Chrysler Theatre*, revealed a major talent in his prime. Perl also produced *East Side/West Side*, the crusading social worker drama that liberated a number of writers, actors, and directors from the blacklist, including Millard Lampell, who wrote a searing episode about racism in the supposedly liberal suburbs.

East Side/West Side lasted for only a single season. It debuted in 1963, a year in which a raft of liberal, topical shows could be found on the major networks: Reginald Rose's *The Defenders* and Rod Serling's *The Twilight Zone*, an in-your-face legal drama and a sly allegory from the two most political of the TV playwrights; the issues-driven medical series *Breaking Point* and *The Nurses*; *The Lieutenant*, a peacetime military dramas that shipped its main character off to Vietnam in the final episode; and *Route 66*, an unclassifiable beat-influenced show whose heroes wandered through parts of rural America not depicted on television before or since. After the fear and hysteria of the McCarthy fifties, the palatable progressiveness of

Camelot was an environment where intellectual and political content could bubble under the surface of television's basically escapist framework.

However, all of these series were off the air by 1965—the same year that the networks quietly dismantled the last vestiges of their clearance bureaucracy. Artists returning from the blacklist often found little on television to stimulate their talent, with sitcoms and action shows largely replacing serious dramas and the occasional challenging program falling victim to network squeamishness (*The Smothers Brothers Comedy Hour*) or low ratings (*The Senator*). Millard Lampell used a pseudonym for his second *East Side West Side* script not because he had to, but because it was rewritten to give the show's working-class hero a glamorous actress girlfriend. Blacklisted writer Richard M. Powell found himself supervising scripts for *Hogan's Heroes*, the prison camp comedy that was arguably the era's most tasteless outing. *Judd For the Defense*, a prestige item created by live TV veteran Paul Monash, spun itself as a successor to *The Defenders*, but an early episode about a blacklisted writer used the character's political past as the motive in a murder mystery rather than an avenue for political comment. One of *Judd*'s producers was Charles Russell—finally fired by CBS for his defiance of the blacklist, he was nearing the end of a slide into alcoholism and inactivity. It was as if television's power brokers had engineered a Faustian bargain: radicals could come back in, but their politics had to be checked at the door.

It is not farfetched to suggest that this defanging of television in the late sixties was in part a result of the blacklist. The McCarthy era coincided with the period during which the first generation of television's power brokers established themselves. Those on the blacklist were excluded from this opportunity, while friendly witnesses bought with their testimony the time needed to ascend within the ranks. Roy Huggins, for instance, had been the *de facto* creative head of television for two studios (Warner Bros. and Fox) by the time the blacklist was broken, and spent most of the sixties and seventies as a producer at Universal responsible for *The Virginian*, *Run For Your Life*, and *The Bold Ones*. Lloyd Bridges starred in the long-running *Sea Hunt* and acquired enough clout to launch his own eponymous half-hour drama. Talent agent Meta Rosenberg became a "packager" of hit TV shows including *Ben Casey* and *Hogan's Heroes*, then attached herself to James Garner as a producer and director on *The Rockford Files*. Is it a coincidence that these three friendly witnesses, who had traded their principles for their careers, came to be associated with "quality" programming that was literate and polished—but resolutely apolitical? Crucially, no blacklistee attained a position of authority in television equal to that of Huggins, Bridges, or Rosenberg.

The dream of a generation of leftist producers and stars creating and controlling politically engaged programming was the most grievous casualty of the television blacklist. One turns inevitably to the output of the returning blacklistees for clues as to what, precisely, might have been lost. Of many possible examples, one of the most intriguing can be seen in the key credits of two blacklisted writers, Abram Ginnes and Oliver Crawford. Both men were typical mid-century leftist intellectuals: each an urban-born child of immigrant Russian Jews, each radicalized as a teen, each conflicted about his faith in an industry where a name change (from Ginsburg and Kaufman, respectively) was a reluctant concession to anticipated anti-Semitism. Crawford, rarely given to autobiographical or introspective projects, nevertheless turned to his own faith for his most personal television work, two scripts (on *Here Come the Brides* and *Death Valley Days*) that examined Jewish-gentile marriage in an unlikely western setting. Ginnes, recruited in 1961 by the police drama *Naked City*, methodically diagrammed a multiracial Manhattan in a series of thirteen scripts, each set in a different ethnic community and many contrasting the clash of old-world customs with the demands of living in a modern metropolis. The first, "The Night the Saints Lost Their Halos," told the story of an unmarried female doctor isolated within her Lower East Side Jewish community because she has defied tradition to pursue a career. The segment begins with a quote from the Talmud: "Given only one life to live, how should we live it?"

The ethnic homogenization of television during the 1950s, as programs like *The Goldbergs*, *Mama*, and *Marty* gave way to more than a decade of prime time in which non-WASP characters were rare and always objects of uneasy scrutiny, has generally been viewed as an inevitable consequence of the technological expansion of television from the country's urban centers to its heartland. It is worth considering that the industry's corps of blacklisted talent, had it retained its voice, might have turned the tide the other way, toward the existence of an ethnically diverse televisual landscape in which Americans could have seen evidence of the civil rights movement in their living rooms at the same time it was unfolding outside their windows.

FURTHER READING

Barnouw, Erik. *Tube of Plenty: The Evolution of American Television*. 2nd rev. ed.; New York: Oxford University Press, 1990.

Bernstein, Walter. *Inside Out: A Memoir of the Blacklist*. New York: Da Capo, 1996.

Buhle, Paul and Dave Wagner. *Hide in Plain Sight: The Hollywood Blacklistees in Film and Television*. New York: Palgrave Macmillan, 2003.

Kisseloff, Jeff. *The Box: An Oral History of Television 1920–1961*. New York: Penguin, 1995.

McGilligan, Patrick and Paul Buhle. *Tender Comrades: A Backstory of the Hollywood Blacklist*. New York: St. Martin's Griffin, 1997.

Skutch, Ira, Ed. *The Days of Live: Television's Golden Age as Seen By 21 Directors Guild of America Members*. Metuchen, NJ: Scarecrow, 1998.

Smith, Sally Bedell. *In All His Glory: The Life & Times of William S. Paley and the Birth of Modern Broadcasting*. New York: Touchstone, 1990.

Chapter 14

Jewish Comedy Writers of the 1950s and 1960s
Kathy M. Newman

Sanford Pinsker, Shadek professor of Humanities at Franklin and Marshall College, remembers watching TV in the 1950s in a suburb of Pittsburgh, Pennsylvania, on his family's ten-inch screen Dumont television. His father, who did not want the television set, soon became a fan of *The Goldbergs*. As a child, however, Pinsker found *The Goldbergs* too "goody goody"; it reminded him of a scolding aunt. Pinsker never saw any families on TV that looked like his. Ozzie Nelson wore cardigan sweaters after dinner and never seemed to work, Pinsker's father "eked out a meager living" as a dry goods peddler, and was never relaxed enough to don a cardigan. The sixties, Pinkser remembers, continued to offer saccharine, unrealistic portrayals of the American family, with shows like *The Brady Bunch* and *The Partridge Family*. Only *All in the Family*, Pinsker claims, had "dashes of realism" and "doses of political liberalism." "Is it of no consequence," Pinsker asks, that *All in the Family* was created by "Norman Lear, a Jewish American shaper of the popular culture?"

It is of great consequence that *All in the Family* was created by Norman Lear, a Jewish television writer. But Pinsker might be surprised to learn that nearly every comedy he watched as a child, from the 1950s to the 1970s, was created, produced, and written by a veritable army of television artists who were Jewish. Even *The Brady Bunch*. Sherwood Schwartz, who created and produced *The Brady Bunch*, grew up in an upper-middle-class Jewish family in Pasaaic, New Jersey, and transferred to DeWitt Clinton high school in the Bronx when his father lost his business during the Depression. Schwartz dreamed of becoming a doctor. He could not get into medical school, because he refused to change his name to something that did not sound Jewish and write "Unitarian" under the religion column on his application to medical school. There was no quota on the number of Jews who were becoming radio writers, and hence Schwartz joined his brother, Al Schwartz, as a writer on Bob Hope's radio show in 1938. Instead of a becoming a medical doctor, Sherwood Schwartz became a joke doctor.

However, Sanford Pinsker is right in his more general point. His Yiddish-speaking, short-tempered, working-class father was no Ozzie Nelson or Mike Brady. Although much of the 1950s and the 1960s television comedy (both stand-up and situation comedy) was created, written, produced, and performed by Jews—it rarely represented the "real life" of Jewish American immigrants. As David Zurawik has argued in *The Jews of Primetime*, despite the powerful presence of Jewish television executives, and the high concentration of Jewish writers and producers in the television industry, "there were no clearly identified Jewish leading characters in a weekly network television series from 1954 to 1972, and 1978 to 1987."

So what did it mean, then, that so many of the earliest television creators/writers/producers were Jewish? What did it mean that so many of them were from Brooklyn, Brownsville, Bushwick, and the Bronx? What did it mean that so many of them had Eastern European parents and grandparents who spoke Polish, Russian, and Yiddish? What did it mean that so many of them were from working-class families—or middle-class families that had been brought down by the Depression? What did it mean that most of them served in the entertainment wing of the U.S. military during WWII? How can we understand the cultural influence of this social formation on mainstream American culture?

Jewish comedy writers invented a new form of comedy in the immediate postwar period: television sketch comedy. This included both the "blackout sketch"—a two-to-twenty-minute character-driven "sketch," which was performed as part of a variety show, and the situation comedy. This new form was drawn, in part, from radio—but it also drew from traditions established by the Yiddish and working-class theater movements of the Depression and World War II era. Television sketch comedy also took some of its influence from avant-garde movements in music and theater; from the "method acting" of the Group Theater, and the jazz saxophone riffs and syncopated rhythms that permeated Sid Caesar's work on *Your Show of Shows*. Jewish writers contributed to every major television comedy hit of the 1950s and 1960s—and a lot of the flops, as well. They wrote for all the stand-up comedians, and most of the situation comedies, too, from *I Love Lucy* to *Ozzie and Harriet* and *Leave It to Beaver*. Jewish writers, in essence, created the iconic images that still persist today of white, Anglo-Saxon, middle-class, Protestant life. Barbara Billingsley in her pearls. Lucy and Ethel watching TV. Dick Van Dyke tripping over the couch.

On the other hand, the situation comedies that we associate with the placid, suburban ideology of the 1950s, like *Leave It to Beaver*, *Ozzie and Harriet*, and *The Donna Reed Show*, were not among the most popular comedies of the decade. The most highly rated comedies of the 1950s included *I Love Lucy* (which was frequently in the top five); it also included *Texaco Star Theater* (Milton Berle), *Your Show of Shows* (Sid Caesar), *The Jackie Gleason Show*, *The Red Buttons Show*, *The Red Skelton Show*, *The Martha Raye Show*, and *The Ed Sullivan Show*. The family situation comedies that were rated in the top fifteen included *Mama, Amos 'n' Andy, Life with Luigi, The Danny Thomas Show*, and *The Real McCoys*. Of these comedies, most of them had writing staffs made up of almost exclusively Jewish writers, and many of them featured Jewish stand-up performers. In addition, many of them had Jewish producers.

Moreover, many of these comedies did not reinforce the white, Anglo Saxon, Protestant, placid, suburban, domestic, child-centered, consumerist, and conformist ideology that we associate with the 1950s. The Brooklyn-born children of immigrants, Jewish writers on *Your Show of Shows* featured Sid Caesar's performances in European "double speak," his parodies of European films, his nutty German professors, and his contentious sketch wife, Doris Hickenlooper. Jewish writers created the constantly arguing, hopeless urban honeymooners, Ralph and Alice Kramden—and all of the other characters that Jackie Gleason played on *The Jackie Gleason Show*. They created *The Danny Thomas Show*: a situation comedy starring a Lebanese American nightclub comedian, his WASP wife, and his children who see him so rarely they call him "Uncle Daddy." They created *The Phil Silvers Show*: a lowbrow antifamily comedy set on a Kansas military base and starring the fastest talking most Yiddish-inflected burlesque trained comedian on the small screen. They created *The Dick Van Dyke Show*, Carl Reiner's tribute to the "writer's room" on *Your Show of Shows*, with the wise-cracking Rose Marie as Sally Rogers and the Jewish comedian Morey Amsterdam as Buddy Sorrell.

BETTER IN THE POCONOS

Less well known than the Catskills, where vaudeville and burlesque performers fled to escape the sweltering New York City summers, the Poconos were also part of the infamous "Borscht Belt." Moreover, it was here, in the Poconos, at Camp Tamiment, that television sketch comedy was born. The camp started as a leisure offshoot of the Rand School of Social Science. It was a camp for singles only (as opposed to families), with a governing board titled "the People's Educational Camp Society." Although it started with a left-leaning social mission it quickly became profitable, too, "drawing middle-class, urban Jews, mostly graduates of New York University and City College." When Tamiment workers started building the camp, Ben Josephson remembers that they told the lumberyard owner that there were three reasons he might not want to sell to them: (1) "We're New Yorkers"; (2) "We're radio New Yorkers"; and, (3) "We're Jewish." To his surprise the lumberyard man answered "No problem." Later on, however, the Camp Tamiment founders had trouble buying dynamite to blow up tree stumps. The storeowner "suspected we were reds . . . It took some effort to change his mind."

Max Liebman had been working as an entertainment director in the Poconos for nine years when he was recruited to work at Camp Tamiment from the Camp Log Tavern in Milford, PA, in 1933. When Liebman took over at Tamiment the weekly Saturday night entertainment was nothing special. Under Liebman's influence, however, it began to make history: "At Tamiment, he devoted his energies to perfecting his own particular review 'formula,' a method by which a new Broadway quality review was written, rehearsed and performed in a fully-staged production within one week." Liebman, born in Vienna in 1899, the son of a furrier, went to the Boys High School in Brooklyn and wrote school musicals with Arthur Schwartz, who went on to write successfully for Broadway. Liebman had a special brilliance for spotting and organizing talent. At Camp Tamiment he recruited rising stars like Danny Kaye (who had worked as a "tummler" at White Roe Lake), Carol Channing, Imogene Coca, Carol Burnett, Bea Arthur (who starred years later on *The Golden Girls*), and writers like Neil Simon, Woody Allen, Mel Tolkin, and Lucille Kallen. With stars and writers like these Liebman produced two shows that would make it to Broadway: *The Straw Hat Review* and *Once Upon a Mattress*, a spoof of "The Princess and the Pea."

During World War II Liebman served in the U.S.O., where he produced a musical review, *Tars and Spars* for the Coast Guard in 1945. Although working for the U.S.O., Liebman met Sid Caesar, a young saxophone-playing Jew from Yonkers who had developed an ear for European languages while working at his father's luncheonette. For *Tars and Spars* they created a nine-minute stage routine in which Caesar mouthed all the sound effects for a fleet of German and American bombers as well as their human targets on the ground. Caesar also performed a conversation in "double talk," the strange dialect that become of the signature of his comedic style, between Adolf Hitler and Donald Duck. Liebman told Caesar to look him up when the war was over. "If I survive the war," Caesar replied, "I certainly will."

After the war Liebman brought all of his great talent together to produce a television show, *The Admiral Broadway Review* for two networks: Dumont and NBC. It starred Sid Caesar and Imogene Coca and it was sponsored by an upstart television producer, The Admiral Corporation. *The Admiral Broadway Review* was well received by critics and audiences, but it folded after nineteen weeks, in July of 1949. According to Caesar, who met with the president of Admiral, the success of the show was creating a greater demand for Admiral televisions than the company could supply. The company dumped the show and put the money it took to produce *The Admiral Broadway Review* into building more factories. Caesar claims it was perhaps the only time in the history of television that a show was cancelled for being too successful.

However, Sylvester "Pat" Weaver at NBC had come to believe in Max Liebman and his team. The cast and crew came back to create *Your Show of Shows* for NBC in 1950. Caesar was again paired with Imogene Coca, and Liebman finally found an acceptable "straight man" for Caesar, the towering 6-foot-4-inch Carl Reiner. Sid Caesar himself was a big, strong man (his strength was the stuff of legends that included stories of Caesar picking up cars and punching a horse) and Liebman believed that the straight man had to be taller than the comic 6-foot-2-inch Caesar. From 1950 to 1954, *Your Show of Shows* boasted a writing staff that included Mel Brooks, Larry Gelbert (who later created *M*A*S*H*), Neil Simon, and his brother Danny Simon. In 1954 Liebman, Caesar and Imogene Coca all parted ways, and Caesar continued to star in a variety show that was now titled: *Caesar's Hour*. Brooks, Gelbart, and the Simon brothers stayed with Caesar; in addition, Woody Allen, barely out of high school, was added to the team, Carl Reiner became a writer, and Selma Diamond, with her smoky, gravelly voice, replaced Lucille Kallen (who left to write for Imogene Coca) in order to provide what Caesar called the "requisite woman's point of view."

Years later, when Larry Gelbert (who was only twenty-two years old when *Your Show of Shows* first debuted) was asked why all of the writers on the show were "young and Jewish," he suggested that it was probably because all of their parents were "old and Jewish." In truth, however, the television shows that starred Sid Caesar had some of the highest concentrations of Jewish writers in the industry. On *Your Show of Shows* Tony Webster was the "token *goy*" (out of eleven writers) and on *Caesar's Hour* that role was filled by Charlie Andrews. Andrews remembers being called "the tamed Gentile." In an ironic twist of fate it was Andrews who helped the blacklisted Jewish television writer, Louis Solomon, get a job on the *Caesar's Hour*'s summer replacement for a few weeks, until he found him a more permanent job on *The Wide Wide World*. Andrews wanted to help Solomon: "Aaron Ruben and Phil Sharp asked me to hire Lou. He wasn't a comedy writer but he was such a sweet guy. It could have blown up in my face, but I didn't have much to lose. Then I introduced him to Bob Bendick (who hired Solomon for *The Wide, Wide World*). In order to hire him on a show as big as that was chancy for Bob, but he did it anyway."

It was also remarkable that both *Your Show of Shows* and *Caesar's Hour* each had a woman writer since few television comedies had *any* women writers. Lucille Kallen, who wrote for *Your Show of Shows*, was also part of the organic origins of the show, since she had been discovered by Max Liebman in 1948 when she was writing for a nightclub review in New York. At Camp Tamiment she met her husband, Herbert Engel, who was working there as a soda jerk, and they were married in 1952. When Kallen left *Your Show of Shows* the first time it was to have her first baby—at which point Neil "Doc" Simon and his brother Danny were brought in to replace her. Kallen came back to write for *Your Show of Shows*, and then left again to write for

Imogene Coca when Coca split with Caesar. Kallen wrote again for TV in 1956 for a short-lived series *Stanley* (starring Buddy Hackett and Carol Burnett) and for a music show on NBC, *The Bell Telephone Hour*, which ran from 1959 to 1968. Kallen wrote a funny, feminist novel in 1964 about her struggles to combine career and family called *Outside There, Somewhere!*—which she dedicated to "Herb and Paul and Lise" (her husband and children) and "the two people without whom this book could not have been written: My Baby-Sitter and My Cleaning Lady."

Although penned and performed by mostly Jewish writers and actors, *Your Show of Shows* and *Caesar's Hour* were not overtly "Jewish." There were few recognizably Jewish characters, and most of the national publicity surrounding Caesar himself made virtually no reference to his ethnic origin. However, the comedy on Caesar's two successful programs was distinct from most other comedies on television in the 1950s. First of all, the comedy had a kind of madcap, immigrant Eurocentrism. Caesar was famous for his "double talk"—his ability to imitate the sound, rhythm, and cadence of German, Russian, French, Polish, etc. Caesar, who started as a saxophone player and joined the New York musician's union in 1940, believed that comedy was a lot like music. One of his most memorable sketches involves a German commander who speaks in an unintelligible German double talk. He orders his servant to dress him, polish his boots, and his brush off his medals. As the scene comes to an end we see the fastidious commandant tending a revolving door at a hotel. As it turns out, he was just a doorman all along.

This skit was typical of another aspect of Caesar's comedy. Caesar and Coca tried to turn domestic clichés—the staple ingredient in 1950s television comedy—on their heads. According to Caesar, Coca "sounded like she came from the Midwest and always spoke in clichés. So we began to develop satires of clichés and platitudes." Here is an example of a husband and wife twisting the dialogue at a clichéd wedding:

Coca:	You know how they met, it was so romantic. He was picking up the garbage. At that moment he fell in love with her.
Sid:	Did you hear, her father is opening a store for him.
Coca:	You think she's that beautiful?
Sid:	With a store, she's beautiful enough.

Likewise, The Hickenloopers, the mismatched couple who argued about everything, were not a sweet, loving, saccharine couple, like Ozzie and Harriet Nelson, or Ward and June Cleaver. In one sketch the Hickenloopers have an argument in which no words are spoken—it is an argument of breaking plates, splintering vases, crashing chairs, and banging silverware. It ends after three days when Doris and Charlie Hickenlooper realize they have forgotten what they were arguing about. As Caesar points out, "What set us apart was that we weren't afraid of showing the emotional and crazy sides of married life."

Born in a Jewish, Socialist summer camp, the comedy and musical review style of *Your Show of Shows* and *Caesar's Hour* would continue to provide a blue print for sketch comedy for years to come; many argue it was the model according to which *Saturday Night Live* was first constructed. The lasting impact of Caesar's comedy on American popular culture can also be found in careers of the Jewish writers and comedians who wrote their first jokes for TV in the writer's room. Although Woody Allen and Mel Brooks both anglicized their names (from Allen Konigsberg and Mel Kaminsky, respectively), they emerged in the late 1950s and 1960s as "openly" Jewish stand-up comedians and filmmakers. Likewise Neil Simon became strongly identified as a Jewish playwright in the 1960s; his play about his days in the "writers' room," *Laughter on the 23rd Floor*, was made into a Showtime movie. Carl Reiner also memorialized the writers' room with his successful television comedy, *The Dick Van Dyke Show*; most recently he played Saul Bloom, an aging Jewish con man in *Ocean's Eleven* and *Ocean's Twelve*. Lucille Kallen had a successful career as a writer of comic detective novels featuring the heroine C.B. Greenfield in the 1980s. She dedicated the first novel in this series to Max Liebman. Selma Diamond wrote a funny book about her life in (and on) television, *Nose Jobs for Peace*, and played the memorable Selma Hacker on *Night Court*. Larry Gelbart, who went on to become one of the creators of *M*A*S*H*, is eloquent about what it meant to be in Max Liebman's writers' room in the 1950s: "We certainly didn't think of ourselves as the greatest writing team in history. We were just a bunch of gifted, neurotic young Jews. Punching our brains out."

"TO THE MOON, ALICE!"

If there was ever a 1950s television couple that nearly came to blows it was Ralph and Alice Kramden. With the Irish American Jackie Gleason playing Ralph Kramden and the Episcopalian child-of-missionaries Audrey Meadows as Alice Kramden, the Kramdens would never be mistaken for *The Goldbergs*. And, yet, *The Honeymooners* had more in common with *The Goldbergs* than they did with their more suburban compadres, like the residents of *The Donna Reed Show* or *Father Knows Best*. Like the Goldbergs, the Kramdens and the Nortons lived in a cramped apartments, yelled out their windows at each other, and were created by a bunch of young Jewish writers from New York.

According to most accounts the skit titled "The Honeymooners" was the creation of Jewish television writer Harry Crane. Born in Brooklyn, Crane started as a stand-up comedian in the Catskills. During World War II, he worked on the script for *Air Raid Wardens* (1943), starring Laurel and Hardy, *Lost in a Harem* (1944), starring Abbott and Costello, and *Ziegfeld Follies* (1946), with Fred Astaire, Lucille Ball, Ziegfeld and Fanny Brice. Crane started writing material for Jerry Lewis and Dean Martin when they were performing at Slapsie Maxie's, a club that was one of the centers for burlesque comedy in Los Angeles. Jackie Gleason was also a frequent performer/customer at Slapsie Maxie's, and, in 1950, when the Dumont Network was looking for a new host for its Friday night show, *Cavalcade of the Stars*, Crane suggested Gleason for the job.

But Crane did not write for Gleason during his first year on the Dumont Network. Gleason's first comedy writers on *Cavalcade of the Stars* worked as a team, Arnie Rosen and Coleman Jacoby (sometimes spelled Jaacoby). Rosen had been writing comedy since he was in high school. There was no "doctor-lawyer" tradition in his family, so his parents—especially his mother—supported his choice of career. He edited his college humor magazine, and, after the Marine Corps, he wrote for a dozen radio shows to try to break into television. In an interview, Rosen once explained that there was a connection between his place of birth and his career as a comedy writer: "[I was born in] Brooklyn—which usually gets a laugh. Unless you were born there. It seems to help if you come from the East coast and you're Jewish. That would be a study in itself, I imagine."

When Rosen and Jacoby started working with Gleason the DuMont network did not know what to do with their new star. According to Jacoby: "They had a lot of trouble in the beginning with Gleason . . . so Arnie and I started inventing. Our first sketch was a Reggie Van Gleason sketch. We wrote up a contract where we owned the characters we created. Unfortunately, when it came time to sue him, which we did, because he used those characters forever, we didn't get a quarter. The contract Arnie drew up was no good." Jacoby had every right to be bitter. The characters Rosen and Jacoby created included "The Poor Soul," a *schlub* of a man who puckered his eyebrows up in the middle and sighed a lot; The Bachelor was a "poor soul" but without dialogue—a character Gleason performed in pantomime as a tribute to his boyhood screen heroes, Charlie Chaplin and Buster Keaton. Joe the Bartender was the neighborhood tavern psychologist who parted his hair down the middle and contorted his face into dozens of expressions; he was the sort of bartender that Gleason had grown up with, and the customers he addressed in his witty monologues were also drawn from Gleason's youth. Rudy the Repairman was a clumsy stooge; Charlie Bratton the Loudmouth was a lecherous lout; and Reggie Van Gleason the III was a snooty, spoiled, no-account aristocrat who insulted his mother, drank with abandon, and wore a top hat, furry mustache, and large cape.

After one year on *Cavalcade*, Harry Crane joined the ranks of Gleason's writers. One of the producers, Joe Cates, remembers that *The Honeymooners* was inspired by a popular radio series written by Phil Rapp, *The Bickersons*. But Crane argues that *The Bickersons* had nothing to do with it: "I had written a sketch called "The Beast When the Honeymoon Is Over" about a bus driver and wife. That was my mother and father. I wrote about my life. I saw these people every day when I was growing up, fighting and scratching for their lives, and the arguments." According to some accounts, Gleason resisted the idea of doing *The Honeymooners*, at first. According to Gleason's account *The Honeymooners* sketch was Gleason's idea: he claimed that Alice and Ralph Kramden were based on his unhappy, squabbling parents.

In the end, Gleason and Crane had a lot in common in when it came to upbringing. Gleason was born and raised in the Bushwick section of Brooklyn, a neighborhood whose hardscrabble poverty would haunt him for the rest of his life. "'I don't ever remember starving,' Jackie recalls. 'But even so, the only the thing my parents ever fought over was money. There was really never enough to go around.'" His only brother died when Gleason was three; his father walked out on the family—never to be heard from again—when Gleason was eight. And his mother, who was forced to take a job as a token clerk in the subway after her husband deserted her, died from an untreated skin infection when Gleason was nineteen. The day she died Gleason claimed he had only a few cents to his name. Likewise, Crane was also from a poor neighborhood in Brooklyn: "I grew up in Brownsville. There was no affluence, no swimming pools. If you wanted to cool off in the summer, you went up to the roof and sat under the line of wet wash."

One thing was for certain: *The Honeymooners* sketch was a hit. In October of 1951, when *The Honeymooners* had just appeared on *Cavalcade* for the first time, the show's ratings were climbing, teenagers all over the country were imitating Gleason's signature phrase, "And awa-a-ay we go!" and the bigger networks were coming a calling. At first, it was reported that Gleason was moving to NBC for $300,000 for several years; one month later, *Variety* reported that Gleason had made a deal with CBS for $300,000 *per year*. Gleason did not get to keep all of that money for himself; he had to pay a lot of the production costs of the show for that amount. But Gleason was on record as one of the highest-paid performers of all time.

The Honeymooners, with exception of having a new Alice (Pert Kelton, the original Alice, lost her job to Audrey Meadows under a cloud of blacklisting rumors and a subsequent heart attack), did not change much in the move from the downscale DuMont network to the upscale studios of CBS. The set retained its depressing, Depression-era feel, with few amenities, old furniture, and bare windows. Women felt so sorry for Alice that they sent her curtains to adorn her apartment. Audrey Meadows had fond memories of their sympathetic gestures: "American's women were so sorry for me in that drab Bensonhurst apartment that they wanted to cheer it and me up a little. I got everything from dotted swiss and regal semidrapes to merry chintz with tiebacks. One dear lady must have thought Ralph and Alice were really up against it. She enclosed ten cents to buy a curtain rod, since, while she could buy one locally, it would be too awkward to mail." These gifts of homemade curtains suggest that one key to the popularity of

The Honeymooners was the pathos it inspired in its viewers. Viewers did not just laugh at Ralph and Alice; they empathized with the couple.

Over the next few years, from the fall of 1952, to the spring of 1955, *The Jackie Gleason Show* rose to become the second most popular television show in the country—with an audience estimated at 13 million—and second only to *I Love Lucy*. CBS found that the Nielsen ratings peaked for the show during *The Honeymooners* sketches, and so in 1953 the average length of the sketch increased from about ten minutes per sketch to about thirty-five to forty minutes per sketch. In 1954, Gleason toppled Milton Berle; Buick Motor Company, which had been sponsoring Berle's *Texaco Star Theater*, became the new sponsor of *The Jackie Gleason Show*, thus intensifying a rivalry between Gleason and Berle, which had been simmering for years. Then, during the 1955–1956 season, Gleason and company filmed individual episodes of *The Honeymooners*, which have become known as the "classic thirty-nine." During this season, *The Honeymooners* aired at 8:30 on Saturday nights, following a revised half-hour variety show. Oddly, on their own, *The Honeymooners* sketches dropped in the ratings to number twenty—just behind their Saturday night competition, Perry Como. Nonetheless, while the filmed episodes themselves were not as highly rated in their first run, they constitute the most widely rerun serial in television history; the "classic thirty-nine" episodes have virtually never been off the air.

Leonard B. Stern, who wrote episodes for the classic thirty-nine, has quipped that if "he knew they were going to become classics he might have written them a little better." Stern, who was one of Gleason's gambling pals in Vegas, was a scriptwriter for Abbott and Costello films as well as the popular Ma and Pa Kettle films before working with Gleason. Besides Stern, there were five additional writers who stayed with Gleason for most of the run of *The Jackie Gleason Show*, and what later became *The Honeymooners*: Marvin Marx, Walter Stone, Harry Crane, Sydney Zelinka, and A.J. Russell. Gleason met Russell when he was doing a serious drama for the Studio One Playhouse. As Audrey Meadows remembered it, Russell and Gleason had a strong, hometown connection: "Writer J.J. 'Andy' Russell might have had a more profound awareness of what made Jackie think and act the way he did than the rest of us, because he was a Brooklyn neighborhood boy who had lived near enough to Bushwick to be a fellow member of the ghetto, 'only we didn't call it that.'" Jack Philbin, one of Gleason's executive producers, remembered that the others writers shared many social roots with Gleason: "[Harry] Crane, [Marvin] Marx and [Walter] Stone were an interesting combination . . . Harry was from Brooklyn, the same part as Gleason. Marvin and Walter were from Jersey, and Gleason had all these ties with Jersey from working in places like the Club Miami in Newark. These writers were so close to Jackie that they took all his personality and almost made it their own."

Some have argued that what made *The Honeymooners* so popular during this period—and since—is the fact that the episodes were "timeless," making few references to political, social, or cultural climate of the 1950s. One Gleason biographer has argued that Ralph, Alice, Ed, and Trixie had little in common with the "real" blue-collar workers of the era: "In the middle of the postwar economic boom, neither couple seems to be experiencing much financial uplift . . . the Kramdens and Nortons seem mired in tenement squalor. In the midst of the baby boom, neither couple makes much noise about becoming parents." Indeed, in the comic plots of *The Honeymooners*, Ralph and Alice struggled to make ends meet on Ralph's bus driver salary; they had trouble finding enough money to pay taxes, pay the rent, donate to charity, buy a television, get Alice a new dress, or go out to a fancy nightclub for a birthday celebration. Ralph fought with his boss, had trouble negotiating a raise, did not always get the shifts he wanted, and lived in fear that he would be fired. Ed and Trixie had a nicer apartment than Ralph and Alice, but in one episode Ed explained that he had to buy everything on credit. On the other hand, perhaps audiences loved *The Honeymooners* not because The Kramdens and the Nortons were so different from themselves, but because they were so similar.

Gleason denied that these plots had any political significance. "Gleason professed to see no political agenda in his depiction of the poverty and thwarted materialism of the working classes." He insisted that Ralph was "no symbol, no metaphor," just "a poor moax" who loved his wife and wanted to please her but had no money to shower indulgences as he wished. Perhaps because of the hardscrabble background of the show's Jewish writers, Ralph and Alice were a world apart from other sitcom couples. They lived in the city. They did not have children. They did not have pets (except once, when Ralph got a puppy). They did not have corny, polite, or mawkish misunderstandings, like middle-class couples on suburban sitcoms: they had the kind of brawls, as Gilbert Seldes once wrote, "that were heard on back porches just before doors slam or crockery is mashed." They did not partake in the consumer madness that was supposedly overtaking the nation—even though they wanted to. Their Spartan existence suggested that perhaps not everyone in America had access to the American dream: to the house, the children, the gadgets, and the gentility.

At times *The Honeymooners* bordered on down right anticonsumerism. Although Ralph and Alice griped that they did not have the consumer conveniences they wanted, when they got them, it never turned out well. When they got a television, Ralph lost sleep every night watching the late late show. When they got a telephone, Ralph suspected that Alice was cheating on him when he found out that she had given out their number to a strange man. When they got a refrigerator, it was part of a scheme to convince an adoption agent that they would be "worthy" parents. However, the agent said "yes" to their application, even when she found out that their "real" refrigerator was just an icebox. Consumer goods did not lead to greater happiness on *The Honeymooners*. Maybe, just maybe, for Ralph and Alice, the American Dream was not all it was cracked up to be.

The Honeymooners also retained an imprint of the progressive political climate of the 1930s and 1940s. In one episode, it was explained that Ralph and Alice met for the first time at a WPA meeting. In another episode it was revealed that Ralph did not get along with Alice's brother because they worked together on a road crew for the WPA, and that Alice's brother had bilked Ralph out of a raise. In another episode, Alice remembered how much Ed Norton helped Ralph when he and his fellow bus workers went out on strike. As Leonard Stern remembers, the comedy he wrote for Gleason appealed to a "common denominator" and the plight of "working stiffs." Stern also remembers the "commonality of humor" shared by ethnic groups in this period, which he describes as "the love and reverence of words, the use of hands and the desire to talk endlessly." Stern acknowledges that there were a lot of taboo ethnic subjects that their comedy could not address, but that they actually had more in common with network executives in the early days of television: "We complained about being restricted but actually that was just a way of venting our frustrations when we couldn't find the right jokes or develop the plot correctly. It was nothing compared to what has happened now because the initial people that represented the networks were respectful of us."

The Honeymooners represented the working class man as a defeated, powerless *schlub*. Ralph Kramden was a loser, what one biographer described as the "biggest loser, and the biggest dreamer, in television history." But Gleason was banking on the fact that there were "far more losers in the nation than winners." Gleason believed his audience would relate to Ralph Kramden as an "Everyman," as a "fatso with thin ideas that never work." Ralph had more than the sympathetic appeal of the lovable loser. He also had temper. Moreover, when he was not angry at Alice, or his pal Ed Norton, he was angry about his station in life: he was angry that he could not control which bus route he had to drive, or which shift he would work, or his salary. He was angry about his rent and the landlord's poor upkeep of his apartment. He was angry at tax time—about how much he had to pay, and how complicated they were to figure out. And in this anger, it seems, Ralph was not alone. His audience laughed at his failures, but they also felt his pain.

MAKE ROOM FOR DANNY

Strangely enough, one of the most "Jewish" television comedies of the 1950s and the 1960s starred a Lebanese American comedian Danny Thomas. *Make Room for Daddy*, renamed *The Danny Thomas Show*, is the fourth longest-running situation comedy in television history (following *The Simpsons*, *My Three Sons*, and *The Adventures of Ozzie and Harriet*). Thomas was born to Lebanese immigrant parents, but early in his comedic career he often passed for Jewish, and was surrounded by Jewish producers, nightclub owners, agents, and writers. As Thomas liked to tell it, he was born Muzyad Yakhoob "on a horse farm in Deerfield, Michigan, over Mrs. Feldman's bakery in Toledo, Ohio." His parents worked as peddlers until they could save enough to buy a horse farm. When Thomas's older brother, William, nearly drowned; he was saved by a local Irish boy, Amos Hurley. Impressed with the bravery of young Amos, Thomas's father renamed his fifth son, Muzyad Yakhoob, Amos Jacobs, and changed the entire family's surname to Jacobs.

In an incident so comically tragic that it could have happened to Ralph Kramden, Thomas's father lost the family's horse farm in a poker game when Thomas was six years old. The new Jacobs family moved to a small apartment over Mrs. Feldman's baker in Toledo, Ohio. Here Thomas listened to Mrs. Feldman. "She told us stories—mostly about her relationship with her in-laws, but sometimes about life in the Polish shtetl in which she grew up. The stories were both hilarious and sad. It was my first introduction to the marvelous subtleties of Yiddish humor, which I have used copiously in my own storytelling ever since I began to work as an entertainer." Thomas changed his name to Danny Thomas when he got his first big break as a stand-up comedian in Detroit. He wanted to make sure that no one back home in Toledo would recognize him just in case his act was a failure, so he used the first names of two of his eight brothers to create the stage name Danny Thomas.

Thomas had a successful three-year run as a stand up comedian at Chicago's 5100 club during the Depression. It was there that he was "discovered" by the infamous William Morris Agent, Abe Lastfogel, who represented Thomas, and whom Thomas called "Uncle Abe," for the rest of his career. Lastfogel sent Thomas on a U.S.O. tour with Marlene Dietrich, and, after the war, Thomas played the role of Jerry Dingle the Postman on Fanny Brice's radio show, *The Baby Snooks Show*. Sherwood Schwartz was one of the young writers on the show—and so was Larry Gelbart, at the age of sixteen. Gelbart, the son of Thomas's barber, always spoke fondly of Thomas's generosity: "Thomas gave me my first professional writing job in 1945. . . . He did it as a favor to my father, who . . . had taken it into his head that I could do such a thing. And so Thomas obliged him. He generously handed a career and a sense of purpose to the son of his barber." Thomas also had a few successful screen roles, but studio executives like Harry Cohn at Columbia kept telling him "to get your beak chopped off already, for crying out loud." Thomas resisted, but he was also beginning to weary of the cross-country, hotel-bound, nightclub life. He begged Lastfogel to find him a job on television, so he could stay close to his wife, Rose Marie, and his three children.

Lastfogel obliged. He made a deal with ABC for the network to hire Ray Bolger, who was a hot property in the early 1950s, and Danny Thomas, a much lesser known entity—both for situation comedies. In the end Bolger's *Where's Raymond?* was short-lived, while Thomas went on to become one of the most beloved of television fathers. The premise of *Make Room for Daddy* was based on Thomas's real life. He played a nightclub performer,

Danny Williams, who spent so much time away from home that his children called him "Uncle Daddy." His character retained his Lebanese ethnicity, embodied by Williams's Lebanese "Uncle Tonoose" who was played by the well-known character actor Hans Conried.

Thomas faced much of the same kinds of racism that Jewish performers faced, especially when it came to his trademark *schnozz*. Interestingly, though, he embraced his quasi-Jewish persona in a commanding performance reprising Al Jolson's role in *The Jazz Singer* in 1952. (Leonard Stern, before writing for Gleason, worked *The Jazz Singer* script.) The *New York Times* review of the film made no mention of Thomas's Lebanese ethnicity; it is merely noted that Thomas, "who does not pretend to emulate Jolson, obviously prefers his own delivery." In the end, the *New York Times* pronounces the film "well dressed" and "well mounted" but "nothing new or especially exciting." In retrospect, however, it seems fairly surprising that one of the epic tales of struggle between Hollywood stardom and Jewish religious identity would be performed by a cast made up entirely of Gentiles and Catholics! And, as it has been argued, if Al Jolson's blackface allows him to become more "white" in 1927, Thomas's reprisal of Jolson's role allowed him, in a way, to become "Jewish." Perhaps by 1952 being Jewish was less ethnically inappropriate than being Lebanese, at least on TV.

Another fascinating aspect of the Danny Thomas story is his longtime collaboration with Jewish television producer Sheldon Leonard. According to Leonard's memoir, Thomas bristled at the idea of having Leonard, who had been typecast as an ethnic gangster actor in a number of films, as his director. However, according to Thomas's memoir it was the "real life" husband of his first TV wife, Jean Hagen, who objected: "I don't want my wife to be directed by that gangster actor." Regardless, Leonard came on board, and Thomas and Leonard developed one of the most successful partnerships in television history. With the money they made from *The Danny Thomas Show* they produced *The Dick Van Dyke Show*, *The Andy Griffith Show*, *Gomer Pyle*, and *The Mod Squad*. Their first collaboration, *Make Room for Daddy*, won the Emmy for Best New Program in 1954 and continued to win Emmys (Best Actor, 1955 and Best Director, 1961) and an additional ten nominations throughout its long run.

Thomas and Leonard, pioneers in the situation comedy genre, developed a comedy technique they called the "treacle cutter." Thomas, famous for his sentimental delivery, could not afford to play his fatherly role too sweetly. Therefore, Leonard and his team of writers would always give Thomas a line at the end of a scene, which "cut the treacle" (a term for molasses). One of the signature lines from the show is, "I love you, you little jerk." Another example is from one of the classic episodes in which Thomas's son, Rusty, runs away from home. When Thomas finds his son in an orphanage (using the name Elvis Earp) he promises he will take his son fishing, swimming, and to a baseball game. At the end of the line he cuts the treacle: "And we'll have dinner together, with you standing up because your bottom will be so sore from the tattoo I'm going to beat on it." With this technique, the burlesque antics of Sheldon Leonard as Thomas's agent, Phil Brokaw, and the hilarious performances of Hans Conried as the Lebanese Uncle Tonoose, *The Danny Thomas Show* maintained a stylistic blend of the sickly sweet sitcoms, like *The Adventures of Ozzie and Harriet* and *Leave It to Beaver*, and the more lowbrow, burlesque-inspired situation comedies, like *I Love Lucy*, *The Honeymooners*, and *The Phil Silvers Show*. Although many of the episodes had a mundane, domestic premise, like "some money is missing and Rusty is accused of stealing it" or "Kathy has a date," in the fourth season, when Thomas's first screen wife, Jean Hagen, leaves the show, Thomas is cast as a lonely widower. His subsequent dating, which leads to his choice of the actress Marjorie Lord to play his new wife, allows *The Danny Thomas Show* to address more substantive issues, such as the problems faced by "blended families." The show even takes on ethnic prejudice in a 1958 episode, "Pardon My Accent," for which Leonard won another directing Emmy.

Leonard was connected to left-wing writers and progressive causes throughout his acting, producing and writing career. The blacklisted John "Julie" Garfield was a close friend of Leonard's during his early career in New York; they performed together in Abraham Polonsky's *Force of Evil* (1948). As a producer in the 1950s and 1960s, Leonard was able to employ several blacklisted writers, including Mac Benoff (a friendly witness) and Frank Tarloff. Later in his career, Leonard expressed his anger about what the "red scare" had done to Hollywood: "The HUAC did its bit toward the reduction of the creative community. It terrorized the colony. People were afraid to express their beliefs. Conversation at social events became vapidly noncontroversial. Many of the most talented and sensitive artists were driven out of the community because their hatred of Fascism on the right had sent them toward the left." At the same time, Leonard was proud of the work he did to help blacklisted writers. In his memoir, he quotes at length from a dialogue between Andy Griffith and Don Knotts, which he then explains was written by a blacklisted writer. Leonard appreciated the "forbidden" talent that he harbored on his productions: "I love that kind of writing. It was done by a blacklisted writer, bearing a name selected from page 326 of the Los Angeles phonebook."

Frank Tarloff, who worked under a pseudonym with Leonard on *The Danny Thomas Show*, *The Dick Van Dyke Show*, and *The Andy Griffith Show*, was from a Jewish family that had emigrated from Poland. His father, who had worked in the needle trades, ran a candy store in New York City after he became ill. He died when Tarloff was twelve years old. At sixteen, Tarloff went to college, where he did poorly in math. But it was in college that he would become friends with two communists and write his first left-wing cabaret, "Academic Epidemic." During the war, Tarloff made his way to LA, where he was hired as a writer for MGM. It was at MGM that he joined the Communist Party: "I was welcome at 'the red table' at MGM, where all the left-wing writers ate. Everybody knew who the left-wingers were . . . I have never regretted, to this day, having joined the Party." During his early days in Hollywood Tarloff began to recognize the unique social formation that was writing for radio in the 1940s: "In radio, all the comedy was being done by about a hundred guys, and we all got to know each other. They were 99 percent Jewish, almost all from the same background, all very, very good friends. It stayed that way during the blacklist."

Tarloff appreciated the freedom he had when working with Leonard. He would tell Leonard the basic idea and Leonard would tell him to "go write it," which surprised Tarloff. "Most writers had to provide a full outline of a script, but I was always able to avoid that." After Tarloff had been working on *Make Room for Daddy* for a few years he began to feel anxious. He asked Leonard: Does Danny know? Leonard decided it was time for Tarloff to write under an assumed name, rather than give a portion of his profits to a "front." Tarloff chose his son's name, Eric Shepard. But Leonard rejected this name because it sounded "too *goy*." "It's not a Jewish name," Tarloff was told. "Get one like every other comedy writer's name. So I came up with David Adler instead." A few years later Tarloff ran into Norman Lear and Larry Gelbart at Schwab's, the popular hang out on Sunset, and they asked him who he was working with. "David Adler," replied Tarloff. They both said, "He's great." Jewish stand-up comedians frequently changed their names (as did Danny Thomas). However, television writers, as Tarloff's case powerfully demonstrates, were expected to have Jewish-sounding names. Otherwise they might be suspected of being closeted Communists.

Danny Thomas, once he knew about Tarloff's taboo status, would tease him by calling him mixed up names, like "Tarloff David." Tarloff remembers that Thomas "wasn't sympathetic politically but he was friendly to my predicament." On the other hand, in his memoir, *Make Room for Danny*, Thomas writes with pride about harboring blacklisted writers. "Two of our best writers were Frank Tarloff and Mac Benoff. Unfortunately, those were the days of McCarthyism, 'Red Channels,' and the Hollywood blacklist. Frank and Mac were on the list—God knows why, because I never heard them say anything more subversive than 'Richard Nixon is a jerk.' But they couldn't work anywhere else in the industry." Thomas remembered that Tarloff was grateful to Sheldon Leonard and himself for allowing giving him a way to support his family. "Later, when the industry honored Sheldon and me for all the shows we made . . . everybody got up and thanked us. However, Frank Tarloff got to his feet and yelled, 'Wait a minute. We've all got some reason to thank these two guys. But I have got the *real* reason. Without them, there would have been no food on the table.'"

Tarloff did not see his contribution to *The Danny Thomas Show* as particularly subversive. He argued that "you couldn't do much politically on television." And, despite his radical politics, he was not bothered by the commercial aspect of television writing: "Working in comedy, being oriented commercially as I have been, I never, never aspired to be a fine writer . . . My attitude has always been, 'What will they buy?'" On the other hand, there was a mildly radical subtext to *Make Room for Daddy*. The character played by Danny Thomas had not one but two interracial—or at the very least interethnic—marriages. And, though it was not meant to be shocking, when the fictional Williams family treated their black maid, Louise, with some humanity, they received a lot of hate mail. Finally, Thomas's character chose a woman for his second wife who already had a child. Years before *The Brady Bunch*, Sheldon Leonard and the gang were already tackling the situation comedy of divorce. In a very real way, Thomas's sitcom "made way for Danny," a Lebanese American with a distinctive ethnic look, and a TV family that was both interethnic and blended. It also made way for Marlo Thomas, Danny's real-life daughter, who, though she succumbed to the nose job, was still a feminist television pioneer with her starring role on *That Girl*. And, in a way, *Make Room for Daddy* made way for Sheldon Leonard and Frank Tarloff, too—at least behind the scenes. Leonard went on to produce the pathbreaking *I Spy*, giving Bill Cosby his first big role on TV, and Frank Tarloff was both a frequent contributor to *The Andy Griffith Show* and one of the head writers on *The Dick Van Dyke Show*.

YOU'LL NEVER GET RICH

Phil Silvers, who had been wildly successful playing the Milton-Berle-esque character, Jerry Biffle, in the musical *Top Banana*, was a pal of Jackie Gleason's from his Los Angeles days, and a comedian with a long, burlesque career. In 1955, when Gleason was filming the "classic thirty-nine," Phil Silvers teamed with one of the best TV comedy writers in the business, Nat Hiken, to produce *You'll Never Get Rich*. This was a lowbrow workplace comedy, which featured the finagling hijinks of a dishonest but affable army sergeant stationed in Kansas named Sergeant Bilko. Silvers played Bilko, who was surrounded by a ragtag bunch of former boxers-turned-actors, including Allan Melvin, who would later play Sam the butcher on *The Brady Bunch*.

You'll Never Get Rich, later named *The Phil Silvers Show*, brought together two Jewish comedy greats. Nat Hiken was a veteran comedy writer who was born in Chicago and raised in Milwaukee, the son of two hard-working, politically Left parents. Hiken's mother Minnie was devoted to left-wing politics, "the more uncompromising the better," and Hiken's father was merely progressive in comparison, refusing to "wear a yarmulke at family weddings and bar mitzvahs." They both belonged to the Workmen's Circle, the Jewish socialist organization, though Minnie, Hiken's mother, became increasingly devoted to Soviet-style communism, and even traveled to Russia in the 1930s. Hiken's father, Max, ran the South Side

Leather Company, a supply store for shoe repair shops, and in 1932 Hiken started college at the University of Wisconsin in order to "avoid selling shoe supplies." Hiken eventually migrated to Los Angeles, where he took refuge with his favorite cousin, Sandy Rothblatt, and he conceived of and wrote a local morning radio program called *The Grouch Club*, which was sponsored by Sam the Credit Man. *The Grouch Club* attracted the attention of the sardonic radio star, Fred Allen, who hired Hiken to be one of his writers.

Hiken met his wife, Ambur Dana, at a political meeting for indigent agricultural workers. (Ambur Dana was also the first cousin of Aaron Ruben, who worked as director on *The Danny Thomas Show* for Sheldon Leonard.) They married in 1941, and lived in New York, where Hiken was working for Allen. In 1947, he quit the Fred Allen show and created the first radio hit for Milton Berle, whose previous attempts had bombed. It was here that Hiken first worked with Pert Kelton (the first Alice Kramden). As Hiken's biographer has noted, Kelton had "a flavorful, blue collar way of tossing a line that was so well attuned to his dialogue style."

It might have been this interest in class tension—or possibly the left-wing politics of his mother, his wife and his cousin—which won Hiken an entry into the blacklisting handbook, *Red Channels*, when it was published in 1950. The entries for Hiken did not paint him as much of a communist threat. He was listed as a sponsor of a May Day parade in the magazine *PM* in 1947 and as a sponsor of the "Scientific and Cultural Conference for World Peace" in 1949. Hiken had supported the activities of his more radical cousin, Sandy, "when it came to such issues as civil rights or aid to the poor." According to Hiken's biographer, after Hiken would write Sandy a check he would kid her: "Remember, when you're up there before the tribunal, when they drag me in, you're going to speak up for me." However, the tribunal, when it came, fingered Nat, and there was little Sandy could do to help him.

Sandy was disappointed with the way Nat handled the blacklist; he sought the help of the infamous anticommunist, George Sokolsky, who acted as an intermediary for blacklistees who were looking for a way to clear their names. Nat agreed to publish a letter in *Variety* stating that he "was not, and had never been a member of the Communist party, and to denounce all that communism stood for." Sandy said that her "heart just dropped to [her] stomach" the day she saw the letter in print, but Nat was able to continue writing for his next gig, NBC's *All Star Revue* "without further harassment."

The job that Hiken was permitted to keep was that of writing for the lowbrow comedienne, Martha Raye, who was one of the rotating hosts of NBC's *All Star Revue*. A natural clown, Raye had appeared in films in the 1940s with Abbott and Costello and Charlie Chaplin. She was also a drinking buddy of Jackie Gleason's. Hiken wrote a part for Raye that made her into a lovable, man-hungry, lowdown character who lived in a "rat trap apartment in Flatbush" with a Jewish neighbor named Mrs. Storecheese. In his first show for Raye, Hiken paired her with the Metropolitan Opera star

Ezio Pinza and sent them on a brow bending date that went from a posh nightclub to the "bucket of blood" nightclub, where Raye's character worked. Hiken finally left the show in 1956, lured away by a promise from CBS to give him more credit—and more responsibility—than he would ever have (or want) again. CBS also promised him a bankable star: the balding, quick-witted, burlesque performer and Broadway sensation Phil Silvers.

Silvers got his start in show business at the age of eight when he was contracted to sing at a getting-out-of-prison party for a Jewish gangster named Little Doggie. Silvers was the youngest of ten, raised by Jewish immigrant parents who had to be whisked out of Russia after Silvers's father threatened (or killed?) a Russian soldier; show business was a way for Silvers to get out of the ghetto—or at least a way into the most interesting parts of it. Silvers's father was an ironworker, and learned to combine Yiddish with the Irish brogue sported by most of his coworkers ("Vell, I tell ye, bejabbers . . ."). Like Hiken's parents, Silvers's parents joined the Jewish Socialist benefit organization, the Workmen's Circle, and his father devoted himself to the cause of the Socialist leader Eugene V. Debs—paying his young son Phil a quarter for every soapbox speech he delivered on Debs's behalf.

As a young man Silvers worked as a comic in burlesque theaters, including a stint at the famous Minsky's Burlesque. Burlesque, according to Silvers, "was about the only steady work in 1932." Silvers wrote that most comics were evaluated not according to "how funny" they were, but "how often" they could be funny. Most burlesque comedians, he observed, were "hokey, rigid and vulgar." But, according to Silvers, a few rose above the medium, including "Abbott and Costello, Rags Ragland, Herbie Faye, Danny Thomas, Bobby Clark, Ed Wynn, Red Skelton, Joe E. Brown, Eddie Cantor. And Fanny Brice." Many of these comedians—Abbott and Costello, Herbie Faye, Danny Thomas, Ed Wynn, and Red Skelton—had successful television careers.

Silvers got his first chance to be a star in the musical *Yokel Boy*, in which he played a Hollywood press agent with New York roots named Punko Parks. The success of *Yokel Boy* led Silvers to Hollywood in 1939. According to Silvers, when he showed up on the MGM lot, where he had just been signed, he was asked to audition for the part of the Vicar in *Pride and Prejudice*. Needless to say, he did not get the part. His Hollywood years led to dozens of bit parts, a few memorable roles, and many big-name friends, including Judy Garland, Mickey Rooney, Frank Sinatra, Bing Crosby, and Orson Welles (it was Silvers's belief that Welles had a secret ambition to be the straight man in a burlesque comedy team). It was in Los Angeles that he first started drinking with Jackie Gleason at Slapsie Maxie's. A few years later Silvers performed with Jackie Gleason at the Copa in New York when Silvers's partner and friend, Rags Ragland, drank himself to death. The first night that Gleason filled in for Ragland the audience—filled with the top comedians in burlesque—began to trade barbs with Gleason, and, as Silvers told it, a mock-fight broke out: "Milton Berle came to my side to heckle

Gleason. Joe E. Lewis joined in. Henny Youngman picked up a violin and went into his routine. Gleason turned a seltzer bottle on Berle who slipped to the floor, and they went into an artificial resuscitation bit. I thought Gleason was really throttling Berle—I knew they had a genuine feud about money—so I tried to pull Gleason away by his tie."

After wowing audiences in *Top Banana*, in 1954 Silvers was asked to be the Master of Ceremonies for the annual show that radio and television correspondents produced for the President of the United States. Silvers, after he was "cleared to make sure [he] had no leftist connections," made Eisenhower laugh hard—twice. This impressed Hubbell Robinson, Jr., the CBS vice president in charge of programming. When Robinson approached Silvers with an offer to star in a television show, Silvers remembered that he was "hooked with two words: Nat Hiken." Hiken and Silvers mulled over dozens of scenarios for the comedy, including casting Silvers as a sergeant in an Army camp. "Oh no," Silvers groaned. "That's Abbott and Costello." But finally the pair settled on the military premise, and Sergeant Bilko was born. Silvers soon learned that "comedy on television is a lot like comedy in burlesque. It's not how funny are you, it's how many weeks can you be funny?" Silvers and company managed to be funny for four years.

In the beginning they filmed a series of trial episodes in front of a live audience until CBS found a sponsor (Camel cigarettes) and a time-slot (8:30 Tuesday nights). This put *You'll Never Get Rich* head-to-head with "Mr. Television" Milton Berle. When Berle found out that he would be competing with the new show he said, "They shouldn't do that to you, Phil." Silvers agreed. When Silvers found out that he was going up against Berle, he "had a hot flash in [his] stomach as if [he'd] swallowed a pack of Camels, already lit." The first week that *You'll Never Get Rich* aired it received a 14.6 share of the rating, while Berle received 23.6. The second week was worse: 14.4 for Bilko, and 28.6 for Berle. But by the end of November the ratings were better: *You'll Never Get Rich* received a 29 share, which beat Berle, who received a 27.4. At the end of the season NBC announced that Berle would be off the air on Tuesday nights. As Berle said to Silvers when it was all over: "You rat. You had to go on Tuesday?"

The title of the show, *You'll Never Get Rich*, was changed after the show had been on the air for a few months to a new title, *The Phil Silvers Show*. But the original title was taken from the popular military song, "You're in the Army Now," and the lyric, "You'll never get rich from digging a ditch, you're in the Army now. . . ." The title also referenced the fact that Sergeant Bilko, even though he was always trying to "bilk" someone for cash, never got rich. And, finally, the title had a slightly ironic quality; you'll never get rich, but then again, maybe you shouldn't want to be? As with the many plots of *Amos 'n' Andy* and *The Honeymooners* that ended in failed "get rich" schemes, the moral of the story of *You'll Never Get Rich* was that friendship, and, especially, fraternity, were more important than money.

Hiken and Silvers figured that they would have a built-in audience of current and former GIs who would appreciate the military setting, and, perhaps, the plebian message. According to Silvers, he and Hiken "didn't want it to be a 'charming' story and they didn't want [Bilko] with a family of kids." Instead, *You'll Never Get Rich* was a workplace comedy. It was a mostly male world, except for the occasional wife, sweetheart, or showgirl, (and the lovely "WACS" [Women's Army Core]). Surprisingly, it was also an interracial world. Hiken insisted on casting black actors, male, and female, to complete the staff at the army base. They had few (if any) lines in most episodes, but their presence was controversial enough to have the show banned in some Southern locals.

The Phil Silvers Show was rife with lowbrow themes, plot twists, and lowdown characters. Gambling, in the form of card playing and horse racing, was a pervasive theme, and, like Ralph Kramden, Bilko always had a foolproof scheme to get-rich-quick that usually misfired. The army base made for a highly malleable setting; the base was an entire world—a whole society—unto itself. And thus Hiken was able to include almost every lowbrow convention into his plots, including gangsters, card sharks, hypnotists, UFOs, a spiritualist named Madam Zaboda, boxing, corrupt politics, diners, nightclubs, failed business ventures (including a uranium cache and a gold mine), and dubious medical potions (a hair tonic, a face cream, and a tranquilizer to cure Bilko's gambling addiction).

The Phil Silvers Show was the pinnacle of the lowbrow comedy genre. It incorporated many of the themes, plots, and characters that had been used on shows like *Amos 'n' Andy* and *The Honeymooners*. This was, in part, because Hiken was able to hire some of the most accomplished "lowbrow" television writers in the business, including Leonard Stern, Arnie Rosen, and Coleman Jacoby, the comedy team that started with Gleason at *Cavalcade* and who had created many of his most enduring characters, Sydney Zelinka and A.J. Russell, two additional alumni of *The Jackie Gleason Show*, Arnold Aurbach, a one-time comedy writer for Milton Berle, and Vincent Bogart, who had written for the lowbrow bar spoof, *Duffy's Tavern*.

According to Leonard Stern, *The Phil Silvers Show* also had a social conscience. Stern remembered that Hiken "tried to touch on race relations and other issues of the day." Sometimes it was hard to see the social "issues" beneath the slapdash zaniness of plots that revolved around eating contests, talent shows, counting jelly beans in a jar, a chimpanzee who was accidentally admitted to the Army, or a $10,000 prize poodle. However, beneath the con-games and contests Hiken and his team of writers did take on such issues as racial and class discrimination. In an episode that highlighted class tensions, "The Blue Blood of the Bilkos," Bilko rushed to the defense of an army buddy who was banned from his own son's wedding "due to the snobbery of the bride's family." Bilko made a sojourn to Philadelphia, where he discovered that "the bride's family [was] not as blue-blooded as [it] seem[ed]."

In other episodes Hiken emphasized one of his favorite themes: the clash of the highbrow vs. the lowbrow. In "Bilko's War Against Culture," Bilko had to find a way to bring his men back to gambling after they were "lured away" by the "art and dance classes run by two beautiful WACs." In another episode, "The Twitch," the "Colonel order[ed] lectures on Beethoven as a punishment for gambling." In another episode, "Bilko's Godson," Bilko used his vast con-man resources to ace the entrance exam to Stanford University. Finally, on the issue of racial integration, Hiken stood by his decision to include black actors in bit-part roles. When Southern stations started to protest, and "one of the advertising agencies sponsoring the show got jittery," Hiken and company were asked to remove the black actors. They refused. As Hiken's biographer explained, "Nat had never been a political zealot, and he may have sidestepped a showdown with industry blacklisters a few years earlier, but he believed in certain progressive principles within his own personal dealings and was willing to stand by them."

HEAD OF THE FAMILY

The story of Jewish television writers in the 1950s and 1960s comes full circle with Carl Reiner's creation, *The Dick Van Dyke Show*. Carl Reiner intended to write about his own life, and starred in a failed pilot for the show, titled *Head of the Family*. As David Marc has brilliantly explained, by the end of the 1950s Reiner could see that the variety show was on the wane, and that a family situation comedy might still have a place on TV. His idea for the show came to him during his commute: "I was driving my car downtown from New Rochelle, wondering what grounds do I stand on that no one else stands on? I thought I am an actor and writer who worked on the Sid Caesar shows." Reiner had been in a reflective mood for some time. In 1958, he had completed his first autobiographical novel, *Enter Laughing*, about an actor named David Kokolowitz. Like his novel, *Head of the Family* was rooted in Reiner's own life—only this time, it was more focused on the space between Manhattan, the work place, and the suburbs of New Rochelle, where Reiner lived. The pilot was funded in part by Kennedy money; Joe Kennedy had screened the pilot at Hyannis Port and had written a large check to help get it on the air. The pilot debuted in the middle of television's dreaded dead zone, July 1960, and later that fall CBS declined to pick it up.

According to David Marc, Reiner's agent, Harry Kalcheim, "persuaded Reiner to meet with another of his clients, Sheldon Leonard." Leonard struggled to tell Reiner the painful truth: "The only think I could say was 'Carl, you're not right for what you wrote for yourself! I believe that if recast, the show would have every chance of making it. Do you mind if I try to wrap the package?'" David Zurawik, in *Prime Time Jews*, suggests that this incident has reverberated within the industry—that it's become the apocryphal story told to Jewish writers in order to persuade them to "tone down" the Jewishness of a character or a story line. Zurawik may be right. According to Leonard Stern, when Stern was producing the pilot episode of *Lanigan's Rabbi*, a short-lived TV series in 1976 starring an aging Art Carney as Lanigan, an Irish cop who makes regular visits to his neighborhood Rabbi, Stern received a memo asking: "Can we make the Rabbi less Jewish?" The answer, of course, was yes, and Stuart Margolin was brought in to play the "less Jewish" rabbi.

In the end, Sheldon Leonard and Carl Reiner were willing to play the TV game, even if it meant making Rob Petrie "less Jewish." In fact, it is hard to imagine a "less Jewish" actor than Dick Van Dyke, the jello-limbed, loose-lipped, physical comedian, master of the pantomime and the double take. All of the "Jewishness" of the original Rob Petrie was deflected into the part of Alan Brady, the show's Max Liebman, played by Reiner, and Maurice B. Buddy Sorrell, the wacky, tacky Mel Brooks of the writers' room, played by the variety show veteran, Morey Amsterdam. Buddy had a platonic relationship with the sexless Sally Rogers, played by Rose Marie Mazetta, who had been in show business since the age of three. The Rogers character was a condensation of the woman writers who worked with Sid Caesar, Lucille Kallen and Selma Diamond. Rogers, portrayed as perpetually and tragically single, was probably closer to Diamond in terms of her biography (since Kallen was married with children, and Diamond was not), though Diamond displayed a sexy sophistication about her love life that Rose Marie's character was lacking (see Diamond's *Nose Jobs for Peace*). By the 1960s, however, Kallen must have been a forgotten contributor to the writers' room, since even Rose Marie had never heard of her: "I knew about Selma Diamond, but I never knew about the other one."

Perhaps the most Jewish of all *The Dick Van Dyke Show* episodes is the one in which Buddy finally gets bar mitzvahed as an adult. Some have suggested that this episode further minimizes Buddy's character—implying that he is suspended in a kind of perpetual adolescence, and drawing attention to his Jewishness in a negative way. On the other hand, Elliot B. Gertel discovered that the idea of giving Buddy a "grown up" bar mitzvah came from one of the show's Jewish writers, Art Baer: "According to the oral histories that I conducted, the idea of giving Buddy a bar mitzvah ceremony came from the mother of the writer Art Baer, who regretted that her son lacked both the time and the funds to have a bar mitzvah instruction, due to his need to work and to help out the family.... *The Dick Van Dyke Show* had a warmth and egalitarian quality that came through even, or especially, in its most biting humor."

Despite the changes Reiner and Leonard made to *The Dick Van Dyke Show*, and perhaps because of them, the comedy that starred a gangly guy with Dutch heritage formed the bedrock of Reiner's later successes. "I don't know what would have happened if I hadn't done *The Dick Van Dyke Show*," Reiner reflects. "I think that is the show that formed my career more than anything." Moreover, today Reiner is able to connect his Jewish identity to his choice of comedy writing as his strategic tool for fighting discrimination: "Jews have always fought back," Reiner says. "Comedians fight with their mouths. . . . You win the day by making other people laugh."

FURTHER READING

Buhle, Paul and McGilligan, Patrick. *Tender Comrades: A Backstory of the Hollywood Blacklist.* New York: St. Martin's Press, 1997.
Caesar, Sid. *Caesar's Hours: My Life in Comedy, With Love and Laughter.* New York: Public Affairs, 2003.
Diamond, Selma. *Nose Jobs for Peace.* Englewood Cliffs, N.J: Prentice Hall, 1970.
Everitt, David. *King of the Half Hour: Nat Hiken and the Golden Age of TV Comedy.* Syracuse, NY: Syracuse University Press, 2001.
Fry, William and Allen, Melanie. *Make 'em Laugh: Life Studies of Comedy Writers.* Palo Alto, CA: Science and Behavior Books, 1975.
Gelbart, Larry. *Laughing Matters: On Writing MASH, Tootsie, Oh, God! and a Few Other Funny Things.* New York: Random House, 1998.
Kallen, Lucille. *Outside There, Somewhere!* New York: Macmillan, 1964.
Leonard, Sheldon. *And the Show Goes On: Broadway and Hollywood Adventures.* New York: Limelight Editions, 1995.
LoMonaco, Martha Schmoyer. *Every Week, A Broadway Revue: The Tamiment Playhouse, 1921–1960.* Westport: Greenwood Press, 1992.
Marc, David. *Comic Visions: Television Comedy and American Culture.* Boston: Unwin Hyman, 1989.
Pinkser, Sanford. "My immigrant family, the popular culture, and me," *Judaism* (Number 174, Volume 44, Spring 1995).
Sid Caesar Collection: Inside the Writer's Room. Beverly Hills, CA: SidVid, 2000.
Silvers, Phil. *This Laugh Is on Me: The Phil Silvers Story.* Englewood Cliffs, NJ: Prentice-Hall, 1973.
Stern, Leonard and Robinson, Diane. *A Martian Wouldn't Say That.* New York: Price Stern Sloane, 1994.
Thomas, Danny. *Make Room for Danny.* New York: Putnam, 1991.
Zurawik, David. *The Jews of Prime Time.* Hanover, NH: Brandeis University Press, 2003.

Chapter 15

Bring in the Klowns: Jewish Television Comedy since the 1960s

Vincent Brook

1960s AND 1970s: INTERMARRIAGE, INC.–*BRIDGET LOVES BERNIE* AND *RHODA*

Periodically, Jewish survivalist angst, ever simmering on the edges of communitarian debate, erupts into crisis. One of the more volatile of these eruptions in the United States occurred in the 1960s, fueled by a series of late-1950s population studies detailing "soaring" intermarriage rates, on which *Look* magazine based a 1964 cover article titled "The Vanishing American Jew" (Morgan 42–43). Unmentioned in the brouhaha was another "crisis" of Jewish survival, on America's television screens. No sitcom or other episodic series *with explicitly identified Jewish protagonists*—the definition, in this chapter, of a "Jewish" program—had aired on any of the major networks since the demise of *The Goldbergs* in 1956. Gone also by the late 1950s were the Jewish-hosted, Yiddish-spiced variety shows that together with the live anthology dramas had dominated early TV, most notably Milton Berle's *Texaco Star Theater* and Sid Caesar's *Your Show of Shows*. The implicitly Jewish comedy series *The Jack Benny Program* made it into the 1960s, but Benny's Jewishness, like George Burns's of *The Burns and Allen Show* remained "closeted" and undisclosed (Berger 99). A full-ledged "Jewishcom" would not resurface on American TV until the early 1970s, when *Bridget Loves Bernie* (1972–1973) hit the air.

This intermarriage sitcom about a Jewish young man and an Irish-Catholic young woman was a curious way to attempt a re-Judaization of prime time. Not that the theme was an unfamiliar, or historically unpopular, one to Jewish or non-Jewish audiences. *Bridget Loves Bernie* was essentially an updating of the 1924 Anne Nichols play *Abie's Irish Rose*, which had spawned a host of imitators and itself had been adapted for the big screen in 1928 and again in 1946 (Erens 106–107). TV itself had dealt with Jewish outmarriage as early as 1948, the first year of network television, and on occasional episodes and anthology dramas thereafter (Pearl and Pearl 195–196). In the context of the survivalist crisis of the 1960s, however, it is not surprising that the reaction to the show, from virtually the entire spectrum of American religious Judaism, was instant and resoundingly negative: Jewish leaders met with CBS officials and demanded that *Bridget Loves Bernie* be withdrawn, one rabbi threatened to organize a boycott, and the show's producers reportedly even received bomb threats (Fiske E8, McClain 94).

Receiving less publicity than the intermarriage issue but more troubling to some Jewish critics was "a new kind of crisis" the show exemplified: hyper-assimilation. For Robert J. Milch of *The Jewish Spectator*, *Bridget Loves Bernie* accurately conveyed the sense that "the state of being Jewish has become so attenuated that for many the very term 'intermarriage' has no meaning" (26). Furthermore, not only had Bernie, like the preponderance of third-generation American Jews he represented, been de-Semitized, but his second-generation parents' ethnicity had been rendered atavistic as well. "Why are you suddenly acting so Jewish?" Bernie asks of his suddenly Yiddish-spouting, *matzah ball*-serving family at the dinner intended to introduce them to his betrothed (9/16/72).

In spite of, or sparked by, the controversy, *Bridget Loves Bernie* was the highest-rated new show on TV, ranking as high as fourth among all TV series and fifth for the season. At the end of March, however, at the height of the Jewish protest and the show's popularity, CBS announced that *Bridget Loves Bernie* would not be renewed for the next season. Defying credibility with the aplomb of a presidential press secretary, CBS President Bob Wood explained that the decision to cancel the show was "absolutely removed, independent, and disassociated from criticism of the show from some Jewish groups" (Montgomery 40).

Just as the attempt at a Jewish sitcom was part of the overall TV industrial turn to "relevance" and ethnically specific programming, the reaction of Jewish advocacy groups to *Bridget Loves Bernie* was part of a larger trend. The settlement of the landmark WLBT case in 1969, after a decade-long struggle between African Americans and a white-owned and -oriented Jackson, Mississippi TV station, finally granted minority groups the right to challenge station-licensing renewal by the Federal Communication Commission (FCC). The WLBT case sparked a movement for media advocacy among the various segments of American society whose minority consciousness had been raised by the civil rights movement. As a result, "virtually every ethnic group mobilized against prime-time TV" by the late 1960s and early 1970s (Montgomery 25).

The rise of image monitoring in general, and the virulent reaction to *Bridget Loves Bernie* in particular, makes *Rhoda*'s prime-time existence, much less its survival for five comparatively controversy-free years (1974–1979), all the more perplexing. Spun-off from the hugely popular *Mary Tyler Moore Show* (1970–1977), *Rhoda* starred Valerie Harper (a non-Jew, as was Bernie portrayer David Birney) as a dark-complexioned, nasal-inflected Jewish Woman in Search of Marriage. At least this was the stereotypical role she had played for four years on *Mary Tyler Moore*, as the New York Jewish "wry" to best buddy Mary Richards' white-bread, Minnesota WASP. Just two months into her own series, however, Rhoda Morgenstern of the Bronx was exchanging vows with an Italian Catholic construction company owner Joe Girard (played by the Jewish David Groh).

The most common explanation for why Jewish media monitors let the intermarriage issue slide on *Rhoda* but not on *Bridget Loves Bernie* is that while the latter show was *premised* on intermarriage, the former show was not: Rhoda herself—a familiar, much-beloved character from her days on *Mary Tyler Moore*—was the crux of her sitcom; *who she was* rather than *what she did* was of primary importance on this, as on most other James L. Brooks/Allan Burns "character-driven," shows (e.g., *Mary Tyler Moore, Phyllis, Taxi*). The show's writers did strive for a certain Jewish "sensibility"— a strong sense of family, Rhoda's self-deprecating humor, her warmth and sensuality—but the show's overall Jewishness, as Executive Producer Charlotte Brown related in an interview, "was just 'set dressing'—Ida's brisket, her plastic on the furniture."

For me, however, it is precisely Rhoda's Jewishness, rather than her lack thereof and more than her character's popular pedigree, that explains the disparate reactions to Rhoda's and Bernie's intermarriage—Jewishness, that is, combined with gender. Based on the Jewish tradition of matrilineal descent, a Jewish male who intermarries is inherently more problematic, from a survivalist standpoint, than a Jewish female. According to the matrilineal principle—since revised by the Reform movement but the normative position of organized Jewry in the 1970s—the children of an intermarried Jewish woman are considered Jewish, while those of an intermarried Jewish man are not, and these can only reclaim their Jewishness through formal conversion. The Jewish Population Survey of 1970 further suggested that an intermarried Jewish mother rather than Jewish father was a greater guarantor of Jewish continuity because she was more likely to raise her offspring Jewish (Steinberg 34–35). Narratively speaking, therefore, whatever remained of Rhoda's Jewishness had a much better chance of being "passed on" than Bernie's, making her if not exactly a positive role model for Jewish survivalism, at least far less of a threat.

In other gender-specific ways, Rhoda served as a proactively positive Jewish role model. Given that the Jewish Princess stereotype of the possessive, demanding woman had come into vogue in the 1970s, the fact that Rhoda resisted its pejorative pull was itself significant (Barr 91). As *Jewish Journal* columnist Marlene Marks reminisced in 1991: "Rhoda, still lovingly remembered by the mass of American women, Jewish or not, between 30 and 50, proved there was more to the Jewish woman than the stereotype. She was not a princess. She was not a shrew. Yes, she was an underdog, but not a loser" (33).

Overall, however, critical assessment of the media effect *Rhoda* had on and for Jewish women, and Jews as a whole, was and remains decidedly mixed, with negative stereotyping and assimilation providing the main bugaboos. Rhoda's mother Ida (also played by a non-Jew, Nancy Walker) exemplifies the post-*Goldbergs* downshift from the nurturing *Yiddishe Momme* to the overbearing Jewish Mother, while Rhoda herself is, for many, the very embodiment of assimilation. TV historian Howard Suber likens Rhoda's "nominal Jew" to Diahann Carroll's "White Negro" in the late 1960s series *Julia* (14); or as Rick Mitz puts it, comparing *Rhoda* to another late 1960s show starring Marlo Thomas: "[Rhoda] went from being 'That Nice Jewish Girl' to *That Girl*" (287).

INTERCHANGEABLE ETHNICS: *BARNEY MILLER, WELCOME BACK, KOTTER*, AND *TAXI*

As it had with the studios through much of American film history, the statistical fact and popular perception of Jewish "over"-representation in the U.S. television industry exacerbated the tendency toward Jewish "under"-representation on TV screens, largely due to fears of anti-Semitic backlash. This "self-protective" attitude among network executives persisted, moreover, even as commercial considerations in relation to ethnic pluralism were revised upward and anti-Semitism, by most measures, was revised downward. Suber, in a 1975 article titled "Hollywood's Closet Jews," lambasted Jewish film and TV executives for continuing to "pass" as non-Jews, symbolically and literally, in their de-Judaizing and de-Semitizing of the media (14). In "Television's Interchangeable Ethnics," another article he wrote the same year, Suber decried the homogenizing tendencies of *all* ethnic television depictions, not merely Jewish ones. Likening TV's then-current "obsession with minorities" to Hollywood's rash of pluralist platoon-movies during World War II, Suber found "that it didn't really matter which ethnic groups were represented. . . . Characters 'happened' to be Jewish, or 'happened' to be Polish, or 'happened' to be black . . . as if by accident" (53).

Barney Miller (1975–1982), *Welcome Back, Kotter* (1975–1979), and *Taxi* (1978–1983) offer classic examples of the platoon-type show with a nominally

Jewish lead. Of the three, *Barney Miller* was and continues to be regarded in the bulk of the Jewish discourse as a quintessentially de-Judaized show. This view was given added weight by series creator Danny Arnold's oft-cited claim that, in the face of network resistance to the casting of the Jewish (and allegedly Jewish-looking) Hal Linden as Barney, "we deliberately called him Miller because it was an ethnic/nonethnic name.... We never said Barney was Jewish and we never said he wasn't" (quoted in Gitlin 186). Yet someone at some point decided to spill the Manischewitz, for on one Christmas episode, Barney "came out," explaining that his lack of enthusiasm for the holiday resulted from his being a Jew. The status of *Welcome Back, Kotter* and *Taxi* as Jewishcoms rests on similarly shaky grounds, with rare episodes in each series making off-handed reference to the eponymous Gabe Kotter's (Gabriel Kaplan) or *Taxi* co-protagonist Alex Rieger's (Judd Hirsch) Jewishness.

The simultaneously foregrounded and disguised ethno-racial dynamic of cultural pluralist sitcoms such as *Barney Miller, Welcome Back, Kotter*, and *Taxi*, in which the quasi-Jewish protagonists' backgrounds are left the haziest of all the ethnically specified characters', that speaks most directly to the tenuousness of 1970s Jewish televisual representation. And even more tenuous determinations could easily be, indeed have been, applied. Adopting the notion of an antic and cerebral Jewish "style" to television comedy, Erik Breitbart has deemed Sgt. Bilko of *The Phil Silvers Show* (1955–1959) and even the de-Judaized *Dick Van Dyke Show* (1961–1966)—with endorsement from Dick Van Dyke himself—as essentially (if secretly) Jewish (35–36). The idea of a Jewish "sensibility" in *The Odd Couple* (1970–1975) is supported by Neil Simon's claim that he was "writing Jewish" in giving character Felix Unger "Jewish idiosyncrasies, phraseology, martyrdom, self-pity" (quoted in Altman 61–62). And if de-Judaized Jewish actors such as Bea Arthur of *Maude* (1972–1978), Peter Falk of *Columbo* (1971–1978), and Jack Klugman of *Quincy, M.E.* (1976–1983) have been "perceived as Jews" on their shows (Elkin 23, O'Connor 23), then Penny Marshall and Cindy Williams of *Laverne and Shirley* (1976–1983) certainly should be. Despite the eponymous duo's apparent identity as working-class Italian (Laverne DeFazio) and Irish (Shirley Feeney), the two women regularly refer to themselves in the opening-credits sequence as *schlemiel* and *schlimazel*—Yiddish terms for two traditional types of comic fool.

Seeking to avoid the pitfalls of both the all-is-Jewish and almost-nothing-is camps, I have charted a dialogical course between the two: one that acknowledges a Jewish hand, on many levels, in American television production, but that also seeks, and seeks to assess, the Jewishness of that production. By such criteria, as an overall judgment of Jewish television comedy in the 1960s and 1970s, one could usefully reverse Edith Bunker's famous quip in an episode of *All in the Family* about the social progress of African Americans—"They've come a long way ... on TV!"—and conclude about America's Jews: "They've come a long way ... except on TV!"

1980s THROUGH THE PRESENT: THE "JEWISH" SITCOM TREND

The situation changed dramatically—literally and figuratively—in the 1980s, largely due to the smash-hit 1978 mini-series *Holocaust*. Piggybacking on the phenomenally successful 1977 African American saga *Roots*, *Holocaust* was alternately denounced for trivializing an "ontological" event by Elie Wiesel (Auster 66) and lauded as "the most powerful drama ever seen on TV" by *Washington Post* columnist Tom Shales (Auster 66); but the series' epochal significance for Jewish televisual representation was unanimously acknowledged at the time—"turning point," "watershed event," "cataclysmic shift"—and retrospectively—"It legitimized the presentation of Jews and Jewish subjects on television" (Auster 67); "The perception and portrayal of Jews . . . on television was to be forever altered [by *Holocaust*]" (Pearl and Pearl 230).

An onslaught of Jewish-themed made-for-TV movies and miniseries followed: *Playing for Time* (1980), *The Diary of Anne Frank* (1980), *Skokie* (1981), *Golda* (1982), *Ellis Island* (1984), *Wallenburg* (1985), *Escape from Sobibor* (1987), among others. Yet this indisputable Jewish TV-*movie* trend must be contrasted, and reconciled, with a comparative death of, indeed decline in, Jewish *episodic* programming over the same period, certainly with regard to the situation comedy. As for dramatic series, the number of recurring Jewish characters increased slightly, if significantly: Mick Belker and Henry Goldblume on *Hill Street Blues* (1981–1987); Stuart Markowitz and Dr. Rebecca Meyer on *L.A. Law* (1986–1994) and *Buck James* (1987–1988), respectively; Joe Kaplan on *Our House* (1986–1988); Paul Pfeiffer on *The Wonder Years* (1988–1993). Drs. Daniel Auschlanger and Wayne Fiscus were arguably the first Jewish protagonists (albeit in a large ensemble cast) in a dramatic series, on *St. Elsewhere* (1982–1988), and they were followed by the yuppie adman Michael Steadman (and his insecure cousin Melanie) on *thirtysomething* (1987–1991). But between the 1979 finale of *Rhoda* and the debut in July 1989 of *The Seinfeld Chronicles* (later *Seinfeld*), all Jewish sitcoms had to show was the quasi-Jewish *Taxi* (1978–1983) and the extremely short-lived *Harry* (March 4–25, 1987), starring Alan Arkin as the Jewish purchasing agent at a New York City hospital. For the generic bulwark of Jewish representation on U.S. television, at least, it appeared that the more things changed, the more they stayed the same.

As did the reasons for the representational stasis: Jews' numerical dominance of the management and creative end of the business, and anxiety over anti-Semitic reaction to this perceived imbalance. NBC President Brandon Tartikoff acknowledged as much in 1985, when he stated that a main cause for few TV series being devoted to Jews and Judaism was that "so many Jews are behind the camera" (Elkin 1985, 25). The long-standing aversion among Jewish executives to drawing "attention to themselves" had been exacerbated by the *Bridget Loves Bernie* affair. "They don't want to be bothered," opined Eric Goldman, director of the Jewish Media Office, by the sort of controversy that befell the ill-starred intermarriage-com. As for the paradoxical rise in Jewish-themed TV movies, Goldman suggested that occasional rather than regular treatment of Jewish characters and issues was permissible for Jewish executives, because it allowed for a "uniqueness" of presentation but was comparatively "safe" (Elkin 1985, 25).

Even *Seinfeld*, the show that would help launch the Jewish sitcom trend, was initially rejected by Tartikoff and other NBC execs for its alleged "too Jewishness": the eponymous star's Jewish name and features, his stand-up comic occupation, and the show's "Jew York City" location amounted to ethnic overkill for the network brass (Kronke and Gauthier C13). *Seinfeld*, of course, not only survived NBC's self-imposed anti-Semitism but would go on to become one of the super-novas of the 1990s and arguably the decade's defining series. Moreover, *Seinfeld* was far from a one-hit Jewish wonder. The period from 1989 through the mid-2000s would see an unprecedented surge in sitcoms featuring explicitly Jewish protagonists, many of them major critical and/or ratings triumphs: for example, *Brooklyn Bridge* (1991–1993), *Mad About You* (1992–1999), *The Larry Sanders Show* (1992–1998), *The Nanny*, (1993–1999), *Friends* (1994–2003), *Dharma and Greg* (1997–2002), *Will and Grace* (1998–2006), *Curb Your Enthusiasm* (2000–), *Arrested Development* (2002–2006). In all, close to forty Jewish sitcoms would air on prime-time network and cable between 1989 and 2005, compared to a grand total of seven such shows in the previous forty years (please see list at the end of the chapter).

As for the main determinants of this explosion in Jewish programming, I offer the following: (1) *a new generation of Jewish television personnel*, more secure in their position as Jews in American society and less defensive about portraying "themselves" on U.S. television; (2) *the green light from Jewish advocacy groups*, which rose briefly to help sink the Jackie Mason-starring intermarriage-com *Chicken Soup* (1989) but otherwise were kept at bay; (3) *high ratings*, as can be judged by the mega-hits listed above, and of course nothing breeds a trend like endorsement from the Nielsens; (4) *the Jewish stand-up legacy*, as an astonishing number of the Jewish sitcom stars possessed this "pre-sold" dimension: Jerry Seinfeld, Jackie Mason, Richard Lewis (*Anything But Love*, 1989–1992), Jay Thomas (*Love and War*, 1991–1993), Paul Reiser (*Mad About You*), Garry Shandling (*The Larry Sanders Show*); (5) *industrial competition*, from new or enhanced programming sources—cable and satellite, increased independent stations, a fourth network, Fox (and eventually a fifth and sixth, UPN and the WB)—and new technologies—video tape (later DVD), remote control (and eventually the Internet)—forced the once cozy network triopoly out of its shell of complacency; (6) *audience reconfiguration*, begun in the 1970s but spurred by the competitive factors just mentioned, heightened the shift toward "narrowcasting" and "niche" programming that "helped spawn the need for cultural- and ethnic-specific styles" (Caldwell 9); (7) the "*Cosby* moment," a term Herman Gray uses to explain the Black sitcom wave propelled by *The Cosby Show* (1984–1992), can be seen as laying the groundwork for more ethnic-oriented fare in general; and (8) *the multicultural/assimilationist dialectic*, to me the most complex and significant factor and one which demands closer scrutiny.

Jews' widespread acceptance in mainstream white America in the 1980s and 1990s came at a moment when a revitalized identity politics was putting a heightened premium on difference. These opposing integrationist and separationist tendencies not only reinforced but also threatened Jews' historically unique insider/outsider status in American society. The commercial and cultural constraints of American television necessarily muted the particularist aspects of the Jewish TV revival, but this very muteness reveals the contradictions inherent in Jews' double investment in assimilation and multiculturalism. For, ultimately, Jews' socioeconomic and cultural success was achieved not through the flaunting but rather the shedding of cultural specificity, a process that not only contradicts identity politics but is also, perhaps, irreversible. The "closeted" or de-Judaized Jews of early television—George Burns, Jack Benny, and Carl Reiner—though they may have rejected religious Judaism and the immigrant experience, bore its distinctive traces nonetheless—the inflections, the Yiddishisms, the bodily mannerisms and manifestations. By contrast, the open, even proud Jews of the Jewish sitcom trend, though they may have had less to hide, on TV as in U.S. society, also have had less to show. Television's Jews confronted, as the Pearls out it, "a stark and alarming reality: they no longer possessed a unique identity to distinguish them. Now that they and the characters they created had achieved acceptance and sameness . . ., both onscreen and off, [they] were faced with a searing question: 'Now that we are like everyone else, *who are we?*'" (Pearl and Pearl 231).

SEINFELD AND COMPANY

"Who we are," it turns out, was a range of things—almost all, in some way, still distinctively Jewish. Surely one of the most overtly and sympathetically Jewish of the trend shows was also one of the earliest, *Brooklyn Bridge*. Betraying its generic roots in the seminal *Goldbergs*, *Brooklyn Bridge* was creator Gary David Goldberg's serio-comic homage to his mid-1950s New York childhood. A "quality" sitcom with no laugh track and a TV-movie look, the show, while set among an extended Jewish family living in a heavily Jewish neighborhood, refrains from "ghettoizing" the environment as exclusively Jewish. Irish, Italian, and other ethnic families are not only prominently displayed, but a *Bridget Loves Bernie*-like romance between the teenaged Jewish protagonist, Alan Silver (Danny Girard), and his Irish

Catholic neighbor and sweetheart, Katie Monahan (Jenny Lewis), forms the throughline of the series. *Brooklyn Bridge* is set in 1955–1956, the same year that *The Goldbergs* was leaving the air. Thus an intertextual throughline of assimilation is also established, with *Brooklyn Bridge* extending the Americanizing notion developed in *The Goldbergs* by reflecting it back onto the inner-city environment from which the suburban-bound Goldberg family was ostensibly "movin' on up." By "bringing it all back home," *Brooklyn Bridge* thus functions as a nostalgic (thus anachronistic) bridge between assimilationist and multiculturalist agendas. Assimilation need not mean homogenization, *Brooklyn Bridge* proclaims; through ritualistic remembrance—a time-honored Jewish practice that the comedic form itself is said to approximate (Marc)—ethnic identity can be maintained.

Historical connections with Blackness provide the strongest link to multiculturalism. Besides the recurring character of the Black school teacher, Mr. Grier (Brent Jennings), African American elements permeate the series. Indeed, from protagonist Alan's perspective, the sitcom essentially exists under the dual signs of Jewishness and Blackness. Jewishness—personfied by the pogrom-surviving matriarch, Grandma Sophie (Marion Ross)—provides the moral core; Blackness—embodied in sports, popular music, and poetry—supplies the pleasure. In the end, however, the multicultural trope is truncated. With the exception of a brush with Greenwich Village–style neo-radicalism (in "On the Road"), the show's commingling of Jewishness and Blackness is ultimately subsumed within the cultural politics of assimilation rather than diversity. As genuine and potentially transformative as the Silvers' inter-racial romance with American cultural forms and figures may be, it essentially functions as neo-blackface, enabling the immigrant family to maintain a modicum of difference within an integrationist America that (anachronistically) no longer excludes Blacks. This historical slippage is significant, for it not only elides the bitter struggles of the civil rights movement but also posits a prelapsarian image of ethnoracial harmony as an antidote to the contentious multiculturalism of the 1990s. "Why can't we all just get along?" the show's black-Jewish connection seems to plead—although, unlike Rodney King, with a nod to an idealized past rather than to a utopian future. Or as Mr. Grier, after Eisenhower's 1956 landslide presidential victory, counsels Alan's all-white class (only two of whom know anyone who voted for Ike): "What unites us is stronger than what divides us!" ("War of the Worlds, Part II").

An even more complex assimilationist/multiculturalist stratgems inform the "decade-defining" *Seinfeld*. Here, "particularist" Jewishness, mocked at a distance in interfaith-romance shows like the contemporaneous *Anything But Love*, has been transformed into a "universalist" Jewishness that can be derided more openly, not because Jewishness has been absorbed into the mainstream but rather the reverse: because the mainstream has become Jewish. This transformation from "assimilatee" to "assimilator" in *Seinfeld* has ramifications not only for postmodern Jewish identity, but for the historical moment of the show's original run.

Seinfeld's Semitic bone of contention, George Costanza (played by the Jewish Jason Alexander), brings the Judaization process of the show "about nothing" into sharp relief. Is George now or has he ever been Jewish? Textually and extratextually, nobody knows for sure. Even George's "parents"—both the diegetic Mr. and Mrs. Costanza—and the show's creative personnel contradict one another on the issue. The Jewish Estelle Harris (who played Mrs. Costanza) ambiguously averred in an interview: "We're not supposed to be Jewish. I once asked Larry David [the show's Jewish co-creator], '*What are we, Jewish?*' He said, 'What do you care?'" (quoted in Fretts 44). Series co-producer Gregg Kavet, however, declared categorically that George *is* Jewish by virtue of the fact that "his mother was written as a Jewish character" (quoted in *Jewish Telegraphic Agency* 11). Carla Johnson framed an entire *Journal of Popular Film and Television* article around George's archetypal connection to the *schlemiel*, the classic existential fool of Yiddish folklore and literature. And Jason Alexander himself has admitted to basing his performance of George on a combination of Woody Allen and Larry David (Zehme 44). Papa Costanza-portrayer Jerry Stiller perfectly captured the paradox of the Jewish Question in regard to George when he joked, "I think we're a Jewish family living under the Witness Protection Program under the name Costanza" (Fretts 44).

More important than outing George, or his TV family, as Jewish, for our purposes, is determining how the "in-joke" of his Jewishness or non-Jewishness is used to structure the production and circulation of ethnicity in the show. For network executives squeamish over "too-Jewishness," and desirous of broadening audience appeal, George's "double identity" obviously allowed them, once again, to have their Jewishness and disavow it, too. For media watchdog groups concerned over offensive Jewish portrayals, George's stereotypically Jewish characteristics—short, balding, bespectacled appearance; bumbling, miserly, and misanthropic behavior—become tolerable under cover of hybridity. And for analysts of the Jewish sitcom trend, George's *goyish* Jewishness (or Jewish *goyishness*) can be taken as another sign that the whole country is being Judaized.

The same ethnoracial sensitivity that has allowed Jews to withstand adverse social conditions over the millennia, Johnson observes, has turned them into a sociocultural barometer of these conditions as well. The accuracy of the measurement in the case of *Seinfeld*, socioculturally and institutionally, was uncanny. The show's ratings ascension coincided with a steep downturn in the U.S. business cycle, culminating in the recession of 1992. As for the much-touted economic boom beginning in 1993 and lasting through the 1990s, this financial upswing primarily benefited the already-wealthy while continuing leaving the average American ever further behind. It wouldn't be until the late 1990s that the rising tide from the "longest boom in post-World War II

American history" would begin (for a brief time) to lift all boats, instead of only all yachts (Healy A16). On the TV-industrial front, the multicultural incursions into *Seinfeld* and company's once-privileged white middle-class space are also uncannily reflective of the networks' shrinking audience share in the face of the cable, technology and niche-programming revolutions. The show's ethnospatial implosion can thus be taken as a metaphor not only for the overall middle-class economic contraction but also for the breakdown of the network hegemony as well.

UNDER THE SIGN OF *SEINFELD*: *MAD ABOUT YOU* AND *FRIENDS*

Seinfeld did not instantly catch fire with TV audiences, ranking a respectable but far from "decade-defining" thirty-eighth among prime-time episodic series in its second full season (1991–1992) and only breaking into the top ten midway into its third season. The following season marked the onset of what *Time* magazine termed the "*Seinfeld* era," with five consecutive seasons in the top three, two of these at number two, and two at number one—a remarkable stretch that unquestionably contributed to the profusion of Jewish sitcoms over the same period (Staiger 25). Besides its commercial encouragement to pursue explicitly Jewish projects, *Seinfeld* offered itself in other ways as a model for emulation—or rejection. The darkly satirical sitcom had broken a cardinal rule of the business, what Jane Feuer calls the "likeability factor" (Feuer 52). While an occasional comedy series, such as the short-lived *Buffalo Bill* (1983–1984), had featured an unsympathetic protagonist, the difference with *Seinfeld*, besides its longevity, was that not just the protagonist but all four main characters were an insult to humankind. Despite *Seinfeld*'s breakthrough success in defying the "likeability factor," however, the *Seinfeld* era is more noteworthy for other Jewish shows' reaction against rather than for *Seinfeld*'s predilection for moralisms. Ironically, nowhere is the commitment to redressing *Seinfeld*'s breach of characterological etiquette more pronounced than in the two other "Must See" Jewish sitcoms cited as *Seinfeld* clones—*Mad About You* and *Friends* (Rapping 110).

Although the main characters on *Mad About You* and *Friends* main characters may collectively share some of *Seinfeld*'s hedonism and social irresponsibility, where they noticeably differ is in their pointed rejection of the latter's "no hugging, no learning" premise. *Mad About You*'s lovers and *Friends*' friends are precisely that, indeed both of these things, to one another—just the opposite of *Seinfeld*'s foursome, for whom sex and friendship are mutually exclusive and love a four-letter word. Yet while *Mad About You* and *Friends*' multiple protagonists certainly trump *Seinfeld*'s in regard to "likeability," how they compare in terms of Jewishness is another matter.

Mad About You's discursive claims to Jewishness rest mainly on the presumed Jewishness of Paul Buchman, whose character is patterned after his portrayer, the show's co-creator, Paul Reiser—"he of the way overdone Jewish accent and mannerisms" (Kaplan 16). This largely implicit sense of Jewishness is reinforced through Paul Buchman's "noodgy" mother, Sylvia (Cynthia Harris), and European-accented father, Burt (*Brooklyn Bridge*'s Louis Zorich), who on one occasion recalls walking in on his son as a youngster playing with his *shmecky* (Yiddish for prick). The family's Jewishness is conjured most strongly through Paul's Uncle Phil, played by Mel Brooks. Besides Brooks' inter- and extra-textual associations with Jewishness, his character knows German and comes from an explicitly Polish immigrant background. And while Reiser and other of the show's producers have admitted to consciously avoiding Jewish references ("Producer," 6), *Mad About You* never disclaims the Buchman family's Jewishness. The discursive field is thus free to describe Paul's character as a "glib, neurotic" Jewish comic or the "unmistakably New York Jewish hero" to his wife Jamie's (Helen Hunt's) "cooler WASP goddess," and to label Paul's mom as the "take-charge," "intrusive, overbearing" Jewish mother (Solomon 30; Hammer and Schwartz 88–89; O'Connor 1993, C20; Hanania AR35). Joyce Antler even finds a rare "positive image" of Jewishness in Paul's sister Debbie (Robin Bartlett), although "her proud lesbianism is more openly flaunted than her Jewishness" (250).

This tendency to erase female, as opposed to male, markers of Jewishness, is also at work in *Friends*' high-school-chums-turned-roommates, Monica Geller and Rachel Green (the non-Jewish Courteney Cox and Jennifer Aniston). What ultimately renders Monica and Rachel most Jewish (or half-Jewish) is an emergent form of Jewish representation I term "conceptual Jewishness." Partly an extension of Herbert Gans's notion of "symbolic Judaism" (244), "conceptual Jewishness" refers sociologically to recent Jews' ever more abstract and attenuated links to identifiable ethnic and cultural, never mind religious, expression. Televisually, the term derives from the fact that in sitcoms like *Friends*, "Jewish" characters are literally *conceived*, more than *represented*, as Jews, which is precisely how *Friends* co-creators Marta Kauffman and David Crane describe the genesis of the Jewish characters they have helped bring to televisual life.

The "midwives" or "surrogate parents" in this textual procreation are the characters' sitcom mothers and fathers, and the actors who portray them, for casting is a prime ethnic determinant. "In our minds," Crane explained in a 1996 *Lilith* interview, "the back story is that Ross is half-Jewish because Elliott Gould [Ross's father] is Jewish, and Christina Pickles [Ross's mother] sure ain't. So he and Monica are half-Jewish." Rachel's case is more complex: although her neurologist father (played by Ron Leibman, a Jew) is "clearly Jewish," her mother (played by the non-Jew Marlo Thomas) can pass for Jewish yet is "possibly non-Jewish" (quoted in Mandel 6).

While "conceptual Jewishness" may be *Friends'* unique contribution—for better or worse—to Jewish representation, the show's propensity for what I call "perceptual Jewishness" clearly relates, once again, to *Seinfeld*. "Perceptual Jewishness" occurs when characters are perceived as Jewish—by Jews or non-Jews—despite their *not* having been conceived as such. George Costanza's pan-Semitic *schlemiel* provided the prima facie case in this regard, at least from a male standpoint. From the female standpoint, two characters from *Friends*—Ross and Monica's mother, and Chandler's girlfriend Janice—offer further striking evidence of the conceptual/perceptual divide. These latter figures, for Antler at least (and I would agree about Janice), are the "two unambiguously Jewish female characters" on the show: Mrs. Geller "belongs to the pantheon of overbearing Jewish mothers"; the "nasal, crass, and overdressed" Janice is the paradigmatic Jewish princess to Rachel's JAP manqué (Antler 250). As we have seen, however, Mrs. Geller was consciously conceived as non-Jewish; while Janice, according to co-creator Kauffman in a phone interview, although she is outed in the series' finale as "nee Hosenstein," was conceived not as Jewish but as "simply New York."

Friends' "perceptual Jewishness" diverges from *Seinfeld*'s in another important aspect: instead of auguring the "Jewification" of America as the affirmation of a "Jewish sensibility or point of view that permeates the nation," as was arguably the case for *Seinfeld* (Lichtenstein 4). Janice's and Mrs. Geller's *performance* of Jewishness compensates for the lack—or at least extreme dearth—of identifiable Jewishness. "Perceptual Jewishness" converges on the two shows in their mutual displacement of undesirable "Jewish" traits onto non-Jews, which serves a protective purpose by deflecting potential protests from the Jewish community. Kauffman alluded to such concerns in our interview, specifically in regard to the Ross Geller character. Ross has generally been praised in Jewish circles for his long-term romance with a Jewish woman, Rachel, yet at a Jewish Youth conference on Jewish representation, Kauffman found herself attacked for making Ross "too geeky." It was David Schwimmer (Ross's portrayer) who chose to take his character in a somewhat "shlubby" direction, Kauffman explained, although she admits to learning a sobering lesson: "It's a bit of a slippery slope with a character like that, as to how far their stereotypical Jewishness should show."

THE NANNY: GOOD OR BAD FOR THE JEWS?

Just how far stereotypical Jewishness *could* show and still succeed, both with Jewish and non-Jewish audiences, was demonstrated by another popular Jewish-trend sitcom, *The Nanny*. Despite what was for many a demeaning portrait of a Jewish American princess by the show's co-creator and star Fran Drescher, *The Nanny* also proved a major breakthrough in female

Jewish representation. Despite Drescher's character's loud dress, gold-digging aim, and "accent that could etch glass, and her even more outrageous and opportunistic mother (played by Renee Taylor), *The Nanny* not only proved popular with many Jews, including Jewish critics, but it sailed through the media-monitoring shoals largely unscathed. The key to the paradox, as with *Rhoda*, relates to gender.

In 1997, four years into *The Nanny*'s run, a perceived crisis in Jewish female representation led to the formation of an industry watchdog group, called the Morning Star Commission, to monitor and, if possible, improve Jewish women's media portrayals. Given the scarcity of Jewish women characters on television, compared to men, during this portion of the trend period, the commission naturally scrutinized *The Nanny* closely and, counterintuitively, gave it generally high marks. Although admitting that Drescher's characterization was "a Jewish stereotype if ever there were one," commission members found it generally inoffensive, with one member, Claudia Caplan, pronouncing it positively "funny and fine and terrific" (quoted in Beyette E4). *Forward* columnist Robin Cembalist went so far as to call Drescher "a conceptual artist" who "is not merely rehashing stereotypes but questioning them"(9), and critic Susan Glenn cited Drescher as the "only reigning Jewish actress on television with the chutzpah to celebrate her ethnic 'otherness'" (quoted in Antler 247). However, where Drescher's nanny most crucially parts company from the stereotypical Jewess is in an area few critics have mentioned: sexuality. Hyper- rather than de-sexualized, as was the standard Jewish woman, Drescher managed to create a variation on the Jewish American Princess whose body is possessed of more than oral appetites and whose persona is—nasal whine and all—romantically desirable.

The Jewish American Princess (or JAP), Riv-Ellen Prell argues, emerged in the 1970s as a response to a burgeoning Jewish-American middle class consumed by the pressure to consume yet frustrated in its ability to do so by the decline of postwar affluence. With women still cast as consumers and men as producers, the "woman's body, freed from labor but requiring others to work," became the horn of the dilemma for the put-upon middle-class male. An embittered Jewish humor that viewed men as "victimized by women and their insatiable wants" arose, in Prell's view, essentially as a displacement of middle-class men's ensnarement in a consumption-driven economic system that had rendered both them and their spouses unproductive (1995, 84). Where Prell's description and Drescher's representation of the Jewish princess part is in the realm of sexual desire—both her own and that which she elicits in others. The standard JAP joke—"What's the difference between a Jewish princess and jello? Jello moves when you touch it"—couldn't be less applicable to the jiggly nanny. Neither is a companion quip—"How do you get a JAP to stop having sex? Marry her"—apropos in Fran's case; she is as eager to bed down her boss after their wedding as before (Prell 1995, 84).

Fran Fine's working-class status has led some to question whether her nanny character qualifies as a Jewish princess, since this type is conventionally regarded as wealthy and spoiled, upper-middle rather than working class. Prell's own historical gloss, however, conjures two New York working-class precursors of the Jewish princess, the 1920s Ghetto Girl and the 1930s Young Jewish Woman in Search of Marriage, both of which fit the 1970s-emergent JAP and Drescher's nanny like a sheer-fitting gown. The earlier types were characterized as "Trolley Car Girls with Rolls Royce Tastes," as "garish, excessively made up, too interested in her appearance, and too uncultivated to dress smartly," with voices whose nasal tones and shrill expression rendered them even more unacceptable to "good society," and with insatiable material desires "leading her to drive away men of her class who might not measure up, or to yoke a man to ceaseless work to satisfy her wants" (Prell 1999, 23, 24, 48, 90). Drescher's "Subway Car Girl with Rolls Royce Tastes," rather than defying the JAP's "acceptable" class, thus can be seen as reclaiming this caricature's ontological roots in working-class sexuality.

By no means ideal as a revisionist Jewish-feminist text, *The Nanny* must nonetheless be credited with challenging the postwar myth of Jewish female passivity and frigidity embodied in the Jewish princess stereotype.

GAYFACE (AND JEWFACE) IN *WILL AND GRACE*

Although the eponymous lead character of *Ellen* (1994–1998) was the first regular prime-time protagonist, and portrayer (Ellen DeGeneres), to openly disclose her/his gayness, this epochal outing occurred near the end of the series' original run. The Jewish sitcom *Will and Grace* (1998–2006) was the first network series to *originate* with an openly gay protagonist, the non-Jewish Will Truman (played by Eric McCormack). Through its leading lady Grace Adler (Debra Messing), the show introduced another unique sitcom character: the Jewish fag-hag. Naomi Seidman's essay "Fag Hags and Bu-Jews: Toward a (Jewish) Politics of Vicarious Identity" offers a useful frame for exploring the fag-hag phenomenon from a Jewish perspective. One solution for the liberally inclined yet multiculturally rejected Jew, Seidman suggests, was to secure "him/herself a place in the multiculture through a different kind of blackface, lifting a marginality wholesale from elsewhere and making it serve other (and Other) interests"(260).

The multiculturally overdetermined Jewish fag-hag finds her televisual analog in the heterosexual Grace Adler, who dotes on the homosexual Will Truman to the extreme. She not only lives with (or just across the hall from) Will through most of the series, but also dated him (pre-coming out) in college, and persists in loving him—passionately. In the pilot episode (9/21/98), Grace breaks off her marriage to another man largely due to her vestigial love for Will, which she communicates through a wishful, though unrequited, wet kiss at the end. Subsequent episodes reinforce the fact that Grace's love life remains severely crimped because all her prospective beaus, in comparison with Will, invariably come up short (no pun intended). The issue is epitomized in an episode (1/4/01) that begins with Will, upset over Grace's over-dependency on his credit card, complaining, "You might as well be my wife!" and ends at a wedding of gay friends with Will and Grace professing their own love for each other as if *they* were the couple getting married. It certainly comes as no surprise that when Grace's marriage to a Jewish doctor (played by Harry Connick, Jr.) is finally "written into" the series, it is a bumpy ride from the get-go and barely makes it through a single season.

Unlike Seidman's Jewish fag-hag, however, whose vicarious identification with queer culture comes at the expense of and even as partial compensation for Jewish particularism, Grace's Jewishness is more than parenthetical and her Jewish-gay connection is to a considerable extent reciprocal. Overt references to Grace's ethnicity outnumber those of all Jewish-trend protagonists with the possible exception of *The Nanny*. Grace attended Camp Ramah (Jewish summer camp) as a child and frequently and fondly alludes to having been bar-mitzvahed. She has a keepsake of that coming-of-age ritual, a music box that plays the Jewish folk song "Havah Nagilah" on her mantel. As for reciprocity, Will is in many ways as romantically, and carnally, obsessed with Grace as she with him. Besides the quasi-marriage episode in which the couple all but exchanges vows, an entire episode revolves around Will and Jack vying for the title of Grace's favorite, culminating with Grace jumping on Will and wrapping her legs around him, to which Jack jibes, "I'm going to leave so you two can make love" (12/7/00). The couple comes close to all-out sex in two other episodes: in one, Will's bedding down with Grace, in an apparent *menage à trois* with her macho lover Nathan (Woody Harrelson), turns out to be, from Will's end, only for moral support (9/26/01); in another, Will and Grace's torrid love-making is revealed as "only" Will's sex dream (5/9/00).

Sexual affinities between gays and Jews in general are implied when Grace calls Will "a disgrace to your people" for his lackluster sex life (12/7/99), then vows to polish up her own by saying "goodbye to Prudie McPrude and hello to Slutty Sluttenstein" (11/9/00). As for explicit examples of Jewface: upon moving across the hall from Will, Grace laments, "I'm going to miss the 'Jewish soup' you always made me when I was ill" (12/7/99); in campaigning against Grace for president of their tenants association, Will pretends to be a rabbi to gain the vote of a hospitalized tenant (9/28/99); when Will impersonates sitcom-character Rhoda to convince Grace it's okay to ask Nathan to marry her, Grace exclaims, "Wow, you'll use any excuse to do a Rhoda impression!" (11/8/01).

Jewish/gay bonding is, from an historical and institutional standpoint at least, a "natural" fit. That the Jewish male already "resembles the homosexual" through physical imputations of effeminacy is well documented (Gilman; Boyarin, Itzkovitz, and Pellegrini). Just as evident, though perhaps less well documented, is the historical "affinity with the closet" the Jewish and gay (sub)cultures have shared (Seidman 265), and the degree to which Jews and gays *in conjunction with one another* have dominated the entertainment industry. "You couldn't do better than grow up Jewish and gay if you want to be in show business," bluntly states gay-Jewish TV writer/film director Don Roos (*The Opposite of Sex, Bounce*). "It's one of the industries in America that has a disproportionate number of gay [and Jewish] people in it." As for TV specifically, Jews and gays, often in the same person, are common in upper-level executive and creative positions.

Will and Grace has inscribed the Jewish/gay interrelationship in its very conception. According to co-creator Kohan, he and creative partner Mutchnick (who is gay) intended the title "Will and Grace" as a play on the words "will" and "grace." Beyond their generic resonance, the double entendres additionally refer to the work of Jewish philosopher Martin Buber, one of Kohan's inspirations in college. In his magnum opus, *I and Thou*, Buber speaks of the interdependence of will and grace in achieving a fully realized and spiritual "I-Thou" (as opposed to a purely material and more impersonal "I-It") relationship between two people. Such an intersubjective relationship requires a *coming together* of will and grace, Kohan explained in our interview: the will to seek the "I-Thou" and the grace to fulfill its transcendence. Will and Grace, like gays and Jews, need each other more than they know, Kohan and Mutchnick appear to be saying. Each group must acknowledge the other in themselves and the self in the other; particularism must be mutually asserted and received, to achieve "postethnic" brother and sisterhood.

The alternative, especially for Jews, is multicultural suicide. As Seidman writes: "In a culture that equates the battle for representation and rights with political progressivism, the Jew who resists a straightforward identity politics in exchange for participation in the struggle of 'someone else' opens herself up to the charges of assimilation, self-hatred, and parasitism" (266). The peril for the "post-Jewish" Jew is thus both multicultural and multifold: s/he must wrestle not only with whiteness but also with Jewishness. Otherwise, again per Seidman, "The very absence of any apparent ethnic self-interest becomes cause for suspicion, revealing itself as the symptom of an apparently Jewish pathology" (266).

Pathological Jews: *Curb Your Enthusiasm* and *Arrested Development*

Four of the eight Jewish sitcoms that premiered in the late 1990s—*Dharma and Greg* (1997–2002), *Alright Already* (1997–1998), *Will and Grace* (1998–2006), and *Rude Awakening* (1998–2001)—featured Jewish female protagonists. Given that all four women—Dharma Finkelstein (Jenna Elfman), Carol Lerner (Carol Leifer), Grace Adler (Debra Messing), and Billie Frank (Sherilyn Fenn)—were attractive and sexually confident indicates that post-*Seinfeld*-era Jewish sitcoms were, at least initially, taking their ethno-cultural cues less from the "decade-defining" show than from *The Nanny*. *Seinfeld*'s influence was far from spent, however. Besides its own perpetuation in endless reruns and its imprint on gentler, kinder "clones" like *Mad About You* and *Friends*, *Seinfeld*'s "unlikeability" factor has been resurrected, and then some, in two of the most recent Jewishcoms, *Curb Your Enthusiasm* (2000–) and *Arrested Development* (2003–2006).

Although not pathological in Seidman's sense, these two shows do carry dysfunctionality to comedic extremes. Created and starring *Seinfeld* co-creator and George Costanza model Larry David, *Curb Your Enthusiasm* confirms whence the earlier show's darkly absurdist thrust derived. Working without observational comic Jerry Seinfeld's ameliorative influence and with the greater creative license cable affords (the show airs on HBO), David has given his Kafkaesque proclivities full rein and allowed a postmodern fudging of fact and fiction—he plays himself as the famous and wealthy producer of the earlier show—to predominate. The result is one of the gems of television comedy—Jewish or otherwise—in which an accretion of existential calamities comment simultaneously on the perils of schlemieldom, the contradictions of U.S. society, and the absurdities of the human condition. *Arrested Development*'s ambitions may approach *Curb*'s, but its attainments—critical encomiums notwithstanding—are more measured. A meaner, nastier, upscale *Married With Children*, airing on a Fox network given, in the interest of counterprogramming, to pushing the outrageousness envelope, *Arrested* is most noteworthy not as a barometer of social or human conditions but rather of how far Jews have—or have not—come in twenty-first-century America. If they can present themselves in as scathing a fashion as the filthy rich and just plain filthy Bluth family are on *Arrested*, and not only can get away with it but be universally lauded—the show even received a Jewish Image award!—then U.S. Jews, as a people, have surely "arrived" (Byers and Krieger).

We have also arrived, it would seem, at a new primary setting for Jewish TV: Southern California. *The Larry Sanders Show* pioneered the move with its L.A.-based location in the early 1990s (Brook 2006), but this program remained a rare exception until a spate of mid-to-late-1990s Jewish sitcoms broke the decades-long hold of New York City on the genre: *Dharma and Greg* (San Francisco); *Clueless*, *Rude Awakening*, and *It's Like, You Know . . .* (Los Angeles). A wholesale exodus westward appears to have occurred in the new millennium. Besides *Curb* (Beverly Hills) and *Arrested* (Newport Beach), other 2000s Jewish shows making Greater Los Angeles their home include *Bette*, *Three Sisters*, *Wednesday 9:30 (8:30 Central)*, *Listen Up*, and *Living with Fran*. Other recent Jewish sitcoms *Good Morning, Miami* and *State of Grace* (North Carolina), not to mention the hit Jewish dramas *The O.C.* (Newport Beach) and *Everwood* (Everwood, Colorado), further confirm that a Jewish show no longer has to be set in the Big Apple to be believable. Indeed, *Will and Grace*, a holdover from the 1990s, was the lone remaining show (as of 2006) set in that once obligatory Jewish TV locale.

This seismic geographical shift is, in a larger sense of course, more a return than an arrival. Given the entertainment industry's long-time and ongoing production headquarters in Hollywood/Los Angeles, a place teeming with Jews from its inception as the movie capital, it is really about time that Jewish representation reflected this reality. The "reality"-show wave of the early 2000s has no doubt spurred recent Jewishcoms' heightened verisimilitude, with the former's mix of the quotidian and the quest for celebrity meshing neatly with several of the latter's focus on the everyday lives of show-biz types: *It's Like, You Know* for example, features a producer of a cable show called *Pay Per Jew*; the narrator of *Three Sisters* is a television writer; as is the protagonist of *Wednesday 9:30 (8:30 Central)*; and Bette Midler stars as herself in *Bette*. *Curb* takes the "reality" concept further by incorporating it into its form as well as its content. The show is shot on location in hand-held, verite style, and the dialogue is improvised. One significant reality gap, of course, is that David's wife not only is not played by David's actual Jewish wife, Laurie; neither her character nor the actor who portrays her (Cheryl Hines) is Jewish.

Curb's "real-life" celebrity aspect has additional historical resonance with 1950s "real life" sitcoms such as *The Adventures of Ozzie and Harriet*, *Burns and Allen* and *Jack Benny*. A major difference, in Jewish-sitcom terms, is that "reality" for Burns and Benny meant extruding their ethnicity; for David it means exposing his—often in self-critical ways. In a second-season episode of *Curb,* for example, a Jewish neighbor of David's attacks the nebbisher producer for whistling a Wagner tune in public: "You wanna know what you are? You're a self-loathing Jew!" Nonplussed and enraged by the charge, David hires an orchestra to play Wagner on the neighbor's front lawn in the middle of the night; then, paraphrasing Kafka via Woody Allen, shouts at the man: "I do hate myself, but it has nothing to do with being Jewish!" ("Trick or Treat").

Arrested also plays on the notion of Jewish self-hatred, but in reverse. George Sr. (Jeffrey Tambor), the Bluth family patriarch, is, from the outset of the series, incarcerated for embezzlement—one meaning of the sitcom's title. Adding irony to insult, prison is also where the heretofore hyperassimilated felon discovers his Jewish roots. Not one to shun publicity, or the chance to make a buck, George heralds his "spiritual rebirth" by hawking "Caged Wisdom" videos that depict him spouting pseudo-inspirational inanities from his cell while wearing a *yarmulke* (prayer cap), a *talit* (prayer shawl), and *tefillin* (prayer receptacles strapped to the arms and head). This scene provides, without question, one of the more bizarre images in the history of American Jewish television. It also begs the question....

WHERE TO FROM HERE?

We began our overview of Jewish television since the 1960s with the "Vanishing Jew" crisis of that decade. To gauge where Jewish representation might be headed in the 2000s requires revisiting and updating the survivalist debate. A national conference, sponsored in 2000 by Hebrew Union College and the USC Department of Jewish Studies, was titled "The Reappearing American Jew." Given the Jewish National Population Survey's shocking findings of a decade earlier that the intermarriage rate had surpassed 50 percent (later revised to 42 percent) for the first time, the conference title was dripping with irony. The conference's object and certainly its outcome, however, were neither to glorify Jewish renewal nor to debunk it. What the event revealed was the degree to which issues of assimilation and multiculturalism, exacerbated by the 1990 survey, continue to haunt Jewish life. The overriding question was not whether the American Jew was reappearing—in a variety of culture forms, she/he surely had—but rather which of the forms this "reappearance" was taking were good, or bad, for the Jews.

The answer to such a question is fundamentally irresolvable, given the subjectivity of the criteria and the increasingly multiple and contradictory nature of Jewish identity, but—two Jews, three opinions notwithstanding—this much seems indisputable. Since Jews, through the process of assimilation, have relinquished much of the minority claim on which a significant portion of their identity was based, they may no longer have to, in Prell's phrase, "fight to become Americans." But another struggle, less of the body politic than of the soul, has taken center stage, one in which Jewish television comedy will continue to play a substantial role: the struggle to be, and to define what it means to be, Americans *and* Jews.

FURTHER READING

Altman, Sig. *The Comic Image of the Jew: Explorations of a Pop Cultural Phenomenon*. Rutherford, N.J.: Farleigh Dickenson University Press, 1971. 61–62.

Barr, Terry. "Stars, Light, and Finding a Way: The Emergence of Jewish Characters in Contemporary Film and Television." *Studies in Popular Culture* 15, no. 2, 1993. 87–99.

Berger, Maurice. "The Mouse That Never Roars: Jewish Masculinity on American Television." *Too Jewish? Challenging Traditional Identities*. Ed. Norman L. Kleeblatt. New Brunswick, New Jersey: Rutgers University Press, 1996. 93–107.

Beyette, Beverly. "Image Make-Over." *Los Angeles Times*. 9 Nov. 1998: E4.

Boyarin, Daniel, Daniel Itzkovitz, and Ann Pelgrini, Eds. *Queer Theory and the Jewish Question*. New York: Columbia University Press, 2003.

Breitbart, Eric Breitbart. "The TVnik Talks Jewish." *Shmate* 6. Summer 1983. 35–36.

Brook, Vincent. *Something Ain't Kosher Here: The Rise of the "Jewish" Sitcom*. New Brunswick, N.J.: Rutgers University Press, 2003.

———. "'Y'All Killed Him, We Didn't!' Jewish Self-Hatred and The Larry Sanders Show." *You Should See Yourself: Jewish Identity in Postmodern American Culture.* Ed. Vincent Brook. New Brunswick, N.J.: Rutgers University Press, 2006.

Brownfield, Paul. "As Minorities TV Presence Dims, Gay Roles Proliferate." *Los Angeles Times.* 21 July 1999: A16.

Byers, Michele and Rosalin Krieger. "Something Old Is New Again? Postmodern Jewishness in *Curb Your Enthusiasm, Arrested Development,* and *The O.C.*" *You Should See Yourself: Jewish Identity in Postmodern American Culture.* Ed. Vincent Brook. New Brunswick, N.J.: Rutgers University Press, 2006.

Caldwell, John Thornton. *Televisuality: Style, Crisis, and Authenticity in American Television.* New Brunswick, N.J.: Rutgers University Press, 1994.

Cembalist, Robin. "Big Hair, Short Skirts—and High Culture: Taking Fran Drescher Seriously." *Forward.* 14 Feb. 1997: 9.

Elkin, Michael. "Jews on TV: From 'The Goldbergs' to 'Hill Street's' Cops." *Jewish Exponent.* 28 June 1985: 25.

———. "Chassidism and Hollywood." *Jewish Journal of Greater Los Angeles* (September 25–October 1 1992). 23.

Erens, Patricia. *The Jew in American Cinema.* Bloomington: Indiana University Press, 1984, 106–107.

Feuer, Jane. "The MTM Stye." *MTM: 'Quality Television.* Jane Feuer, Paul Kerr, and Tise Vahimagi. London: BFI, 1984. 52.

Fiske, Edward B. "Some Jews Are Made at Bernie." *New York Times.* 11 Feb. 1973: E8.

Fretts, Bruce Fretts. "Cruelly, Madly, Cheaply." *Entertainment Weekly.* 4 May 1998: 44.

Gans, Herbert J. "American Jewry: Past and Future." *Commentary.* May 1956: 244.

Gilman, Sander. *The Jew's Body.* New York and London: Routledge, 1991.

Gitlin, Todd. *Inside Prime Time.* New York: Pantheon, 1985, 186.

Hammer, Joshua and Josh Schwarz. "Prime-Time Mensch." *Newsweek.* 12 Oct. 1992: 88–89.

Hanania, Joseph. "Playing Princesses, Punishers, and Prudes." *New York Times.* 7 Mar. 1999: AR35.

Healy, Melissa. "Incomes Up as Poverty Hits 11.9%, Lowest Rate Since '79." *Los Angeles Times.* 27 Sept. 2000: A16.

Jewish Telegraphic Agency. "Who's Jewish, Who's Not on 'Seinfeld.'" *Jewish Journal of Greater Los Angeles* (May 5–21 1998): 11.

Johnson, Carla. "Luckless in New York: The Schlemiel and the Schlimazl in Seinfeld." *Journal of Popular Film and Television* (Fall 1994): 116–124.

Kaplan, Susan. "From Seinfeld to Chicago Hope: Jewish Men Are Everywhere, but the Few Jewish Women Perpetuate Negative Stereotypes." *Forward.* 29 Nov. 1996: 16.

Kronke, David and Robert Gauthier, "There's Nothing to It." *Los Angeles Times.* 29 Jan. 1995: C13.

Lichtenstein, Gene. "A Furor Over Religion, Politics, and Identity." *Jewish Journal of Greater Los Angeles* (November 25–December 1, 1988): 4.

Mandel, Nora Lee. "Who's Jewish on 'Friends.'" *Lilith* (summer 1996): 6.

Marc, David. *Comic Visions: Television Comedy and American Culture.* 2nd Ed. Malden, Massachusetts and Oxford, UK: Blackwell, 1997.

Marks, Marlene Adler. "Where's Rhoda Now?" *Jewish Journal of Greater Los Angeles* (November 29–December 5, 1991): 33.

McClain, Ellen Jaffe. *Embracing the Stranger: Intermarriage and the Future of the Jewish Community*. New York: Basic Books, 1995.

Milch, Robert J. "Why Bridget Loves Bernie." *Jewish Spectator* (December 1972): 26.

Mitz, Rick. *The Great TV Sitcom Book*. New York: Perigree, 1988.

Montgomery, Kathryn C. *Target: Prime Time: Advocacy Groups and the Struggle over Entertainment Television*. New York: Oxford University Press, 1989. 25, 40.

Morgan, Thomas P. "The Vanishing American Jew." *Look* (May 5, 1964): 42–43.

O'Connor, John J. "Jewish Heroes Make It to Television." *Jewish Journal of Greater Los Angeles* (August 3–9 1990): 23.

_____. "This Jewish Mom Dominates TV, Too." *New York Times*. 14 Oct. 1993, C20.

Pearl, Jonathan and Judith Pearl. *The Chosen Image: Television's Portrayal of Jewish Themes and Characters*. Jefferson, North Carolina: McFarland & Company, 1999. 195–196, 230, 231.

Pfefferman, Naomi. "Norman Lear on Comedy, TV and His Mother." *Jewish Journal of Greater Los Angeles* (May 14 1999): 28.

Prell, Riv-Ellen. "Why Jewish Princesses Don't Sweat: Desire and Consumption in Postwar American Jewish Culture." *Too Jewish? Challenging Traditional Identities*. Ed. Norman Kleeblatt. New Brunswick, N.J.: Rutgers University Press, 1995. 74–92.

_____. *Fighting to Become Americans: Jews, Gender, and the Anxiety of Assimilation*. Boston: Beacon, 1999. 23, 24, 48, 90.

"Producer, Director, 'Something Wilder' Creator—Barnet Kellman," *Jewish Televimages Report* (March 1995): 6.

Rapping, Elayne. "The Seinfeld Syndrome." *The Progressive* (September 1995): 37–38, 110.

Seidman, Naomi. "Fag Hags and Bu-Jews: Toward a (Jewish) Politics of Vicarious Identity." *Insider/Outsider: American Jews and Multiculturalism*. Eds. David Biale, Michael Galchinsky, and Susannah Heschel. Berkeley and Los Angeles: University of California Press, 1998. 254–268.

Solomon, Lois K. "Farewell Fleishman," *Jewish Journal of Great Los Angeles* (March 3–9, 1995): 30.

Staiger, Janet. *Blockbuster TV: Must-See Sitcoms in the Network Era*. New York: New York University Press, 2000. 25.

Steinberg, Kerri. "Photography, Philanthropy, and the Politics of American Jewish Identity." Ph.D. diss. University of California, Los Angeles, 1995. 34–35.

Suber, Howard. "Hollywood's Closet Jews." *Davka* (Fall 1975): 12–14, 53.

_____. "Television's Interchangeable Ethnics: 'Funny, They Don't Look Jewish.'" *Television Quarterly* (Winter 1975): 53.

Zehme, Bill. "Jerry & George & Kramer & Elaine: Exposing the Secrets of Seinfeld's Success," *Rolling Stone* (8–22 July 1993): 44.

Sitcoms

Other Jewish sitcom-trend shows, listed chronologically, include *Chicken Soup* (1989), *Anything But Love* (1989–1992), *The Marshall Chronicles* (1990), *Singer & Sons* (1990), *Princesses* (1990), *Dream On* (1990–1996), *Flying Blind* (1992–1993), *Room for Two* (1992–1993), *Love and War* (1992–1995),

Daddy Dearest (1993), *Something Wilder* (1994–1995), *Ned and Stacey* (1995–1997), *Dr. Katz: Professional Therapist* (1995–1999), *Clueless* (1996–1999), *George and Leo* (1997), *Alright Already* (1997–1998), *You're the One* (1998), *Conrad Bloom* (1998), *LateLine* (1998–1999), *Rude Awakening* (1998–2001), *It's Like, You Know . . .* (1999–2000), *Bette* (2000–2001), *Inside Schwartz* (2001), *Three Sisters* (2001–2002), *Wednesday 9:30 (8:30 Central)* (2002), *Good Morning, Miami* (2002–2003), *Listen Up* (2004–2005), *Living with Fran* (2005–). An unprecedented number of dramatic series with Jewish protagonists have also aired during the sitcom-trend period, including *Northern Exposure* (1990–1995), *Beverly Hills 90210* (1990–2000), *Reasonable Doubts* (1991–1993), *The X-Files* (1993–2002), *Chicago Hope* (1994–2000), *Relativity* (1996–1997), *Once and Again* (1999–2002), *100 Centre Street* (2000–2003), *The Education of Max Bickford* (2001–2002), *Everwood* (2002–), *The O.C.* (2003–), and *Numb3rs* (2006–).

Index

Aaronson, Gilbert Max, 5
ABC television, 225
Abel, Richard, 6
Abie's Irish Rose, 51, 238
Abrams, Ray, 97
Abramson, Ivan, 21
Actors Studio, 187
Adler, Jacob P., 17
Adler, Stella, 39
Adorno, Theodore, 149
Advertising: animation used in, 100–1; on Jewish radio, 130–32
Alda, Robert, 51, 65
Aleichem, Sholom, 190
Alexander, Jason, 246
Allen, Fred, 151, 230
Allen, Gracie, 149, 150, 151
Allen, Mel, 153
Allen, Woody, 39, 101, 216, 217, 219
All in the Family, 213
All the World's a Stooge, 81
American Film Institute, 110, 111–12
Americanizing, 73–74
American Movies Theater, 19–20
American Soviet Film Initiative, 114
The American Jewish Hour, 125
Amos 'n' Andy, 147
AMPWU. *See* Animated Motion Picture Workers Union (AMPWU)
Amsterdam, Morey, 215, 235
Andrews, Charlie, 217
Animated Motion Picture Workers Union (AMPWU), 92
Animation, 85–106; in advertising, 100–1; assembly line technique, 87; beginnings of, 86–87; early series, 87; Rotoscope technique, 90; television series, 100–1; three-hole peg system, 89
Anti-communism sentiment. *See* Blacklisting
Anti-Jewish hostility, early film industry, 3–10
Anti-Nazi films, 76–77
Anti-Semitism, 184; congressional, 55; films dealing with, 73–84; in Hollywood, 37–59; peak of, 74; Walt Disney, 97–98, 99
Ants in the Pantry, 81
Archer, Wes, 105
Arendt, Hannah, 8, 9
Arlen, Harold, 62, 66
Armstrong Circle Theatre, 205
Arnheim, Rudolf, 131, 138
Arnold, Danny, 241
Arrested Development, 253–54, 255
Arthur, Bea, 216
Artist's Union, 92
Ashman, Howard, 103
Askoldov, Alexander, 117
Auerbach-Deutsch, Debbie, 165–66
Aurbach, Arnold, 233
Aurthur, Robert Alan, 190, 196
Automatic Vaudeville Company, 14, 15
Avenue B Theater, 17, 18
Avery, Tex, 95

Index

Awad, Mubarak, 113
Aware, Inc., 203, 208

Babbitt, Art, 97, 98, 104
Baer, Art, 235
Bakshi, Ralph, 101
Balaban, Barney, 31
Ball, Lucille, 201
Balsam, Martin, 187
Bara, Theda, 1, 27
Barney Miller, 240–41
Barr, Esther, 105
Barre, Raoul, 89
Barry, Claire, 123
Barry Sisters, 123, 134
Bart, Jan, 134
Basis, Howard, 101
Baumann, Charles O., 6, 8
Bayne, Martha Collins, 131, 138
Beck, Jerry, 104
Beckerman, Howard, 91, 101, 104
Beiman, Nancy, 101
Bein, Albert, 185
Bellamy, Ralph, 26
Ben-Ami, Jacob, 49
Benny, Jack, 77, 96, 151–52, 244
Benoff, Mac, 227, 228
Berg, Gertrude, 39, 146, 147–48, 152, 202
Berk, Harvey, 158, 165–66
Berle, Milton, 230, 231–32, 237
Berlin, Irving, 62
Berliner, Alan, 110
Berman, Pandro S., 32
Bernstein, Leonard, 63
Bernstein, Walter, 186, 187, 189, 201–2, 205, 206, 207
Berry, Alfred, 204
Besser, Joe, 79
Betty Boop, 90, 92
Biberman, Herbert, 58
Biblical spectaculars, 56
Big Eight, 3, 9, 25
Big Five, 25
Bikel, Theodore, 157
Bingham, Theodore, 13
Bird, Brad, 103, 105
Birns, Julie, 148

Birth of a Nation, 9
Black-Jewish connection, 245
Blacklist industry, television, 201–4
Blacklisting: CBS television, 202–4; end of, 207–11; Hollywood, 37–39, 41, 55–59, 100, 199–211, 228, 230; resistance strategies, 204–7; return from, 207–11; in television, 187, 189, 199–211
Blackton, James Stuart, 85–86, 89
Blackton, John Stuart, 8
Blanc, Mel, 94–96, 146, 152
Blankford, Henry, 52
Blue Sky, 106
Bluth, Don, 103, 105
B'nai B'rith, 158, 165–67
Bodner, Alan, 104
Bogart, Humphrey, 41
Bogart, Vincent, 233
Bolger, Ray, 225
Bond, Ward, 207
Booth, Marlene, 110
Bordowitz, Greg, 117
Bornstein, Sheldon, 101
"Borscht Belt," 215
Bousutow, Steve, 100
Bowery Boys, 41
Bowser, Eileen, 8
Box Office Attractions, 27
Brandeis, Louis, 9
Brandt, Joseph, 32
Bray, John Randolph, 87, 89, 90
Brecher, Irving, 207
Breen, Joseph L., 75, 76
Brenner, Zev, 157–58, 163–65, 170, 177
Brice, Fanny, 149, 150, 225
Bridges, Lloyd, 210
Bridget Loves Bernie, 237–39
Brodkin, Herbert, 186, 192, 194
Brooklyn Bridge, 244–45
Brooks, Mel, 73, 77, 101, 217, 219, 248
Brooks, Richard, 52
Broun, Heywood, 136
Brown, Himan, 148
Brucker, Eli, 92
Brynner, Yul, 187, 188

Buber, Martin, 253
Buchman, Sidney, 41, 45, 58
Buchwald, Sam, 94
Bugs Bunny, 94–95
Buloff, Joseph, 190, 191
Bunim, Meyer, 126
Burnett, Carol, 216
Burns, George, 149, 150, 151, 244

Cabin in the Sky, 57, 64
Caesar, Irving, 63
Caesar, Sid, 73, 214, 215, 216, 217, 218, 235, 237
Caesar's Hour, 217–18, 219
Cafe Society, 56, 57
Cageny, James, 149
Cahan, Abraham, 136
Cahn, Sammy, 63–64, 69, 71
Camp Tamiment, 215–19
Cantor, Eddie, 61, 75, 96, 146, 148, 149, 150–51, 231
Capra, Frank, 32, 41
Cartoon factory, 87
Cartoon Network, 106
Catalog of Independent Jewish Cinema, 116
CBS radio, 137, 147
CBS television, 202–4, 206, 208, 232, 238
Censorship: in movies, 2, 75; in television, 187; of The Three Stooges, 83
Champion Studios, 1, 5
Channing, Carol, 216
Chaplin, Charlie, 33, 56, 76–77, 80
Charles Mintz Studio, 95
Chase, William Sheafe, 10
Chayefsky, Paddy, 188, 189–91, 193, 196, 200
Cheap Amusements (Peiss), 6
Chekhov, Michael, 190
Children of Fate, 21
Clampett, Bob, 95
Clannishness, 7, 8
Clift, Montgomery, 54
Cobb, Lee J., 199
Coca, Imogene, 216, 217, 218
Coe, Fred, 185, 186, 190, 194, 195, 196, 204, 205

Cohen, Doris, 123
Cohen, Karl, 104
Cohen, Lizabeth, 127, 128
Cohl, Emile, 86, 89
Cohn, Harry, 26, 32–33, 56, 73, 79, 81–82, 225; attempts to protect writers, 55; social statement films, 41
Cohn, Jack, 26, 32–33
Columbia Pictures, 25, 26, 32–33, 79
Comden, Betty, 64
Comedy shows (*see also* Sitcoms): *Arrested Development,* 253–54, 255; *Barney Miller,* 240–41; *Bridget Loves Bernie,* 237–39; *Brooklyn Bridge,* 244–45; *Curb Your Enthusiasm,* 253–54, 255; *The Danny Thomas Show,* 224–29; *The Dick Van Dyke Show,* 234–36; *Friends,* 247, 248–49; *The Goldbergs,* 213, 219, 244–45; *The Honeymooners,* 219–24; Jewishcoms, 237–40; *Mad About You,* 247–48; *The Nanny,* 249–51; non-New York-based, 254–55; *The Phil Silvers Show,* 229–34; *Rhoda,* 239–40; *Seinfeld,* 243, 244–47; *Taxi,* 240–41; *Welcome Back, Kotter,* 240–41; *Will and Grace,* 251–53
Comedy writers, television, 213–36. See also *specific writers*
Commodore Theater, 21, 22
Confessions of a Nazi Spy, 76
Congressional hearings on influences in Hollywood, 37–38
Conried, Hans, 226, 227
Conte, Richard, 54
Cook, Fielder, 196
Cook, Lorna, 101, 105
Correll, Charles, 147
COSMOS, 102
Counterattack, 187, 188, 202, 205
Cousins, Norman, 44
Cowl, Jane, 2
Cox, Wally, 101
Crane, David, 248
Crane, Harry, 219–22, 222
Crawford, Oliver, 211
Crosby, Bing, 62, 147, 231
Crossfire, 51–52

Crypto-Jewish films, 39
Crystal Hall, 15
Cuddihy, John Murray, 74
Cukor, George, 32, 44–45
Cultural Jews, 118
Curb Your Enthusiasm, 253–54, 255
Curtis, Tony, 55

Daffy Duck, 94
Dana, Ambur, 230
Danger, 187, 188, 203, 206
The Danny Thomas Show, 224–29
Dardenne, Luc, 116
Da Silva, Howard, 39
David, Larry, 246, 254
David, Tissa, 104
Davis, Arthur, 89
Davis, Marc, 98, 99
Debs, Eugene, 136, 137, 231
The Defenders, 208, 209, 210
The Defiant Ones, 58
Deitch, Gene, 101
Delancey Street Theater, 17, 18
DeMille, Cecil B., 5
Deneroff, Bill, 92
Deneroff, Harvey, 104
Depatie-Freleng, 85
Depotism, film industry, 26
Depression, 42, 92–93
DeRita, Curly, 79
Der Tog, 124–25, 128, 134, 136, 137
Deutsch, Esther, 127
Dewey, John, 136
Dewey Theater, 16
Diamond, Selma, 217, 219, 235
The Dick Van Dyke Show, 234–36
Dietrich, Marlene, 44, 225
Dietz, Howard, 70
Dintenfass, Mark, 5, 6
Directors, social statement film, 44–46
Disney, Walt, 88, 97–100
The Disney Version (Schickel), 98
Displaced persons (DPs), 140–41, 191
Dmytryk, Edward, 53
Doherty, Thomas, 77, 82–83
Douglas, Melvyn, 37, 52
DPs. *See* Displaced persons (DPs)

Dramatic television, 183–96
Dranko, Bob, 100
Draper, Paul, 202
DreamWorks SKG, 85, 105–6
Drescher, Fran, 249–51
Dreyfuss, Richard, 40, 103
Dubin, Al, 71
Duke, Vernon, 64
Durante, Jimmy, 149
Dyer, Frank L., 7, 8

Eastman, George, 86
Eastman, Phil, 100
Ebb, Fred, 66
Eckhardt, Joseph, 8
Edison, Thomas, 1, 3, 7, 85, 86
Edison trust, 3, 5, 6, 8
Eisner, Michael, 103, 105
Elliot, Maxine, 2
Elliott, Peter, 98
An Empire of Their Own (Gabler), 3
The Enchanted Drawing, 86
Encyclopedia of Radio, 156
Engel, Herbert, 217
Engel, Jules, 97, 100
Epstein, Julius, 50
Epstein, Lawrence J., 82
Epstein, Phillip, 50
Erens, Patricia, 6, 75
Essanay studio, 6, 7

Fag-hag, 251–52
Fain, Sammy, 64, 66
Fairbanks, Douglas, 33
Famous Players Company, 17
Famous Players in Famous Plays, 17, 30, 94
Famous Studios, 94
FCC, 138, 156, 238
Feiffer, Jules, 101
Feinberg, Larry, 78–79
Felix the Cat, 87–88
Ferber, Edna, 140
Ferrand, Jacques, 128
Ferrer, Jose, 54, 70, 190
Fiddler On the Roof, 48
Fields, Dorothy, 64–65, 70
Film. *See* Motion picture industry

264

Filmation, 101
Film Supply Company, 8–9
Finian's Rainbow, 66, 67, 68
Fink, Charlie, 103, 104
Fink, Phil, 158–59, 166–68
Finklehore, Florence, 96
Finkleman-Cox, Penny, 105
Fischinger, Oscar, 97
Fisher, Bud, 86, 87
Flamm, David, 124
Flamm, Donald, 132
Fleischer, Dave, 89–91
Fleischer, Edith, 93
Fleischer, Max, 88, 89–94, 97, 98, 148
Fleischer, Richard, 97
Fleming, Michael, 78
Fleury, Eugene, 100
Fly, James Lawrence, 138
Foote, Horton, 190, 194, 196, 200
Ford, Henry, 10, 75, 87, 99, 151
Foreman, Carl, 58
Fort Lee (NJ), 1–2, 5, 6, 9
Foster, Warren, 95
Fox, Eytan, 117
Fox, William, 3, 4, 6, 8, 10, 14, 15–16, 17–18, 21, 26–28
Fox Film Corporation, 26, 27, 42
Frankel, Doug, 104
Franken, Al, 155
Frankenheimer, John, 194
Frankenstein, 26
Freed, Arthur, 28, 65, 68
Freedman, Dave, 150
Frees, Paul, 101
Freleng, Friz, 95–96, 100
Friedman, Ed, 101
Friedman, Lillian, 101
Friedman-Astor, Lillian, 92, 93
Friends, 247, 248–49
Fromer, Seymour, 110
Fuchs, Wilhelm. *See* Fox, William
Furniss, Maureen, 104

Gabler, Neal, 3, 25, 35, 75, 82
Garden, Mary, 2
Garfield, John, 28, 39, 40, 47, 52, 53, 54, 55, 199, 227
Garfinkle, Jay, 166

Garland, Judy, 63, 231
Garner, James, 210
Geffen, David, 105
Gelbart, Larry, 217, 219, 225, 228
Gelbfisz, Schmuel. *See* Goldwyn, Samuel
General Film Company, 7, 8
Gentlemen's Agreement, 27–28, 52
Gershwin, George, 51, 58, 63, 65, 67
Gershwin, Ira, 54, 62, 65, 67, 71
Gimbel, Ben, 147
Ginnes, Abram, 207, 211
Gitai, Amos, 117
Gleason, Jackie, 215, 219–24, 229, 231
Goetz, William, 29
Goldberg, Eric, 104
Goldberg, Gary David, 244
Goldberg, Rube, 87
Goldberg, Steve, 104
The Goldbergs, 213, 219, 244–45
Goldenson, Solomon, 156
Goldman, Eric, 243
Goldman, Frank, 89
Goldman, Sol, 96
Goldman-Sigall, Martha, 96
Goldsmith, Beatrice, 126, 132
Goldstein, Debbie, 106
Goldstein, Gary, 101
Goldstein, Jennie, 126
Goldwyn, Samuel, 3, 4, 5, 6, 17, 32, 56
The Golem, 111, 120
Gollub, Morris "Moe," 103
Gone With the Wind, 29, 43, 56, 57
Goodman, Benny, 96, 153
Gordon, Larry, 159, 168–69
Gosden, Freeman, 147
Gould, Elliot, 248
Gould, Manny, 89
Grand Theater, 16, 18
Grant, Bob, 180
Grant, Joe, 97, 98, 99, 106
Grant, Lee, 187, 207, 208–9
Graphic Films, 101
Greater M & S Circuit, 20–22
The Great Dictator, 76–77, 80
Green, Adolph, 64
Green, Paul, 185
Griffith, D. W., 9, 33

Grimes, William, 73
Groening, Matt, 105
Gross, Milt, 87, 97, 148
Group Theater, 41, 214
Gruber, Bernie, 96
Gruene Felder, 48, 49
Guedel, John, 152
Guttman, Lee, 96
Guys and Dolls, 67, 68

Hagen, Jean, 226, 227
Halper, Donna, 156–57
Hammermesh, Mira, 113
Hammerstein II, Oscar, 69–70
Hanna & Barbera, 85, 100
Hannity, Sean, 180
Hans Christian Andersen, 61, 68, 70
Harburg, Yip, 57, 62, 66
Harman, Larry, 101
Harper, Valerie, 239
Harris, Estelle, 246
Harris, Julie, 187
Hart, Lorenz (Larry), 69
Hart, Moss, 28
Hartnett, Vincent, 203
Harveytoons, 94
Hayes, Helen, 26
Hayworth, Rita, 149
Healy, Ted, 78, 79
Hearst, William Randolph, 86, 87
Heavenly Daze, 83
Hecht, Ben, 186
Heinze, Andrew, 130, 134
Helfand, Judith, 116
Hellman, Lillian, 41
Hepburn, Katharine, 32, 43, 45, 149
Herman, Felicia, 75
Hertz, Lou, 101
Heumer, Dick, 97
Hickenloopers, 215, 218
"Hidden Jews," 40
Higher Than a Kite, 81
Hiken, Nat, 229–30, 232, 233, 234
Hiken, Sandy, 230
Hikind, Dov, 159–60, 170–71
Hilberman, David, 97, 98, 100
Hill, George Roy, 196
Hillquit, Morris, 136
Hirsch, Judd, 241

Hirschbein, Peretz, 49
Hirschfeld, Harry, 148
Hitler, Adolf, 74, 76, 80
Hoadly, Harold, 10
Hodkinson, W. W., 31
Hoff, Max "Boo Boo," 147
Hoffman, Daniel, 120
Hoffman, Dustin, 40
Hoffman, Michael, 160
Hogan's Heroes, 77
Holden, William, 46
Holiday, Billie, 56, 57, 58
Holliday, Judy, 54–55, 199, 205
Hollywood: animation studios, 89; anti-Semitism, 37–59; attempt to combat anti-Semitism, 82–84; avoidance of Judaism, 74–75; Biblical spectaculars, 56; blacklisting, 37–39, 41, 55–59, 100, 199–211, 228, 230; Communist influence in, 37–38; Congressional hearings on influences in, 37–38; effect of Depression on, 42; Golden Age, 22, 25; Jewish roles, 50–55; musicals, 61–72; prejudice theme in, 51–52; pre-war, 73–84; Production Code Administration (PCA), 75; "secret" role in, 37; social statement films (*see* Social statement films); studio sabotage, 52
Hollywood 10, 51
Holocaust (mini-series), 242
The Honeymooners, 219–24
Hoover, J. Edgar, 38, 55
Horkheimer, Max, 149
Horn, James W., 21
Horne, Lena, 57, 64
Horowitz, Jerome "Curly," 78–81
Horowitz, Meyer, 149
Horowitz, Moses "Moe," 78–81
Horowitz, Samuel "Shemp," 78, 79
Horvath, Ferdinand, 97
House Committee on Un-American Activities (HUAC), 37–38, 51, 55, 99–100, 138, 187, 200, 207, 227
Howard, Moe, 73
HUAC. *See* House Committee on Un-American Activities (HUAC)
Hubley, John, 100
Huggins, Roy, 210

Index

Hughes, Howard, 32
Humoresque, 54
Hunter, Ian McLellan, 206
Hunter, Kim, 187, 203, 208
Hurtz, Bill, 98, 100
Hussey, Jimmy, 148
Hyperassimilation, 238

I'll Never Heil Again, 80–81
Immigration, 153
IMP. *See* Independent Moving Picture Company (IMP)
Independent filmmakers, 109–10
Independent Moving Picture Company (IMP), 34
Intermarriage, 237–40
Internet: effect on Jewish Film Festival, 120; radio, 155, 166, 174, 181
Interracialism, 56–59
Irwin, Lew, 97

The Jackie Gleason Show, 221
Jacoby, Coleman, 220, 233
JAP (Jewish American Princess), 249, 250
Jay Ward, 100
The Jazz Singer, 30, 42, 51, 56, 94, 150, 226
Jessel, George, 150, 151
Jesse L. Lasky Feature Play Company, 5
Jewish American Princess (JAP), 249, 250
Jewishcoms, 237–40
The Jewish Daily Foward, 135–37, 146
Jewish Film Festival, 109–21; *Catalog of Independent Jewish Cinema,* 116; early years, 110–13; intent of, 110; international forays, 113–16; Madrid production, 115–16; Moscow production, 113–15; obstacles encountered, 113; programming, 110; proliferation of, 118–19; sponsorship, 118
Jewishness, 84; in Hollywood, 39–40; represented on television, 189; *Rhoda,* 239–40; *The Three Stooges,* 73
Jewish Philosopher, 125, 126, 131
Jewish roots, hiding of, 4–5

Jewish supremacy, 10
Jews-as-Other, 40
Johnson, Laurence, 203
Jolson, Al, 61, 63, 146, 149, 150, 226
Jones, Chuck, 95, 96–97
Josephson, Ben, 215
Judah Magnes Museum, 110

Kachivas, Lou, 101
Kallen, Lucille, 216, 217–18, 219, 235
Kalmar, Bert, 70
Kander, John, 66
Kanin, Garson, 190
Kaplan, Esther, 174
Kaplan, Gabriel, 241
Kaplan, Shmuel, 160, 171–73
Kaplan, Yvette, 104
Karin, Rita, 126
Katz, Mickey, 157
Katz, Ray, 96
Katzenberg, Jeffrey, 103, 105–6
Kauffman, Marta, 248, 249
Kaye, Danny, 32, 37, 56, 61, 216
Kelly, Selby, 101
Kelton, Perl, 230
Kempner, Aviva, 116
Kennedy, Madge, 2
Kern, Jerome, 66–67
Kessel, Adam, 6, 8
Kestin, Sam, 134
Khleifi, Michel, 117
Kimmelman, Phil, 101
Kingsley, Sidney, 41
Kinkelstein, Louis, 157
Kinoy, Ernest, 191, 194, 208
Kirkpatrick, Theodore, 202
Kirshner, David, 103
Klein, Bert, 104
Klein, Isidor "Izzy," 89
Klein, Phil, 89
Kleine, George, 8, 10
Klynn, Herb, 100
Knietel, Seymour, 94
Koch, Howard, 51
Kohn, Morris, 5
Kosher Kitty Kelly, 21
Kraft, Hy, 57
Krantz, Steve, 101
Krisel, Gary, 103

Index

Kuperschmidt, Alex, 104
Kurtz, Bob, 101
Kurtz & Friends, 101

Lady In the Dark, 54
Laemmle, Carl, 2, 3, 5–10, 25, 26, 34–35
Laemmle, Carl Jr., 25, 43
Lahr, Bert, 61
Lampell, Millard, 208, 209, 210
Lane, Burton, 67, 68
Lantz, Walter, 89
Lardner, Ring, 206
Lasky, Blanche, 5, 6, 10
Lasky, Jesse, 17
Lastfogel, Abe, 149, 225
Lawrence, Florence, 34
Lawson, John Howard, 46
Lazarsfeld, Paul, 149
Leachman, Cloris, 187
Leaf, Caroline, 104
Lear, Norman, 213, 228
Lees, Robert, 209
Leifer, Miriam, 131
Leonard, Sheldon, 39, 226–27, 228, 229, 235
Leon Schlesinger Studio, 85
Lerner, Alan Jay, 68
Lessing, Gunther, 98
Lester, Julius, 164
Levant, Oscar, 54
Levene, Sam, 39, 51, 53
Leventhal, J. F., 89
Levi, Harry, 156
Levinson, Barry, 40
Levitow, Abe, 100, 101
Levy, Al, 206
Levy, Dani, 116
Lewis, Richard, 243
Lieberman, Joseph, 38
Liebermann, Kalman, 4, 5
Liebman, Max, 216, 217, 219
Limbaugh, Rush, 171, 180
Linden, Hal, 241
Little Three, 25
"Living Life Between the Lines" (Goldman), 96
Livingstone, Mary, 151
Loeb, Phillip, 152, 202, 208

Loesser, Frank, 61, 67–68
Loew, Arthur, 5, 6, 10, 15–18
Loew, Marcus, 3, 4, 5, 14, 18, 21, 22, 27, 28, 30
Loewe, Frederick, 68
Loew's Consolidated Enterprises, 17
Looney Tunes, 94–96
Lord, Marjorie, 227
Louvish, Simon, 75
Love, Ed, 97
Love, Harry, 97
Lovejoy, Frank, 140
Lubin, Sigmund, 5, 8
Lubinsky, Herman, 149
Lubitsch, Ernst, 27, 47, 69, 77
Lumet, Baruch, 129, 133, 188–89
Lumet, Sidney, 130, 133, 188, 196
Luxury items, 130

McCay, Winsor, 86, 89
McCarthyism, 201, 228
McDougall, Maude, 2
McClellan, Brinton, 2, 13
McManus, George, 86
Mad About You, 247–48
Make Room for Daddy, 224–29
Maltese, Michael, 95
Maltin, Leonard, 104
Maltz, Albert, 41, 56, 57
Mamet, David, 40
Mankiewicz, Joseph L., 27
Mann, Abby, 195, 196
Mann, Daniel, 187
Mann, Delbert, 186, 191, 194, 195
Manoff, Arnold, 189, 206, 209
Marc, David, 234
March, Fredric, 53, 140
Marchand, Roland, 130, 135
Marcus, Sid, 89, 96
Markell, Bob, 208
Marks, Marlene, 240
Marks, Sadie, 151
Marsh, Mae, 2
Marx, Chico, 82, 152
Marx, Groucho, 39, 76, 88, 152
Marx, Harpo, 82
Marx, Marvin, 222
Marx, Zeppo, 151

Index

Marx Brothers, 75, 82
Mason, Jackie, 243
Matthau, Walter, 149
Matusow, Harvey, 203
Max Fleischer Studio, 85
Mayer, Louis B., 3, 5, 14, 28–29, 42, 56, 99, 100
Meadows, Audrey, 219, 221
Meeropol, Abel, 56–57
Melendez, Bill, 94
Melvin, Allan, 229
Men In White, 41
Menken, Alan, 103
Menken, Yaakov, 160–61, 173–74
Mercer, Jack, 91
Mercer, Johnny, 62
Merman, Ethel, 71
Merrie Melodies, 94
Messing, Debra, 251
Messmer, Otto, 87
Method acting, 41, 55
MGM, 3, 5, 15, 25, 28–29; acquisition of Columbia Pictures, 33; animation studio, 97; merger with United Artists (UA), 34; Thalberg System, 43
Mickey Mouse, 89, 92, 95
Midler, Bette, 255
Milch, Roberty J., 238
Milestone, Lewis, 44, 45–46, 69
Miller, Arthur, 190
Miller, J.P., 186, 190, 194
Miller, Ruth, 97
Miner, Worthington, 185–86, 196
Minsky, Abraham, 19
Mintz, Charles, 88–89
Mishkin, Lee, 101
Mix, Tom, 27
Mograbi, Avi, 117
Moguls, 40–43, 75. *See also specific individuals*
Monash, Paul, 210
Montor, Max, 47
Morgan, Henry, 208
Morning Star Commission, 250
Mosel, Tad, 189, 190, 194
Mostel, Zero, 39
Motion Picture Distributing and Sales Company, 8

Motion picture industry: animation (*See* Animation); blacklisting (*See* Blacklisting); early history, 1–10; ethnic origins, 1–10; Fort Lee years, 1–10; growth of, 13–23; Hollywood (*see* Hollywood); Jewish Film Festival (*see* Jewish Film Festival); Jews portrayed as Jews, 50–55; New York City theaters, 13–23; social statement films (*see* Social statement films); studio system, 25–35
Motion Picture Patent Company (MPPCo), 3, 6, 7, 9, 27, 34
Movies. *See* Motion picture industry
MPPCo. *See* Motion Picture Patent Company (MPPCo)
M & S theaters, 21–22
Muir, Jean, 202, 204
Mulligan, Robert, 194
Muni, Paul, 40, 46, 48, 52
Murdoch, Rupert, 28
Muses, Ken, 97
Musicals, Hollywood, 61–72
Mutts to You, 83
Mutual Film Company, 8
My Fair Lady, 68

The Naked Dawn, 50
The Nanny, 249–51
Nash, Ogden, 25
Nathan, Robert, 140
National Board of Censorship, 2
National Conference of Jewish Film Festivals, 119
National Foundation For Jewish Culture's Fund for Jewish Democracy, 119
Nazi American Bund meetings, 98
Nazis, films dealing with, 74, 76, 80
NBC radio, 137, 146, 147–48, 150, 153, 156
NBC television, 216–17, 243
NBC Universal, 35
Neimark, Marilyn Kleinberg, 155–56, 161, 174–76
Nepotism: film industry, 25–26; Louis Mayer, 29

New Apollo Theater, 21–22
New Fourteenth Street Theater, 20
New Jewish Filmmaker Project, 119
News Corp., 28
New York, New York, 66
New York City theaters, 13–23
New York Community Campaign, 6
Nine Old Men, 98
Niven, David, 149
Novick, Morris, 149
Novros, Les, 101–2
Nye, Gerald P., 38, 76

Odeon Theater, 21
Opatashu, David, 130, 186
Out of the Inkwell, 88, 90
"Over the Rainbow," 62, 65, 66
Oysher, Moishe, 133
Ozark, Jack, 92, 101

Packer, Victor, 127, 131
Palace Theater, 20, 22
Paley, William, 136, 146–47, 208
Paradise Theater, 25
Paramount Case, 22
Paramount Decision, 26
Paramount Pictures, 3, 14, 25, 30–31, 42; animation division, 90, 93–94
Paramount Studios, 94
Paramount Theater, 25
Pasternak, Joseph, 43, 44, 68–69
Patriarchies, film industry, 25–26
Paul, Elliott, 51
PCA. *See* Production Code Administration (PCA)
Pearl Harbor, 74, 76
Peck, Gregory, 27, 53
Peiss, Kathy, 6
Penn, Arthur, 190, 194, 196
Pentecost, Jim, 103
People's Vaudeville Company, 15
Pepe LePew, 96–97
Perl, Arnold, 208, 209
Perlov, Betty, 128, 129, 133
Perry, Joan, 33
Persoff, Nehemiah, 187
Philbin, Jack, 222
Philco-Goodyear Playhouse, 190, 196

Philco Television Playhouse, 184, 185, 189, 205
The Phil Silvers Show, 229–34
Pickford, Mary, 33
Picon, Molly, 48, 134
Pierce, Ted, 95
Pierre, Jean, 116
Pinsker, Sanford, 213, 214
Pintoff, Ernie, 101
Pixar, 104, 106
Playhouse 90, 194–95
Pluralism, 83
Poconos, Camp Tamiment, 215–19
Polonsky, Abraham, 189, 206, 227
Popeye, 91, 92, 94
Popular Front, 44, 56
Porgy and Bess, 65
Posner, Barney, 97
Powell, Dick, 149
Powell, Richard M., 210
Prell, Riv-Ellen, 250–51
Preminger, Otto, 27, 65
Prescott, Norm, 101
Presley, Elvis, 149
Pressman, David, 204, 208
Pressman, Larry, 38
Previn, André, 69
Procter & Gamble, 204
Producers, social statement film, 43–44
Production Code Administration (PCA), 75
Project Geneis, 160, 173
Prolifka, Bernyce, 100
The Public Is Never Wrong (Zukor), 14

Questel, Mae, 90, 93

Rabins, Sandra, 105
Radio: advertising, 130–32; on the air Jews on, 149–53; *The American Jewish Hour,* 125; behind the scenes Jews on, 146–49; celebrity creation, 133; child stars, 134–35; cultural debates, 135–37; *Daf Hashevua,* 126; decline of Jewish, 141–44; *Der Tog,* 124–25, 128, 134, 136, 137; dramatic shows, 132–34; ethnic bonding through, 127–29; FCC regulation,

138–39; foreign-language broadcasting, 124–44; future direction of, 181; image of, 135–37; introduction to, 123–44; Jewish oral tradition, 127; Jewish Philosopher, 125, 126, 131; Jewish programming, 124–25; *The Jewish Daily Foward*, 135–37, 146; Jews on (1920–1953), 145–53; KDKA, 156; musical programs, 134–35; participatory nature of, 129; refugees broadcasting on, 139–41; satellite, 166, 169, 181; Sirius satellite radio, 166; Socialism on, 136–37; talk radio (*See* Talk radio); theatrical spinoffs, 133; "time-broker" system, 143; WABC, 136; WARD, 128; WBAI, 175–76; WBBC, 128, 132; WBNX, 124; WCAU, 147; WEAF, 156; WEVD, 125–29, 131–33, 135–37, 139, 143, 149, 157, 164, 166, 169, 176; WFMU, 178; WHN, 124, 125, 134; WHOM, 142; WINS, 127; WJZ, 137; WLTH, 127, 128, 131, 133, 134, 139; WMCA, 124, 126, 128, 132, 140; WNYC, 139; WRNY, 124–25; during WWII, 137–39; XM satellite radio, 169; Yiddish, 124–44, 152
Ragland, Rags, 231
Rakhlin, Yosef, 135
Rankin, John, 37
Rapf, Maurice, 97, 98
Rapp, Phil, 150, 220
Rapper, Irving, 51
Rathner, Janet, 165–66
Raye, Martha, 230–31
Raymond, Art, 141, 161, 167, 176
RCA, 146
Reagan, John Neil, 204
Reagan, Ronald, 204
"Real" Jews, 40
Ream, Joseph, 204
Reardon, Jim, 105
Red-baiting, 202
Red Channels, 187, 202, 230
Red Pepper Sam, 91
Red Seal Pictures, 90
Reed, Alan, 101

Refugees, radio broadcasts, 139–41
Rehberg, Eddie, 101
Reiner, Carl, 101, 215, 217, 219, 234–36, 244
Reiser, Paul, 243, 248
Remarque, Erich Maria, 53
Rhapsody in Blue, 51, 54, 57, 65
Rhoda, 239–40
Richler, Mordecai, 104
Righteous Persons Foundation, 119
Riskin, Robert, 41
Ritt, Martin, 187–88, 196, 203, 205, 206, 207
RKO, 3, 25, 31–32, 42
The Robe, 56
Robinson, Edward G., 37, 96, 149
Robinson, Hubbell, Jr., 232
Rodgers, Richard, 69–70
Rodman, Howard, 207
Rogers, Will, 147, 149
Romberg, Sigmund, 70
Rooney, Mickey, 231
Rosanka, Vera, 129, 133
Rose, Reginald, 191, 192–93, 194, 196, 200, 201, 208, 209
Rosen, Al, 76
Rosen, Arnie, 220, 233
Rosenberg, Meta, 210
Rosenberg, Samuel, 4
Rosenberg, Stuart, 208
Rotoscope, 90
Roxy Theater, 25
Royal Theater, 16
Rubinstein, Sholom, 125, 128, 130, 137
Ruby, Harry, 70
Rumann, Sigfried, 82
Rumshinsky, Joseph, 134
Russell, A.J., 222, 233
Russell, Charles, 206, 210
Ryan, Robert, 51

Sagan, Carl, 102
Sahl, Mort, 101
Saint, Eva Marie, 187
Salkin, Leo, 101
Sandburg, Carl, 44
Sanders, Gavriel, 162, 176–78
Sandler, Adam, 106

Index

San Francisco Jewish Film Festival, 111, 118, 119–20
Sarnoff, David, 31–32, 136, 141, 146–47
Satellite radio, 181; Sirius, 166; XM, 169
Schaffner, Franklin, 194, 196
Schary, Dore, 29, 53
Scheimer, Lou, 101
Schenck, Joseph, 5, 6, 26, 27, 33
Schenck, Nicholas, 5, 26, 27
Schenckman, Ben
Schickel, Richard, 97–98
Schlesinger, Leon, 94–96
Schneider, Peter, 103
Schumacher, Tom, 103
Schwartz, Al, 214
Schwartz, Arthur, 70, 216
Schwartz, Jack, 97, 98
Schwartz, Sherwood, 213–14, 225
Schwartz, Zack, 100
Schwarz, Steven, 103
Schwimmer, David, 249
Scooler, Zvee, 127, 133
Scott, Joan, 207
Screen Cartoonist Guild, 98
Screenwriters, social statement film, 46–50
Seeger, Hal, 101
Segal, Nachum, 162, 178–79
Segal, Steve, 104
Seibert, Fredeneroff, Harvey, 104
Seidman, Naomi, 251, 252, 253
Seinfeld, 243, 244–47
Seinfeld, Jerry, 106, 243
Selby, Margaret, 97, 98
Seldes, Gilbert, 223
Selig, William, 6, 8
Selzer, Eddie, 96–97
Selznick, Arna, 104
Selznick, David O., 29, 32, 43, 45, 56, 99, 204
Selznick, Lewis J., 3, 4, 5, 6, 10
Serling, Rod, 191, 193–94, 195, 196, 200, 201, 209
Shandling, Gary, 243
Sharpsteen, Ben, 89, 98, 99
Shaw, David, 190, 194, 208
Shaw, Irwin, 185

Sherman, Richard, 97, 98
Sherman, Robert, 97, 98
Shoah, 73
Showmen, Jewish, 14–23
Shubert, Lee, 5
Silverman, David, 105
Silverman, Hal, 101
Silvers, Phil, 39, 229–34
Simon, Danny, 217
Simon, Neil, 216, 217, 219
The Simpsons, 105
Sinatra, Frank, 57, 61, 63, 69, 149, 231
Singin' in the Rain, 64
Sirius satellite radio, 166
Sitcoms: 1960s and 1970s, 237–41; 1980s to present, 242–55; *Barney Miller*, 240–41; *Bridget Loves Bernie*, 237–39; reasons for increase during 1980s, 243–44; *Rhoda*, 239–40; *Seinfeld*, 243; *Taxi*, 240–41; *Welcome Back, Kotter*, 240–41
Sklar, Marty, 97
Skulnik, Menashe, 152
Slapsie Maxie's, 220, 231
Sloane, Allen E., 208
Smith, Albert, 8
Smith, Gerald L. K., 75
Social statement films, 40–59; decline of, 55–59; directors, 44–46; moguls, 40–43; producers, 43–44; screenwriters, 46–50
Sokolsky, George, 230
Solomon, Charles, 104
Solomon, Louis, 217
Sondheim, Stephen, 70–71
Song Car-Tunes, 90
Sony Pictures Entertainment, 29
Sparber, Izzy, 92, 94
Spence, Irv, 97
Spielberg, Steven, 103, 105–6, 119
Spivak, Yaakov, 162–63, 179–81
Spoor, George, 6, 7
Stapleton, Maureen, 187
Star system, 34
Steig, William, 106
Steiner, Charles, 14, 18–23
Stern, Howard, 155
Stern, Leonard B., 222, 224, 233, 235

272

Stiller, Jerry, 246
Stone, Walter, 222
"Strange Fruit," 57
Strasberg, Lee, 41
Streisand, Barbra, 55, 61
Studio One, 184, 185, 186, 189, 204
Studio owner, movie, 3–4
Studio sabotage, 52
Studio system, motion picture, 25–35
Stutchkoff, Nchum, 133
Styne, Jule, 66, 71, 101, 153
Suber, Howard, 240
Sullivan, Barry, 54
Sullivan, Ed, 202
Sullivan, Pat, 88
Susskind, David, 190, 205–6
Sutherland, Hal, 101
Swanson, William, 7, 8
Swift, David, 190

Talent Associates, 205
Talkline Communications Network, 157, 163
Talk radio, 155–82; cast of characters, 157–63; historical overview, 156–57; political leanings of, 155–56; women in, 155
Tarloff, Frank, 209, 227–29
Tarras, Dave, 134
Tartikoff, Brandon, 242, 243
Taxi, 240–41
Taylor, Elizabeth, 56
Taylor, Frederick, 87
Teague, David, 101
Television: *Actors Studio,* 187; blacklist industry, 201–4; blacklisting, 187, 189, 199–211; Broadway theatricality, 186–87; censorship, 187; "clean American look," 186, 187; comedy shows (*see* Comedy shows); comedy writers, 213–36; dramatic, 183–96, 242; early dramatic shows, 184–85; experimentation with, 186–87; gay characters, 251–53; Jewishcoms, 237–40; made-for-TV movies and mini-series, 242; *Philco-Goodyear Playhouse,* 190, 196; *Philco Playhouse,* 184, 185, 189; *The Phil Silvers Show,* 229–34; *Playhouse 90,* 194–95; sitcom trend, 242–55; sponsorship, 187, 195–96; *Studio One,* 184, 185, 186, 189; as transformitive medium, 183; variety shows, 214–19
Television playwrights, 200
Tendlar, Dave, 92
Terrytoon, 101
Thalberg, Irving, 28, 35, 43
Thalberg System, 43
Thomas, Danny, 149, 224–29, 231
Thomas, Jay, 243
Thomas, Marlo, 229
Thomas, Norman, 137
The Three Stooges, 73, 74, 77–84
Time Warner, 30
To Be or Not To Be, 77
Tolkin, Mel, 216
Tracy, Arthur, 151
Tracy, Spencer, 29, 149
Triangle Film Corporation, 9
Trickfilms, 86
Trumbo, Dalton, 207
Tucker, Sophie, 149, 150
Turner, Lana, 149
20th Century Fox, 3, 25, 26–28
Tyne, George, 53
Tytla, Bill, 98

UAA. *See* Unemployed Artists Association (UAA)
UCLA Film Archives, 110
Ulmer, Edgar G., 44, 47–50
Unemployed Artists Association (UAA), 92
Unions: Animated Motion Picture Workers Union (AMPWU), 92; Artist's Union, 92; Fleischer Studio, 93; Walt Disney, 98–99
United Artists (UA), 3, 5, 25, 33–34
United Productions of America (UPA), 85, 100
United Service for New Americans (USNA), 140
Universal City, 35
Universal Film Manufacturing Company, 8

Universal Pictures, 1, 3, 25, 34–35
UPA. *See* United Productions of America (UPA)
USNA. *See* United Service for New Americans (USNA)

Van Allsberg, Chris, 105
Van Dyke, Dick, 235
Van Fleet, Jo, 187
"Vanishing American Jew" crisis, 237–38, 256
Vanzoff, Max, 205
Verhoeven, Michael, 117
Vernick, Edith, 92
Viacom, 31
The Vicious Circle, 52
Vidal, Gore, 190
Vitaphone, 30
Vladeck, B. Charney, 136, 137, 146

Waldman, Leybele, 133
Waldman, Louis, 137
Waldman, Myron, 92
Waletzky, Josh, 110
Wallach, Eli, 187
Waller, Fats, 57
Wallis, Hal B., 43
Walt Disney, 85, 89, 91, 94, 97–100, 103–4
Walt Disney, The Dark Prince (Elliott), 98
Wanger, Walter, 33, 44
Warburg, Edward, 140
Warfield, David, 15
Warner, Abe, 29
Warner, Harry, 26, 29–30
Warner, Jack, 26, 29–30, 42, 51, 94
Warner, Sam, 29–30
Warner Bros., 25, 26, 29–30, 76; animation studio, 94–97; social statement films, 42
Warren, Harry, 71
Wasserman, Lew, 50
Waters, Ethel, 57
Wayne, John, 27, 83
Weaver, Sylvester "Pat," 208, 217
Webster, Tony, 217
Weill, Kurt, 71–72
Weimar, Pat, 56

Weinstein, Hannah, 206
Weiss, Barry, 105
Weiss, Bill, 101
Weiss, Jules, 80
Welcome Back, Kotter, 240–41
Welles, Orson, 231
West, Mae, 149
West Side Story, 63, 71
White, Jules, 80
"White Christmas," 62
Whiteman, Paul, 147
Whitfield, Stephen, 84
Wiesel, Elie, 242
Wilk, Max, 52, 186
Will and Grace, 251–53
William Morris Agency, 149
Williams, Esther, 26
Winant, Ethel, 205
Winkler, George, 88
Winkler, Margaret, 88–89, 90
Wischengrad, Morton, 148
Wise, Stephen S., 5, 156
The Wizard of Oz, 61, 62, 65
WLBT case, 238–39
Wolf, Bernie, 97
The Woman in Brown, 52
Wood, Bob, 238
Woolery, Ade, 100
World Film Corporation, 5
Wyler, William, 32, 41
Wyman, David, 74
Wynn, Ed, 152–53, 231

XM Satellite Radio, 169

Yiddish, 73
Yiddish films, 47–49
Yiddishisms, 73
The Yolk's on Me, 83
You'll Never Get Rich, 229
You Nazty Spy, 80, 81
Youngman, Henny, 232
Young & Rubicam, 204, 205
Your Show of Shows, 214, 215, 217–19, 237

Zanuck, Darryl, 27
Zashlove, Alan, 100

Zeleznik, Lewis. *See* Selznick, Lewis J.
Zelinka, Sydney, 222
Zemeckis, Robert, 105
Zimet, Julian, 50
Zinnemann, Fred, 53, 149
Zionist Organization of America, 6

Zukor, Adolph, 3–6, 8, 10, 30–31; rise to power, 14–18; standards, 17
Zukor, Lou, 92, 101
Zukor, Mildred, 5
Zurawixk, David, 214, 234–35

About the Editor and Contributors

Paul Buhle is Senior Lecturer in the History and American Civilization Departments at Brown University, a Distinguished Lecturer for the Organization of American Historians, and author or editor of twenty-nine previous books, including *Popular Culture in America* and *Encyclopedia of the American Left*. He is Contributing Editor to *Tikkun* magazine and a contributor to *The Forward, Jewish Currents*, the *San Francisco Chronicle*, the *Chronicle of Higher Education, The Guardian*, and many other publications.

Barry Blitt's illustrations have appeared in *Entertainment Weekly, Sports Illustrated*, the *New York Observer*, and frequently grace the cover of *The New Yorker*. He has also published illustrated books for children and adults, including *The 39 Apartments of Ludwig von Beethoven, Once Upon a Time, The End (Asleep in 60 Seconds)*, and *Baby's First Tattoo: A Memory Book for Modern Parents*.

Steven W. Bowie is a freelance writer and researcher with a B.A. in film and television studies from the University of Southern California. His work has appeared in *Filmfax, Scarlet Street, Television Chronicles*, and *Senses of Cinema*. He is currently compiling oral histories with early television writers and directors for publication.

Dan M. Bronstein, a 1996 ordainee of the Hebrew Union College–Jewish Institute of Religion, is a Congregational Scholar at Congregation Beth Elohim in Brooklyn, New York, and is completing his Ph.D. at the Jewish Theological Seminary of America. Along with teaching at the seminary, Rabbi Bronstein has published and spoken on a variety of topics, especially American Judaism and popular culture.

Vincent Brook has a Ph.D. in film and television from the University of California-Los Angeles. He has worked as a film editor and a screenwriter and currently teaches film, television, and cultural studies at UCLA and the University of Southern California. He has written numerous articles for anthologies and leading media journals and is the author of *Something Ain't Kosher Here: The Rise of the "Jewish" Sitcom*, and the editor of the anthology *You Should See Yourself: Jewish Identity in Postmodern American Culture*.

Bernard F. Dick holds a Ph.D. in Classical Languages from Fordham University and is presently Professor of Communication and English at Fairleigh Dickinson University's Metropolitan Campus in Teaneck, New Jersey, and coordinator of the M.A. Program in Media and Professional Communication. He is the author of a number of books of film history, including *The Star-Spangled Screen: The American World War Two Film* (1985) and *Forever Mame: The Life of Rosalind Russell* (2006). He is currently writing a biography of Claudette Colbert.

Ariana Green is a 2006–2007 Fulbright Scholar, working toward an MA in International Journalism in London. A 2004 magna cum laude graduate of Brown University, she hosted and produced Brown's first feminist talk radio program and wrote her history honors thesis about radio's impact on black-Jewish relations. She has worked for ABC News, the *New York Times*, *San Juan Magazine*, *Popular Science Magazine*, PBS, and the *Cambridge Chronicle*.

Deborah Kaufman is an award-winning film producer, director, and writer whose documentaries, *Thirst*, *Secrets of Silicon Valley*, and *Blacks and Jews*, have been broadcast on PBS and around the world. She founded and was for thirteen years Director of the San Francisco Jewish Film Festival, the first and largest festival of its kind. Kaufman is a graduate of the University of California, Hastings College of the Law, and a member of the California Bar.

Ari Y. Kelman is an Assistant Professor of American Studies at the University of California at Davis. He is the author of *Station Identification: A Cultural History of Yiddish Radio*, and he has written and spoken widely on Jewish culture in the United States.

Dennis B. Klein has written several studies on the nexus between Jews and modernity and is the founding editor of *Dimensions: A Journal of Holocaust Studies*. He is professor of History and director of the Jewish Studies program at Kean University.

Kathy M. Newman is Associate Professor of English/Literary and Cultural Studies at Carnegie Mellon University. Her first book is *Radio Active: Advertising and Consumer Activism*. In her spare time she works as a freelance writer, a political activist, and a linoleum block artist.

Harvey Pekar, author-editor of the long-running comic series *American Splendor*, and personage of the award-winning film of the same name, lives in Cleveland and is currently collaborating with Paul Buhle on two volumes, *The Beats* and a history of Students for a Democratic Society. He has scripted many works of comic art, including *Ego & Hubris: The Michael Malice Story* and *The Quitter.*

Janis Plotkin programmed and produced the San Francisco Jewish Film Festival from 1982 through 2002. Her prior work as a community organizer led her to develop an interest in the use of media as a tool for communicating values, history, and culture. Since her departure from the SFJFF she has continued her work as a film curator and a teacher of Jewish subject cinema.

Henry Sapoznik is an award-winning author, radio and record producer, and performer of traditional Yiddish and American music. He coproduced the ten-part series the *Yiddish Radio Project* for National Public Radio's *All Things Considered* in the spring of 2002, winner of the Peabody Award. His three-CD box set for Sony Columbia/Legacy of legendary country music pioneer Charlie Poole was nominated for three Grammy awards.

Tom Sito is a veteran animator, teacher, and author. His movie screen credits include *The Little Mermaid* (1989), *Beauty and the Beast* (1991), and *Shrek* (2001). He teaches and writes about animation and is an adjunct professor in the cinema departments of the University of Southern California and University of California, Los Angeles. The three-term President of the Hollywood Animation Guild Local 839, he has also written the book *Drawing the Line: The Untold Story of Animation Unions from Bosko to Bart Simpson.*

Judith Smith is Professor of American Studies and director of the American Studies MA program at the University of Massachusetts, Boston, where she teaches courses on the history of film, recent American culture, and women's history. She has written on immigration and ethnicity, urban and family history, and most recently on postwar film, drama, and television drama in *Visions of Belonging: Family Stories, Popular Culture and Postwar Democracy, 1940–1960.*

Judith Thissen is an Assistant Professor in Media History at Utrecht University, Netherlands. She has published on a variety of subjects relating to Jewish immigrant audiences and is currently completing a book on the politics of popular entertainment on New York's Lower East Side.

Dave Wagner, a founder of the journal *Cultural Correspondence,* is coauthor of four books on the lives and work of the Hollywood Blacklistees.